# THE ROLE OF BUSINESS IN GLOBAL SUSTAINABILITY TRANSFORMATIONS

Drawing on contributions from more than thirty scholars and experts in the field, this book examines the role of business as an enabler, as an inhibitor, and ultimately as a co-actor in global sustainability transformations expected over the next few decades.

*The Role of Business in Global Sustainability Transformations* employs several theoretical perspectives and provides abundant examples and cases to discuss a variety of emerging concepts, phenomena, and trends shaping business sustainability. Weaving through the chapters, the editors present core tensions and sources of inertia towards transformative change, and acknowledge that envisioning multiple solutions and pathways are possible and desirable. They advocate for the need to align visions, actions and time horizons between policy, society and business in addressing the interlinked socio-ecological challenges that our society currently faces.

This book will be an important resource for scholars and professionals working in the field of sustainability and sustainable business, and a vital educational text for students interested in this discipline.

**Dalia D'Amato** is an Adjunct Professor at the Department of Forest Sciences, Faculty of Agriculture and Forestry, University of Helsinki (Finland), and a member of the Helsinki Institute of Sustainability Science (HELSUS). Since Autumn 2022, she has been employed by the Finnish Environment Institute (SYKE). Current research interests include solution-oriented sustainability narratives, such as the green, circular, and bioeconomy, and related societal and organisational transformations; business sustainability in the forest sector and other land use-intensive sectors; biodiversity-underpinned ecosystem services and the governance of socio-ecological systems.

**Anne Toppinen** is Professor in forest economics and business and Vice Dean of research affairs and doctoral education at the Department of Forest Sciences, Faculty of Agriculture and Forestry, University of Helsinki (Finland). During 2018–2021, she served as Director of the Helsinki Institute of Sustainability Science (HELSUS). Her research interests focus on sustainability pathways and resilience of forest-based value networks, corporate responsibility questions in a broad sense, and emergence of new sustainability-driven business models. She has published widely in the fields of corporate responsibility and forest bioeconomy.

**Robert Kozak** is a Professor and Dean of the Faculty of Forestry at the University of British Columbia. His research and teaching revolve around sustainable business management and business-based solutions to complex problems related to sustainable development, forestry, wood products, and the emerging conservation economy. He was awarded the International Union of Forest Research Organization's Scientific Achievement Award (2014), a Doctor of Agriculture and Forestry *honoris causa* from the University of Helsinki (2022), and the Killam Teaching Prize (2001, 2014).

# Routledge Research in Sustainability and Business

For more information about this series, please visit: www.routledge.com/
Routledge-Research-in-Sustainability-and-Business/book-series/RRSB

# THE ROLE OF BUSINESS IN GLOBAL SUSTAINABILITY TRANSFORMATIONS

*Edited by*
*Dalia D'Amato, Anne Toppinen*
*and Robert Kozak*

Routledge
Taylor & Francis Group

LONDON AND NEW YORK

from Routledge

Cover image: Photo by Dalia D'Amato: G20 Green Garden installed by the Food and Agriculture Organization (FAO) in the Caffarella Park (Appian Way Regional Park) in Rome, Italy.

First published 2023
by Routledge
4 Park Square, Milton Park, Abingdon, Oxon OX14 4RN

and by Routledge
605 Third Avenue, New York, NY 10158

*Routledge is an imprint of the Taylor & Francis Group, an informa business*

*British Library Cataloguing-in-Publication Data*
A catalogue record for this book is available from the British Library

ISBN: 978-0-367-43482-3 (hbk)
ISBN: 978-0-367-43483-0 (pbk)
ISBN: 978-1-003-00358-8 (ebk)

DOI: 10.4324/9781003003588

Typeset in Bembo
by codeMantra

Dedicated to our seventh generation.

# CONTENTS

# FIGURES

# TABLES

# CONTRIBUTORS

**Kahlil Baker** is the Co-founder and CEO of Taking Root, a purpose-driven organisation that uses carbon markets to accelerate the restoration of the world's forests. Kahlil has spent the last 15 years working with farmers in the tropics to develop economic systems that promote the integration of trees on farms. He also serves as an Advisor for leading forest carbon standards, including Plan Vivo and the Gold Standard. A featured CBC changemaker and a recipient of Canada's Meritorious Service Cross, Kahlil holds an MSc and a PhD in forestry from the University of British Columbia, and a BA in Economics from Concordia University.

**Michael Barkusky** holds a BA (Honours) in economics from the University of Cape Town, an MBA degree from the University of British Columbia, and the Canadian professional accounting designation of CPA, CGA. He divides his time between a professional public accounting and management consulting practice, part-time teaching of ecological economics at the post-secondary level (with a managerial economics focus being a speciality), and volunteer work with sustainability-focused NGOs. He was the lead author on 'The Economic Logic of Corporate Social Responsibility' *(International Journal of Environment Workplace and Employment (2006))* and served as Secretary-Treasurer of the Canadian Society for Ecological Economics (CANSEE) from 2006 to 2015.

**Benjamin Cashore** holds the Li Ka Shing Chair in Public Management at the Lee Kuan Yew School of Public Policy, National University of Singapore. He is also Director of LKYSPP's Public Policy Initiative on Environment and Sustainability (PPIES). He specialises in global and multi-level environmental governance, comparative public policy, and transnational business regulation/corporate environmental social governance (ESG) innovations. His substantive research interests include climate policy, biodiversity conservation/land use change, and sustainable environmental management of forests and related agricultural sectors. His geographic focus includes Southeast Asia, North America, Latin America, and Europe. Cashore's theoretical interests include the potential of anticipatory policy design for identifying path-dependent policy mixes capable of ameliorating 'super wicked' environmental problems; the legitimacy and authority requirements of non-state market-driven (NSMD) global governance; and the influence of economic globalisation on domestic environmental policies.

**Dalia D'Amato** is an Adjunct Professor at the Department of Forest Sciences, Faculty of Agriculture and Forestry, University of Helsinki (Finland), and a member of the Helsinki Institute of Sustainability Science (HELSUS). Since Autumn 2022, she is also employed by the Finnish Environment Institute (SYKE). Before gaining her PhD in forest economics and marketing at the University of Helsinki (2016), she completed two MSc degrees related to ecology and biodiversity management from the University of Sussex (UK) and the University of Roma Tre (Italy). Current research interests include solution-oriented sustainability narratives, such as the green, circular, and bioeconomy, and related societal and organisational transformations; business sustainability in the forest sector and other land use-intensive sectors; biodiversity-underpinned ecosystem services and the governance of socio-ecological systems. She serves as an editor for the journal *Circular Economy and Sustainability* (Springer), the journal Frontiers in Sustainability (Frontiers) and the journal *Canadian Journal of Forest Research* (Canadian Science Publishing). @Dalia_DAmato

**Francesca Govoni** graduated in law at Roma Tre University in 2015, writing a final dissertation on the EU Environmental Policy. After completing her BA, she obtained a master degree in international relationships in Rome at LUMSA University, focusing mostly on European and international law, bioeconomy, environmental law, and environmental economics. In 2016, she won a scholarship from Lazio Regional Government to attend a training programme on 'EU policies and funding schemes' in Brussels. She is currently employed at Unitelma Sapienza University of Rome working on the preparation of project proposals and on the financial and administrative management of EU and national funded projects.

**Marko Hakovirta** is currently Professor at the College of Natural Resources at NC State University. His teaching and research interests are in sustainable business and bioeconomy, with a focus on carbon neutrality. Hakovirta has a broad experience in different sectors in business, academia, and large research institutions. He previously served as SVP (Innovation) at Stora Enso Corporation and Group VP (Technology, Environment and Quality) at Metso Corporation. Hakovirta has also held academic leadership positions in NC State University,

Auburn University, and Georgia Tech. He received his PhD and MSc from the University of Helsinki, Finland, and MBA from Emory University, Atlanta.

**Eric Hansen** is Professor of forest products marketing and Department Head of Wood Science and Engineering at Oregon State University (OSU). He received a BS in forest products business management from the University of Idaho in 1990 and a PhD in 1994 from Virginia Tech, specialising in forest products marketing. He is Co-author of the textbook *Strategic Marketing in the Global Forest Industries* and Editor of *BioProducts Business*, a journal published by the Society of Wood Science and Technology.

**Liina Häyrinen** is Research Scientist of business economics, bioeconomy, and environment at the Natural Resource Institute Finland (Luke). Her special expertise is in marketing, with empirical focus, for example, on timber construction, non-industrial private forest ownership, and human–nature relationship.

**Ari Jantunen** is a Professor of strategy research at LUT University, School of Business and Management, Finland. Industry dynamics, entrepreneurship, innovation, and organisational renewal have been central themes in his research. His current primary areas of research interest are in the organisational cognition, dynamic capabilities, and strategic renewal of companies.

**Jaana Korhonen** is a Research Fellow at the Oak Ridge Institute for Science and Education in the United States. Her research interests include sustainability transition and sustainable business management of biobased industries, with a special focus on the global forest sector. She currently serves in the editorial board of Forest Science and in the scientific board of *Journal of Forest Business Research*.

**Kaisa Korhonen-Kurki** works as at Finnish Environment Institute, where she is a Programme Director for the programmes: Adaptation and Resilience for a Sustainable Growth under the Strategic Research Council, and where she is a Head of system transformation unit. She is also an Adjunct Professor at the Helsinki Institute of Sustainability Science (HELSUS), University of Helsinki. She has a wide experience on knowledge co-production activities in various science policy interfaces, and she has published widely on environmental and forest policy, Sustainable Development Goals, and sustainability transformation.

**Angelina Korsunova** works as a University Instructor in forest bioeconomy and business at the Department of Forest Sciences, University of Helsinki, and is also a member of the Helsinki Institute of Sustainability Science (HELSUS). She holds a doctorate in economics and management. Her research interests include sustainability-oriented innovation and new economic models, stakeholder engagement, and consumer–company interactions on sustainability, as well as motivating the transition to sustainable lifestyles. She is currently leading an international project on Circular Citizens, exploring how to support active citizen participation in a circular economy. She has extensive experience in societal impact activities and coordinates HELSUS Youth initiative, aimed at increasing the accessibility and attractiveness of sustainability research to youth.

**Robert Kozak** is a Professor and Dean of the Faculty of Forestry at the University of British Columbia and the former Associate Dean, Academic, and Head of the Wood Science Department. His current research and teaching interests, as part of the Forests and Communities in Transition Lab, revolve around sustainable business management practices and issues and providing business-based solutions to complex problems related to sustainable development, forestry, wood products, and the emerging conservation economy. Currently, his work focuses on the wellbeing of forest-dependent communities, international development and poverty alleviation strategies, forest certification, corporate social responsibility, and forest sector sustainability and competitiveness. He has published and presented his work widely, and is actively involved in service to the university and the broader academic community. In recognition of his work, he was awarded the International Union of Forest Research Organization's Scientific Achievement Award in 2014 a Doctor of Agriculture and Forestry *honoris causa* from the University of Helsinki in 2022, and is a two-time recipient of the Killam Teaching Prize in 2001 and 2014.

**Noriko Kusumi** is a PhD candidate at the Department of Environmental Science, Policy, and Management, Rausser College of Natural Resources, University of California, Berkeley. Her research interest is the global political economy of multinational corporations. Her recent research focuses on the practical and political role of corporate social responsibility (CSR) and socially responsible investment (SRI) in global environmental governance. She formerly worked as an SRI analyst and consultant at investment research firms in Washington, D.C., and San Francisco.

**Katja Lähtinen** is Research Professor of business development and economics at the Natural Resources Institute Finland (Luke). Her key area of research is strategic management within the scope of circular bioeconomy and sustainable urbanisation, especially from the perspective of wood-based value chain businesses.

**Piergiuseppe Morone** is Full Professor of economic policy at Unitelma Sapienza, with a strong interest in green innovation and sustainable circular bioeconomy pushing his research at the interface between innovation economics and sustainability transitions, an area of enquiry that has attracted growing attention over the last decade. His work regularly appears in prestigious innovation and environmental economics journals. He is the Coordinator of the Bioeconomy in Transition Research Group (BiT-RG) and the Director of the School of

Sustainability Studies and Circular Economy (SUSTAIN). Moreover, he is/was involved in several European projects (including H2020, BBI-JU, Life, Erasmus+, COST, Horizon Europe, and CBE-JU) acting as Scientific Coordinator, Vice-Chair, and WP Leader. He was Economic Advisor to the Italian Minister of the Environment, Land and Sea Protection till February 2021. He is now Local Unit Scientific Coordinator in the LIFE EBP project (2020–2024) and Scientific Committee Member of BIOVOICES and Biobridges projects (BBI JU CSAs). Piergiuseppe is Associate Editor of *Cleaner and Circular Bioeconomy* and Member of the Editorial Boards of *Current Opinion in Green and Sustainable Chemistry* (ELSEVIER) and *Open Agriculture* (De Gruyter Open) and acts as Guest Editor for various journals, including the *Journal of Cleaner Production* (ELSEVIER) and *Sustainability* (MDPI). Since April 2022, Piergiuseppe has been the Vice-Chair of the Circular Bio-based Europe Joint Undertaking (CBE JU) Scientific Committee.

**Iana Nesterova** is a Postdoctoral Researcher at Umeå University, Department of Geography. Her research on business and degrowth transformations has been published in the leading journals in the field of sustainable organisations, including *Ecological Economics, Journal of Cleaner Production,* and *Futures.*

**William Nikolakis** is an Assistant Professor in the Department of Forest Resources Management, Faculty of Forestry at the University of British Columbia, Canada, where he supports the development of the Bachelor of Indigenous Land Stewardship program. William is a Practising Member of the Law Society of British Columbia. His focus is on the intersection between Indigenous rights, governance, and natural resources law. William has published in diverse peer-reviewed journals, including *Governance, Land Use Policy, Ecosystem Services, Business Strategy and the Environment, Organization & Environment,* and *the Journal of Hydrology* (among others).

**Rajat Panwar** (*pronounce: he/him/his; pronunciation: R-u-jh-u-t P-un-w-aa-r*) is an Associate Professor of sustainable business management and corporate social responsibility at Oregon State University.

**Romana Rauter** is Associate Professor on sustainability and innovation management at the University of Graz, Austria. In her research, she explores ways of how companies can advance on sustainability, which includes, amongst others, managing sustainability innovations or developing new and sustainable business models. She is co-Chair of the NBM Conference Series and Associate Editor for the *Journal Business and Society Review.*

**Ben Robra** is a Postdoc Researcher at the Universidade de Vigo's Post-growth Innovation Lab. He is also an Affiliate at P2P Lab as well as one of the founding editors at *Degrowth* journal. Ben's research focuses on economic organisations and innovation in connection to degrowth as well as postgrowth. He holds a BA in business administration from the Hamburg School of Business Administration as well as an MSc in ecological economics and a PhD in sustainability from the University of Leeds. @BenRobra

**Tomas Santa-Maria** is a PhD candidate at the Institute of System Sciences, Innovation and Sustainability Research of the University of Graz, Austria, and a Senior Researcher at the Know-Center research center for data-driven business and AI. His research has been focused on sustainable and circular business models, and more lately, on data-driven business models, understanding the drivers and challenges for circular business model innovation, exploring the needed dynamic capabilities, and developing design-thinking based tools to support innovation processes.

**Fabian Schipfer** is a Postdoctoral Scientist at Technische Universität Wien. Since 2012, his research has focused on the nexus between the biosphere and technosphere. His current work aims at providing decision support for anthropocentric transformation strategies. He pursues his objectives with fundamental research on system flexibilisation and resource uncertainty, modelling synergies between the circular bioeconomy and renewable power sectors and interdisciplinary transformation research.

**Josef-Peter Schöggl** currently works as a Postdoctoral Researcher at the Christian Doppler Laboratory for Sustainable Product Management in a Circular Economy at the University of Graz, Austria. He holds a PhD in environmental systems sciences, during which he conducted research on supply chain-wide sustainability assessment. In his current research, he focuses on the role of digital technologies and interorganisational collaboration in corporate sustainability management and the development of concepts for data-driven sustainability assessment and design.

**Mario D. Schultz** is a Postdoctoral Researcher at the Ethics and Communication Law Center (ECLC), Faculty of Communication, Culture and Society, Università della Svizzera italiana (CH), External Lecturer at the SDI München (DE), and Guest Lecturer at the University of Applied Sciences and Arts Northwestern Switzerland (CH). He studied International Business Administration at the University of Amsterdam (NL), the University of Vienna (AT), and the Singapore Management University (SG). His current research focuses on corporate social responsibility (CSR) and business ethics related to digitalisation, information, and communication technologies.

**Peter Seele** is Professor of corporate social responsibility and business ethics at USI Lugano, Switzerland. Peter holds a PhD in economics from the University of Witten/Herdecke (D) and a PhD in philosophy from the University of

Düsseldorf (D). Before working at USI, he was Assistant Professor at the University of Basel (ZRWP) and prior to that Postdoc at the Institute for Advanced Studies in the Humanities (KWI) in Essen (D). He has studied at the University of Oldenburg (D) and at Delhi School of Economics (IND) and worked for two years as Business Consultant in Frankfurt/M.

**Ellen Stenslie** is pursuing a PhD at the Department of International Environment and Development Studies at the Norwegian University of Life Sciences (NMBU). She has a BBA and an MSc in international environmental governance. Her research explores sustainability-driven hybrid organisations and their role in a postgrowth economy, drawing on diverse fields like institutional economics, sustainability entrepreneurship, and law. Stenslie has been a Visiting Researcher with The Centre for the Understanding of Sustainable Prosperity (CUSP) and the Sustainability Research Institute (SRI) in the UK. She is engaged in Rethinking Economics and the European Society for Ecological Economics (ESEE) and is interested in topics like circular and regenerative economy and business models for sustainability.

**Maria Fernanda Tomaselli** is a Lecturer at the University of British Columbia (UBC), Faculty of Forestry, and the Coordinator of UBC's Land One program. Her research about the green economy and postgrowth communication has been published in the Journals *International Forestry Review* and *Ecological Economics*. She holds a BSc in environmental communication from San Francisco de Quito University and an MSc and a PhD in forestry from the University of British Columbia.

**Anne Toppinen** finished her PhD in 1998 and since 2008 she has been Professor in forest economics and business at the University of Helsinki. Starting 2022, she is also a Vice Dean of research affairs and doctoral education, Faculty of Agriculture and Forestry. Prior to this, she has served as Director of the Helsinki Institute of Sustainability Science (HELSUS) during 2018–2021, a Research Program Manager at the European Forest Institute (2017), and a Researcher at the Finnish Forest Research Institute (1991–2006). Her research interests focus on sustainability pathways and resilience of forest-based value networks, corporate responsibility questions in a broad sense, and emergence of new sustainability-driven business models. She has published widely in the fields of corporate responsibility and forest bioeconomy. She currently coordinates a large-scale interdisciplinary DECARBON-HOME consortium funded by the Strategic Research Council. Anne is also a Member of the Academy of Finland's Biosciences, Health and Environment Research Council (2022–24) and a member of the Finnish Academy of Science and Letters since 2020.

**Anni Tuppura** is an Associate Professor at LUT University, School of Business and Management. Her research interests are in strategic management and sustainable business. Currently, her work focuses on how the companies and industries renew towards sustainability. She has published research articles (e.g., in Business Strategy and the Environment, Corporate Social Responsibility and Environmental Management, and International Business Review, among others) and book chapters that focus on sustainability, corporate responsibility, and strategy.

**Peter Wood** has worked in the field of international forest policy, human rights, and sustainability for over two decades in a variety of roles, including with non-governmental and intergovernmental organisations. He was a Lead Author on the Global Expert Panel on International Forest Governance (IUFRO), and has served on Forest Stewardship Council technical committees for the development of certification standards and policy. As a Team Leader and Editor with the International Institute for Sustainable Development's Earth Negotiations Bulletin since 2005, he has reported on dozens of key international negotiations related to forests, biodiversity, and climate change. Currently, he is an Adjunct Professor at the Faculty of Forestry at the University of British Columbia. He holds a PhD from the University of Toronto, and wrote his dissertation on international influences in domestic forest policy and management.

**Gülşah Yilan** is a Researcher in the bioeconomy in Transition Research Group at Unitelma-Sapienza University of Rome (Italy) and also a Research Assistant at Marmara University (Turkey). She holds a PhD in chemical engineering where she studied the country-wide environmental impacts of electricity generation technologies along with sustainable future scenarios for Turkey. Her current research interests include circular economy, renewable energy, sustainability assessment, and waste management.

# ACKNOWLEDGEMENTS

We wish to acknowledge our host institutions: the University of Helsinki, the Helsinki Institute of Sustainability Science (HELSUS), and the University of British Columbia.

This book was made possible by the generous support of the following funders: Academy of Finland, which funded project 'OPerationalising Ecosystem services in business Sustainability: drawing from green and circular bioeconomy' (OPES, funding decision 315912); ORBIT ('Orchestrating sustainable user-driven bioeconomy: policy, transformation and benefits', funding decision 337480); NordForsk, which funded project 'Green forests policies: a comparative assessment of outcomes and trade-offs across Fenno-Scandinavia' (GreenPole, funding decision 103443); and Nordic Forest Research, which funded project 'Transdisciplinary co-production in forest policy research' (ForPol, funding decision SNS-128).

We are grateful to Kone Foundation for providing the financial resources to publish this book in open access format (funding decision 201902831).

We thank all the devoted co-authors of individual chapters and many anonymous reviewers who supported the development of these chapters. We also thank Alice Lehtinen for the language revision of this book.

# PART 1
# Business Sustainability Today

# 1

# A LITTLE CHAPTER ON THE BIG PICTURE

*Robert Kozak, Anne Toppinen, and Dalia D'Amato*

If you are reading this book, we probably don't need to convince you that this planet is in heaps of trouble. By the time you've leafed through this chapter, we know that our ecosystems will be a little less biodiverse, our air and water will be a little more polluted, and our global temperature will keep inching upwards. Simply put, if we don't put an end to these alarming trends today, we will not be able to sustain ourselves in the future.

At the same time, capitalism is increasingly becoming the only game in town, and the neoliberal models which favour free market enterprise, globalisation, and development continue unabated. Businesses are here to stay; they anchor economic growth through the provision of incalculable positive socioeconomic outcomes – jobs, profits, taxes, community wellbeing, and so forth. And they support the voracious consumption of goods by a swelling population.

But herein lies the problem; a 'wicked' problem in every sense of the word.

Businesses are extractive in nature, reliant on the bounty of natural capital and related ecosystem services that our planet offers. This leads to all kinds of eyebrow-raising questions. How can businesses continue to exist in a world that is desperately seeking sustainable solutions? What is their role in this existential crisis that we now find ourselves facing? If businesses are an important part of the problem, can they not also be an important part of the solution?

This book sets out to provide some clarity around these paradoxical questions. We approach this topic through a distinctive lens. While this is categorically not a forestry or forest bioeconomy book, each of the editors is a business researcher with a background in forest sciences. In other words, we have spent our careers thinking about socio-ecological systems along complex temporal and spatial scales, and we are part of a tradition that has infused into business thinking the sustainability ethos that has been present, in one way or another, in the field of forestry for centuries.

DOI: 10.4324/9781003003588-2

It is through this unique perspective that we explore whether it may be possible to enable a paradigm shift that allows us to move away from the *status quo* industrialised approaches of renewable resource extraction, production, delivery, and consumption to more holistic, systems-based approaches of sustainable business management and practices. In other words, how can we negotiate the transformation of moving the notion of sustainable business from the realm of a hypothetical construct to a more practical reality? We argue that the beginning point in such an exercise is with some agreement on terminology.

Context and definitions are important, especially in a nascent field like sustainable business management. Clarity, sharpness, and a common understanding of terms form a necessary cornerstone in advancing burgeoning sustainability concepts forward in a meaningful way. Without such a foundation in place, and at least some degree of accord among researchers and practitioners, how can we even begin to measure progress towards a more sustainable future that continues to provide economic opportunities? To that end, we begin the book with a close look at what we are seeing in this field today.

It doesn't take a huge leap to understand that a logical starting point would be the ubiquitous Sustainable Development Goals (SDGs) adopted by the United Nations in 2015, which have fast-become a beacon guiding sustainable business management, practices, and logics all over the world. One of its core goals, flagging the importance of sustainable consumption and production, is displayed on the cover of this book. We see the principles set forth in the SDGs being adopted in contexts ranging from small and medium enterprises to multinational corporations, from small community-based organisations to highly developed economies. Chapter 2 explores not only the efficacy of SDGs to deliver sustainability outcomes, but the business impetus for engagement. This leads into a discussion of the broader, but equally, compelling topic of sustainable business models (SBMs). In Chapter 3, we scan the current business literature and highlight some of the emergent approaches for theorising and implementing SBMs, with the ultimate aim of trying to create a common language for understanding how business management and practice can and should align with notions of sustainability and responsible stewardship of our planet's ecological systems.

Next, the book further contextualises the issues of sustainable business management by proffering some current conceptualisations for framing and managing sustainability within the context of business operations. Chapters 4 and 5 take a deep, critical dive into the transformational potential of the green economy and the circular bioeconomy, related terms which have become increasingly pervasive, but perhaps also increasingly misconstrued. While a green economy model explicitly places the value of ecosystem services squarely at the nexus of business decision-making, a circular bioeconomy economy model refers to a biomass-based system which incorporates efficiencies through recycling and the use of waste and byproducts in industrial processes. Both of these models offer the promise of increased coordination and collaboration along the supply chains, but also maintain the *status quo* neoliberal paradigm of continuous economic growth led by the private sector, which ultimately may be incompatible with sustainability thinking.

And, so, while these models may not be transformational as such, they do offer businesses novel strategic opportunities to aim for loftier goals related to sustainability approaches. Two such opportunities are discussed in further detail in Chapters 6 and 7, respectively, as potentially influential transition pathways. Downstream along the value chain, brand owners and retailers can tailor their marketing strategies to better capitalise on society's demands for more environmentally benign and climate-friendly products. Servitisation, the process of providing customers with comprehensive product-service systems, also offers a good deal of promise, not only as a means of enabling co-creation and added value along the supply chain, but as a way of cultivating new economic paradigms like the green economy and circular bioeconomy models by enhancing the competitiveness of businesses that participate in these economies. Notably, while the domain of both of these business practices has the makings of moving the needle forward on sustainable solutions, they remain vastly understudied and not particularly well understood.

Equally perplexing is the role that governance and policy mechanisms play in fostering an enabling environment for sustainable businesses to thrive. The past decades have seen an undeniable shift towards the use of private sector policy innovations, like finance- and market-driven tools (FMDs) and third-party certification schemes, being utilised to address critical issues related to environmental degradation and the overall health of our planet, as articulated in the United Nations SDGs. Results have been, at best, mixed in terms of curbing global deforestation, emissions, or environmental degradation, even when these efforts are part of larger governmental or intergovernmental initiatives. While it has been speculated that continued sustainability challenges are the result of poor policy design, Chapter 8 postulates that it may have more to do with a number of competing conceptions of sustainability and competing notions of what exactly should be transformed in order to create a more sustainable future for all.

We use examples from forestry and forest products to illustrate our points, although the results are portable and applicable to other sectors. We then supplement this broad supposition with two very focused illustrations, also residing squarely within the world of forestry and forest industry. First, borrowing from the case of third-party forest certification, Chapter 9 takes a closer look at the degree to which businesses and non-government organisations (NGOs) can cooperate to produce sustainability-oriented rules and solutions. Second, using an example of insect infestation, Chapter 10 outlines the transformative potential of networked surveillance and digital data exchange in addressing some of the grand challenges of our time. In both cases, the importance of collaboration among stakeholders in achieving sustainable solutions is highlighted.

We end the book with three distinct prognostications, each varying in subject matter and critical stance, on how business sustainability could manifest in the not-too-distant future. The opening volley is a deep dive into the world of sustainability-oriented innovations, which Chapter 11 argues occurs within a broader context of business innovations, and may not – on their own – necessarily be the panacea to tackle the existential threats of an unsustainable planet. Chapter 12 then takes a more radical view by suggesting that, as it stands, businesses and the profit motive cannot co-exist with the notion of a strongly sustainable society. The goals of each with respect to material growth and capital accumulation are diametrically opposed and, consequently, will require a transformational shift in our understanding of what businesses do and how we, as a society, interact and interrelate with our planet. Finally, Chapter 13 takes a more modulated perspective with a consideration of how social and environmental logics can better be incorporated into the business function. One mechanism that shows a good deal of promise is the hybrid organisation. These are businesses with a societal purpose, which focus not on profit maximisation, but on creating a meaningful sustainability orientation.

Our planet is a complicated place – more so now than ever. But it's the only planet that we have, and we must do our utmost to leave a legacy that is not centred around diminishment and increasingly challenging choices. As Chapter 14 reminds us, we must strive for sustainability and solutions that are long-term and intergenerational.

This will not be easy. It will require fresh thinking, bold ideas, innovative solutions, and courageous action. Here, we present some of these ideas – some aligned, some contradictory, all thought-provoking – focusing on the role that business can play in a sustainable world.

We began with a thorny question related to how to reconcile the two seemingly irreconcilable constructs of business and sustainability. This is indeed a grand challenge, and we don't pretend to have all of the answers. But we hope that readers of this book – students, academics, researchers, and practitioners – will take something from it that makes this world a little more sustainable, or at least a little less unsustainable.

We owe it to the planet and the future generations that inhabit it to give it a try.

# 2

# TOWARDS THE IMPLEMENTATION OF THE SUSTAINABLE DEVELOPMENT GOALS IN BUSINESS STRATEGY AND OPERATIONS

*Angelina Korsunova and Kaisa Korhonen-Kurki*

## 1 Introduction

The Sustainable Development Goals (SDGs), also known as the Global Goals, were adopted by all United Nations Member States in 2015 as a universal call to action to end poverty, protect the planet, and ensure that all people enjoy peace and prosperity by 2030. The 17 Sustainable Development Goals and 169 targets demonstrate the scale and ambition of the Agenda 2030 (Figure 2.1).

The SDGs are the first Global Goals that are targeted at all nations in the world – compared to their predecessors Millennium Development Goals (MDGs) that were designed mainly for developing nations. The goals are intended to be treated as universal but also indivisible. The principle of indivisibility means that the implementation of the Agenda 2030 should be based on integrated approaches rather than on siloed knowledge and policy-making (Bennich et al., 2020). Compared to MDGs, SDGs are more inclusive in thinking of where 'sustainable development' should take place. First, they acknowledge the importance of context for considerations of poverty and the experiences of people living in poverty. Second, they concern the expansion of environmental considerations to reflect the responsibility of the richer nations and repositioning of the global development agenda away from the economically poorest countries of the world (Willis, 2016). However, SDGs have been targeted with criticism too. There has been concern that the targets included in the SDGs are not the right ones: it has been suggested that in economic terms, efforts to achieve some of the targets would be 'poor value for money' and they should be changed or dropped entirely (Lomborg, 2014). Furthermore, the agenda has been criticised for not being able to enhance human rights or to reduce gender inequalities in Africa (Struckmann, 2018). Studies of corporate reporting on SDGs point out that there is too little information on corporate policies targeted at eliminating corruption

DOI: 10.4324/9781003003588-3

and action to protect human rights (Tsalis et al., 2020). More importantly, some authors are concerned that SDGs are more representative of 'weak sustainability', which assumes full substitutability of foregone resources with higher income, and do not sufficiently address 'strong sustainability' (also discussed in Chapter 12), that calls for drastic limitations in the use of physical resources (Spangenberg, 2017). Despite these issues, the SDGs now stand as new global development goals agreed to by world leaders and therefore represent a beacon for business activities.

The implementation of SDGs requires collaborative efforts of all stakeholders, and the design of the goals indeed involved broad multi-stakeholder consultations between national governments, the international community, the private sector, civil society organisations (CSOs), and academic institutions (Scheyvens et al., 2016). However, there are also some concerns regarding the donor-driven nature of Agenda 2030 and the uneven involvement of the private sector and CSOs in its design process (Willis, 2016). While the goals were formulated for the national-level purposes, the framework is widely adapted by the cities, and also companies, to track, guide, and boost sustainability activities.

This chapter provides an overview of the complexities associated with SDGs' interconnectedness and their implementation on multinational, national, and individual company levels. Next, it discusses the potential of businesses to contribute to implementation of Agenda 2030 and to advance also those SDGs that are typically considered to be the public policy domain. Further, it offers insights on existing ways to measure progress in SDGS framework implementation by businesses and reviews the benefits of implementing Agenda 2030 in partnerships. In addition to the theoretical framings, the chapter is enriched with managerial insights from a prominent bioeconomy player – Stora Enso – a company producing solutions based on wood and biomass (Box 2.1).

## 2 Levers of Business Involvement with the SDGs

For businesses, SDGs represent an opportunity to renew and discover more avenues for growth aligned with benefits for the society and the environment (Scheyvens et al., 2016). The Business and Sustainable Development Commission estimated that new economic opportunities of engaging with SDGs could amount up to US$12 trillion, hence the rhetoric of creating shared value (Porter and Kramer, 2011). Business consultancies, such as Ernst & Young, emphasise that harnessing the SDGs can help to drive growth, manage risks by re-examining the supply chains, and attract capital as the investment flows are expected to follow the global development challenges (E&Y, 2017). Although SDGs represent an opportunity to develop the corporate capacity for systems change and holistic thinking (Schramade, 2017), sometimes SDGs can just be a box-ticking activity. Embracing Agenda 2030 requires companies to think in terms of broader systemic challenges related to their value chains and meeting societal expectations, beyond the cherry picking of SDG labels to existing CSR activities.

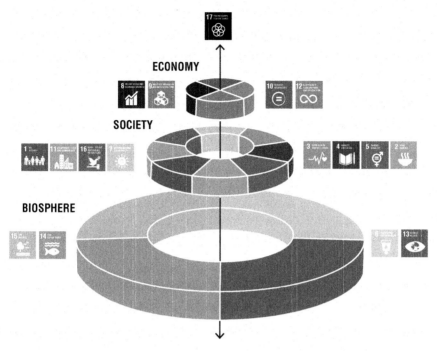

**FIGURE 2.1**   The illustration by the Stockholm Resilience Centre (SRC) implies that economies and societies are embedded in the biosphere.
*Source*: SRC 2017.

The idea that businesses voluntarily engage in creating value for the common good is not paradoxical: it has been shown that participation to non-committal schemes, for example, the UN Global Compact, creates a number of benefits for the companies (e.g. Van der Waal and Thijssens, 2020). It facilitates reputation management, but also corporate learning with a clearly defined policy agenda for sustainability. While certified management systems have been guiding companies for decades on quality-assured ways of engaging with environmental and social issues, many times these processes can be perceived as bureaucratic exercises and can lead to a checklist mentality, reducing the capacity for innovative thinking (Martinuzzi and Schönherr, 2019). In this sense, a global agenda with a delimited set of goals and targets is a tangible opportunity for establishing new connections within the industry and beyond to explore new opportunities for development in the direction of sustainability.

## 3 Nexus Thinking for Interconnected SDGs Implementation

The 17 SDGs are designed to be integrated in a way that they recognise that action in one area will affect outcomes in others, and that development must balance social, economic, and environmental sustainability. There are also strong arguments that no goal should be taken out of the framework without giving thought to its connectedness with others. Nevertheless, there are various attempts to classify the goals to different categories. For example, the Stockholm Resilience Centre classifies the goals to those of environmental scope (biosphere) SDG15, 14, 6, and 13, society SDG1, 11, 16, 7, 3, 4, 5, and 2, and economy SDG8, 9, 10, 12 – all leading to SDG17 (partnerships).

Different methodologies have been developed to assess the interactions, synergies, and trade-offs between different goals. For example, there are methodologies that assess interactions between selected goals and those that focus on correlations between national-level SDGs indicators designed to describe all 17 goals. There are also observations based on voluntary national reviews that the links between the SDGs are subject to divergent interpretations. Synergies and trade-offs have been studied by incorporating experts' opinions to identify the relationships between the SDGs, by analysing the trade-off in SDGs in forest nexus context and by using indicator data to evaluate the interconnectedness of SDGs (e.g. Nilson et al., 2016; Pradhan et al., 2017; Dörgö et al., 2018; Kumar et al., 2018). Finally, the Global Sustainable Development Report (GSDR, 2019) draws together about 200 global studies and assessments addressing interactions between SDGs targets.

The main message from these assessments is that most of the relationships within the SDGs framework are synergistic ones: activities aiming to reach one goal or target tend to improve, directly or indirectly, opportunities to reach other goals or targets. However, some trade-offs have been identified, and often there is a masking effect caused by the parallel existence of synergies and trade-offs. For example, increasing the proportion of renewable energy (SDG7) with forest-based bioenergy may help to replace fossil fuels and mitigate climate change (SDG13), but at least temporarily, it might reduce forest carbon sinks and cause other harmful environmental effects (SDG14, SDG15; Kangas et al., 2018).

'Nexus thinking' is one of the approaches called for to assist in more systemic achievement of SDGs. Originally, it has been applied under the Food-Energy Nexus Programme in 1983 to find integrated solutions to food and energy scarcity, but since then multiple authors have been developing the approach to tackle the interconnected sustainability challenges (Bowen et al., 2017). The essence of the nexus approach is focusing on the interconnections to solve the issues at hand, while applying systemic thinking to make sense of the potential synergies and trade-offs (Liu et al., 2018). As sustainability challenges spread across borders, the nexus approach suggests focusing on the goals, rather than on geographical boundaries. This calls for a multi-centric perspective (Pahl-Wostl, 2019), comprising a balanced negotiation of interests between diverse actors and across sectors. Framing the challenges as an arena for collective action may prove more effective, without placing all responsibility on any single type of actor.

The Global Sustainable Development Report (GSDR, 2019) emphasises the decision-making power, which lies in the private sector to do 'good', and the possibility that businesses have in sharing responsibility for human well-being. For businesses, tackling SDGs coherently and applying nexus thinking would mean mapping all of their products and operations against different sustainability challenges to build assessments of co-benefits and spill-over effects on the scale of different regions or administrative areas (Dahlmann and Bullock, 2020). Negative spillovers can be considered as externalities in economic terminology, and have been debated in sustainability literature for decades. However, positive spillovers – the so-called handprints – have not been discussed as widely and represent positive societal and environmental impacts the companies have.

Currently, in the business context, coherent thinking regarding SDGs is advancing slowly. In particular, there seems to be a divide between small sustainability-driven start-ups and larger companies with more complex structures and impacts. Recent findings suggest that many companies are just beginning to pick up on the interdependencies between sustainability challenges (Dahlmann and Bullock, 2020). Businesses are not the only relevant actors in the sustainability crisis, but it's important for them to be able to review their own contributions to sustainability on regional or global scale (Dyllick and Muff, 2016). Otherwise, the result is a discrepancy between small-scale sustainability activities by businesses and the macro-scale climate emergency. For businesses, building a comprehensive picture would help to recognise and report on the progress towards SDGs in fuller scale, reflecting on synergistic effects. Nexus thinking and adopting multi-centric perspective (examining the problem from the point of view of more than one sector) help to identify the gaps and encourage seeking partnerships with the most relevant actors for the issues in question.

## 4 The Role of Businesses in Advancing Agenda 2030

Although the SDGs 2030 framework is not a reporting tool *per se*, an increasing number of companies worldwide mention SDGs in their reporting (PwC, 2019). PricewaterhouseCoopers has looked at more than 1,000 companies worldwide from a range of different industries and found that 72% of the studied companies mentioned the SDGs in their reporting, but only 14% of the studied companies included specific SDGs targets, while just 1% went as far as measuring the performance against the SDGs targets. This correlates with the findings by Schramade (2017) that corporate use of targets and key performance indicators (KPIs) on the SDGs is very limited despite the increasing importance of SDGs for investment decisions (Betti et al., 2018).

In terms of the number of SDGs, there is no fit-for-all solution: larger companies typically commit to seven or eight SDGs (PwC, 2019), taking into consideration their global operations and complexity. It is also obviously a question of resources, where larger companies are capable of tackling more issues, while smaller companies are more selective, but might engage deeply with the selected SDGs. There also exist examples of companies that have taken all the SDGs and classified all their operations under the goals in such a way that all the goals include several operations. This leads to 'everything relates to everything' – type of analysis, which does not advance companies in their sustainability work and has been referred to as 'rainbow washing'. The Global Reporting Initiative noted that small- and medium-sized companies tend to be more active in measuring and reporting their impact, while multinational companies and large nationals most often go for sustainability reporting and measuring performance (GRI, 2016). Notably, Chapters 12 and 13 in this book, argue that small-scale businesses may be more compatible with the strongly sustainable society. Other proponents of strong sustainability simply suggest that in order for the Agenda 2030 to be operational, it is necessary to impose legally binding targets for the private sector and make all CSR reports verifiable to avoid the danger of 'rainbow washing' (Spangenberg, 2017).

The traditional perception of businesses' role in the society is related to provision of goods and employment. Therefore, it is not surprising that a study by PwC (2019) finds the majority of companies explicitly committing to SDG8 (Decent Work & Economic Growth) and to SDG12 (Responsible Consumption & Production), while SDG1 (No Poverty) and SDG2 (Zero Hunger) remain as the least popular among company commitments. As climate emergency is driving the global sustainability agenda, SDG13 (Climate Action) is among the leading SDGs in terms of expressed corporate commitment (PwC, 2019), despite the fact that earlier this area has been perceived as the responsibility of policymakers (Donoher, 2017). Engaging corporate leaders to the development of the global sustainability agenda makes their political role as apparent as the economic one. Thus, there is hope that businesses will contribute to the diverse range of SDGs. Although certain industries relate to very specific SDGs, still there are many SDGs that are not specific to an industry or market (Schramade, 2017), yet their societal salience is tremendous and so is the potential for corporate contributions towards them.

There remains room for companies to explore how their activities contribute to the SDGs traditionally seen as belonging to the public policy (e.g. SDG6 Clean Water & Sanitation, SDG10 Reduced Inequalities). For instance, promising business opportunities are connected to SDG1 (No Poverty) through microfinance and the bottom of the pyramid solutions (Kolk et al., 2017). Moreover, using the lens of political CSR, SDGs represent an opportunity for addressing human rights using the due diligence thinking and analysing existing institutional voids (Buhmann et al., 2018). It is possible to expand the due diligence analysis to identify not just human rights *risks* related to company's activities and operations, but also human rights *needs* that are non-related to the company, yet potentially within its capacity and contextual strength, offering potential SDGs contributions. Considering the needs calls for cooperation with the wider network of stakeholders, such as the UNDP, local municipalities, local CSOs, and communities to respond to local voids with solutions, improved access to opportunities, or enhanced standards of operating.

## 5 Measuring Progress in SDGs Implementation

At the national level, the progress in SDGs is measured, e.g. through SDG Index, where all the countries are assessed by using global databases (Sachs et al., 2020). At first look, Nordic countries tend to be at the top. However, more recent assessments start to take into account the spill-over effects, referring to the extent of positive or negative effects of the countries' actions on other countries' ability to achieve the SDGs (Sachs et al., 2020). Looking from this perspective, Nordic countries are not performing that well, as many of the actions taken in the industrialised countries often affect negatively to less affluent countries. This reflects the interconnectedness of the goals and the world itself.

Different tools and guides have been developed to advise companies on aligning company strategies with the SDGs (Table 2.1). The SDG Compass Guide, designed jointly by GRI, United National Global Compact (UNGC) and the World Business Council for Sustainable Development (WBCSD), offers a five-step process for getting to know the SDGs, relating them to the core business operations, supporting better anchoring of the SDGs within the business, and general advising on reporting. Also, it highlights how SDGs explicitly call on businesses to solve sustainability challenges through their innovation and creativity. However, since the tracking of progress takes place on the national levels, businesses are facing a nontrivial challenge of reinterpreting and translating SDGs to the business realms (Redman, 2018). The all-encompassing nature of the SDGs framework has proved challenging for establishing a comparable system of measuring progress, even in the public sector (Allen et al., 2017), let alone the private one. Global value chains of business activities complicate the development of measurement systems that would be equally relevant in different national contexts and interfere with the coherency of reporting on business contributions to the progress of SDGs (Schönherr et al., 2017). Since the SDGs are being measured in terms of national progress, transnational businesses face the challenge of trying to quantify their impacts separately for each nation, while being encouraged to always take their global value chains into account (Redman, 2018).

Further on, one of the key problems is that most metrics that companies rely on are still about company-level operations, while measuring progress of SDGs calls for measuring impacts, where the unit of analysis is broader than the company and its operations (Betti et al., 2018). Even the rating organisations for CSR often end up basing their rankings on the formal policies, principles, and various CSR-related activities of the companies, overlooking the actual sustainability performance (Halme et al., 2018). In other words, measuring impact is about shifting the focus from what companies do for sustainability, to what they achieve – linking company-level data to higher-level data on sustainability trends (Schönherr et al., 2017). But in reality, although many of the targets in Agenda 2030 are worded in terms of impacts and appear to be outcome-oriented, proposed indicators are more conservative and oriented towards inputs and outputs

**TABLE 2.1** Examples of existing tools and guides for Sustainable Development Goals (SDGs) implementation and reporting

| | For whom? | Goal | Starting point | Developed by | Free or subject to charge |
|---|---|---|---|---|---|
| *Short guides* | | | | | |
| Eight ways the private sector can apply the Sustainable Development Goals by Cory Searcy | Businesses | To outline the key steps for supporting the SDGs (combined guidance from SDG Compass and guides). | A process map of what company does upstream and downstream of the value chain | International Institute of Sustainable Development | Free |
| How your company can advance each of the SDGs | Businesses | To guide companies and other stakeholders to action-oriented platforms and tools that support SDG implementation. | Getting to know each SDG, relevant cases, platforms, and linked tools | United Nations Global Compact | Free |
| Why Sustainable Development Goals should be in your business plan now | Businesses | To show how organisations can harness the SDGs to drive growth, address risk, attract capital, and focus on purpose. | Identifying the SDGs that have the biggest impact in terms of risk and opportunity over the long term, and the area in which the company has the greatest ability to contribute to the progress towards the goals. | Ernst & Young | Free + customised paid services |

Guides

| | | | | | |
|---|---|---|---|---|---|
| Integrating the SDGs into corporate reporting: a practical guide | Businesses | To embed the SDGs in existing business and reporting processes. | Defining priority SDG targets for reporting. | Global Reporting Initiative | Free |
| SDG guide for business leaders | Businesses | To introduce the SDGs and explain how they can be translated into business value. | Considering how value can be created: 1) through organisational performance; 2) risk management; 3) growth; 4) return on capital | McKinsey & Company | Free + customised paid services |
| Navigating the SDGs: a business guide to engaging with the UN global goals | Businesses | To introduce the SDGs and their implications for business, how each goal is relevant to business; how business leaders can mitigate the risks and grasp the opportunities offered by SDGs. | Getting to know the relevance of SDGs in each country of the world (link to insights and tools offered by PWC) | PricewaterhouseCoopers | Free + customised paid services |
| The UN SDGs: a why, when, and how guide for business | Businesses | To give business leaders the tools they need to understand why the SDGs are relevant to their enterprises, and suggestions for how best to approach these goals. | Defining company priorities and relevant SDGs. | The SDG Business Hub /The Silicon Valley Community Foundation (SVCF) | Free |

(Continued)

**TABLE 2.1** Examples of existing tools and guides for Sustainable Development Goals (SDGs) implementation and reporting (Continued)

| | For whom? | Goal | Starting point | Developed by | Free or subject to charge |
|---|---|---|---|---|---|
| SDG compass | Focus on large multinationals. | To support companies in aligning their strategies with the SDGs and in measuring and managing their contribution (with links to tools and cases). | Understanding the SDGs and getting to know each one. | Global Reporting Initiative, United Nations Global Compact, World Business Council for Sustainable Development | Free |
| Roadmaps | | | | | |
| Chemical sector SDG roadmap | Chemical sector companies | To offer a collective vision for the sector of the key impact opportunities to contribute to its most material SDGs and specific SDG targets – from product innovation to process improvement through to innovative public–private partnerships. | Describing chemical sector's relevance for every SDG. | A group of companies and industry associations from the chemical sector | Free |

| | | | | | |
|---|---|---|---|---|---|
| Forest group's roadmap | Forest sector companies | To articulate a joint vision of the most impactful contributions the forest sector can make through process, product, and partnership innovation to help realise the Agenda 2030 ambitions. | Identifying key SDGs for the sector. | Forward-looking member companies of the Forest Solutions Group (FSG). | Free |
| Roadmap for localising the SDGs: implementation and monitoring at subnational level | Cities and regions | To outline a range of strategies that can be adapted to the specific contexts and needs of different regions. | Raising awareness of local (subnational) SDGs | gtf2016.org Global Task Force of Local and Regional Governments, UNDP, UN Habitat | Free |

Tools

| | | | | | |
|---|---|---|---|---|---|
| SDGs impact assessment tool (learning tool) | Any | To visualise self-assessment of how an activity, organisation, or innovations affects SDGs. | Deciding on the setting and context for the assessment | Gothenburg Centre for Sustainable Development, at Chalmers University of Technology and University of Gothenburg, together with SDSN Northern Europe and Mistra Carbon Exit, Region Västra Götaland | Free |
| SDGs lens (digital tool) | Businesses or others | To guide self-assessment regarding the SDGs. | Prioritising the SDGs most relevant for the business. | Versaus DNV GL | Fee-based |

(Redman, 2018). The input–output language is closely linked to the sets of company activities and operations, which are easy to report, but require an additional effort to be translated into broader societal impacts. In general, the complexity of translating from company-level to system-level of planetary boundaries is the practical challenge where most companies need assistance and strong guidance (Haffar and Searcy, 2017). It has been found that industry sector affects the reporting practices adopted by businesses concerning SDGs (Tsalis et al., 2020). Thus, sector-level decisions and sector-specific guidelines for companies have a huge potential to direct the companies towards good practice (Bjørn et al., 2017).

In the academic literature, materiality assessment is suggested to be an effective method for determining and prioritising sustainability issues, and better enabling the measurement and management of sustainability impacts (Schönherr et al. 2017; Topple et al., 2017). Also, tools like life cycle assessment are relevant for estimating trade-offs and related impacts (Baumgartner, 2019). Linking corporate quantitative indicators to the changes in societal-level sustainability indicators is a complex task, involving the acquisition of comparable and relevant statistical data, sometimes from multiple nations. While there exist a number or impact-oriented tools that provide frameworks for assessing the impact of companies' strategies and operations, they are still limited in their scope and therefore the results of their evaluations must be considered carefully (Temmes, 2019). As the scope of each tool deals only with a specific set of issues, assessing all different impacts might require companies to employ a variety of tools to complete the impact puzzle, which is very resource-intensive. Among examples of impact-oriented tools are the LBG Model, WBCSD Measuring Impact Framework, FICAT, and the Human Rights Compliance Assessment (Temmes, 2019).

Initial steps have been made on the national levels as some countries have performed a gap analysis, looking at the differences between the data they collect, and the data typically found in corporate reporting. Moreover, in some cases, governments work in cooperation with business associations to collect the most relevant data from the private sector to reflect on the SDGs progress (GRI, 2016). Such approaches demonstrate that closer cooperation with companies under the SDG framework is mutually beneficial, because it sends clear signals to the companies on what types of data they should collect and disclose, while it allows governments to complement national statistical information with the data from the private sector to reflect on the SDGs progress.

## 6 Harnessing SDG Opportunities through Partnerships

The UN Development Programme's registry of partnerships has seen a rapid increase in numbers after SDGs have come into play (Bull and McNeill, 2019). It is not surprising, given that SDG17 is devoted to partnerships for the SDGs. In the forest sector, the great importance of partnerships has been recognised in emerging production countries, like Brazil (Tauszig and Toppinen, 2017). However, it is also very important to distinguish between the different types of partnerships to be able to assess their impacts. For example, partnerships focusing on traditional charity activities are considered to have less of a transformative potential than the ones seeking to change production practices and markets (Bull and McNeill, 2019). While changing the standards in the industries can be a lengthy and complicated process, breakthrough innovations usually act as catalysers changing the patterns in the industry and related sectors.

As also discussed in Chapters 3 and 11 in this book, innovating successfully requires companies to go beyond their own boundaries. In fact, focusing on company's own processes and products can only have limited impact, and it is only by engaging in collaborative partnerships, on a sectorial or cross-sectorial levels that businesses can have a wide-reaching sustainability impact – by sharing best practices, defining new rules and standards for operations (Dyllick and Muff, 2016). Dealing with wicked interconnected challenges leads to situations where it is often not clear who should take the responsibility for finding solutions. Under such circumstances interacting with relevant societal stakeholders, understanding societal needs and existing institutional voids can lead companies to disruptive innovations and new organisational forms (Van Tulder, 2018). Research also suggests that businesses that reach out to a diverse range of stakeholders (such as municipalities, NGOs, and educational institutions) and try out different partnering arrangements are better enabled to go beyond business-as-usual and pursue collaborative innovation, allowing multiple actors to advance a shared sustainability agenda (Goodman et al., 2017).

Further, partnerships represent a way to gain additional expertise and share the risks when dealing with complex interconnected issues. While implementation of SDGs requires action from all actors, partnerships and dialogue between actors can help to ensure commitment and accountability. Universities, for example, are particularly important in facilitating the cross-sectoral implementation of SDGs since they are both influential yet neutral actors (El-Jardali et al., 2018). In the midst of political negotiations for prioritising SDG implementation, universities can serve as platforms for cross-sectoral dialogue between government, businesses, academia, and the civil society. Typically, businesses consider universities as secondary stakeholders, as they are not deemed essential for the survival of the business (Clarkson, 1995). Yet, in the context of SDG implementation, universities gain in salience due to their expertise in all sectors of SDGs, and their capability to translate the SDGs into business context, helping businesses to negotiate their role in SDG implementation. For the businesses operating in a transnational context, partnering up with local universities could significantly facilitate building coherent thinking regarding business contributions to SDGs, potential synergies, and spill-overs on the scale of regions where they operate. Nevertheless, university–business collaboration needs to be carefully designed in order to achieve a mutually beneficial process. Universities are not to be used as sustainability validators of the business activities, but to help businesses realise the strategically important areas for their own SDG work and provide critical insights for a company that it could learn from.

Overall, it has been found that sector-specific public–private partnerships can help to develop approaches for measuring impact, taking into account the specifics of the sector (Redman, 2018). Setting sectoral-level standards for reporting impacts is beneficial for all: it is about creating a space where businesses can be honestly accountable and comparable, and allows ambitious goal setting in the future.

## Box 2.1 Stora Enso: managerial insights into SDG integration into company strategy and operations

Stora Enso is a bioeconomy player that develops and produces renewable solutions in packaging, biomaterial, wooden construction, and paper. It is one of the largest private owners of biological assets in the world and all its wood comes from sustainable sources only. Stora Enso's Sustainability Reports are in the top ten in the WBCSD's global ranking.

How has Stora Enso experienced translating Agenda 2030 to suit its core activities?

Although Stora Enso supports all 17 SDGs, it estimates that it contributes the most to three strategic goals: Responsible Consumption and Production (SDG12), Climate Action (SDG13), and Life on Land (SDG15). Stora Enso had a series of workshops to match its own business topics to the SDGs along the entire value chain. These proved to be a useful foresight tool:

> 'The SDGs brought a vision of the world from the highest possible level. We've used this as a strategic tool in different contexts. It helps to see the overall ambition and goals developed for the world. And then, how future-proof our own aims are in relation to this'.

What are some of the challenges Stora Enso has faced when working with the SDGs?

The interconnectivity of the SDGs is something that stands them apart from all other frameworks. This complexity can feel overwhelming, but is actually one of the main strengths of the framework:

> 'I think the great strength of the SDGs is that they highlight the interconnectivity of the sustainability agenda – that we cannot achieve certain environmental goals if we don't progress in social topics. This is a very positive thing, but that said - of course, to make it somehow doable and meaningful in a business context we need to prioritise which areas of our business and our competencies can really make a difference, contribute the most'.

There are multiple challenges related to the measurement and tracking of the progress of the SDGs in the private sector. Depending on the actual products and solutions produced by the company, it may be difficult to develop comparable metrics, even within the same sector:

> *'The measurement of progress – I think it's a big challenge for the private sector, because there are no specific metrics for the framework like there are for the public sector. So, we are working with our own metrics, and our existing disclosures, basically. If we think of external disclosure – then we think of GRI and SASB, because the SDGs don't provide a reporting framework'.*

The net climate benefit is a metric under development, that is especially relevant to all products manufactured from renewable materials and not fossil fuels. It enables highlighting and quantifying the positive contributions that companies make towards the SDGs. Stora Enso has been calculating the substitution effect of its products in terms of climate benefit, i.e. in terms of avoiding the emissions that these products may create.

> *'Measuring impact – that's really challenging. It's something the private sector is moving towards. But it requires this sort of topic-specific work, like the substitution effect mentioned earlier. How do you measure the impact? We are at different stages in this… And often it boils down to the availability of data, and in some cases, the price of data'.*

What are some of the benefits of committing to Agenda 2030?

Agenda 2030 is an opportunity for companies to join new networks and form collaborations with new stakeholders, and for example, work together on the development of more meaningful metrics for tracking the progress of the SDGs:

> *'I think that the SDGs have done this really well: the private sector has also been actively welcomed to the process, which has made it easier for companies. It's like this – it's been taken on by so many stakeholder groups that it has helped Stora Enso feel closer and be closer to certain stakeholder groups, speak the same language more easily – when we've had this framework'.*
>
> *'One concrete benefit of the SDG roadmap was that the forest sector, or the member companies of that group, actually agreed to look into more meaningful targets and KPIs for the sector, which better support their contribution to the SDGs'.*

## 7 Conclusions

There is no doubt that the private sector has an important role in SDG implementation. Engagement of companies to the development of Agenda 2030 has made it explicit that they have both economic and political power in directing societal transitions. The critics towards SDGs view the voluntary engagement basis as insufficient to fully achieve the ambition of Agenda 2030 and call for stricter binding targets for all different actors, including businesses. At the same time, Agenda 2030 is especially valuable as an outcome of a voluntary collaborative development process, with participants publicly recognising their responsibilities and committing to take an active part in achieving the goals. SDGs are both a high-level vision and a contract for companies to adhere to.

The complexity and interconnectedness of the SDGs pose a number of practical challenges for companies. Large multinational players especially may struggle, as adopting coherent approaches to global value chains is complicated by the different ways of assessing and measuring progress in the national contexts. Moreover, companies are facing the task of learning to translate their sustainability activities into sustainability impacts across geographical borders and different sectors. The tools for assisting companies on this journey are still developing and can be intensive in terms of time and data collection. Sector-level guidance and standards on measuring impacts and SDG contributions are crucial to support businesses of various sizes in their SDG-related efforts.

It is still the case that SDGs are sometimes being used only as a communication tool or as a 'sustainability label'. Minimising the superficial use of the SDGs may require institutional-level innovation: a combination of report audits, taxation, legislation, incentives for well-performing businesses. If the integration of SDGs into business strategies starts from local societal needs and institutional voids (rather than own processes only), it may lead to truly disruptive innovations. While nexus thinking and the multi-centric approach help to overcome the silo mentality, they may also assist in singling out more demanding and innovative partnerships, aimed at changing the markets and production patterns. Prioritising these types of partnerships over simple charity projects has a bigger potential for achieving synergies between the SDGs and allowing multiple actors to advance a shared sustainability agenda, while also exploring new sustainable business opportunities.

## References

Allen, C., Nejdawi, R., El-Baba, J., Hamati, K., Metternicht, G. and Wiedmann, T. (2017) 'Indicator-based assessments of progress towards the sustainable development goals (SDGs): A case study from the Arab region', *Sustainability Science*, 12(6), pp. 975–989. https://doi.org/10.1007/s11625-017-0437-

Baumgartner, R. (2019) 'Sustainable development goals and the forest sector - a complex relationship', *Forests*, 10(2), 152. https://doi.org/10.3390/f10020152.

Betti, G., Consolandi, C. and Eccles, R. (2018) 'The relationship between investor materiality and the sustainable development goals: A methodological framework', *Sustainability*, 10, 2248. https://doi.org/10.3390/su10072248.

Bjørn, A., Bey, N., Georg, S., Røpke, I. and Hauschild, M. Z. (2017) 'Is Earth recognized as a finite system in corporate responsibility reporting?', *Journal of Cleaner Production*, 163, pp. 106–117. https://doi.org/10.1016/j.jclepro.2015.12.095.

Bowen, K. J., Cradock-Henry, N. A., Koch, F., Patterson, J., Häyhä, T., Vogt, J. and Barbi, F. (2017) 'Implementing the "sustainable development goals": Towards addressing three key governance challenges—collective action, trade-offs, and accountability', *Current Opinion in Environmental Sustainability*, 26, pp. 90–96.

Buhmann, K., Jonsson, J. and Fisker, M. (2019) 'Do no harm and do more good too: Connecting the SDGs with business and human rights and political CSR theory', *Corporate Governance*, 19(3), pp. 389–403.

Bull, B. and McNeill, D. (2019) 'From market multilateralism to governance by goal setting: SDGs and the changing role of partnerships in a new global order', *Business and Politics*, 21(4), pp. 464–486. https://doi.org/10.1017/bap.2019.9.

Clarkson, M. E. (1995) 'A stakeholder framework for analyzing and evaluating corporate social performance', *Academy of Management Review*, 20(1), pp. 92–117.

Dahlmann, F. and Bullock, G. (2020) 'Nexus thinking in business: Analysing corporate responses to interconnected global sustainability challenges', *Environmental Science and Policy*, 107, pp. 90–98.

Donoher, W. (2017) 'The multinational and the legitimation of sustainable development', *Transnational Corporations*, 24(3), pp. 49–60.

Dörgö, G., Sebestyén, V. and Abonyi, J. (2018) 'Evaluating the interconnectedness of the sustainable development goals based on the causality analysis of sustainability indicators', *Sustainability*, 10, 3766.

Dyllick, T. and Muff, K. (2016) 'Clarifying the meaning of sustainable business: Introducing a typology from business-as-usual to true business sustainability', *Organization & Environment*, 29(2), pp. 156–174.

El-Jardali, F., Ataya, N. and Fadlallah, R. (2018) 'Changing roles of universities in the era of SDGs: Rising up to the global challenge through institutionalising partnerships with governments and communities', *Health Research Policy and Systems*, 16(38). https://doi.org/10.1186/s12961-018-0318-9.

Ernst & Young (No date) 'Why sustainable development goals should be in your business plan now'. *Short Guide*. https://www.ey.com/en_gl/assurance/why-sustainable-development-goals-should-be-in-your-business-plan.

Global Reporting Initiative (2016) 'Measuring impact: How business accelerates the sustainable development goals'. https://www.globalreporting.org/resourcelibrary/Meassuring%20Impact_BCtA_GRI.pdf.

Global Reporting Initiative ( 2018) 'Integrating the SDGs into corporate reporting: A practical guide'. https://www.globalreporting.org/resourcelibrary/GRI_UNGC_Reporting-on-SDGs_Practical_Guide.pdf.

Goodman, J., Korsunova, A. and Halme, M. (2017) 'Our collaborative future: Activities and roles of stakeholders in sustainability-oriented innovation', *Business Strategy and the Environment*, 26(6), pp. 731–753.

Gothenburg Centre for Sustainable Development, at Chalmers University of Technology and University of Gothenburg, in collaboration with SDSN Northern Europe and Mistra Carbon Exit, Region Västra Götaland (No date) 'SDG impact assessment tool'. https://sdgimpactassessmenttool.org7.

Haffar, M. and Searcy, C. (2018) 'Target-setting for ecological resilience: Are companies setting environmental sustainability targets in line with planetary thresholds?' *Business Strategy and the Environment*, 27, pp. 1079–1092. https://doi.org/10.1002/bse.2053.

Halme, M., Rintamäki, J., Knudsen, J. S., Lankoski, L. and Kuisma, M. (2018) 'When is there a sustainability case for CSR? Pathways to environmental and social performance improvements', *Business & Society*. https://doi.org/10.1177/0007650318755648.

International Institute of Sustainable Development. (No date) 'Eight ways the private sector can apply the sustainable development goals'. https://www.iisd.org/articles/eight-ways-private-sector-can-apply-sustainable-development-goals.

Kangas, H-L., Lyytimäki, J., Saarela, S-R. and Primmer, E. (2018) 'Burning roots: Stakeholder arguments and media representations on the sustainability of tree stump extraction in Finland', *Biomass and Bioenergy*, 118, pp. 65–73.

Kolk, A., Kourula, A. and Pisani, N. (2017) 'Multinational enterprises and the sustainable development goals: What do we know and how to proceed?' *Transnational Corporations*, 24(3), pp. 9–32.

Kumar, P., Ahmed, F., Singh, R. K. and Sinha, P. (2018) 'Determination of hierarchical relationships among sustainable development goals using interpretive structural modelling', *Environment, Development and Sustainability*, 20(5), pp. 2119–2137.

Liu, J., Hull, V., Godfray, H. C. J., Tilman, D., Gleick, P., Hoff, H., Pahl-Wostl, C., Xu, Z., Chung, M. G., Sun, J. and Li, S. (2018) 'Nexus approaches to global sustainable development', *Nature Sustainability*, 1(9), pp. 466–476.

Lomborg, B. (2014) 'The United Nations needs a shorter, stronger game plan for humanity', *The Washington Post*, 21 November, https://www.washingtonpost.com/opinions/the-united-nations-needs-a-shorter-strongergame-plan-for-humanity/2014/11/21/a65e14d4-6f7611e4-ad12-3734c461eab6_story.html.

Martinuzzi, A. and Schönherr, N. (2019) 'The sustainable development goals and the future of corporate sustainability', in N. Schönherr and A. Martinuzzi (eds.), *Business and the Sustainable Development Goals: Measuring and Managing Corporate Impacts*. Cham: Springer International Publishing.

McKinsey&Company (2019) 'SDG guide for business leaders'. https://vl.dk/wp-content/uploads/2019/06/20190612-SDG-Guide-full-version.pdf.

Nilsson, M., Griggs, D. and Visbeck, M. (2016) 'Map the interactions between sustainable development goals', *Nature*, 534(7607), pp. 320–322.

Pahl-Wostl, C. (2019) 'Governance of the water-energy-food security nexus: A multi-level coordination challenge', *Environmental Science & Policy*, 92, pp. 356–367.

Porter, M. E. and Kramer, M. R. (2011) 'The big idea: Creating shared value. How to reinvent capitalism and unleash a wave of innovation and growth', *Harvard Business Review*, 89(1), pp. 2–17.

Pradhan, P., Costa, L., Rybski, D., Lucht, W. and Kropp, J. P. (2017) 'A systematic study of sustainable development goal (SDG) interactions', *Earth's Future*, 5, pp. 1169–1179.

PricewaterhouseCoopers (2019) 'The SDG challenge 2019. Creating a strategy for a better world. How the sustainable development goals can provide the framework for business to deliver progress on our global challenges'. https://www.pwc.com/sdgchallenge.

PricewaterhouseCoopers (2016) 'Navigating the SDGs: A business guide to engaging with the UN global goals'. https://www.pwc.com/gx/en/sustainability/publications/PwC-sdg-guide.pdf.

Redman, A. (2018) 'Harnessing the sustainable development goals for businesses: A progressive framework for action', *Business, Strategy and Development*, 1(4), pp. 230–243.

Scheyvens, R., Banks, G. and Hughes, E. (2016) 'The private sector and the SDGs: The need to move beyond "business as usual"', *Sustainable Development*, 24(6), pp. 371–382.

Schönherr, N., Findler, F. and Martinuzzi, A. (2017) 'Exploring the interface of CSR and the sustainable development goals', *Transnational Corporations*, 24(3), pp. 33–47.

Schramade, W. (2017) 'Investing in the UN sustainable development goals: Opportunities for companies and investors', *Journal of Applied Corporate Finance*, 29, 87e99. https://doi.org/10.1111/jacf.12236.

Spangenberg, J. H. (2017) 'Hot air or comprehensive progress? A critical assessment of the SDGs', *Sustainable Development*, 25, pp. 311–321. https://doi.org/10.1002/sd.1657.

Stockholm Resilience Centre, SRC (2017) 'Stockholm resilience centre's contribution to the 2016 Swedish 2030 agenda HLPF report Stockholm'. https://www.stockholm-resilience.org/download/18.2561f5bf15a1a341a523695/1488272270868/SRCs%20 2016%20Swedish%202030%20Agenda%20HLPF%20report%20Final.pdf.

Struckmann, C. (2018) 'A postcolonial feminist critique of the 2030 agenda for sustainable development: A South African application', *Agenda*, 32(1), pp. 12–24. https://doi.org/10.1080/10130950.2018.1433362.

Tauszig, J. and Toppinen, A. (2017) 'Towards corporate sustainability under global agenda 2030: Insights from Brazilian Forest companies', *BioProducts Business*, 2(7), pp. 65–76.

Temmes, A. (2019) 'Managing what matters: Integrating impact measurement into corporate sustainability management', in N. Schönherr and A. Martinuzzi (eds.), *Business and the Sustainable Development Goals: Measuring and Managing Corporate Impacts.* Cham: Springer International Publishing.

The SDG Business Hub / The Silicon Valley Community Foundation, SVCF. (No date) 'The UN SDGs: A why, when and how guide for business'. https://sdghub.com/project/report-the-un-sdgs-a-why-when-and-how-guide-for-business/

Timko, J., P. Le Billon, H. Zerriffi, J. Honey-Rosés, I. de la Roche, C. Gaston, T. Sunderland and Kozak, R. A. (2018) 'A policy nexus approach to forests and the SDGs: Tradeoffs and synergies', *Current Opinion in Environmental Sustainability*, 34, pp. 7–12.

Topple, C., Donovan, J. D., Masli, E. K. and Borgert, T. (2017) 'Corporate sustainability assessments: MNE engagement with sustainable development and the SDGs', *Transnational Corporations*, 24(3), pp. 61–71.

Tsalis, T. A., Malamateniou, K. E., Koulouriotis, D. and Nikolaou, I. E. (2020) 'New challenges for corporate sustainability reporting: United Nations' 2030 Agenda for sustainable development and the sustainable development goals', *Corporate Social Responsibility and Environmental Management*, 27, pp. 1617–1629. https://doi.org/10.1002/csr.1910.

UNDP. (No date) 'Roadmap for localizing the SDGs: Implementation and monitoring at subnational level. Global Task Force of Local and Regional Governments'. *UN Habitat*. https://www.uclg.org/sites/default/files/roadmap_for_localizing_the_sdgs_0.pdf.

UN Global Compact. (No date) 'How your company can advance each of the SDGs'. https://www.unglobalcompact.org/sdgs/17-global-goals.

Van der Waal, J. W. H. and Thijssens, T. (2020) 'Corporate involvement in sustainable development goals: Exploring the territory', *Journal of Cleaner Production*, 252, 119625. https://doi.org/10.1016/j.jclepro.2019.119625.

Van Tulder, R. (2018) *Business & the sustainable development goals: A framework for effective corporate involvement.* Rotterdam: Rotterdam School of Management, Erasmus University.

Verasus DNV GL (No date) 'SDG lens'. https://www.dnvgl.co.uk/assurance/sustainability-strategy/sdg-lens.html.

Willis, K. (2016) 'International development planning and the sustainable development goals (SDGs)', *International Development Planning Review*, 38, pp. 105–111.

# 3

# SUSTAINABLE BUSINESS MODELS

## State of the Art and Emerging Avenues

*Romana Rauter, Tomas Santa-Maria, and*
*Josef-Peter Schöggl*

## 1 Introduction

Unsustainable global developments, such as climate change, social injustice, and economic imbalances require immediate, impactful, and co-ordinated actions from various societal actors. Only the sum of these actions will help us master the related challenges and transform our societies into more sustainable ones (Köhler et al., 2019). Businesses of various forms and sizes represent one group of actors with a powerful role to play here. However, companies' reported progress towards sustainable development (WCED, 1987) is too slow and results in, for example, stakeholders placing more pressure on companies. Practitioners might argue that there is a lack of suitable strategies and approaches that allow businesses to move towards sustainable development while remaining attractive and competitive on the market. In this context, sustainable business models (SBMs) (i.e. business models for sustainability) have received increasing attention and continuing interest from scholars, managers, entrepreneurs, and policymakers over the last two decades (Lüdeke-Freund and Dembek, 2017; van Bommel et al., 2020). The SBM concept helps to systematically describe, define, and innovate the value creation logic of a firm by acknowledging sustainability as a core principle and stakeholders as essential.

The continued interest in SBM research is mirrored by the considerable number of publications on the topic, including special issues (e.g., Dentchev et al., 2016, 2018; Schaltegger et al., 2016a) and literature reviews (e.g., Nosratabadi et al., 2019; van Bommel et al., 2020). International community-building initiatives fostering exchange and collaboration, such as the New Business Models Conference Series founded in 2016, underpin the relevance and attractiveness of SBMs.

However, the thematic foci vary, and researchers take different conceptual and empirical approaches to investigating SBMs. In the absence of a comprehensive

DOI: 10.4324/9781003003588-4

theory to explain SBMs, stakeholder or transition theories, for example, are used to support research and to find solutions to the challenges in business practice, such as how to successfully innovate a business model (BM) in close co-operation with partners (Dentchev et al., 2018).

While some kind of consensus has been reached on the core elements and functions of SBMs, the SBM research field is still heterogenous and fragmented, and new foci and themes continue to emerge. Two reasons for this are the newness of the field and its interdisciplinarity, and its roots being in several fields of research, such as those of conventional BMs, strategy, innovation, and corporate sustainability (Lüdeke-Freund and Dembek, 2017; Dentchev et al., 2018). Content-wise, scholars emphasise various issues, such as greening BMs or social impacts. Some explore the SBMs of entrepreneurial firms or hybrid businesses, while others focus on the SBM characteristics of established firms. Contextual factors such as economic development and geographical location also influence SBMs.

To convey this diversity and shed light on interesting trends, we provide an overview of the state-of-the-art and emerging themes of SBM research. Our aim is to help readers identify opportunities for future research and to provide examples of SBMs in practice.

## 2 Systematising the Literature on Sustainable Business Models

This section contains an overview of the definitions, themes, topical areas, and empirical contexts in SBM research. Section 2.1 discusses the definition of SBMs, and Section 2.2 presents four core themes that emerged from a literature review. Section 2.3 describes four relevant topical areas related to SBM research and presents a brief example of these topics through three concrete cases (Box 3.2). The empirical contexts (e.g., economic paradigm, industry, or company type) in which SBM research takes place are presented in Section 2.3 (Figure 3.4).

### 2.1 Sustainable Business Model Definition

The BM concept involves questions of a strategic nature, such as what services and products to offer to specific groups of customers and other stakeholders (i.e. value proposition), how to create and deliver the offered value (i.e. value creation and delivery), and how to make a profit out of this (i.e. value capture) (Richardson, 2005). Having a BM in place helps a company create value by using resources and capabilities and organising activities in a meaningful way. This requires customer and stakeholder interfaces, infrastructure, and a viable financial model (Osterwalder et al., 2005; Lüdeke-Freund et al., 2019). Business models serve many different functions; they are understood as a link between strategy and implementation, as a means to connect different innovation actors, as a subject of innovation themselves, or as narratives (Aagaard, 2019). However, a fundamental change is taking place in terms of BM logic: the traditional focus on financial and economic viability is being redefined and extended to capture the environmental and social dimensions of sustainability (Stubbs and Cocklin, 2008; Lüdeke-Freund et al., 2019). This is resulting in a triple bottom line approach to measuring performance (Stubbs and Cocklin, 2008); in adopting practices based on circularity, renewables, sufficiency, and sharing (Bocken et al., 2014); or in defining value according to stakeholders' perceptions (Lüdeke-Freund et al., 2020).

The understanding and interpretations of SBMs differ among scholars and practitioners, but most agree that 'A business model for sustainability helps describing, analyzing, managing, and communicating (i) a company's sustainable value proposition to its customers, and all other stakeholders, (ii) how it creates and delivers this value, (iii) and how it captures economic value while maintaining or regenerating natural, social, and economic capital beyond its organizational boundaries' (Schaltegger et al., 2016).

## 2.2 Core Themes in Sustainable Business Model Research

We next describe the four core themes of SBM research, based on the qualitative analysis of the 35 most influential publications in the field. The papers were selected through a historical citation network analysis, applied to a total of 452 scientific articles that were published in the 4.5-year period between January 2016 and June 2020, and were listed on Scopus. This enabled us to systematically outline the development of the field. Since the field is growing rapidly, a 4.5-year perspective seemed to be reasonable, beginning with the year the international Conference on New Business Models was held for the first time. It was the authors' decision to focus on the 35 most influential articles to cover the diversity of content. Further themes and examples were added on the basis of the selected literature and the authors' expertise.

Figure 3.1 illustrates the variety of the thematic foci of these 35 papers. It shows a keyword co-occurrence network based on 'Keywords Plus'.[1] Each keyword is represented by a node and a co-occurrence is denoted by an edge. The nodes' size illustrates their degree (i.e. the total co-occurrences of a keyword), and the edges' weight shows the frequency of the respective co-occurrence. Box 3.1 provides more details on the two analyses applied.

As Figure 3.1 shows, the keywords can be categorised[2] into three clusters. One cluster forms around the most frequently used keyword 'sustainab*', which pools the keywords 'sustainability' and 'sustainable development'. Further frequent keywords in this cluster, in descending order, are 'sustainable business', '(product) design', 'business innovation', and 'value proposition'. The second cluster forms around 'circular economy' and focuses, in addition to the general keyword 'bms*' (= business model(s)), on aspects of 'collaboration', 'resource use', or 'service-oriented systems'. The third and final cluster groups together publications that focus on environmental impact assessment, as illustrated by keywords such as 'life cycle (assessment)', 'global warming potential', or 'eutrophication'.

## Box 3.1 Methods used for the literature review in this chapter

Methods: Historical citation analysis (Garfield, 2004) using R (R Core Team, 2018) and version 2.2.1 of the 'bibliometrix' package (Aria and Cuccurullo, 2017) for determining the 35 most influential articles on the basis of local citation scores (i.e. the number of times an article was cited within the set of 452 articles). The keyword co-occurrence network analysis of the 35 articles using bibliometrix version 3.0.1 (Aria and Cuccurullo, 2017) and Gephi version 0.9.2 for visualisation (Figure 3.1). Only nodes with a degree higher than 15 were included in the network, to keep the illustration lucid. The full reproducible code of both analyses is available at https://osf.io/txacy/.

Database: Scopus

Time period: January 2016 – June 2020

Search string: 'sustainable business model*' OR 'business models for sustainability' in abstracts, titles, or keywords.

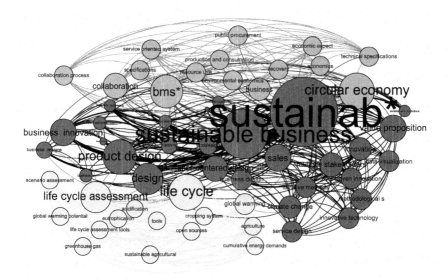

FIGURE 3.1 Keyword co-occurrence network based on the 35 most influential sustainable business model (SBM) articles. The different shades of grey illustrate the three clusters described in the text.

As these three clusters only provide a shallow overview of the field, the four core themes of SBM research denoted in Figure 3.2 were derived in the subsequent qualitative content analysis of the 35 articles. The grouping of the core themes (i.e. thematic groups) is based on the authors' judgement and results from the dataset used for this analysis.

If several publications addressed the same or a similar theme, we grouped them thematically. The aim of this was to provide structured guidance, thus some overlapping is possible, and the grouping is not necessarily comprehensive. Figure 3.2 illustrates these core themes.

The first thematic group consists of publications dealing with *concepts and definitions* of SBM. An example is the previously mentioned definition stating that sustainable value proposition and how to create and deliver it are central (Schaltegger et al., 2016a). In the same year, Upward and Jones (2016) published an ontology for SBMs based on a transdisciplinary literature review. As one result of this review, the authors defined a strongly sustainable firm as an organisation 'that creates positive environmental, social, and economic value throughout its value network, thereby sustaining the possibility that human and other life can flourish on this planet forever' (Upward and Jones, 2016, p. 103 cf. to further literature). As a consequence, organisations can only declare themselves sustainable if they consider their own actions in the context of the wider business network, for which the SBM concept can be helpful. Lozano (2018, p. 6) states that companies realising SBMs need to 'embed sustainability holistically, systemically and integrally into the elements of their BMs' to ensure value creation for both the company and its stakeholders. This needs to be based on attributes such as the cultural, structural, or system-level ones. Abdelkafi and Täuscher (2016) introduced a systems dynamic perspective to advance the understanding of the value

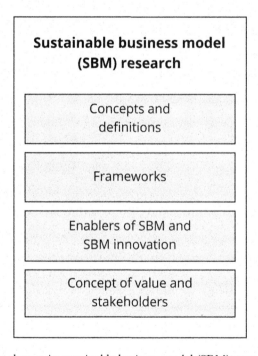

**FIGURE 3.2** Core themes in sustainable business model (SBM) research.

creating logic of SBMs and to model the dynamics of the following four perspectives: the firm, the environment, the decision-maker, and the customer.

The second thematic group focuses on *frameworks* such as canvases, archetypes, and patterns. These help describe and deepen the understanding of the SBM logic and serve as inspiration and tools for change and for innovating SBMs. The Triple Layered Business Model Canvas (Joyce and Paquin, 2016), for instance, combines the original BM Canvas proposed by Osterwalder and Pigneur (2010) with two new additional layers related to the environmental lifecycle and social stakeholder perspectives. The taxonomy of 45 BM patterns, summarised in 11 pattern groups and developed by Lüdeke-Freund et al. (2018), can be helpful for developing SBMs that are independent from contextual factors such as industry or firm size. Examples of such patterns are 'Buy one, give one' or 'Tack back management' (Lüdeke-Freund et al., 2018, p. 153). Yip and Bocken (2018) chose a narrower perspective and developed eight archetypes of SBMs for the banking industry, thus adopting a service-oriented perspective to SBMs. Examples of such archetypes are 'Substitute with digital processes' or 'Resilience in loan granting' (Yip and Bocken, 2018, p. 156). The purpose of the study conducted by Ritala et al. (2018) was to investigate different SBM archetypes (Bocken et al., 2014) employed by US companies listed in the S&P 500 index. Based on a longitudinal data analysis, the findings revealed that these firms were more oriented towards environmental issues and less towards societal and organisational ones (Ritala et al., 2018). To support entrepreneurs in the development of more sustainable firms in the apparel and fashion industry, Kozlowski et al. (2018) developed the reDesign Canvas. As a design tool for sustainability, this canvas consists of building blocks such as '(de)Branding' and 'Prototypes & Product Development' (Kozlowski et al., 2018, p. 200).

*Enablers of SBMs and SBM innovation (SBMI)* make up the third thematic group. Many scholars exploring these themes build on the entrepreneurship and innovation literature, addressing innovation challenges specific to BMs, such as the experimentation approach or entrepreneurial ventures with SBMs. SBMI with strong links to conventional BM innovation (Foss and Saebi, 2016) is a key source of competitive advantage and might be realised in practice in the form of different strategies, such as transforming from one BM to another or implementing a fundamentally new BM (Geissdoerfer et al., 2018b). Despite the fact that innovating BMs differs from process or product innovation (Lüdeke-Freund et al., 2019), the innovation and (sustainable) entrepreneurship literature offers knowledge on how to innovate BMs (Schaltegger et al., 2016b; Dentchev et al., 2018).

Several challenges may arise during the SBMI process. These may include determining how to co-create financial profits and to balance these with social and environmental benefits; how to engage in external relationships with stakeholders; and how to allocate resources appropriately (Evans et al., 2017). This list of questions that managers need to answer continues, as Barth et al. (2017) illustrate in their conceptual framework for SBMI. Franceschelli et al. (2018) applied a single case study in the food industry to explore SBMI within a start-up setting. They identified the following elements as advantageous for SBMI (Franceschelli et al., 2018): using ICT and digital technologies, establishing partnerships, and building the BM around fresh, unique, and sustainable raw materials and specific assets. BM experimentation and design are key tools for determining which new idea or SBM fits best and holds potential for future success (Bocken et al., 2019a). The Ecology of Business Models Experimentation map provides guidance on the experimentation process, on supporting practices such as co-creation sessions, and on outlining the dependencies one should keep in mind, such as interactions with other BMs (Bocken et al., 2019a, p. 1503).

While some scholars specifically addressed SBMI, others investigated the factors that enabled innovating and developing SBMs, although as our analysis revealed, they did not explicitly frame it as SBMI (only). For example, the findings of the empirical case study conducted by Roome and Louche (2016) revealed that three elements were important in the process of developing SBMs: establishing networks and developing 'collaborative practices for learning and action around a new vision'; integrating new external concepts; and 'elaborating an implementation structure within a reconfigured network' (Roome and Louche, 2016, p. 11). Rauter et al.'s (2017) study used a sample of ten Austrian SMEs to explore the characteristics of SBMs. In this context, the following factors were identified as influencing the development of SBMs: legal regulations, leadership, organisational culture, and coherence between corporate strategy and the BM. Todeschini et al. (2017) empirically investigated fashion start-ups to identify the entrepreneurial drivers of SBMs in this industry, such as 'sustainable raw materials', 'capsule wardrobe', and 'recycling' (p. 763). Adopting a social network perspective, Neumeyer and Santos (2018) analysed the influence of individual (e.g., types of network actors) and organisational factors (e.g., types of venture) on the connectivity of ventures in social networks. For this analysis, ventures with both sustainable and conventional BMs were analysed. According to the authors, the results indicated that sustainable entrepreneurs developed 'unique structures, procedures and strategies', supported each other, and created 'a pronounced value system' (p. 4575). Focusing on sustainable entrepreneurship and adopting an evolutionary economics perspective, Schaltegger et al. (2016b) developed a conceptual framework to support the analysis of 'co-evolutionary business model development' (p. 284) for both sustainable niche pioneers and conventional mass market players.

In recent years, an increasing number of studies have been published in which scholars make the *concept of value and stakeholders* the focus of investigation. This is not surprising, considering that the entire discourse on BMs centres around questions of how to create, deliver, and capture value. We grouped these studies as a fourth thematic group. Baldassarre et al. (2017) developed a process model for sustainable value proposition design that combines the principles of user-driven innovation and SBMI. According to them, designing a sustainable value proposition involves the following steps: talking to stakeholders in the network, pondering the sustainability problem, and testing a product/service. The overall aim of this approach is to design and develop sustainable innovations that address sustainability challenges and are accepted by stakeholders. A framework in which different forms of uncaptured value are turned into opportunities for SBMI was elaborated by Yang et al. (2017). It aims to deepen the understanding of the concept of value to promote sustainability. The forms of uncaptured value are: value surplus (such as waste generated), value absence (such as a lack of resources), value missed (such as inefficient use of resources), and value destroyed (such as negative impacts on the environment and society) (Yang et al., 2017). In response to the lack of integration of sustainability domains in the conventional existing BM frameworks, Biloslavo et al. (2018) created the Value Triangle. This triangle exemplifies a company's co-creation and co-delivery of value together with its stakeholders. Brehmer et al. (2018) used a boundary-spanning perspective to BMs to investigate the value exchange (i.e. value transfer) between a focal company and its network partners. Pal and Gander (2018) focused on the environmental value and impact created by BMs in the fashion industry. Strategies such as 'narrowing, slowing and closing the loop of resources' (p. 251) are used to analyse the environmental impact.

## 2.3 Topical Areas Related to Sustainable Business Model Research

SBM research relates to various fields and provides inspiration, knowledge, and support. In the following, we briefly describe four related topical areas in SBM research that resulted from the analysis of the same dataset described in Section 2.1, i.e. the qualitative content analysis of the 35 most influential articles in the SBM scientific literature. Figure 3.3 showcases these topical areas in the form of arrows. At the end of Section 2.3, Box 3.2 presents three real cases reflecting three of the described topics.

The *entrepreneurship and innovation* literature plays an important role in the context of SBMs, and the articles that have addressed these issues were described in Section 2.2 (thematic group: *enablers of SBM and SBM innovation*). For a holistic and complete picture, however, we again list this one topic clearly linked to SBM research.

In recent years, the *circular economy (CE)* has been emerging as one specific context for observing and establishing SBMs. The CE promotes the transformation of waste into resources, thereby addressing environmental, ecological, and social issues (Witjes and Lozano, 2016). Designing and implementing SBMs that support this transformation have gained importance, and 'circular business models' (CBMs) (i.e. BMs for CE) have emerged (Geissdoerfer et al., 2018a). Witjes and Lozano (2016) dealt with the linkages between sustainable public procurement and SBMs in the wider context of CE. They developed a framework that demonstrates how collaboration between procurements and CBMs could lead to reductions in material usage and waste. Adopting a broader perspective, Murray et al. (2017) investigated how CE, as a possible strategy for

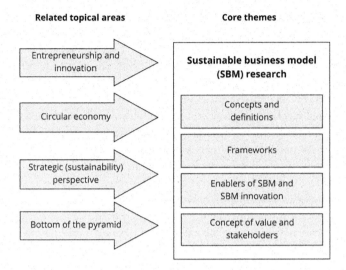

Related topical areas           Core themes

**FIGURE 3.3** Four influential topical areas related to sustainable business model (SBM) research.

contributing to more sustainable BMs, has been applied in business and policy. Geissdoerfer et al. (2018a) compared traditional BMs, SBMs, and CBMs and developed a framework based on case study research that reinforces the links between a single organisation, a specific CBM, and the wider network in which value is created – what they call 'Circular supply chains' (p. 719). The authors also illustrate the overlaps and similarities between the two overarching concepts of sustainable development and CE. Given the importance of the service sector for increased circularity in relating producers to users, Heyes et al. (2018) applied the 'Backcasting and Eco-design to the Circular Economy framework' in an ICT firm located in the UK. This framework, originally developed by Mendoza et al. (2017), is supposed to support companies in the service sector moving towards CE. It illustrates various process steps from envisioning to designing and implementing. Adopting and implementing CBM in the Swedish apparel industry was the focus of a study by Stål and Corvellec (2018). Emerging demands prompt apparel firms to engage with circularity, while decoupling strategies help them buffer this demand and cease closing loops. Decoupling appears in two forms: outsourcing and internal separation (Stål and Corvellec, 2018).

Analysing SBM and SBMI from a *strategic (sustainability) perspective* is another topical area that emerged in the literature. This is in line with the fact that BMs and corporate strategies are linked concepts. França et al. (2017) combined the Framework for Strategic Sustainable Development (FSSD) (Broman and Robèrt, 2017) and the Business Model Canvas (Osterwalder and Pigneur, 2010) with the aim of incentivising and supporting 'business model innovation and design for strategic sustainable development' (França et al., 2017, p. 155). Although they did not merge the two concepts, Rauter et al. (2017) also used the FSSD and the Business Model Canvas to investigate drivers of SBMs. Strategic orientation was found among the drivers on which many respondents agreed. The role and importance of relational leadership for strategic sustainability was addressed in a study by Kurucz et al. (2017). Relational leadership focuses on relationship building, which has the potential to strategically navigate tensions arising from integrating sustainability. The authors used the FSSD (Broman and Robèrt, 2017), the Strongly Sustainable Business Model Canvas (Upward and Jones, 2016), and the Future-Fit Business Benchmark (Kendall and Willard, 2015) in their study.

Finally, of the articles in our dataset, only that by Bittencourt Marconatto et al. (2016) studied the development of SBMs in *bottom of the pyramid* contexts, given the specific governmental programmes and regulations in Brazil. In short, the bottom of the pyramid concept focusses on market segments with people of low income, and initiatives and BMs for how to better serve their needs (Bittencourt Marconatto et al., 2016).

---

**Box 3.2 Three SBM cases reflecting three related topical areas**

Circular economy: IKEA, innovating for circularity
IKEA, the Swedish furniture giant, has committed to being a 'circular and climate positive business by 2030' (IKEA, 2018). To achieve this, it has been experimenting with and implementing SBMs in its different markets. For example, IKEA repair services enable customers to extend product lifetime (more than one million spare parts sold in 2018), and IKEA Japan offers a buy-back service for furniture that is still in good condition, which it then refurbishes and sells at a reduced price.

Entrepreneurship and innovation: Bureo, turning waste to value
Bureo is an innovative start-up that organises the collection of discarded fishing nets from the Chilean coasts, which are later palletised and transformed into products such as Patagonia® hat brims, Humanscale® ergonomic task chairs, and Jenga® blocks (Bureo, 2000). Their SBMI provides income for local fishermen while also cleaning up the ocean and creating value from waste.

Bottom of the pyramid: Aravind Eye Care, putting people first
What started as a social mission-driven 11-bed hospital in 1976 is now one of the largest eye care providers in the world (Aravind Eye Care Systems, 2020). Aravind provides large-volume, high-quality, affordable care to 'eliminate needless blindness'. Two-thirds of its patients receive free care or highly subsidised rates, which are covered by the income generated by the one-third that pays in full.

### 2.4 Contexts of Empirical Sustainable Business Model Research

The SBM concept consists of elements describing the value creation logic of a company. However, the way in which the concept is generally applied – its concrete and specific configuration – depends on the context. This context can be, for example, the economic system or the company's size and purpose. Scholars have chosen different contexts in which to empirically investigate SBMs, and Figure 3.4 showcases these. Figure 3.4 differentiates between overarching contexts that offer principles and inspiration for more sustainable business solutions, such as the already mentioned CE or the sharing economy or bioeconomy. In a sharing economy, the value proposition ranges between product and service orientation as well as between ownership and access (Ritter and Schanz, 2019). The bioeconomy accentuates the potential for sustainability transitions by moving from the use of fossil-based resources to biomass-based ones (D'Amato et al., 2020).

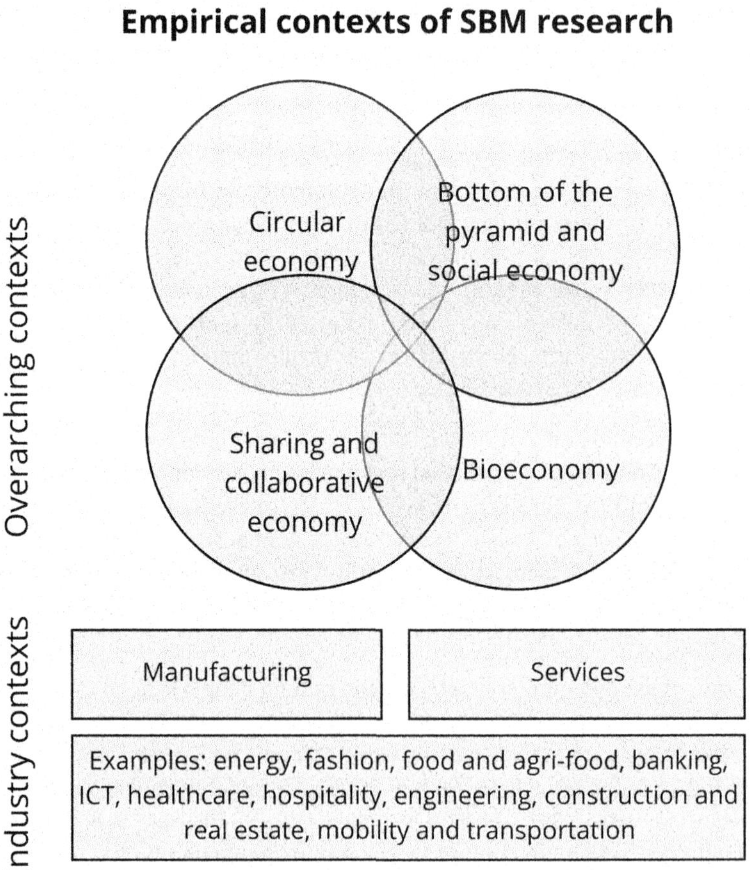

**FIGURE 3.4** Overarching and industry contexts of empirical sustainable business model (SBM) research.

It is worth mentioning that in principle, each business could make its BM more sustainable, regardless of its context. However, certain circumstances in specific areas, such as renewable energy or mobility, might enable SBMs, whereas in other areas, such as in the metalwork industry, this might prove more challenging.

SBM research has so far focused mainly on the energy, manufacturing, and food sectors, which can be explained by the importance of the resources they use and the products and services they provide (van Bommel et al., 2020). Regarding industry contexts in our sample, the fashion and apparel industry (Todeschini et al., 2017; Kozlowski et al., 2018; Pal and Gander, 2018; Stål and Corvellec, 2018) and the food and agri-food sector (Barth et al., 2017; Franceschelli et al., 2018) were used frequently. Service-oriented companies, such as banks (Yip and Bocken, 2018) or ICT companies (Biloslavo et al., 2018; Heyes et al., 2018), were also objects of investigation. Many authors used data from different and mixed samples in their studies (e.g., Rauter et al., 2017; Brehmer et al., 2018; Bocken et al., 2019a). Other industry contexts investigated in recent years have been healthcare, hospitality, engineering, construction and real estate, and mobility and transportation (Nosratabadi et al., 2019).

## 3  Summary and Outlook

Researchers, entrepreneurs, policymakers, managers, and consumers are expressing growing interest in companies' BMs and sustainability issues. Changing and innovating a BM is key for creating business opportunities while considering the positive and negative impacts on the environment and society. Transforming our societies into more sustainable ones will only be successful if multiple actors co-ordinate their activities and efforts in line with the principles of sustainable development and political strategies such as the CE. The overview of the recent literature presented here revealed an array of relevant themes, related topical areas, and contexts that SBM scholars have investigated, and represents the current spotlight on a rapidly growing research area. The analysis suggests that SBM research relates to and is influenced by several fields, such as entrepreneurship and innovation or strategy. Overall, SBM research is becoming increasingly diversified and specific and is changing rapidly, as indicated by the fast-growing number of publications. This can be considered positive for the further establishment of the field, but it might also limit generalisability and impede placement. This overview is intended to help the reader orientate her/himself and to provide ideas and inspiration. To conclude, we highlight some future research avenues that we consider relevant and promising for SBM researchers and practitioners. Figure 3.5 showcases these promising topics in the form of dotted arrows and provides a final summary.

Given the urgency of implementing sustainable development, *social and inclusive business models* (Seelos and Mair, 2005; Yunus et al., 2010; Michelini and Fiorentino, 2012) need to become more important. This would also imply a

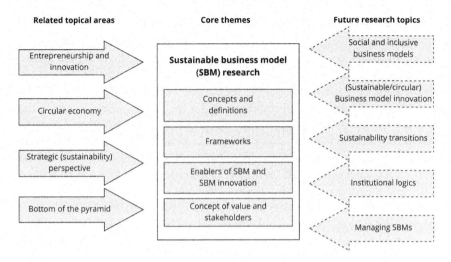

Related topical areas        Core themes        Future research topics

**FIGURE 3.5** Past and future of sustainable business model (SBM) research.

necessary shift in the geographical focus from the northern to the southern hemisphere (van Bommel et al., 2020).

*SBMI and CBM innovation* (CBMI) will remain key topics in the future. However, such innovation is a complex and challenging task, as firms navigate unknown terrain that might involve changing the key building blocks of their businesses and going against the dominant business paradigms. This requires proactive engagement with stakeholders, partnerships throughout the supply chain, and the development of a novel set of organisational capabilities (Bocken et al., 2018, 2019b). Most of these tasks entail going beyond the company's boundaries to innovate successfully and collaboratively (e.g., Velter et al., 2020; Pedersen et al., 2021). A considerable number of tools, methods, and conceptual models have emerged to support this process in recent years, reflected in the 92 approaches reviewed by Pieroni et al. (2019).

Another promising emerging theme within SBM research is its integration with the wider *sustainability transitions* literature. Supported by the understanding of BMs as boundary spanning (beyond the focal firm and in relation to its network), the role of SBMs in socio-technical system transformations is being explored from a multi-level perspective (Bidmon and Knab, 2018; Sarasini and Linder, 2018). This perspective has been explored in the context of mobility services (Sarasini and Linder, 2018), reuse centres (Gorissen et al., 2016), and energy service companies (Bolton and Hannon, 2016).

Recognising the diversity of SBMs and the variety of the *institutional logics* shaping them presents another potential future avenue (Laasch, 2018). Finally, the overall topic of *managing SBMs* will also require attention in the future. Successfully managing SBMs means more deeply understanding the context in which the company is located. This includes internal factors such as resources and strategies and external settings such as political and cultural contexts (van Bommel et al., 2020). Including stakeholders for the purpose of sustainable value creation (Freudenreich et al., 2020; Lüdeke-Freund et al., 2020) and co-creating SBM with ecosystem partners are further examples that have recently been addressed (e.g., Konietzko et al., 2020). Last but not least, metrics and indicators for evaluating the performance and impact of SBMs (e.g., Rauter et al., 2019) and clarifying management responsibilities are also issues worth mentioning.

Addressing sustainability with innovative, promising SBMs will remain key in the future as this builds one element of a societal change that results in a sound development aligned with sustainability principles. This, of course, represents only one possible approach. SBMs might be best understood if considered from a holistic perspective and put into context with notions such as the relations between businesses and a strongly sustainable society (see Chapters 12 and 13), businesses' engagement with the SDGs (see Chapter 2), or the circular bioeconomy (see Chapters 5 and 6).

## Notes

1 These keywords are assigned manually by Scopus and contain fewer specific descriptors of the content of the papers than the author keywords. Therefore, they are generally considered to have a broader meaning, making them suitable for an overview of a research area (Zhang et al., 2016).
2 The three clusters (i.e. modularity classes), illustrated in different shades of grey, were determined using the Louvain algorithm (Blondel et al., 2008) in Gephi.

## References

Aagaard, A. (2019) 'Identifying sustainable business models through sustainable value creation', in A. Aagaard (ed.), *Sustainable Business Models. Innovation, Implementation and Success*. Cham: Palgrave Macmillan.

Abdelkafi, N. and Täuscher, K. (2016) 'Business models for sustainability from a system dynamics perspective', *Organization & Environment*, 29(1), pp. 74–96. https://doi.org/10.1177/1086026615592930.

Aravind Eye Care Systems (2020) 'Genesis. A humble beginning'. https://aravind.org/our-story.

Aria, M. and Cuccurullo, C. (2017) 'Bibliometrix: An R-tool for comprehensive science mapping analysis', *Journal of Informetrics*, 11(4), pp. 959–975. https://doi.org/10.1016/j.joi.2017.08.007.

Baldassarre, B. Calabretta, G., Bocken, N. M. P. and Jaskiewicz, T. (2017) 'Bridging sustainable business model innovation and user-driven innovation: A process for sustainable value proposition design', *Journal of Cleaner Production*, 147, pp. 175–186. https://doi.org/10.1016/j.jclepro.2017.01.081.

Barth, H., Ulvenblad, P. O., and Ulvenblad, P. (2017) 'Towards a conceptual framework of sustainable business model innovation in the agri-food sector: A systematic literature review', *Sustainability*, 9(9), 1620. https://doi.org/10.3390/su9091620.

Bidmon, C. M. and Knab, S. F. (2018) 'The three roles of business models in societal transitions: New linkages between business model and transition research', *Journal of Cleaner Production*, 178, pp. 903–916. https://doi.org/10.1016/j.jclepro.2017.12.198.

Biloslavo, R., Bagnoli, C. and Edgar, D. (2018) 'An eco-critical perspective on business models: The value triangle as an approach to closing the sustainability gap', *Journal of Cleaner Production*, 174, pp. 746–762. https://doi.org/10.1016/j.jclepro.2017.10.281.

Bittencourt Marconatto, D. A., Barin-Cruz, L., Pozzebon, M., and Poitras, J. E. (2016) 'Developing sustainable business models within BOP contexts: Mobilizing native capability to cope with government programs', *Journal of Cleaner Production*, 129, pp. 735–748. https://doi.org/10.1016/j.jclepro.2016.03.038.

Blondel, V. D., Guillaume, J. L., Lambiotte, R. and Lefebvre, E. (2008) 'Fast unfolding of communities in large networks', *Journal of Statistical Mechanics: Theory and Experiment*, p. 10008. https://doi.org/10.1088/1742-5468/2008/10/P10008.

Bocken, N., Boons, F., and Baldassarre, B. (2019a) 'Sustainable business model experimentation by understanding ecologies of business models', *Journal of Cleaner Production*, 208, pp. 1498–1512. https://doi.org/10.1016/j.jclepro.2018.10.159.

Bocken, N., Schuit, C. S. C., and Kraaijenhagen, C. (2018, September) 'Experimenting with a circular business model: Lessons from eight cases', *Environmental Innovation and Societal Transitions*, 28, pp. 79–95. https://doi.org/10.1016/j.eist.2018.02.001.

Bocken, N., Strupeit, L., Whalen, K. and Nußholz, J. (2019b) 'A review and evaluation of circular business model innovation tools', *Sustainability*, 11(8), 2210. https://doi.org/10.3390/su11082210.

Bocken, N. M. P., Short, S. W., Rana, P. and Evans, S. (2014) 'A literature and practice review to develop sustainable business model archetypes', *Journal of Cleaner Production*, 65, pp. 42–56. https://doi.org/10.1016/j.jclepro.2013.11.039.

Bolton, R. and Hannon, M. (2016) 'Governing sustainability transitions through business model innovation: Towards a systems understanding', *Research Policy*, 45(9), pp. 1731–1742. https://doi.org/10.1016/j.respol.2016.05.003.

Brehmer, M., Podoynitsyna, K. and Langerak, F. (2018) 'Sustainable business models as boundary-spanning systems of value transfers', *Journal of Cleaner Production*, 172, pp. 4514–4531. https://doi.org/10.1016/j.jclepro.2017.11.083.

Broman, G. I. and Robèrt, K.-H. (2017, January) 'A framework for strategic sustainable development', *Journal of Cleaner Production*, 140 (Part 1), pp. 17–31. https://doi.org/10.1016/j.jclepro.2015.10.121.

Bureo (2000) 'Bureo'. https://bureo.co/ (Accessed 31 December 2020).

D'Amato, D., Veijonaho, S. and Toppinen, A. (2020) 'Towards sustainability? Forest-based circular bioeconomy business models in Finnish SMEs', *Forest Policy and Economics*, 110, 101848. https://doi.org/10.1016/j.forpol.2018.12.004.

Dentchev, N., Baumgartner, R., Dieleman, H., Jóhannsdóttir, L., Jonker, J., Nyberg, T., Rauter, R., Rosano, M., Snihur, Y., Tang, X. and van Hoof, B. (2016, February) 'Embracing the variety of sustainable business models: Social entrepreneurship, corporate intrapreneurship, creativity, innovation, and other approaches to sustainability challenges', *Journal of Cleaner Production*, 113, pp. 1–4. https://doi.org/10.1016/j.jclepro.2015.10.130.

Dentchev, N., Rauter, R., Jóhannsdóttir, L., Snihur, Y., Rosano, M., Baumgartner, R. J., Nyberg, T., Tangh, X., van Hoof, B., and Jonker, J. (2018, September) 'Embracing the variety of sustainable business models: A prolific field of research and a future research agenda', *Journal of Cleaner Production*, 194, pp. 695–703. https://doi.org/10.1016/j.jclepro.2018.05.156.

Evans, S., Vladimirova, D., Holgado, M., Von Fossen, K., Yang, M., Silva, E. A., and Barlow, C. Y. (2017) 'Business model innovation for sustainability: Towards a unified perspective for creation of sustainable business models', *Business Strategy and the Environment*, 26(5), pp. 597–608. https://doi.org/10.1002/bse.1939.

Foss, N. J. and Saebi, T. (2016) 'Fifteen years of research on business model innovation: How far have we come, and where should we go?', *Journal of Management*, 43(1), pp. 200–227. https://doi.org/10.1177/0149206316675927.

França, C. L., Broman, G., Robèrt, K. H., Basile, G. and Trygg, L. (2017) 'An approach to business model innovation and design for strategic sustainable development', *Journal of Cleaner Production*, 140, pp. 155–166. https://doi.org/10.1016/j.jclepro.2016.06.124.

Franceschelli, M. V., Santoro, G. and Candelo, E. (2018) 'Business model innovation for sustainability: A food start-up case study', *British Food Journal*, 120(10), pp. 2483–2494. https://doi.org/10.1108/BFJ-01-2018-0049.

Freudenreich, B., Lüdeke-Freund, F. and Schaltegger, S. (2020) 'A stakeholder theory perspective on business models: Value creation for sustainability', *Journal of Business Ethics*, 166, pp. 3–18. https://doi.org/10.1007/s10551-019-04112-z.

Garfield, E. (2004) 'Historiographic mapping of knowledge domains literature', *Journal of Information Science*, 30(2), 119–145. https://doi.org/10.1177/0165551504042802.

Geissdoerfer, M., Morioka, S. N., de Carvalho, M. M. and Evans, S. (2018a) 'Business models and supply chains for the circular economy', *Journal of Cleaner Production*, 190, pp. 712–721. https://doi.org/10.1016/j.jclepro.2018.04.159.

Geissdoerfer, M., Vladimirova, D., and Evans, S. (2018b, October) 'Sustainable business model innovation: A review', *Journal of Cleaner Production*, 198, pp. 401–416. https://doi.org/10.1016/j.jclepro.2018.06.240.

Gorissen, L., Vrancken, K. and Manshoven, S. (2016) 'Transition thinking and business model innovation–towards a transformative business model and new role for the reuse centers of Limburg, Belgium', *Sustainability*, 8(2), 112. https://doi.org/10.3390/su8020112.

Heyes, G., Sharmina, M., Mendoza, J. M. F., Gallego-Schmid, A., and Azapagic, A. (2018) 'Developing and implementing circular economy business models in service-oriented technology companies', *Journal of Cleaner Production*, 177, pp. 621–632. https://doi.org/10.1016/j.jclepro.2017.12.168.

IKEA (2018) 'IKEA sustainability report FY18'. https://preview.thenewsmarket.com/Previews/IKEA/DocumentAssets/535135.pdf (Accessed 31 December 2020).

Joyce, A. and Paquin, R. L. (2016) 'The triple layered business model canvas: A tool to design more sustainable business models', *Journal of Cleaner Production*, 135, pp. 1474–1486. https://doi.org/10.1016/j.jclepro.2016.06.067.

Kendall, G. and Willard, B. (2015) *Future-Fit Business Benchmark-Public Draft 1.0.* http://www.truevaluemetrics.org/DBpdfs/Metrics/FutureFit/Future-Fit-Business-Benchmark-Public-Draft-1.pdf.

Köhler, J., Geels, F. W., Kern, F., Markard, J., Onsongo, E., Wieczorek, A., Alkemade, F., Avelino, F., Bergek, A., Boons, F., Fünfschilling, L., Hess, D., Holtz, G., Hyysalo, S., Jenkins, K., Kivimaa, P., Martinskainen, M., McMeekin, A., Mühlemeier, M. S., Nykvist, B., Pel, B., Raven, R., Rohracher, H., Sandén, B., Schot, J., Sovacool, B., Turnheim, B., Welch, D. and Wells, P. (2019) 'An agenda for sustainability transitions research: State of the art and future directions', *Environmental Innovation and Societal Transitions*, 31, pp. 1–32. https://doi.org/10.1016/j.eist.2019.01.004.

Konietzko, J., Bocken, N., and Hultink, E. J. (2020) 'Circular ecosystem innovation: An initial set of principles', *Journal of Cleaner Production*, 253, 119942. https://doi.org/10.1016/j.jclepro.2019.119942.

Kozlowski, A., Searcy, C., and Bardecki, M. (2018) 'The reDesign canvas: Fashion design as a tool for sustainability', *Journal of Cleaner Production*, 183, pp. 194–207. https://doi.org/10.1016/j.jclepro.2018.02.014.

Kurucz, E. C., Colbert, B. A., Lüdeke-Freund, F., Upward, A., and Willard, B. (2017) 'Relational leadership for strategic sustainability: Practices and capabilities to advance the design and assessment of sustainable business models', *Journal of Cleaner Production*, 140, pp. 189–204. https://doi.org/10.1016/j.jclepro.2016.03.087.

Laasch, O. (2018) 'Beyond the purely commercial business model: Organizational value logics and the heterogeneity of sustainability business models', *Long Range Planning*, 51(1), pp. 158–183. https://doi.org/10.1016/j.lrp.2017.09.002.

Lozano, R. (2018) 'Sustainble business models: Providing a more holistic perspective', *Business Strategy and the Environment*, 27(8), pp. 1159–1166.

Lüdeke-Freund, F., Carroux, S., Joyce, A., Massa, L., and Breuer, H. (2018) 'The sustainable business model pattern taxonomy—45 patterns to support sustainability-oriented business model innovation', *Sustainable Production and Consumption*, 15, pp. 145–162. https://doi.org/10.1016/j.spc.2018.06.004.

Lüdeke-Freund, F., and Dembek, K. (2017, December) 'Sustainable business model research and practice: Emerging field or passing fancy?', *Journal of Cleaner Production*, 168, pp. 1668–1678. https://doi.org/10.1016/j.jclepro.2017.08.093.

Lüdeke-Freund, F., Rauter, R., Gjerdrum Pedersen, E. R., and Nielsen, C. (2020) 'Sustainable value creation through business models: The what, the who and the how', *Journal of Business Models*, 8(3), pp. 62–90.

Lüdeke-Freund, F., Schaltegger, S. and Dembek, K. (2019) 'Strategies and drivers of sustainable business model innovation', in F. Boons and A. McMeekin (eds.), *Handbook of Sustainable Innovation*. Cheltenham and Northampton: Edward Elgar Publishing Limited.

Mendoza, J. M. F., Sharmina, M., Gallego-Schmid, A., Heyes, G. and Azapagic, A. (2017) 'Integrating backcasting and eco-design for the circular economy: The BECE framework', *Journal of Industrial Ecology*, 21(3), pp. 526–544. https://doi.org/10.1111/jiec.12590.

Michelini, L., and Fiorentino, D. (2012) 'New business models for creating shared value', *Social Responsibility Journal*, 8(4), pp. 561–577.

Murray, A., Skene, K. and Haynes, K. (2017) 'The circular economy: An interdisciplinary exploration of the concept and application in a global context', *Journal of Business Ethics*, 140, pp. 369–380. https://doi.org/10.1007/s10551-015-2693-2.

Neumeyer, X. and Santos, S. C. (2018) 'Sustainable business models, venture typologies, and entrepreneurial ecosystems: A social network perspective', *Journal of Cleaner Production*, 172, pp. 4565–4579. https://doi.org/10.1016/j.jclepro.2017.08.216.

Nosratabadi, S., Mosavi, A., Shamshirband, S., Kazimieras Zavadskas, E., Rakotonirainy, A. and Chau, K. W. (2019) 'Sustainable business models: A review', *Sustainability*, 11(6), 1663. https://doi.org/10.3390/su11061663.

Osterwalder, A. and Pigneur, Y. (2010) *Business Model Generation*. Hoboken, NJ: John Wiley & Sons.

Osterwalder, A., Pigneur, Y. and Tucci, C. L. (2005) 'Clarifying business models: Origins, present, and future of the concept', *Communications of the Association for Information Systems*, 16, pp. 1–25.

Pal, R. and Gander, J. (2018) 'Modelling environmental value: An examination of sustainable business models within the fashion industry', *Journal of Cleaner Production*, 184, pp. 251–263. https://doi.org/10.1016/j.jclepro.2018.02.001.

Pedersen, E. R. G., Lüdeke-Freund, F., Henriques, I. and Seitanidi, M. M. (2021) 'Toward collaborative cross-sector business models for sustainability', *Business & Society*, 60(5), pp. 1039–1058. https://doi.org/10.1177/0007650320959027.

Pieroni, M., McAloone, T. and Pigosso, D. (2019) 'Business model innovation for circular economy: Integrating literature and practice into a conceptual process model', *Proceedings of the International Conference on Engineering Design, ICED*, 1(1), pp. 2517–2526. https://doi.org/10.1017/dsi.2019.258.

R Core Team (2018) *R: A Language and Environment for Statistical Computing*. Vienna: R Foundation for Statistical Computing.

Rauter, R., Jonker, J., and Baumgartner, R. J. (2017, January) 'Going one's own way: Drivers in developing business models for sustainability', *Journal of Cleaner Production*, 140, pp. 144–154. https://doi.org/10.1016/j.jclepro.2015.04.104.

Rauter, R., Zimek, M., Baumgartner, R. J. and Schöggl, J.-P. (2019) 'Assessing the impacts of sustainable business models: Challenges, key issues and future research opportunities', in N. Bocken et al. (eds.), *Innovation for Sustainability*. Cham: Palgrave Studies in Sustainable Business in Association with Future Earth, Palgrave Macmillan. https://doi.org/10.1007/978-3-319-97385-2_14.

Richardson, J. E. (2005) 'The business model: An integrative framework for strategy execution', *SSRN Electronic Journal*, 17, pp. 133–144. https://doi.org/10.2139/ssrn.932998.

Ritala, P., Huotari, P., Bocken, N., Albareda, L. and Puumalainen, K. (2018) 'Sustainable business model adoption among S&P 500 firms: A longitudinal content analysis study', *Journal of Cleaner Production*, 170, pp. 216–226. https://doi.org/10.1016/j.jclepro.2017.09.159.

Ritter, M. and Schanz, H. (2019) 'The sharing economy: A comprehensive business model framework', *Journal of Cleaner Production*, 213, pp. 320–331. https://doi.org/10.1016/j.jclepro.2018.12.154.

Roome, N. and Louche, C. (2016) 'Journeying toward business models for sustainability: A conceptual model found inside the black box of organisational transformation', *Organization & Environment*, 29(1), pp. 11–35. https://doi.org/10.1177/1086026615595084.

Sarasini, S. and Linder, M. (2018) 'Integrating a business model perspective into transition theory: The example of new mobility services', *Environmental Innovation and Societal Transitions*, 27, pp. 16–31. https://doi.org/10.1016/j.eist.2017.09.004.

Schaltegger, S., Hansen, E. G. and Lüdeke-Freund, F. (2016a) 'Business models for sustainability: Origins, present research, and future avenues', *Organization & Environment*, 29(1), pp. 3–10. https://doi.org/10.1177/1086026615599806.

Schaltegger, S., Lüdeke-Freund, F. and Hansen, E. G. (2016b) 'Business models for sustainability: A co-evolutionary analysis of sustainable entrepreneurship, innovation, and transformation', *Organization & Environment*, 29(3), pp. 264–289. https://doi.org/10.1177/1086026616633272.

Seelos, C. and Mair, J. (2005) 'Social entrepreneurship: Creating new business models to serve the poor', *Business Horizons*, 48(3), pp. 241–246. https://doi.org/10.1016/j.bushor.2004.11.006.

Stål, H. I. and Corvellec, H. (2018) 'A decoupling perspective on circular business model implementation: Illustrations from Swedish apparel', *Journal of Cleaner Production*, 171, pp. 630–643. https://doi.org/10.1016/j.jclepro.2017.09.249.

Stubbs, W. and Cocklin, C. (2008) 'Conceptualizing a 'sustainability business model'', *Organization & Environment*, 21(2), pp. 103–127. https://doi.org/10.1177/1086026608318042.

Todeschini, B. V., Cortimiglia, M. N., Callegaro-de-Menezes, D. and Ghezzi, A. (2017) 'Innovative and sustainable business models in the fashion industry: Entrepreneurial drivers, opportunities, and challenges', *Business Horizons*, 60(6), pp. 759–770. https://doi.org/10.1016/j.bushor.2017.07.003.

Upward, A. and Jones, P. (2016) 'An ontology for strongly sustainable business models: Defining an enterprise framework compatible with natural and social science', *Organization & Environment*, 29(1), pp. 97–123. https://doi.org/10.1177/1086026615592933.

van Bommel, K., Blanson Henkemans, M., Brinkhorst, T. and Meurs, M. (2020) 'A review of sustainable business models: Past accomplishments review of sustainable business models: Past accomplishments and future promises', *Journal of Sustainability Research*, 2(3e200022), 25. https://doi.org/10.20900/jsr20200022.

Velter, M. G. E., Bitzer, V., Bocken, N. M. P. and Kemp, R. (2020) 'Sustainable business model innovation: The role of boundary work for multi-stakeholder alignment', *Journal of Cleaner Production*, 247, 119497. https://doi.org/10.1016/j.jclepro.2019.119497.

Witjes, S. and Lozano, R. (2016) 'Towards a more circular economy: Proposing a framework linking sustainable public procurement and sustainable business models', *Resources, Conservation and Recycling*,112, pp. 37–44. https://doi.org/10.1016/j.resconrec.2016.04.015.

World Commission on Environment and Development (WCED) (1987) *Our Common Future, Our Common Future*. Oxford: Oxford University Press.

Yang, M., Evans, S., Vladimirova, D., and Rana, P. (2017) 'Value uncaptured perspective for sustainable business model innovation', *Journal of Cleaner Production*, 140, pp. 1794–1804. https://doi.org/10.1016/j.jclepro.2016.07.102.

Yip, A. W. H. and Bocken, N. M. P. (2018) 'Sustainable business model archetypes for the banking industry', *Journal of Cleaner Production*, 174, pp. 150–169. https://doi.org/10.1016/j.jclepro.2017.10.190.

Yunus, M., Moingeon, B. and Lehmann-Ortega, L. (2010) 'Building social business models: Lessons from the Grameen experience', *Long Range Planning*, 43(2–3), pp. 308–325. https://doi.org/10.1016/j.lrp.2009.12.005.

Zhang, J., Yu, Q., Zheng, F., Long, C., Lu, Z. and Duan, Z.(2016) 'Comparing keywords plus of WOS and author keywords: A case study of patient adherence research', *Journal of the Association for Information Science and Technology*, 67(4), pp. 967–972. https://doi.org/10.1002/asi.23437.

# PART 2
# Framing and Managing Sustainability

# 4

# POTENTIAL OF THE GREEN ECONOMY DISCOURSE TO ADVANCE SUSTAINABILITY IN BUSINESS

*Maria Fernanda Tomaselli, Kahlil Baker, Michael Barkusky and Noriko Kusumi*

## 1 Introduction

Neoliberal economic theory is predicated on the idea that economic growth improves human welfare. Yet, human well-being is inextricably linked to the health of our environment, and the unfortunate truth is that economic growth is commonly linked to environmental destruction (Whiting et al., 2018). Unprecedented economic growth over the last century has led to a significant increase in material welfare at the expense of the natural world. We have now reached a point at which welfare gains are undermined by welfare losses, driven by increased environmental degradation due to the over-consumption and exploitation of natural resources (Daly, 2015).

The concept of a green economy has emerged through recognition that 'getting the economy right' is key for sustainability (UNEP, 2011). Although the green economy concept dates back to the late 1980s, it has regained prominence in light of the financial crisis of 2008 and the current climate and biodiversity loss emergencies (Merino-Saum et al., 2020). The green economy centres on the idea that environmental externalities should be fully accounted for, with the emphasis on financially driven markets and the private sector.

Many countries have begun adopting this green discourse, which seeks to continue developing economies in tandem with environmental and social sustainability goals. Moreover, trends for greening industries are gaining traction. For example, markets for ecosystem services and certified agricultural and forestry products have more than doubled in the past decade, with an estimated value of annual transactions between USD 36 and USD 42 billion for payment for ecosystem services only (TEEB, 2010b; Salzman et al., 2018).

Despite the uptake of the green economy, it is important to assess how transformational this proposal has actually been. This chapter critically evaluates the

DOI: 10.4324/9781003003588-6

green economy discourse and practice and its potential to steer human economic activity onto a more sustainable path. It discusses the green economy concept at the global, national, and ultimately, the firm level.

The chapter is organised into five main sections. This first section introduces the topic. Section 2 uncovers the most prevalent conceptualisations of the green economy and describes a business case study that incorporates green economy principles into its *modus operandi*. Section 3 explores macro- and micro-level indicators for tracking progress towards green goals, while Section 4 investigates the state of green finance and socially responsible investment (SRI). Finally, Section 5 discusses the limitations and policy opportunities for moving the concept forward.

## 2 Main Conceptualisations and Key Elements of the Green Economy

The green economy is conceptualised in diverse and sometimes contested ways (Georgeson et al., 2017; Merino-Saum et al., 2020). Although it has hundreds of definitions, the United Nations Environment Program (UNEP, 2011) in its seminal report *Towards a Green Economy* provides one of the most prominent and cited interpretations. UNEP (2011, p. 16) describes the green economy as 'low-carbon, resource efficient, and socially inclusive' and presents it as a pathway to increasing equity and well-being while reducing ecological risks and scarcities. Other organisations such as the OECD (2011) and the World Bank (2012) have put forward parallel conceptions, and even the business community has presented its own notions in its *Green Economy Roadmap* (International Chamber of Commerce, 2012).

In most instances, the green economy is equated with green growth and the terms are used almost interchangeably (Death, 2015). However, Merino-Saum et al. (2020) reveal some key differences. First, green growth focuses more explicitly on economic growth, which is not as prominent in some green economy conceptions. Second, most definitions of green growth systematically ignore issues concerning ecological limits, whereas these appear slightly more often in the green economy. Third, the green economy places greater emphasis on social dimensions, whereas in green growth definitions, these are less prominent.

Despite the apparent diversity in interpretations, most green economy conceptions focus on the need to better recognise, demonstrate, and capture the value of natural capital and ecosystem services in decision-making, while assuming a need for continued economic growth. These two key aspects of the green economy will be discussed in turn.

### 2.1 Accounting, Maintenance, and Enhancement of Natural Capital and Ecosystem Services

The green economy recognises that human well-being and long-term socio-economic development are inextricably linked to the continuous provision of ecosystem services (UNEP, 2011). It aims to address the 'invisibility of nature' by recognising the value of natural resources and ecosystem services for economic activity and to promote a more accurate reflection of this value in private and public decision-making (ten Brink et al., 2012). Ultimately, it aspires to better account for, maintain, and enhance natural capital (D'Amato et al., 2019).

To reach this goal, the Economics of Ecosystems and Biodiversity (TEEB) was established in 2007 as a global initiative. Natural capital valuation is central to TEEB's efforts to demonstrate the value of nature to society and the economy (TEEB, 2010a). For instance, TEEB's work on monetary valuation has shown that the benefits of forest conservation are worth trillions of dollars, in comparison to the potential costs of failing to tackle the drivers and potential outcomes of climate change (TEEB, 2010a). Similarly, beekeeping is worth billions of dollars annually, when the services of pollination and other benefits are considered in full (Gallai et al., 2009). In most instances, the economic value of ecosystem services is much higher than their current market value, especially when regulation and other services are taken into account. Non-monetary valuation (e.g., biophysical calculations, sociocultural assessments) can also provide input for rational decision-making concerning ecosystem services, although it is used more marginally than monetary valuation (Kallis et al., 2013).

The business community is increasingly acknowledging the importance of biodiversity and ecosystem services for economic activity. In 2009, only 27% of global CEOs (out of the 1200 surveyed) expressed concern about biodiversity loss and its impact on business growth (TEEB, 2010b). In contrast, the 2020 Global Risk Report by the World Economic Forum (based on a Global Risks

---

## Box 4.1 Integrating ecosystem services into business models: the case of Taking Root

Taking Root is a Canadian-Nicaraguan social enterprise established in 2007 that markets ecosystem services such as carbon credits, fuelwoods, sawn wood, and shade grown coffee (Porras et al., 2015). It has become the largest reforestation effort in Nicaragua and is now expanding to other countries in Latin America and Africa. Taking Root pays farmers over a ten-year period, on the basis that they successfully meet pre-established tree-planting and growth milestones, which are ultimately linked to the carbon that trees sequester. It also helps farmers over this period to create productive, market-oriented agroforestry systems.

Despite the success of Taking Root, it has had to overcome a number of social, political, and market challenges associated with setting up new green economic modes of working. The farmers it works with do not necessarily have any experience in growing market-oriented trees nor can they afford the long-term investments required to support such a business model. To create the right social context, the organisation starts with a bottom-up process of community-led design to identify which species of trees will be grown by whom, where, and how. Different communities design different agroforestry systems that are well adapted to the local climate and way of life. Provided that participants meet a set of eligibility requirements (e.g., the land is not already forested, there are no conflicting land tenure claims), they enter into a performance-based agreement that contains a series of incentives that are delivered over an initial ten-year period. The programme provides support for the farmer over this period, including technical support, low-cost farm inputs, and low- to no-interest rate loans.

Regarding the political context, forestry laws in Nicaragua – as in many other countries – can be burdensome and are often not designed with small-holder needs in mind (Montambault, 2004).

Although these laws are designed to encourage sustainable forest man-agement, they end up discouraging farmers from growing trees as the required permits become too burdensome and unaffordable (Pokorny, 2013). To overcome these challenges, Taking Root has worked closely with farmers, multiple levels of government, and wood consuming businesses to support the formalisation of the sector. This has included automating the process of creating farm management plans to reduce costs, coordinating capacity building workshops for federal and regional government offices, and lob-bying for changes to facilitate the legalisation of the forest industry. After almost a decade of work, Taking Root is now selling some of the country's first smallholder plantation-grown wood under a legally recognised market mechanism.

To increase the international demand and value of its carbon credits, Tak-ing Root has made substantial marketing efforts to create a differentiated product. Rather than selling carbon credits as a commodity without a face or place, the organisation has managed to obtain a significant premium over the market price by leveraging the added social and environmental benefits it creates. For its agroforestry products, it has provided more value-added pro-cessing and continuously improved quality to further differentiate its prod-ucts. Moreover, to lower production costs, economies of scale have been achieved in permitting, transporting, and processing, due to the large num-ber of participating farms.

Taking Root's creative business model shows that it is possible to create multiple environmental values alongside a new thriving economy. Thousands of hectares have been restored into sustainable forestry and agroforestry sys-tems, while sequestering hundreds of thousands of tonnes of $CO_2$ and cre-ating multiple ecological benefits, alongside jobs that increase and diversify farmers' incomes.

Perception Survey of 800 of its members) ranked biodiversity loss and other environmental issues (e.g., climate change, natural disasters) as the top five global risks in terms of likelihood, above other economic, social, geopolitical, and technological risks. This report recognises that 'biodiversity loss has critical implications for humanity, from the collapse of food and health systems to the disruption of entire supply chains' (World Economic Forum, 2020b, p. 7). Nevertheless, most negative impacts of businesses on the environment are still externalised, and the negative externalities of air pollution and carbon emissions are estimated to cost nine trillion dollars annually (World Economic Forum, 2020a).

Although much work needs to be done, several existing successful initiatives could point the way for a green transition. Box 4.1 describes an example of a social business that has successfully integrated the value of ecosystem services into its *raison d'etre* (see also Chapter 3 about sustainable business models). Although this case is specific to a particular socio-political and market context, many of its principles and practices could also be widely applicable outside these contexts.

## 2.2 Economic Growth, Decoupling, and Innovation

A central element in most green economy definitions is the pursuit of economic growth (Merino-Saum et al., 2020). Economic decoupling is central to the assumption that there does not need to be a trade-off between environmental sustainability and economic growth. Some conceptions focus on relative decoupling (i.e., reducing ecological impact per unit of GDP) (OECD, 2011; International Chamber of Commerce, 2012), whereas others emphasise the need for absolute decoupling (UNEP, 2011). Innovation, technological solutions, and eco-efficiency are essential for achieving any form of decoupling (D'Amato et al., 2017; Merino-Saum et al., 2020). As illustrated by the OECD (2012, p. 10): '[...] the ability of reproducible capital to substitute for [depleted] natural capital is limited in the absence of innovation. By pushing the frontier outward, innovation can help to decouple growth from natural capital depletion'. Limitations to the concept of decoupling and eco-efficiency are discussed in Section 5.1.

## 3 Measuring Progress Towards the Green Economy: The State of Green Indicators

Developing good indicators is essential for assessing the policy efficacy and transformative potential of the green economy (Georgeson et al., 2017). At the macro (national) level, the **Global Green Economy Index (GGEI)** ranks 130 countries on four green economy dimensions: (1) leadership and climate change, (2) efficiency sectors, (3) markets and investment, and (4) the environment. It uses a mix of qualitative and quantitative measures and expert assessments. In 2018, Sweden ranked first, followed by Switzerland and then Iceland.

Another national-level measure, the OECD's *Green Growth Monitoring Framework* uses over 30 indicators, including socio-economic context and growth characteristics (e.g., GDP per capita), environmental and resource productivity, natural asset base (e.g., renewable and non-renewable stocks), environmental quality of life (e.g., exposure to air pollution, wastewater treatment plants), and economic opportunities and policies (e.g., technology and innovation, skills and training; Linster, 2012). So far, 23 countries have produced reports using this framework (e.g., Netherlands, Korea), but have adjusted their reporting, depending on local realities (Georgeson et al., 2017).

A related initiative focused on better ecosystem accounting is the *Wealth Accounting and Valuation of Ecosystem Services (WAVES)*, led by the World Bank. This is a global partnership of 70 nations, which aims to develop common methods to account for natural capital and ecosystem services in order to promote the inclusion of these into policy and decision-making. Similarly, the United Nation's *System of Environmental-Economic Accounting (SEEA)* is a global effort to use common accounting standards that report, link, and compare environmental, social, and economic statistics.

At the micro (firm) level, many companies now produce sustainability reports – a trend that has expanded over the past 30 years. Although there are no explicit green economy indicators, the *Global Reporting Initiative (GRI)* is the most widely used and is based on triple bottom line (TBL) accounting, wherein organisations report on their social, economic, and environmental impact. For instance, in the environmental dimension, organisations report on aspects that impact biodiversity, such as the proportion of habitats that are protected or restored, the number of threatened species that are affected by business operations, and the operational sites that are within or adjacent to protected areas (Boiral and Heras-Saizarbitoria, 2017). The GRI has attempted to integrate ecosystem service thinking in its reporting, but many challenges still complicate meaningfully measuring and assessing a business' performance (its dependencies and impact) in terms of ecosystem services (GRI, 2011). Figure 4.1 illustrates some indicators included in each dimension of the GRI.

Despite the progress made in recent decades, green economy indicators are still in their infancy. Significant challenges remain at the macro level to generating rigorous, meaningful, and internationally comparable indicators (Georgeson et al., 2017). Given the scale of transformation needed, most green economy indicators lack measures of the aggregate impact of economic activity on the environment, and many still mainly focus on narrow indicators of environmental quality (e.g., air quality, wastewater treatment) (Georgeson et al., 2017). In addition, some indicators are relative in that they compare one country with another, but provide little information on the absolute rate of change and whether this change is sufficient to avoid ecological breakdown (Stoknes and Rockström, 2018).

At the micro level, sustainability reporting has received a great deal of criticism. Reporting has been labelled a façade, symbolic and lacking sufficient

**SUSTAINABILITY**

| ECONOMIC STANDARDS | ENVIRONMENTAL STANDARDS | SOCIAL STANDARDS |
|---|---|---|
| Economic performance, market presence, indirect economic impacts, procurement practices, anti-corruption behaviours, etc. | Materials used, recycled inputs, reclaimed products and packaging, energy (e.g. consumption, intensity and reductions), water and effluence, biodiversity (e.g. operational sites adjacent to protected areas or areas of high biodiversity, habitats protected or restored), emissions, environmental compliance, etc. | Employment, labour-management relations, occupational health and safety, training and education, diversity and equal opportunity, non-discrimination, child labour, rights of indigenous peoples, human rights, etc. |

**FIGURE 4.1** Examples of indicators included in each dimension of the Global Reporting Initiative (GRI).

and genuine influence on business behaviour (Milne and Gray, 2013; Michelon et al., 2015). It has been pointed out that there is little or no integration between the economic, social, and environmental dimensions of TBL, as these are often reported as separate dimensions. Moreover, organisations rarely report on the environmental and social dimensions with the same quality and seriousness they give the financial dimension (Milne and Gray, 2013). So far, corporate sustainability has largely ignored concepts of ecological limits, carrying capacity, ecological footprints, and equity and social justice (Milne and Gray, 2013; Bjorn et al., 2017; D'Amato et al., 2019). In this sense, there is a significant disconnect between these reports and the scale and urgency of global challenges.

## 4 Financing the Green Economy: Where Are We?

Green finance and investment are integral elements in the green economy. Socially responsible investment (SRI) aims to promote corporate social responsibility (CSR) – including environmental, social, and corporate governance (ESG) policy and practice – through investment discretion and shareholder engagement. Such investment techniques are supposed to influence the environmental and social behaviour of the financed companies and ultimately increase sustainable standards for the wider economy (Richardson, 2008).

SRI emerged in the late 1960s in protest against corporate involvement in the Vietnam War and South Africa's apartheid regime (Markiel and Richard, 1971; Sparkes and Cowton, 2004) and later extended to diverse causes such as environmental pollution, labour protection, and indigenous and local communities' rights (Hollender, 2006; Vogel, 2006).

In the last decades, the SRI market has grown considerably in both assets under management and the diversity of actors in its network. As SRI has become increasingly involved in the mainstream financial industry after the 2000s (especially in North America, Europe, and Australia), this mission- or ethics-based corporate screening method has evolved into a financial risk management strategy in which institutional investors perceive environmental and social issues as forms of financial risks or opportunities.

SRI uses three main mechanisms to direct CSR. First, exclusion (avoidance) and inclusion of company stock from financial portfolios, which alters the cost of the capital of the targeted companies, thereby creating pressure for improved corporate behaviour. Second, investors directly engage in dialogue with corporate management to influence their business strategies. The third channel is shareholder activism (coercion), such as filing shareholder resolutions to demand certain business actions. In addition, public announcement of the divestment of a company share (public disinvestment) is used to denounce a company's irresponsible behaviour (Sparkes and Cowton, 2004; Richardson, 2012). Through these activities, the financial industry, especially institutional investors, have become increasingly influential in norm creation and standard setting for CSR.

Among those leading the move are the most powerful asset owners and managers, including pension funds, insurance companies, sovereign funds, and index brand and accounting firms (Krosinsky and Purdom, 2016). The UN Principles of Responsible Investment (PRI), an investor-led public–private collaboration in partnership with the UNEP Finance Initiative and the UN Global Compact, has also played a substantial role in introducing the ESG concept to mainstream investors. The global initiative encourages institutional investors to take actions to incorporate ESG issues into their conventional investment practices, thereby contributing to the development and diffusion of new knowledge, practices, and norms. As of June 2020, the UN PRI had attracted 3038 global signatories since its launch in 2006, which accounts for over USD 103 trillion in assets under management worldwide (UN PRI, no date). The UNEP Finance Initiative aligns with the idea of SRI as a risk management tool: 'The first [...] reason to integrate ESG issues is to make more money. There is a hypothesis, which we support, that a more thoroughgoing and systematic approach to integrating ESG issues in portfolios will, over time and in general, result in better financial performance' (UNEP FI, 2006, p. 4).

Important players in this field also include standard-setters (such as Global Reporting Initiatives and Sustainable Accounting Standard Board) and rating firms (such as MSCI, Vigeo Eiris, and Sustainalytics) who have set up ESG key performance indicators and measurement models across the industrial sectors based on the perspectives of shareholders and stakeholders. Non-governmental organisations (NGOs) are also active participants in the SRI network, as information providers and watchdogs in a broad range of strategies in various ESG issue areas (MacLeod and Park, 2011).

From a fiduciary institution's point of view, where their 'fiduciary duty' signifies a financial obligation, ESG factors need to be commensurate with financial metrics to be integrated into one bottom line (i.e., financial value) rather than a double or triple line (i.e., society and the environment) (Hawley, 2011). Consequently, there are significant trends in the development of ESG standards and metrics to identify 'financially material' ESG factors (Hawley, 2016; Khan, Serafeim and Yoon, 2016). However, a number of authors have suggested that the SRI industry has been too preoccupied with financial profitability, rather than questioning how SRI might contribute to sustainability goals (Hoepner and Mcmillan, 2009; Capelle-Blancard and Monjon, 2012; Haigh, 2016). Financialised environmental and social values seem to be widely legitimatised among investors, corporations, and the media, typically phrased as 'doing well by doing good', despite the unsubstantiated positive correlation between corporate social performance and financial performance (Fung, 2010; Lydenberg, 2012; Revelli and Viviani, 2015). Issues that may be relevant from a sustainability perspective but are deemed financially non-material may not be considered worthy of attention (Butz and Laville, 2007). The problem is that this materialistic view does not take into account the fundamental economic concept of externalities, which are the subject of CSR activities (Robins, 2008).

For this reason, SRI offers only a limited response to the integration of sustainability in finance. Investors' fiduciary principles that require maximising risk-adjusted returns might inadvertently lead to a reduction in the effectiveness of SRI as a CSR enforcement mechanism (Eccles, 2011). Although there has been an unprecedented growth in the number of participants, the amount of assets under management, and the diversity of players in the SRI network, the progress of making corporations and institutional investors more sustainable and responsible may have been substantially limited by the investors' narrow focus on maximising financial returns.

While the practice of SRI by major institutional investors has important implications for corporate sustainability practices, a high emphasis on the financial performance of SRI rather than on the moral responsibility of businesses to contribute to the long-term collective good potentially limits SRI's contribution to a genuine green economy transformation (Amaeshi, 2010). In order to avoid SRI becoming an empty signifier (Sorsa, 2013), its mainstreaming should not be celebrated as an expression of corporate virtue or the invention of profit-sustainability harmony; instead, it should eventually overcome the conventional notion of a financial fiduciary's duty to truly commit to sustainability and social responsibility as it proclaimed.

## 5 Are We Ready? Limitations and Opportunities of Integrating the Green Economy into Business

The green economy has emerged due to the increasing recognition that changing the dominant unsustainable economic model is key to sustainability. A central element of the green economy is to better recognise, account for, and value ecosystem services and natural capital in private and public decision-making. Another dominant tenet is that economic growth and environmental sustainability can coexist by means of decoupling economic activity from environmental impact, giving an important role to technology and markets.

Despite the uptake of the green economy concept in policymaking, business, and finance, globally, the transformative potential of the practical implementation of the green economy remains limited due to the scale of current challenges.

## 5.1 Limitations in Dominant Green Economy Conceptions

The green economy has been criticised for being weak, reformist, or incrementalistic in that it relies on techno-fixes as a path to sustainability rather than on downscaling human activities to suit the planet's ecological limits. In fact, most green economy conceptions do not move beyond the conventional growth paradigm, nor do they address the question of limits, excluding strong sustainability or post-growth approaches to the economy (Death, 2015; Tomaselli et al., 2017; Merino-Saum et al., 2020). Moreover, they fail to challenge, in any significant way, the current patterns of consumption and production (D'Amato et al., 2017).

Emphasising eco-efficiency can also be problematic, as it may not be sufficient to reduce environmental impacts in absolute terms, due to the rebound effect (Korhonen et al. 2018). The rebound effect occurs when increased efficiency lowers the cost of producing a good or service. Due to the lower price, the consumption of this good or service increases, partially offsetting the beneficial effects of the new technology (Lambin and Meyfroidt, 2011). To address the rebound effect, efficiency gains should be accompanied by adequate policies to effectively reduce consumption. Moreover, efficiency often comes at the expense of resilience in terms of diversity or adaptability, thus potentially compromising sustainability in the long run (Korhonen and Seager, 2008).

More importantly, decoupling economic growth from environmental damage, which is another essential element of the green economy discourse, has no strong empirical support. Although there is some evidence to support relative decoupling, there is little indication that the absolute decoupling required to avoid ecological breakdown can be achieved (Jackson and Victor, 2019). For example, global carbon intensity dropped from 0.47 kg $CO_2$/\$ in 1990 to 0.35 kg $CO_2$/\$ in 2013 (at 2011 constant prices) demonstrating relative decoupling. However, total carbon emissions have not decreased; they plateaued in 2014 and increased again in 2017 as the overall growth of the economy outstripped these gains (Ritchie and Roser, 2018). To keep temperatures within the 1.5°C target, Jackson and Victor (2019) calculate that an average reduction of carbon intensity of 14% per year for the next three decades is required. The maximum ever attained is a 3% reduction in carbon intensity per year and the current average is 1% per year. These authors argue that: 'Proponents of so-called green growth – economic growth that uses natural resources in a sustainable manner – must show that it is possible to effectively eliminate carbon emissions from developed economies in the space of little more than a decade with no impact at all on economic expansion' (Jackson and Victor, 2019, p. 951).

Even the evidence for relative decoupling can be weak in comparison to other indicators of environmental impact (beyond carbon emissions). In the past century, global material intensity decreased from 3.5 kg/USD in 1900 to 1.2 kg/USD in 2000, indicating relative decoupling (UNEP, 2016). However, since the 2000s, material intensity has increased, working 'against the hypothesis of decoupling' (UNEP, 2016, p. 16). For example, in 2000, 1.2 kg of materials were needed per USD, but by 2010, this had increased to 1.4 kg of materials per USD (UNEP, 2016). Using other indicators of environmental impact, the World Bank (2017) concluded that between 1990 and 2015, very few countries achieved strong decoupling. Moreover, most countries show weak decoupling or intensified coupling (i.e., environmental impact increases even faster than economic growth).

In conclusion, '[...] there is little indication that any fundamental decoupling of raw economic growth from material use has occurred' (UNEP 2016, p. 89). Fischer-Kowalski and Steinberger (2017, p. 386) suggest that 'decoupling well-being from biophysical resource use is more achievable than decoupling biophysical resource use from economic activity'. These data seriously question the central tenet of the green economy that economic growth and environmental sustainability could coexist.

## 5.2 Opportunities and the Way Forward

At present, private sector firms face weak incentives to invest in transforming their strategies and operations for greater environmental sustainability. Barkusky and Lorne (2006) showed that these incentives are strongest for firms in oligopolistic markets, where the offerings of all firms are substantively differentiated and competition is focused on product or service features and quality rather than on price. For these firms, genuine 'greening' can be a viable, profit-enhancing strategy to signal quality, durability, and the general credibility of claims that their products or services more consistently embody these positively valued attributes than those of their rivals. However, little can be expected from firms in industries that are more thoroughly monopolistic, in the absence of a concern to pre-empt expected government regulation. Similarly, little can be expected in markets that are more thoroughly price-competitive, as competitors essentially compete on their abilities to restrain costs, and no competitor can survive for long if they voluntarily internalise costs that their rivals still regard as externalities.

All of this highlights the important role of government interventions and public policy to further 'green' the economy by changing the incentive structure faced by the private sector (Droste et al., 2016). Some incentive-structure reforms, such as the introduction of carbon taxes and cap-and-trade schemes, have already been widely discussed, and there may already be some momentum in this direction (Lin and Li, 2011).

Here, we put forward four proposals, some of which have not previously been widely considered, and which may show considerable promise for jumpstarting the process of green innovation. These are meant to be globally applicable, but will require modifications and adjustments to suit national laws and local realities.

*Sustainability-focused quality standards* could be introduced pursuant to a long-term plan, for all products or services, which would heavily tax (and ultimately ban) any products and services that fall below minimum standards (Kronenberg, 2007). One option here could be to implement commodity tax rates that are specifically designed to drive re-engineering or withdrawal of sub-standard products. These tax rates should start low, but rise relentlessly, ideally on a pre-announced schedule. Outright bans should not occur pre-emptively but could definitely be retained in the policy toolkit. If a close alternative, but environmentally superior, product emerges on the market at a roughly equivalent financial cost or at a cost that is only a modest premium over less sustainable options, it is not unreasonable to completely ban the sale of the latter. Consumer preference founded on irresponsible consumer convenience (e.g., when disposable products are often preferred but the consumer does not bear the external cost of disposal) need not be indulged when imposing more punitive tax burdens or outright bans are considered. However, in general, all of these proposals, particularly outright bans, should be implemented cautiously and with lengthy advance notice to consumers and industry.

An *'ecologically competitive' corporate income tax system* borrows from the logic and competitive psychology observed in high-profile sports leagues. Individuals and teams in these sports do not compete to attain minimum standards, they compete to be better than everyone else. This proposal essentially involves creating premium, discounted rates of taxation of business income, and categorising taxpayers in successive tax years into groups on the basis of their relative performance in environmental-impact audits. Initially, participation in such a system could be voluntary, but could become universal and mandatory over time. Firms could be categorised into terciles, such that corporate income tax rates are discounted in the top-performing tercile and are assessed at a premium in the worst-performing tercile, with the central tercile paying the established pre-existing rate. In this proposal, standards could be re-calibrated to keep the system revenue neutral from the point of view of the tax agency. A critical requirement for this to work though would be the development of a solid, credible auditing system.

A *system of waste-intensity benchmarks with rewards and penalties,* sometimes known as volume-based emission pricing, has been implemented fairly weakly in some jurisdictions and has now been adopted by the Canadian federal government in tandem with its federal backstop, carbon tax.[1] This involves fiscal or regulatory 'sticks and carrots' based on measuring performance against emission-intensity benchmarks and is designed to recognise the existing output of firms and apply these fiscal incentives primarily to marginal units of the firm output, so that trade-exposed firms in the jurisdiction in question can still survive, but face an incentive to improve performance if, and as, they seek to expand output.

*Green product preference in the public sector* would establish a strong preference for 'greener' products through public purchasing power (Parikka-Alhola, 2008).

This proposal creates core demand and catalyses economies of scale. Public purchasing, through some kind of 'points system', could recognise ecological-impact attributes, as well as financial purchase cost, and would thus allow new products and services with superior attributes some compensatory leeway when stacked up against financially cheaper competing products and services. Some natural synergy between performance quality and durability on the one hand, and ecological impact on the other, would mitigate the financial impact of environmentally superior products, gaining an edge over financially cheaper (but more unsustainable) ones, on aggregate public expenditure in the medium to long term. Learning curve effects and conventional economies of scale should, over time, help environmentally superior products and services become more financially competitive and thus also win new customers in the private sector.

These proposals are hardly exhaustive, but they could quite easily be integrated into a common sustainability strategy. All four rely on the government setting and on enforcing goals and rules, but they also depend largely on private sector responses to make their investments, and to design, develop, manufacture (in the case of products), and market the improved products and services. The introduction of all of these could also be eased by the existence of a macroeconomic policy environment in which there is a consensus that increased fiscal stimulus is needed, yet none are primarily dependent on any large and sustained increase in public spending (with the consequent significant future tax burden).

We are still far from a genuine transformation into an ecological macro-economy. The current global COVID-19 pandemic has quite dramatically highlighted the collision course that humanity may well be on with respect to its natural environment, as well as serious faults in socio-economic cohesion. It is definitely an opportune moment for governments and business leaders to seriously reconsider 'business as usual' and to contemplate major, and possibly radical, reforms that could lead society onto a more sustainable path (Cohen, 2020; Gore, 2020).

## Note

1 For more information on Canada's output-based pricing system, see: https://www.canada.ca/en/environment-climate-change/services/climate-change/pricing-pollution-how-it-will-work/output-based-pricing-system.html

## References

Amaeshi, K. (2010) 'Different markets for different folks: Exploring the challenges of mainstreaming responsible investment practices', *Journal of Business Ethics*, 92(1), pp. 41–56.

Barkusky, M. and Lorne, F. (2006) 'The economic logic of corporate social responsibility', *International Journal of Environment Workplace and Employment*, 2(2/3), pp. 148–179.

Bjorn, A., Bey, N., Georg, S., Røpke, I. and Hauschild, M. Z. (2017) 'Is Earth recognized as a finite system in corporate responsibility reporting?', *Journal of Cleaner Production*, 163, pp. 106–117.

Boiral, O. and Heras-Saizarbitoria, I. (2017) 'Best practices for corporate commitment to biodiversity: An organizing framework from GRI reports', *Environmental Science and Policy*, 1, pp. 244–255.

ten Brink, P., Mazza L., Badura T., Kettunen M. and Withana S. (2012) *Nature and Its Role in the Transition to a Green Economy*. Institute for European Environmental Policy.

Butz, C. and Laville, J. (2007) *Socially Responsible Investment: Avoiding the Financial Materiality*. Ethos Fund, Geneva, Switzerland.

Capelle-Blancard, G. and Monjon, S. (2012) 'Trends in the literature on socially responsible investment: looking for the keys under the lamppost', *Business Ethics: A European Review*, 21(3), pp. 239–250.

Cohen, M. (2020) 'Does the COVID-19 outbreak mark the onset of a sustainable consumption transition?', *Sustainability: Science, Practice and Policy*, 16(1), pp. 1–3.

D'Amato, D., Droste, N., Allen, B., Kettunen, M., Lähtinen, K., Korhonen, J., Leskinen, P., Matthies, B. D. and Toppinen, A. (2017) 'Green, circular, bio economy: A comparative analysis of sustainability avenues', *Journal of Cleaner Production*, 168, pp. 716–734. https://doi.org/10.1016/j.jclepro.2017.09.053.

D'Amato, D., Korhonen, J. and Toppinen, A. (2019, December) 'Circular, green, and bio economy: How do companies in land-use intensive sectors align with sustainability concepts?', *Ecological Economics,* 158, pp. 116–133. https://doi.org/10.1016/j.ecolecon.2018.12.026.

Daly, H. (2015, June) 'Economics for a full world', *Great Transition Initiative*, 15.

Death, C. (2015) 'Four discourses of the green economy in the global South', *Third World Quarterly*, 36(12), pp. 2207–2224. https://doi.org/10.1080/01436597.2015.1068110.

Droste, N. et al. (2016) 'Steering innovations towards a green economy: Understanding government intervention', *Journal of Cleaner Production*, 135, pp. 426–434.

Eccles, N. (2011) 'New values in responsible investment', in Vandekerckhove, W. et al. (eds.), *Responsible Investment in Times of Turmoil*. Heidelberg, London, New York: Springer, Dordrecht, pp. 19–34.

Fung, H. (2010) *Socially Responsible Investment in a Global Environment*. Cheltenham: Edward Elgar Publishing Limited.

Gallai, N., Salles, J. M., Settele, J. and Vaissière, B. E. (2009) 'Economic valuation of the vulnerability of world agriculture confronted with pollinator decline', *Ecological Economics*, 68(3), pp. 810–821.

Georgeson, L., Maslin, M. and Poessinouw, M. (2017) 'The global green economy: A review of concepts, definitions, measurement methodologies and their interactions', *Geo: Geography and Environment*, 4(1). https://doi.org/10.1002/geo2.36.

Gore, C. (2020) 'Virus reveals the ecology of global economic life', *Financial Times*.

GRI (2011) *Approach for Reporting on Ecosystem Services: Incorporating Ecosystem Services into an Organizational Performance Disclosure*. Amsterdam, Holland: Global Reporting Initiative.

Haigh, M. (2016) 'Challenges in responsible investment research', in Hebb, T. et al. (eds.), *The Routledge Handbook of Responsible Investment*. Abingdon: Routledge, pp. 536–542.

Hawley, J. (2011) 'Reclaiming fiduciary duty balance', *Rotman International Journal of Pension Management*, 4(2), pp. 4–16.

Hawley, J. (2016) 'Setting the scene: The basics and basis of responsible investment', in Hebb, T. et al. (eds.), *The Routledge Handbook of Responsible Investment*. https://doi.org/10.4324/9780203104415-51.

Hoepner, A. and Mcmillan, D. G. (2009) 'Research on "responsible investment": An influential literature analysis comprising a rating, characterisation, categorisation and investigation', *SSRN Electronic Journal*, 84.

Hollender, J. (2006) *What Matters Most: How a Small Group of Pioneers Is Teaching Social Responsibility to Big Business, and Why Big Business Is Listening*. New York: Basic Books.

International Chamber of Commerce (2012) *Green Economy Roadmap: A Guide for Business, Policymakers and Society*. International Chamber of Commerce.

Jackson, T. and Victor, P. A. (2019) 'Unraveling the claims for (and against) green growth', *Science*, 366(6468), pp. 950–951. https://doi.org/10.1126/science.aay0749.

Kallis, G., Gómez-Baggethun, E. and Zografos, C. (2013) 'To value or not to value? That is not the question', *Ecological Economics*, 94, pp. 97–105. https://doi.org/10.1016/j.ecolecon.2013.07.002.

Khan, M., Serafeim, G. and Yoon, A. (2016) 'Corporate sustainability: First evidence on materiality', *The Accounting Review*, 91(6), pp. 1697–1724.

Korhonen, J., Honkasalo, A. and Seppälä, J. (2018) 'Circular economy: The concept and its limitations', *Ecological Economics*, 143, pp. 37–46. https://doi.org/10.1016/j.ecolecon.2017.06.041.

Korhonen, J. and Seager, T. P. (2008) 'Beyond eco-efficiency: A resilience perspective', *Business Strategy and the Environment*, 17(7), pp. 411–419. https://doi.org/10.1002/bse.635.

Kronenberg, J. (2007) *Ecological Economics and Industrial Ecology – A Case Study of the Integrated Product Policy of the European Union*. Abingdon, Oxfordshire: Routledge.

Krosinsky, C. and Purdom, S. (Eds.) (2016) *Sustainable Investing: Revolutions in Theory and Practice*. 1st ed. London: Routledge. https://doi.org/10.4324/9781315558837

Lambin, E. F. and Meyfroidt, P. (2011) 'Global land use change, economic globalization, and the looming land scarcity', *Proceedings of the National Academy of Sciences*, 108(9), pp. 3465–3472. https://doi.org/10.1073/pnas.1100480108.

Lin, B. and Li, X. (2011) 'The effect of carbon tax on per capita $CO2$ emissions', *Energy Policy*, 39(9), pp. 5137–5146.

Linster, M. (2012) *Monitoring Progress Towards Green Growth: OECD Indicators*. https://www.oecd.org/greengrowth/monitoring progress towards green growth-indicators.pdf.

Lydenberg, S. (2012) *On Materiality and Sustainability: The Value of Discllusure in the Capital Markets*. Cambridge, MA: Initiative for Responsible Investment, Hauser Center for Nonprofit Organizations at Harvard University.

MacLeod, M. and Jacob, P. (2011) 'Financial activism and global climate change: The rise of investor-driven governance networks', *Global Environmental Politics*, 11(2), pp. 54–74.

Markiel, B. and Richard, Q. (1971) 'Moral issues in investment policy', *Harvard Business Review*, 49(2), pp. 37–47.

Merino-Saum, A., Clement, J., Wyss, R. and Baldi, M. G. (2020) 'Unpacking the green economy concept: A quantitative analysis of 140 definitions', *Journal of Cleaner Production*, 242, 118339. https://doi.org/10.1016/j.jclepro.2019.118339.

Michelon, G., Pilonato, S. and Ricceri, F. (2015) 'CSR reporting practices and the quality of disclosure: An empirical analysis', *Critical Perspectives on Accounting*, 33, pp. 59–78. https://doi.org/10.1016/j.cpa.2014.10.003.

Milne, M. J. and Gray, R. (2013) 'W(h)ither ecology? The triple bottom line, the global reporting initiative, and corporate sustainability reporting', *Journal of Business Ethics*, 118(1), pp. 13–29. https://doi.org/10.1007/s10551-012-1543-8.

Montambault, J. R. (2004) *Sustainable Forest Management in Rural Nicaragua: Self-reported Household Behaviour and Stated Management Preferences in Santo Tomás, Chontales*. Master of Science Thesis, University of Florida.

OECD (2011) *Towards Green Growth*. OECD Publishing.

Parikka-Alhola, K. (2008) 'Promoting environmentally sound furniture by green public procurement', *Ecological Economics*, 68, pp. 472–485.

Pokorny, B. (2013) *Smallholders, Forest Management and Rural Development in the Amazon*. 1st ed. London: Routledge.

Porras, I., Amrein, A. and Vorley, B. (2015) *Reforestation, Carbon Sequestration and Agriculture: Can carbon Financing Promote Sustainable Smallholder Activities in Nicaragua?* International Institute for Environment and Development & Hivos.

Revelli, C. and Viviani, J.-L. (2015) 'Financial performance of socially responsible investing (SRI): What have we learned? A meta-analysis', *Business Ethics: A European Review*, 24(2), pp. 158–185.

Richardson, B. J. (2008) *Socially Responsible Investment Law: Regulating the Unseen Polluters*. New York: Oxford University Press.

Richardson, B. J. (2012) *Are Social Investors Influential?*, SSRN Scholarly Paper. New York.

Ritchie, H. and Roser, M. (2018) $CO_2$ *and Other Greenhouse Gas Emissions, Our World in Data*. https://ourworldindata.org/co2-and-other-greenhouse-gas-emissions (Accessed 15 April 2018).

Robins, N. (2008) 'The emergence of sustainable investing', in Krosinsky, C. and Robins, N. (eds.) *Sustainable Investing: The Art of Long-Term Performance*. London: Routledge, p. 16.

Salzman, J., Bennett, G., Carroll, N., Goldstein, A. and Jenkins, M. (2018) 'The global status and trends of payments for ecosystem services', *Nature Sustainability*, 1, pp. 136–144.

Sorsa, V.-P. (2013) 'Social responsibility and the political: Studying the politics of social responsibility in institutional investment', *Journal of Sustainable Finance & Investment*, 3(3), pp. 223–237.

Sparkes, R. and Cowton, C. (2004) 'The maturing of socially responsible investment: A review of the developing link with corporate social responsibility', *Journal of Business Ethics*, 52(1), pp. 45–57.

Stoknes, P. E. and Rockström, J. (2018, April) 'Redefining green growth within planetary boundaries', *Energy Research and Social Science*, 44, pp. 41–49. https://doi.org/10.1016/j.erss.2018.04.030.

TEEB (2010a) *Mainstreaming the Economics of Nature: A Synthesis of the Approach, Conclusions and Recommendations of TEEB*. United Nations Environment Program, p. 39.

TEEB (2010b) *The Economics of Ecosystems and Biodiversity: TEEB for Business*. United Nations Environment Program, 217.

Tomaselli, M. F., Hajjar, R., Ramón-Hidalgo, A. E. and Vásquez-Fernández, A. M. (2017) 'The problematic old roots of the new green economy narrative: How far can it take us in re-imagining sustainability in forestry?', *International Forestry Review*, 19(S1), pp. 1–13.

UN PRI (No date) *About the PRI*. https://www.unpri.org/pri/about-the-pri (Accessed 27 June 2020).

UNEP (2011) *Towards a Green Economy: Pathways to Sustainable Development and Poverty Eradication*.

UNEP (2016) *Global Material Flows and Resource Productivity. Assessment Report for the UNEP International Resource Panel*. https://doi.org/10.1111/jiec.12626.

UNEP FI (2006) *Show Me the Money: Linking Environmental, Social and Governance Issues to Company Value*. Geneva, Switzerland: UNEP Finance Initiative Asset Management Working Group.

Vogel, D. (2006) *The Market for Virtue the Potential and Limits of Corporate Social Responsibility*. Washington, DC: Brookings Institution Press.

Whiting, K., Konstantakos, L., Carrasco, A. and Carmona, L. G. (2018) 'Sustainable development, wellbeing and material consumption: A stoic perspective', *Sustainability*, 10(2), pp. 474–494. https://doi.org/10.3390/su10020474.

World Bank (2012) *Inclusive Green Growth: The Pathway to Sustainable Development*. Washington, DC: World Bank.

World Bank (2017) *Atlas of Sustainable Development Goals 2017: From World Development Indicators*. Washington, DC: World Bank Group.

World Economic Forum (2020a) *The Future of Nature and Business*. Geneva, Switzerland: World Economic Forum.

World Economic Forum (2020b) *The Global Risks Report 2020*. http://wef.ch/risks2019.

# 5

# THE CIRCULAR BIOECONOMY

## Company-Level Strategic Perspectives

*Ari Jantunen and Anni Tuppura*

## 1 Introduction

Global sustainability challenges force societies to reassess their functions and values. Importantly, this relates to the current market system, which has become crucial for creating and delivering welfare in Western economies. In the consumer goods market, the current system has created a situation in which producing something new is relatively cheap and fixing a broken article is relatively expensive, and from the business point of view, more value is created when a new item is sold than when a used item is repaired. To curb the devastating influences of overconsumption, it has been suggested that societies should strive to drastically decrease the use of non-renewable resources by moving towards a circular bioeconomy (from here on CBE): a renewable resource-based economy that aims to maximise utility and minimise material loss and energy consumption by using an integrated production–consumption system with cyclical material flows. Such a 'comprehensive societal transformation' (Priefer et al., 2017, p. 2) will not happen overnight, and it is likely that political discussion and decisions will greatly influence how the CBE will materialise in terms of, for example, sustainability (see discussion, e.g., Temmes and Peck, 2020).

From the business actor's point of view, as the circular economy is inherently more systemic than a linear economy (Antikainen and Valkokari, 2016), it calls for more cooperation and coordination between companies and other parties. The emphasis of value creation in value chains is also different, as the circular economy is more complex in terms of variety of business operations and business models than the linear system, due to the increased role of complementary assets in business activities and the need to align the interests and activities of multiple interdependent actors (see Lüdeke-Freund et al., 2018; Konietzko et al., 2020; see also Chapters 3 and 6 in this book).

DOI: 10.4324/9781003003588-7

The fundamental issue that every company manager faces is how to achieve and sustain profitability and competitive advantage and thereby ensure business survival. The related strategic decisions concern questions about the businesses with which the company chooses to engage, and which activities are performed in-house and which are sourced from markets. Further, managing the resources and capabilities needed in business (i.e., obtaining and coordinating the use of these assets to create value) is at the core of companies' strategic management. Adapting to the CBE can create new business opportunities, but whether these opportunities are utilised depends first on recognising the opportunity and then on (company-specific) motivations and the ability to take the required actions.

In this chapter, we use strategic management frameworks, in particular, those related to *organisational cognition, transaction costs,* and *capabilities*, to discuss the elements of a circular economy (CE) from the bioeconomy (BE) business actor perspective, and to develop a better understanding of the kinds of barriers that may slow down the transformation from a linear economy to a CBE. Specifically, we ponder *how operating in a CBE differs from operating in a linear economy from the company perspective, and what the most important company-level strategic decisions related to operating in a CBE are.*

## 2 What Is a Circular Bioeconomy?

The meaning of CBE is still somewhat unestablished, even though the term has been used in a number of scientific, policy, and industry documents (see Giampietro, 2019). Stegmann, Londo, and Junginger (2020) recognise three different perspectives of how the literature defines the relationship between a BE and a CE in a CBE. The first is that a CBE can be seen as a part of a CE; the second that a CBE is more than a sum of its parts, and third that a CBE is the intersection of a BE and a CE. In this chapter, we adopt a perspective that recognises both the individual backgrounds of the concepts and the synergies in which the combination may result.

The word *bioeconomy* has many interpretations. Bugge et al. (2016) identify three (although, not completely distinct) visions attached to the word in the academic literature: (1) a bio-technology vision, which focuses on the research and application of bio-technology and aims to create economic growth and job creation; (2) a bio-resource vision, which emphasises the research related to biological raw materials, and the potential of upgrading and converting them, and aims to create economic growth and sustainability; and (3) a bio-ecology vision, which emphasises 'the importance of ecological processes that optimise the use of energy and nutrients, promote biodiversity, and avoid monocultures and soil degradation' and underlines the potential for integrated processes. The aim of this latter vision is ecological sustainability (for a discussion on the different meanings of BE, see also Vivien et al., 2019). In this study, we adopt McCormick and Kautto's (2013, p. 2590) definition, according to which the BE represents an 'economy where the basic building blocks for materials, chemicals and energy are derived from renewable biological resources'.

A BE has been seen as a means to decrease dependence on fossil resources and reduce greenhouse gas emissions (Pfau et al., 2014). Political discussions have also presented a BE as a possible means of creating economic growth (European Commission, 2012). However, the EU policy framework has been criticised for brushing aside the possible environmental and social consequences when highlighting a BE's economic possibilities (Ramcilovic-Suominen and Pülzl, 2018). The relationship between sustainability and a BE is not straightforward. In the literature, the visions of this relationship vary from a BE as inherently sustainable to a BE having a negative impact on sustainability (Pfau et al., 2014). Empirical evidence shows that increased biomass production can have unintended negative environmental or social consequences (e.g., Danielsen et al., 2008; Obidzinski et al., 2018) and reveals a lack of information on how much biomass can be produced sustainably overall, as well as uncertainty regarding how biomass usage should be prioritised (Priefer et al., 2017). However, adding elements of a CE to BE applications would increase their sustainability, as 'circularity framing can highlight areas where value can be preserved, and sustainability functions improved' (Temmes and Peck, 2020, p. 10).

A *circular economy* refers to a production and consumption system in which the need for raw materials for producing the same amount of utility is lower than in the prevailing linear economic system, due to circular material flows. Geissdoerfer et al. (2017, p. 759) define a CE as 'a regenerative system in which resource input and waste, emission, and energy leakage are minimised by slowing, closing, and narrowing material and energy loops. This can be achieved through long-lasting design, maintenance, repair, reuse, remanufacturing, refurbishing, and recycling' (for further discussion on the definitions of a CE, see Kirchherr et al., 2017). The argued sustainability of a CE is based partly on diminished production owing to the longer lifecycle of products granted through repair and refurbishing, and the existence of a sharing economy and less waste through better design and more effective utilisation of waste streams. Further, once extracted, the resources circulate longer in the system, thanks to reuse, remanufacturing, and recycling. Consumers refusing or reducing consumption has also been seen as part of a CE (e.g., see Reike et al., 2018). Box 5.1 depicts examples of how CE principles have been applied in a BE context.

The CE has been criticised for, for example, conceptual fragmentation, over-simplicity, and neglecting thermodynamic limits (for a review, see Giampietro, 2019; Inigo and Blok, 2019). Despite its limitations, a CE 'has a great inspirational strength and equipped with critical sustainability assessment it can be important for global net sustainability' (Korhonen et al., 2018, p. 45). By studying the barriers to businesses and policymakers implementing a CE, Kirchherr et al. (2018) have identified cultural issues such as a lack of consumer interest and awareness and a hesitant company culture and market issues such as low prices of raw materials and high upfront investment costs as the most pressing

---

## Box 5.1 New value-adding uses of different bio-based side streams

In recent years, interest has been growing in utilising different bio-based by-products or waste- and side streams to create new value-adding products. In the food industry, new business has been developed from the fruit and vegetable waste of groceries and farms. Independent producers collaborate with groceries to collect fruits and vegetables that are not fit for sale (e.g., because of their unattractive appearance) but are still fit to eat, and the groceries then sell these waste-based food products to consumers, for example. Side streams of different bio-based industries and agriculture have been further developed into fertilizers and soil improvement products to substitute synthetic fertilizers. In the textile industry, recent solutions enable recycling raw materials such as cotton fibre for use in yarn, fabric, and garment manufacturing. Forest industry by-products also have versatile attributes. Tall oil (which is a by-product of pulp production) has recently been further developed for diversified uses, such as the cholesterol-reducing ingredients in margarine and feed to decrease the need to use antibiotics in breeding. New innovations have also been created from spruce sawdust, a by-product which is typically used in energy production. These innovations can be utilised in the food industry, techno-chemical industry, and cosmetics, either to substitute existing ingredients or to create new attributes for the products. These examples depict the potential for creating new value-adding products by utilising the different material flows of bio-based production. Utilising side streams to create value-added products is one aim of the circular economy to achieve more value-based on extracted resources, or resources that are already 'in cycle'.

---

barriers. The authors conclude that governmental interventions would be needed to accelerate the transition towards a circular system.

To cast some more light on the business–level issues that are prerequisites for the transformation to a CBE, we next discuss issues related to company-level strategic decision-making. We look at the CBE from the company-level perspective and explore some central strategic issues that companies' managements must deal with when planning to build new CBE-type businesses or shifting existing businesses towards a CBE. We approach the strategy issues by first introducing the fundamental *transaction cost* approach and then discussing the *organisational capabilities* and *cognition* perspectives on company strategies. Strategy research generally uses these concepts to explain or anticipate the possible decisions and reactions of companies to the changes in their business environments. We then briefly present the relevance of *business models* and *ecosystem* concepts for CBE-related businesses, as for a single business, changing from a linear to a virtual economy may also require reconsidering how value is created and captured. Because maximising the benefits of a CE (e.g., in terms of utilising the side streams) demands the value creation alignment of multiple actors, the role of business ecosystems may become emphasised in a CBE. These perspectives help us understand the nexus of issues that companies face in CBE business.

## 3 Strategic Management in a Circular Bioeconomy

### 3.1 Transaction Cost Approach

According to transaction cost theory (Coase, 1937; Williamson, 1985, 1991), when firms decide whether to source some product or service from the market or produce it within the firm, they consider the benefits and costs of different governance options. Which governance solution is most desirable depends on the *transaction costs* – that is, the costs and risks related to the use of markets. According to transaction cost theory, considerable attention is given to the risk of opportunism and contractual hazards. These are possible risks when making contracts with other parties. Since it is impossible to prepare and enforce contracts that would cover all possible future situations and conditions, the participants of market transactions face the risk of opportunistic behaviour from contractors. According to Williamson (1991), especially transaction determinant factors such as the uncertainty and asset specificity related to the transaction determine the most optimal governance form for the transaction. In addition to exposure to opportunism, market transactions involve other types of transaction costs, including risks, problems, costs related to pricing (Coase, 1937), and the costs of persuading, negotiating, coordinating, and teaching external suppliers (Langlois, 1992). Together, these costs limit the opportunities to source necessary production inputs from markets or to sell the end products. In addition, the markets are sometimes non-existent, meaning that there are no providers for some products or services, inevitably leading to the redefinition of a 'make or buy' decision as a 'to make or not to make' proposition.

The first question to determine whether a company is willing to join a system that assumes strong interrelationships between firms (as a CBE is) is what motivates the individual companies to put their resources and efforts into cooperation that includes various types of transaction costs. The second question is how these interrelationships are organised and governed. From the individual firm's perspective, it is easier to build and coordinate new production processes when value creation and appropriation issues can be handled inside a single firm, as claimed by Helfat (2015, p. 806): '...in a new industry based on a systemic innovation, transaction costs of close coordination through contracting are often prohibitively high, favoring vertical integration'.

A potential transaction cost problem would arise if, for example, a CBE's sub-system consisted of a large-scale industrial production facility and smaller specialised companies that could use, for instance, bio-based side streams of this large-scale production. A large company that recognises the value potential of side streams has two options: to utilise the potential of the side stream by itself (invest in R&D to develop new products based on the side stream as well as production capacity, etc.) or to put the side stream on the market for some other company to utilise. If economic efficiency requires that the side stream is utilised near the production facility, the potential buyer companies have to make the necessary investments on site, hence exposing themselves to risks associated with dependence on a certain location and one raw material provider. When considering this strategic decision, the value potential of the side stream for a smaller company is not the only decisive issue; it is also essential that the company examines the risks associated with dependence on one vendor, as the potential for hold-ups is evident. The potential means of decreasing the risk of opportunism (e.g., a technical solution that decreases dependence on one supplier and a financial arrangement that integrates the actors' economic interests) are not necessarily within reach or feasible for the actors in whose best interests they would primarily be, making the business opportunity uninteresting.

Transaction costs are not stable and merely transaction- or relation-specific; they develop over time in accordance with the industry evolution (Jacobides and Winter, 2005; Helfat, 2015). In the early phase of industry development, operating conditions are characterised by high uncertainty and asset specificity (Helfat and Campo-Rembado, 2016). In addition to industries as units of evolution, also business ecosystems can be seen as units that evolve. In the CBE context, the costs of market coordination activities are high because certain issues in emergent sectors and ecosystems are highly uncertain, for example, the necessary specifications and pricing principles of the intermediate and end products and the future development of their markets. Over time, transaction costs in general may decrease, hence improving the probability that CBE-based business transactions will be realised and ecosystems will grow. Both uncertainty and asset specificity – central factors of increasing transaction costs – decrease with the standardisation of products and their pricing (Helfat, 2015). Furthermore, the predictability of the development of regulation reduces uncertainty and supports the adoption of CBE-type products and business models. For example, the European Union's Circular Economy Action Plan (European Commission, 2020) contains initiatives for promoting circularity by means of mandatory legislation and by supporting a CE with other policy actions. This 'creation and destruction policy mix' (Kivimaa and Kern, 2016) signals that even though the exact details of future pathways are imprecise, the direction is clear, conveying the message that proactive, voluntary, company-level actions for developing CBE-based business will also pay off.

## 3.2 Organisational Capabilities and Cognition

A CBE as an operating context for business, especially when seen as an economic system in which the actors are quite strongly interlinked, can be characterised by a high level of uncertainty in general, as presented above. High uncertainty arises from numerous factors, such as a lack of clarity about the expected roles of different actors and their interaction mechanisms in the system, a lack of descriptions of value appropriation issues, and a lack of specifications and standardisation for intermediate and end-use products. These characteristics together make systemic CBE particularly complex and risky as a business environment, thus reducing incentives for companies to extensively participate in CBE business in practice.

However, firms are not identical in their risk-taking abilities, and their incentives to participate in a CBE differ, depending on their specific position in production factor (resource) markets and product markets. A study by Guerrero and Hansen (2021) of the cross-sector collaboration of forest sector companies with other sector companies shows that both industry-specific and firm-specific factors, such as culture and strategy, influence the drivers and objectives of participating in collaboration. One reason why CBE business opportunities are idiosyncratic for firms is that the effective scale of operations is firm-specific. Secured availability and uniform quality of biomaterial batches or flows is crucial to achieve operational efficiency in production processes. Building new capabilities and justifying the fixed costs of investments for increasing capacity require the right scale of available raw material. The 'right scale' is a firm-specific condition; what is 'too much' for one company (requiring overly large and risky investments related to the company's risk-taking ability) may be 'too little' for another company (business potential not worth building new organisational units for in-house utilisation of material).

For business opportunities to be seized, they must first be recognised. Seizing them, in turn, requires them to appear attractive from the particular company's viewpoint. Many factors relating to the characteristics of operating environments as well as firm-specific features influence how attractive opportunities seem from the firm's perspective (Kaplan, 2008; Eggers and Kaplan, 2013). Of the factors related to conditions in the operating environments, in addition to those mentioned in the transaction cost approach, relative prices, demand, competition, regulation, and expected stability are central. Firm-specific factors are also important: in externally similar conditions firms face dissimilar opportunities and local internal factors affect whether available opportunities are also interpreted as economically viable from the particular firm's perspective (Eggers and Kaplan, 2009).

Opportunities are also strongly firm-specific, because in the same operating environment (e.g., industry sector), firms are heterogeneous, as they have unique capability endowments and distinctive business models. Capability-based approaches, especially the dynamic capability view (Teece et al., 1997), consider the firm to be a repository of organisational capabilities. These capabilities consist of skilled personnel, facilities, and production machinery, systems and processes, and coordination and governance mechanisms that integrate different components to form a coherent whole for carrying out tasks (Teece, 2019).

Firms' capabilities and product portfolios coevolve. As Richardson (1972) points out, firms tend to specialise and grow in *activities* that are in congruence with their existing *capabilities* and can be executed without making major changes to these capabilities. Teece (2019) presents three dimensions of gaps between the capabilities needed to exploit a recognised opportunity and the firm's existing capability portfolio, namely technical distance, market distance, and business model distance, referring to how easily current capabilities can be applied for utilising new opportunities. The more substantial the gap between the existing organisational system and the future option, the riskier and more difficult the new capability development (or acquisition).

When the firm needs to change its capability base by, for example, seizing emerging opportunities, it must reorganise its activities and build, integrate, or reconfigure resources and capabilities. In this adaptation, *dynamic capabilities* are essential, meaning the firm's ability to renew and transform its resource base and activities according to the changing needs of the operating environment (Teece et al., 1997). In addition to internal assets, firms need the ability to manage the external assets owned by others in its value chains or networks. CBE business requires dynamic capabilities, and the firm's internal asset base must also be changed in the orchestration of complementary assets. The need for orchestration skills to coordinate both internal activities and external networks is greater in a systemic CBE business than in the linear economy.

Organisational cognition issues also affect how firms grasp opportunities and make business decisions. The way in which operating environments are interpreted and the firm's internal strengths shape how managers perceive business opportunities and react to them. Hence, strategic actions are responses to 'enacted' operating environments and business opportunities, not only to the 'objective' conditions of the operating environments. The way in which the management conceptualises the firm and its operating environments and allocates resources filters which operating environment changes are seen as potential business opportunities worth closer examination and which changes are ignored, neglected, and dismissed (Prahalad and Bettis, 1986). Existing capabilities and organisational cognition also govern *how* a particular firm will take steps towards a CBE. For example, for the incumbent big pulp and paper conglomerates, it may be relatively easier to consider the side streams of their main production process as valuable raw material for other companies than to invest in building new capabilities to utilise this material internally, if its current business is based on scale economies. The utilisation of side streams might also require investing in R&D activity and adopting a smaller-scale specialised production logic with high value-added products for narrow customer segments. Finding a fit between the different operating modes – exploitative and explorative – can be challenging (March, 1991).

As presented above, whether companies recognise business opportunities and how attractive they see these opportunities as being depends on both the characteristics of business transactions and environments and firm-specific factors, especially cognition and capabilities. When a promising opportunity is recognised and interpreted as viable, the next phase in the strategic decision-making would be to determine whether and how the opportunity would create value and how to capture this value. In other words, using the firm's capabilities to create new products and services also means considering the firm's *business model*.

## 3.3 Business Models

Capabilities and products are intertwined in a firm's value creation and capture system; 'resources and products are two sides of the same coin', according to Wernerfelt (1984, p. 171). A firm's business model describes how value is created (a link between capabilities and products) and monetised (a link between products and customers). A business model can be described as the architecture of a firm's value creation and appropriation activity system (Zott and Amit, 2010). When a company creates a new product or makes significant changes to, for example, the delivery system of an existing product, the company's business model must be adjusted so that the new model design includes a description of how these new innovations create value for target customers and how the firm captures this value (i.e., makes a profit).

The literature on sustainable business models (see, e.g., Bocken et al., 2014; Schaltegger et al., 2016) extends the concept of value – a central element of business models – to cover social and ecological aspects as well as financial aspects. As regards CBE business models, the literature is scarce, even though reviews of the CE business models more broadly cover examples that contain both circular and bioeconomy aspects (see, e.g., Ghisellini et al., 2016; Lüdeke-Freund et al., 2019; DeBoer et al., 2020; Toppinen et al., 2020). From the business model perspective, one of the challenges in systemic CBE is the need to align the business models of several companies to achieve the benefits of the CBE.

Despite the growing attention being paid to sustainable business models in the scientific literature, many questions about how to create and develop sustainable business remain open, especially in the systemic CBE context. As discussed in Chapter 3, the management of sustainable business models deserves more interest in the research literature in the future and this calls for paying more attention to understanding the firm-specific contextual factors that influence value creation and value capture (i.e., business model) at the company level. In the business context, where the value creation of one company is tightly intertwined with the activities of others (i.e., value creation is systemic), developing business models in practice or analysing them from an academic viewpoint requires clarifying the influence of the dynamics between the different actors (e.g., in terms of interdependence, decision-making, negotiation power, and coordination) on value creation. However, although relations with other actors are clearly important in CE business models, 'details about the roles and importance of partners are often absent' in the current literature, as Lüdeke-Freund et al. (2019, p. 56) note.

Furthermore, Korhonen et al. (2018) note that business models attached to a CE would require interorganisational sustainability management, which raises issues regarding coordination and control as well as the distribution of responsibility, risks, and gains related to sustainability management (e.g., how to coordinate the interests of network actors so that what is beneficial for a single firm – in terms of, for example, an environmental management system – is also beneficial for the network). How to form collective decision-making structures that enable the synchronisation of the activities of multiple actors is an open issue.

In their review on existing CBE business model studies, Salvador et al. (2021) found that academic research on CBE has paid very little attention to company-level business issues; the social dimension of sustainability in particular has been ignored (also noted in Chapter 3). Examples of the few studies that approach CBE from the company-level business perspective are those by Näyhä (2020) and D'Amato et al. (2020). These studies focus on business models and other related internal factors of forest-based companies and offer suggestions on how to advance the transformation of business into a CBE and sustainability. Guerrero and Hansen (2021), also focusing on forest-based companies like the two previously mentioned authors, extend the examination to how cross-sectoral innovation collaboration may support the transition to a CBE business and to determining the related challenges in these initiatives. Still, much more research is required to understand what a CBE means to business actors and what is needed from other actors such as public authorities to support CBE business activity.

## 3.4 Business Ecosystems

From the business actor's perspective, a systemic business environment such as a CBE requires deeper and wider coordination and collaboration than the current linear economy. From the perspective of companies, shared goals, strong interdependence between multiple actors, and a systemic approach constitute an *ecosystemic approach* to conducting business. Moore (1996), who introduced the ecosystem metaphor into the business studies literature, describes the business ecosystem in terms of interaction, shared vision, and the coordinated alignment of economic actors in the same direction. Compared to bilateral business relationships, 'an ecosystem is inherently multilateral' (Adner, 2017, p. 42) and multilateralism makes the analysis (as well as the practical management) of interactions complex.

Adner (2017) argues that from the business perspective, at the core of an ecosystem is the value proposition. According to Adner, an analysis of the ecosystemic value proposition includes central structural elements of *activities*, *actors*, *positions*, and *links* in the ecosystem. Economic actors and their strategies can be complementary, contradictory, or competitive. For the business ecosystem to create value for a single firm, the activities in the ecosystem must be *aligned*. An interesting question, which has yet to be answered sufficiently, is how this happens and who coordinates the interests and activities within the ecosystem.

Jacobides et al. (2018, p. 2264) fundamentally define the business ecosystem using complementarities: 'An ecosystem is a set of actors with varying degrees of multilateral, nongeneric complementarities that are not fully hierarchically controlled'. Hence, central to this definition, as to many others, is *multilateral mutual interdependence,* which demands an analysis framework for which the established business studies approaches are not suited. In the existing strategy research literature, the current approaches overlook some or many central elements needed for ecosystem analysis (see Adner, 2017). Research on business ecosystems is still more anecdotal and scattered than systematic and consistent. Such a shortage of theoretical ecosystem analysis frameworks in the literature limits the possibilities to examine the necessary prerequisites of CBE ecosystems and how the ecosystems should be organised in practice.

The concept of the CBE ecosystem combines aspects of the CE, bio-based material usage, and the ecosystemic approach to running a business. The research literature on CBE ecosystems is still very scarce. This is not surprising, as both business ecosystems and CBE ecosystems are somewhat new concepts. However, practical business life already offers some examples that can be defined as CBE ecosystems (see Box 5.2).

In a CBE ecosystem, companies encounter the same questions related to important strategic issues as any other business ecosystem: how to align the

---

## Box 5.2 Circular bioeconomy business ecosystem: case Plänet B

One example of endeavours to build a circular bioeconomy ecosystem is Plänet B in Äänekoski, located in Central Finland. Project Plänet B (http://planetb.fi) aims to bring together different companies and other actors to build a business ecosystem for companies whose business relates to the bioeconomy and/or circular economy, especially companies operating in the field of the forest-based bioeconomy. According to their project plans and communication materials, Plänet B aims to seek new CBE business around the current businesses in Äänekoski. Metsä Group has a bioproduct mill in Äänekoski and the company itself, as well as the wider Plänet B network, explicitly aims to expand the usage of forest-based raw materials and production side streams for creating new business. As well as the bioproduct mill, the area also has a demo plant (joint venture of Metsä Group and Itochu), for instance, which tests wood-based textile fibre production. In addition to its current products and current use of the side streams of production (such as pulp, cellulose derivatives, wood-based chemicals, energy), Plänet B aims to expand the ecosystem and attract start-ups and other companies whose business models enable new ways in which to use the wood-based side streams of industrial processes.

diverging (or conflicting) interests of multiple parties and how to govern business risks that are asymmetric for companies in the same ecosystem. The issues related to incentives, the alignment of activities of different companies, and the risks of being dependent on resource providers or complementary assets and other strategic issues, also presented in this chapter, are important – and complex from the company-level perspective. Explicitly addressing them and finding solutions to them at the level of interfirm relationships or at system level could further the materialisation of the anticipated CBE benefits.

# 4 Summary and a Path Forward

In this chapter, we have used strategic management frameworks to discuss the CBE business context at the company level. We conclude that understanding company-level decision-making (i.e., choices and reasoning) is important when trying to understand and anticipate the transformation process from the linear economy to a CBE. The frameworks offered by the strategic management literature are useful to some extent for analysing the transformation to a CBE from the actor perspective. However, the business studies field still needs frameworks that help us understand the alignment of interests and system coordination in systems that include multilateral mutual interdependence.

As depicted above, a firm's internal characteristics channel its business activities. Strategic moves and directions are shaped by organisational cognition, capabilities, and incentives (Kaplan, 2008). Something must trigger changes to strategic choices or business (Cho and Hambrick, 2006). The deeper cooperation that the CBE requires results in higher transaction costs, especially asset specificity and hold-up problems. Every company must cope with these strategic-level issues, and the way in which they are solved has an impact on the role that the CBE plays in each company. These aspects will not inhibit the transformation towards a CBE if related business opportunities appear sufficiently advantageous in terms of profit or long-term survival (i.e., the expected returns are greater than the assessed costs) to some companies. Businesses differ in terms of resources and capabilities and thus also in their willingness and ability to renew: some companies are better than others at overcoming initial obstacles. The prevailing incentive schemes in the operating environment are also important, and societies can support a sustainability transformation by giving companies the necessary incentive signals to start changing their business activities according to society's sustainability goals. Putting a price (e.g., through regulation or taxation) on the social and environmental costs and benefits of production would be one technology-neutral, efficient way in which to support sustainability transformation.

Innovative business actors can be the motors of change, and the power of the free-market system lies in its ability to funnel the usage of scarce resources effectively, systematically increasing overall economic efficiency. Societies have ways in which to influence companies to adopt more sustainable practices, thus catering to the welfare of a wider group of stakeholders. For example, investing in education and R&D creates tools and accumulates the skills of individuals and companies to strive for a more strongly sustainable society in both everyday life and business practices.

## References

Adner, R. (2017) 'Ecosystem as structure: An actionable construct for strategy', *Journal of Management*, 43, pp. 39–58.

Antikainen, M. and Valkokari, K. (2016) 'A framework for sustainable circular business model innovation', *Technology Innovation Management Review*, 6, pp. 5–12.

Bocken, N. M. P., Short, S. W., Rana, P. and Evans, S. (2014) 'A literature and practice review to develop sustainable business model archetypes', *Journal of Cleaner Production*, 65, pp. 42–56.

Bugge, M. M., Hansen, T. and Klitkou, A. (2016) 'What is the bioeconomy? A review of the literature', *Sustainability*, 8, pp. 691–713.

Cho, T. S. and Hambrick, D. C. (2006) 'Attention as the mediator between top management team characteristics and strategic change: The case of airline deregulation', *Organization Science*, 17, pp. 453–469.

Coase, R. (1937) 'The nature of the firm', *Economica New Series*, 4, pp. 386–405.

D'Amato, D., Veijonaho, S. and Toppinen, A. (2020) 'Towards sustainability? Forest-based circular bioeconomy business models in Finnish SMEs', *Forest Policy and Economics*, 110, 101848.

Danielsen, F., Beukema, H., Burgess, N. D., Parish, F., Bruhl, C. A., Donald, P. F., Murdiyarso, D., Phalan, B., Reijnders, L., Struebig, M. and Fitzherbert, E. B. (2008) 'Biofuel plantations on forested lands: Double jeopardy for biodiversity and climate', *Conservation Biology*, 23, pp. 348–358.

DeBoer, J., Panwar, R., Kozak, R. and Cashore, B. (2020) 'Squaring the circle: Refining the competitiveness logic for the circular bioeconomy', *Forest Policy and Economics*, 110, 101858.

Eggers, J. P. and Kaplan, S. (2009) 'Cognition and renewal: Comparing CEO and organizational effects on incumbent adaptation to technical change', *Organization Science*, 20, pp. 461–477.

Eggers, J. P. and Kaplan, S. (2013) 'Cognition and capabilities: A multi-level perspective', *Academy of Management Annals*, 7, pp. 295–340.

European Commission (2012) 'Innovating for sustainable growth: A bioeconomy for Europe'. https://publications.europa.eu/en/publication-detail/-/publication/1f0d8515-8dc0-4435-ba53-9570e47dbd51.

European Commission (2020) 'A new circular economy action plan - for a cleaner and more competitive Europe'. https://eur-lex.europa.eu/resource.html?uri=cellar:9903b325-6388-11ea-b735-01aa75ed71a1.0017.02/DOC_1&format=PDF.

Geissdoerfer, M., Savaget, P., Bocken, N. M. P. and Hultink, E. J. (2017) 'The circular economy – a new sustainability paradigm?', *Journal of Cleaner Production*, 143, pp. 757–768.

Ghisellini, P., Cialani, C. and Ulgiati, S. (2016) 'A review on circular economy: The expected transition to a balanced interplay of environmental and economic systems', *Journal of Cleaner Production*, 114, pp. 11–32.

Giampietro, M. (2019) 'On the circular bioeconomy and decoupling: Implications for sustainable growth', *Ecological Economics*, 162, pp. 143–156.

Guerrero, J. E. and Hansen, E. (2021) 'Company-level cross-sector collaborations in transition to the bioeconomy: A multi-case study', *Forest Policy and Economics*, 123, 102355.

Helfat, C. E. (2015) 'Vertical firm structure and industry evolution', *Industrial and Corporate Change*, 24, pp. 803–818.

Helfat, C. E. and Campo-Rembado, M. A. (2016) 'Integrative capabilities, vertical integration, and innovation over successive technology lifecycles', *Organization Science*, 27, pp. 249–264.

Inigo, E. A. and Blok, V. (2019) 'Strengthening the socio-ethical foundations of the circular economy: Lessons from responsible research and innovation', *Journal of Cleaner Production*, 233, pp. 280–291.

Jacobides, M. G., Cennamo, C. and Gawer, A. (2018) 'Towards a theory of ecosystems', *Strategic Management Journal*, 39, pp. 2255–2276.

Jacobides, M. G. and Winter, S. G. (2005) 'The co-evolution of capabilities and transaction costs: Explaining the institutional structure of production', *Strategic Management Journal*, 26, pp. 395–413.

Kaplan, S. (2008) 'Cognition, capabilities, and incentives: Assessing firm response to the fiber-optic revolution', *Academy of Management Journal*, 51, pp. 672–695.

Kirchherr, J., Piscicelli, L., Bour, R., Kostense-Smit, E., Muller, J., Huibrechtse-Truijens, A. and Hekkert, M. (2018) 'Barriers to the circular economy: Evidence from the European Union (EU)', *Ecological Economics*, 150, pp. 264–272.

Kirchherr, J., Reike, D. and Hekkert, M. (2017) 'Conceptualizing the circular economy: An analysis of 114 definitions', *Resource, Conservation & Recycling*, 127, pp. 221–232.

Kivimaa, P. and Kern, F. (2016) 'Creative destruction or mere niche support? Innovation policy mixes for sustainability transitions', *Research Policy*, 45, pp. 205–217.

Konietzko, J., Bocken, N. and Hultink, J. E. (2020) 'Circular ecosystem innovation: An initial set of principles', *Journal of Cleaner Production*, 253, 119942.

Korhonen, J., Honkasalo, A. and Seppälä, J. (2018) 'Circular economy: The concept and its limitations', *Ecological Economics*, 143, pp. 37–46.

Langlois, R. N. (1992) 'Transaction-cost economics in real time', *Industrial and Corporate Change*, 1, pp. 99–127.

Lüdeke-Freund, F., Gold, S. and Bocken, N. M. P. (2019) 'A review and typology of circular economy business model patterns', *Journal of Industrial Ecology*, 23, pp. 36–61.

March, J. G. (1991) 'Exploration and exploitation in organizational learning', *Organization Science*, 2, pp. 71–87.

McCormick, K. and Kautto, N. (2013) 'The bioeconomy in Europe: An overview', *Sustainability*, 5, pp. 2589–2608.

Moore, J. F. (1996) *The Death of Competition: Leadership and Strategy in the Age of Business Ecosystems*. New York: Harper Business.

Näyhä, A. (2020) 'Finnish forest-based companies in transition to the circular bioeconomy: drivers, organizational resources and innovations', *Forest Policy and Economics*, 110, 101936.

Obidzinski, K., Andriani, R., Komarudin, H. and Andrianto, A. (2012) 'Environmental and social impacts of oil palm plantations and their implications for biofuel production in Indonesia', *Ecology and Society*, 17, 25.

Pfau, S. F., Hagens, J. E., Dankbaar, B. and Smits, A. J. M. (2014) 'Visions of sustainability in bioeconomy research', *Sustainability*, 6, pp. 1222–1249.

Prahalad, C. K. and Bettis, R. A. (1986) 'The dominant logic: A new linkage between diversity and performance', *Strategic Management Journal*, 7, pp. 485–501.

Priefer, C., Jörissen, J. and Frör, O. (2017) 'Pathways to shape the bioeconomy', *Resources*, 6, 10.

Ramicilovic-Suominen, S. and Pülzl, H. (2018) 'Sustainable development: A "selling point" of the emerging EU bioeconomy policy framework?', *Journal of Cleaner Production*, 172, pp. 4170–4180.

Reike, D., Vermeulen, W. J. V. and Witjes, S. (2018) 'The circular economy: New or refurbished as CE 3.0? — Exploring controversies in the conceptualization of the circular economy through a focus on history and resource value retention options', *Resources, Conversation and Recycling*, 135, pp. 246–264.

Richardson, G. B. (1972) 'The organisation of industry', *Economic Journal*, 82, pp. 883–896.

Schaltegger, S., Hansen, E. G. and Lüdeke-Freund, F. (2016) 'Business models for sustainability: Origins, present research, and future avenues', *Organization & Environment*, 29, pp. 3–10.

Stegmann, P., Londo, M. and Junginger, M. (2020) 'The circular bioeconomy: Its elements and role in European bioeconomy clusters', *Resources, Conservation & Recycling: X*, 6, 100029.

Teece, D. J. (2019) 'A capability theory of the firm: An economics and (strategic) management perspective', *New Zealand Economic Papers*, 53, pp. 1–43.

Teece, D. J., Pisano, G. and Shuen, A. (1997) 'Dynamic capabilities and strategic management', *Strategic Management Journal*, 18, pp. 533–537.

Temmes, A. and Peck, P. (2020) 'Do forest biorefineries fit with working principles of a circular bioeconomy? A case of Finnish and Swedish initiatives', *Forest Policy and Economics*, 110, pp. 1–12.

Toppinen, A., D'Amato, D. and Stern, T. (2020) 'Forest-based circular bioeconomy: Matching sustainability challenges and novel business opportunities?', *Forest Policy and Economics*, 110, 102041.

Vivien, F.-D., Nieddu, M., Befort, N., Debref, R. and Giampietro, M. (2019) 'The hijacking of the bioeconomy', *Ecological Economics*, 159, pp. 189–197.

Wernerfelt, B. (1984) 'A resource-based view of the firm', *Strategic Management Journal*, 5, pp. 171–180.

Williamson, O. E. (1985) *The Economic Institutions of Capitalism*. New York: Free Press.

Williamson, O. E. (1991) 'Comparative economic organization: The analysis of discrete structural alternatives', *Administrative Science Quarterly*, 36, pp. 269–296.

Zott, C. and Amit, R. (2010) 'Business model design: An activity system perspective', *Long Range Planning*, 43, pp. 216–226.

# 6

# STRATEGIES FOR BRAND OWNERS AND RETAILERS IN THE CIRCULAR BIOECONOMY TRANSITION

*Fabian Schipfer, Gülşah Yilan, Francesca Govoni and Piergiuseppe Morone*

## 1 Introduction

The Sustainable Development Goals (SDGs) and the Paris Agreement set the course towards a safe and just operating space under stable environmental conditions (UN/FCCC, 2015; United Nations Development Programme, 2015). We refer to the practices and developments in line with this course of action here as 'sustainable', although some criticism of the integration of SDGs into business strategies is expressed elsewhere in this book (see Chapter 2). As part of the transition from the current economic system to a sustainable and resilient one, the European Union aims, through its Bioeconomy Strategy (EC, 2018), to strengthen and boost biobased sectors, unlocking investments and markets while rapidly deploying local bioeconomies across Europe and improving the understanding of ecological boundaries. By definition, this includes

> all primary production sectors that use and produce biological resources (agriculture, forestry, fisheries, and aquaculture) and all economic and industrial sectors that use biological resources and processes to produce food, feed, bio-based products, energy, and services. To be successful, the European bioeconomy needs to have sustainability and circularity at its heart.
>
> *(EC, 2018, p. 1)*

The combination of these strategies will be further denoted as the transformation towards a circular bioeconomy. The transition implies a plurality of normative and quantitative targets which go beyond eliminating emissions and implementing efficient, circular use of resources, including stable, healthy conditions for individuals and the fair distribution of opportunities among all members of our society.

DOI: 10.4324/9781003003588-8

In the more general sustainable transition process, the role of policymakers and institutional actors, both at the national and regional level, has been broadly discussed (van Vuuren et al., 2015; Gómez Martín et al., 2020; Moyer and Hedden, 2020). However, the setting of framework conditions for economic activities, responsibility and opportunities for producers (including brand owners) and large retailers, are discussed to a lesser extent (Naidoo and Gasparatos, 2018; Istudor and Suciu, 2020). Moreover, studies of the sustainability of economic players have historically concentrated more on primary production, the sourcing of biomass and materials, the nexus of primary and secondary sectors (e.g., manufacturing, final energy supply), and more recently, on businesses in the information and communications sectors (Pohl et al., 2019) or even public administration and defence (SGR, 2020).

This chapter focuses on the significant role that brand owners and retailers play in the circular bioeconomy transition (e.g., in terms of products including apparel, beverages, chemical products, cleaning products, food products, furniture, paper products, plastics, sports goods, textiles, and wood products). Brand owners are businesses that supply well-established and known products in the current economy and they represent key actors in the incumbent regime. Retailers, on the other hand, are important actors and shape the circular bioeconomy through their responsible economic operations. European retailers are taking numerous steps to promote the transition to more circular business practices, including helping to valorise food waste, redesigning their products using recycled or recyclable materials instead of virgin materials, and employing renewable energy alternatives in their processes (Jones and Comfort, in press). With brand owners representing secondary-sector and retailers tertiary-sector actors, this less examined nexus accounts for significant shares of the energy and material flows of economic metabolism and thus deserves particular academic attention in bioeconomy transition research. To set the scene for this field, this chapter aims to excite the reader by asking and hypothesising about brand owners' and retailers' responsibilities, risks, and opportunities in the transition process under various system dynamics.

To clarify the possible roles of retailers and brand owners, in Section 2 we provide a theoretical background to the transition processes in general and offer a comprehensive but simplified typology of possible transition pathways. Based on this typology, in Section 3, we outline our findings regarding the risks and opportunities of brand owners and retailers and underpin them with examples of the circular bioeconomy and other transition processes. The conclusion (Section 4) summarises our findings and distils the primary take-home messages for the reader.

## 2 Beyond Technological Change: Sociotechnical Transitions

Analytical and descriptive approaches to discussing the path from invention to market diffusion are described by, for example, 'strategic niche management' scholars (Kemp et al., 1998), 'transition management' scholars (Perez, 2009), and 'technological revolutions' scholars (Rotmans et al., 2001). Partly building upon these approaches, the 'sociotechnical transition' concept forms a structural context for actively created, (re)produced, and refined activities of human actors who are from different social groups, yet share specific characteristics (Geels, 2005, 2004). Nevertheless, a sociotechnical transition is a multi-dimensional process that includes not only technological but also organisational, institutional, and socio-cultural change to fulfil societal functions such as transport, communication, and nutrition. The transition allows new products, services, businesses, models, organisations, regulations, norms, and user practices to emerge as either complementary or by substituting existing ones (Markard et al., 2016). Hence, retailers and brand owners – inherently social by nature due to their interaction and communication with different stakeholders throughout the value chain – hold a unique position for steering the transition onto a more sustainable pathway.

However, sociotechnical transitions do not occur overnight; they evolve through four developmental phases, which may even take several decades to complete (Geels, 2019). Energy system transitions take, for example, something in the range of 80 (oil/gas/electricity substituting coal steam power) to 130 years (coal steam power replacing pre-industrial energy sources) (Grubler, 2012). Previous studies have aptly described the development phases through which niche innovations pass towards ultimately replacing the incumbent regime (Kemp et al., 1998; Sandén and Azar, 2005; Geels and Raven, 2006; Schot and Geels, 2008; Klitkou et al., 2015; Sengers et al., 2019) and a more detailed discussion of sociotechnical transitions under the concept of sustainability-driven innovation is described elsewhere in this book (see Chapter 11).

In this chapter, we wish to focus on the timing and nature of different multi-level interactions between regimes and niches in the context of brand owners and retailers in the circular bioeconomy. We use the typology developed by Geels and Schot (2007), in which the timing of these interactions is central for determining the fate of niche innovations. Initially, a niche innovation does not act as a threat to the regime; this only happens when the external landscape developments open a window of opportunity by exerting pressure on the incumbent regime. A niche innovation can only break through this window if it is sufficiently developed. Meanwhile, the nature of interaction may have two distinct characteristics. Niche innovations may aim to replace the existing regime in a *competitive* manner, or they may seek to serve as a complementary mechanism to the current regime in a *symbiotic* relationship. Geels and Schot (2007) proposed four different transition pathways as combinations of the time and nature of the interactions between niche innovation development and landscape pressure: transformation (P1), de-alignment and re-alignment (P2), technological substitution (P3), and reconfiguration (P4). To categorise niche innovations into different maturity levels, we adopt terminology from the European Commission's funding schemes such as the Technology Readiness Level (TRL), which enables differentiation of innovation steps from the laboratory, via pilot and demonstration plants, to market introduction (EC, 2014). Figure 6.1 summarises the four

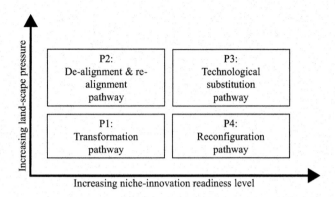

**FIGURE 6.1** Transformation paths described as change types for different combinations of niche readiness level and landscape pressure level.
*Source*: Own illustration.

transformation paths of Geels and Schot (2007) as simplified combinations of landscape pressure and niche readiness levels.

The regime dynamics remain in a stable reproduction process of accustomed practices, leaving minimal space for radical niche innovations if no external landscape pressure exists, i.e., the business-as-usual scenario (BAU). Using the BAU scenario as a benchmark, the *transformation path* (P1: embryonic and symbiotic niche innovations) describes a situation with moderate landscape pressure but no sufficiently advanced solution from the niche level at hand. Good adaptive capacity is essential for incumbent actors to reorient development trajectories in response to gradually increasing landscape pressures and proposed alternatives. The basic architecture of the incumbent regime remains stable, allowing technical variations (i.e., mutations) or adopting symbiotic niche innovations. The *de-alignment and re-alignment path* (P2: embryonic and competitive niche innovations) describes divergent, large, and sudden landscape change. Rapid landscape pressure destabilises (de-aligns) the incumbent regime, thus creating a competition between co-existing niche innovations, until one of them fully develops and re-aligns a new regime. The *technological substitution pathway* (P3: fully developed, competitive niche innovations) describes high landscape pressure, and fully developed niche innovations use the open windows of opportunity to diffuse into the mainstream markets and eventually stabilise the new regime. When the niche innovation substitutes the existing regime, incumbent firms tend to lose their position unless they defend themselves by investing in improvements. Thus, this pathway has a technology-push character. The *reconfiguration pathway* (P4: fully developed, symbiotic niche innovations) describes the transition as being due to the cumulative effect of symbiotic innovations that originated in niches but then came to apply to the regime-level problems as supplementary or substitute components, thus creating 'new combinations' of old and new elements. P1 and P4 have a common characteristic, as the new regime originates from the old one. But, in a transformation pathway (P1), the basic architecture does not change in response to the pressure. These two pathways (P1 and P4) are particularly relevant in the framework of the circular bioeconomy transition, as they describe situations in which landscape pressure is still low. Still, brand owners and retailers can play a crucial role in the transition process by trying to influence and steer trajectory of the innovation process.

The following section discusses the role of brand owners and retailers in the specific context of a sustainable transition towards a circular bio-based economy, based on the multi-level perspective and the four pathways discussed above. It also identifies and highlights potentially relevant synergies and barriers.

## 3 Brand Owners and Retailers in the Circular Bioeconomy Transition

As discussed in the introduction of this chapter, the transition to a circular bio-based economy is a complex and multi-dimensional process, because it requires radical changes in both cognitive and operational *schemas*. This 'transition process' dynamic structure requires innovative technologies from the supply side and regulatory and societal transformations based on a multi-actor 'play' in which brand owners and retailers have vital roles. Based on the phases of the innovation processes and the respective market diffusion characteristics discussed, as well as the theoretical framework of different typologies for the process dynamics (addressed in Section 2), this section employs a theoretical framework to highlight the incumbent regime brand owners' and retailers' responsibilities, risks, and opportunities in terms of either stimulating/accelerating or restraining/slowing down sustainability transitions under various framework conditions. At first, the BAU scenario is discussed from the advantageous position of the incumbent actors via various lock-in mechanisms. Then, the need to combine financial and ecological sustainability aspects in response to the shift in consumer demand for more sustainable products is highlighted. Finally, it depicts some circular bioeconomy examples, along with possible transition pathways under moderate (Section 3.1) and high landscape pressure (Section 3.2).

The BAU scenario contains no landscape pressure to steer production activities in a sustainable direction. Due to the lack of pressure, the incumbent actors (e.g., large brand owners that dominate the industry) do not necessarily feel the need to shift to more sustainable alternatives, and instead prefer to play safe in a stable reproduction process of accustomed practices that leave no space for radical niche innovations to break through.

Techno-economic lock-in mechanisms provide a safe atmosphere for the incumbent regime actors via economies of scale and long-term experience of learning-by-doing, thus yielding low cost and high performance. The regime actors do not take the risk of sunk investments and resist transitional change. Social and cognitive lock-in mechanisms can blind actors to developments outside their routines and mindsets (Geels, 2019). Institutional and political lock-in mechanisms generally favour incumbent regime actors via existing regulations, standards, and policy networks, creating unfair competition for innovations (Kuckertz, 2020). Moreover, influential incumbent actors may use their power through market control or political lobbying to oppose breakthrough innovations. They may even leverage organisations such as industry associations or branch organisations to lobby on their behalf (Unruh, 2000). Concerning the option of lobbying to weaken pressure and thus delay the sustainability transformation, research is starting to reveal social costs, especially for climate policies. For instance, Meng and Rode (2019) empirically analysed US lobbying records and quantified expenses that could be avoided through a more robust climate policy proposal design.

Although the lock-in mechanisms stabilise incumbent firms' positions in the existing regimes, in a sustainability transition process, these firms can play a crucial role – contradicting Schumpeter's dichotomy – provided that emerging economic opportunities and/or attractive financial incentives exist. Legal regulations and public attitudes are also essential for changing the opinions of various types of actors. Therefore, the reorientation of the incumbent actors' financial assets, technical competencies, and political capital may also accelerate sustainability transitions without landscape pressure (Geels, 2019). Sustainability in business management practices can result from optimising the profitability of the firms. For example, Nakao et al. (2007) and Markley and Davis (2007) revealed a positive relationship between financial and ecological sustainability. Mathis (2007) and Youn et al. (2017) already showed that, in return, companies are highly likely to cater to consumers' demands for environmental friendliness and therefore have very good images among consumers. A positive company image can also alter consumer behaviour on the company's behalf. For instance, in their comprehensive research study of 18,980 consumers in 28 countries, the IBM Institute for Business Value (IBV), in association with the National Retail Federation, reported that 'over seven in ten consumers say it's at least moderately important that brands offer "clean" products (78%), are sustainable and environmentally responsible (77%), support recycling (76%), or use natural ingredients (72%)' (Haller et al., 2020).

### 3.1 Brand Owners and Retailers Steering Innovation – Moderate Pressure and Transformation (P1) and Reconfiguration (P4) Pathways

While adaptation and reactive strategies prevail in high-pressure situations, mitigation options and pro-active or 'daredevil' responses are characteristic of moderate pressure circumstances. Whereas the former strategies can be understood as market driven, the latter has the chance to be an investment in market-driving practices. In comparison to COVID-19, the climate crisis continues to exert low to moderate landscape pressure on the incumbent regime as it has done since the beginning of the second decade of the current century. However, its pressure is noticeably increasing in the environment and in society. Moderate landscape pressure offers an opportunity for brand owners to reconsider their actions incrementally. It allows for strategic planning of innovation dynamics and the selection of solutions on the basis of a risk-minimising approach. It aims to maximise revenues from current products and services and incrementally amend them. On the other hand, niche innovations also suffer from low funding and support, as current 'pain points' are not yet painful enough.

Under moderate pressure circumstances, brand owners can still choose from a set of actions and combinations of these. Boiral (2006) differentiates between managerial, socio-political, and technical actions. Managerial action includes brand owners' self-commitment to environmental certification schemes (like ISO 14001 or EMAS – Eco-Management and Audit Scheme). Examples of socio-political actions are image campaigns, lobbying to enforce regulations, and institutional entrepreneurship. Technical action encompasses innovative designs, resource input substitution, and green investments motivated by external pressure and resource availability.

Under moderate landscape pressure and before initiating P1 or P4, corporate social responsibility (CSR) reporting can be understood as an issue that gains traction under retailers and brand owners. As CSR reports seldom follow a standardised approach and the respective information is presented in individual formats, a risk of greenwashing is associated with this type of socio-political action. Still, it can be assumed, and has partly been shown, that CSR reports 'indicate actual sustainability performance' (Papoutsi and Sodhi, 2020). In the new Circular Economic Action Plan to strengthen the European Union consumer law, the European Commission proposes 'further strengthening consumer protection against greenwashing' (in EC, 2020, p. 6). A combination of managerial actions, such as following standardised and certified procedures, can significantly improve the credibility of such reports. Furthermore, Demertzidis et al. (2015, p. 104) propose designing 'specific guidelines to record climate change information in financial and non-financial terms'. The Global Reporting Initiative (GRI) framework for sustainability reporting has developed a set of economic, environmental, social, and governance performance indicators, the aim of which is to represent the actual performance of corporate activities (GRI, 2021).

In their literature review, Istudor and Suciu (2020) analysed the sustainability reports of six of the largest grocery retail corporations in the European Union. They emphasised that the activities of food retailers align with the bioeconomy and circular economy concepts. Auchan Holding, Ahold Delhaize, Carrefour Groupe, and the REWE Group in particular mention the GRI 308 Supplier Environmental Assessment Standard in their sustainability reports. The bioeconomy-related activities in the sustainability reports of the reviewed retailers are clustered into general groups, such as the use of renewable biological sources like electricity provided through the means of solar panels, and the use of methanation reactors to produce biogas from food waste; the use of certified paper stickers instead of plastic wrapping; and the use of recycled materials in the packaging instead of plastic. Since 2014, globally sustainable and environmentally responsible investment has risen by 68%, and in 2019, it exceeded USD 30 trillion (McKinsey, 2019). Nevertheless, it is worth mentioning that the sustainability declarations of companies may misleadingly present their actions, prioritising reputation building rather than the attainment of sustainability goals, especially due to the lack of sector-level guidance and standards on measuring the impacts and contributions to sustainability goals (see also Chapter 2). Once again, it has to be mentioned, a gap may exist between the company's commitment and actual performance – known as greenwashing.

Another essential opportunity for brand owners regarding sustainable transformation can be seen in the current situation (moderate pressure) in institutional or corporate entrepreneurship or intrapreneurship in the case of externally supporting a niche innovation (Macrae, 1976). In contrast to business ecosystems, which focus on value capturing, the mentality of innovation ecosystems circulates around value creation (Gomes et al., 2018), a luxury that can be associated with P1 and P4, rather than with high-pressure pathways P2 and P3. Under moderate landscape pressure, brand owners can still choose whether they want to aim for costly and still risky value capture and direct implementation of deployable solutions or to be on the forefront and at the top of value creation by, for example, supporting and protecting quasi-independent innovation ecosystems, together with or without governmental funding for start-ups and small and medium enterprises. Box 6.1 presents circular bioeconomy examples of the P1 pathway.

---

### Box 6.1 Circular bioeconomy example of initiating transformation pathway (P1)

Brand owners such as Novamont S.p.A., Arkema, Avantium Chemicals BV, Clariant AG, Lego Systems AS, and Henkel KGaA can be named here as actors in a potential P1 pathway and under the Biobased Industries Consortium (BIC) and Biobased Industry Joint Undertaking (BBI JU) flagship projects. This 'partnership aims to invest €3.7B by the end of 2024 - €975M from the [European Commission] Horizon 2020 budget, and the rest from the industry' (Ruiz Sierra et al., 2021 p. 105). It aims to establish a sustainable and competitive bio-based industrial sector in Europe, focusing on bringing together research competencies and industry, but also focusing on market creation via brand owners, retailers, and co-ordination and support measures. Envisaged TRLs are relatively high compared to other R&D funding schemes in BBI JU, and their successor, the Circular Bio-based Europe (CBE) partnership. The advanced solutions need additional investment and development to reach maturity and be appropriate for a P3 or P4 pathway.

Retailers play a unique role as intermediaries between market demand and consumer expectations in such a way that they can force their suppliers to achieve more sustainable business models (see Chapter 3 for a detailed discussion on sustainable business models), as well as promote and encourage changes in consumer behaviour that improve social and environmental issues (Ruiz-Real et al., 2018). Box 6.2 presents circular bioeconomy examples of the reconfiguration pathway.

Mainly on the basis of the P4 examples, we can see that retailers can act as gatekeepers as they determine product standards, communicate with consumers, and provide information on consumers' behaviour towards suppliers (Lai et al., 2010; Youn et al., 2017). As gatekeepers, retailers reduce the value–action gap by introducing sustainable products throughout the supply chain and communicating with customers about sustainability issues (Lee et al., 2012; Gleim et al., 2013; Youn et al., 2017).

However, suppliers are not always willing to co-operate with retailers. For example, Vermeulen and Ras (2006) illustrated the difficulties faced by two Dutch fashion companies in the greening of their global fashion supply chain. The first case was Van Bommel, a shoe producer, who reported that an Indian supplier was unwilling to engage in environmental performance assessment until Van Bommel paid for the cost of the environmental assessment. The other case was a clothing chain store, Peek & Cloppenburg, which was greening its retail range. The firm had to restrict their options inside Europe because the agents and factory tailors in South-East Asia did not co-operate, refusing to give information or identify opportunities for improvement.

Summarising the strategies of the moderate landscape pressure section, it is worth mentioning that a prerequisite for choosing between the various types of actions and being prepared for high sociotechnical landscape pressure is logically knowledge about these options and the operating space for incumbent businesses. Boiral (2006) stresses the importance of building up environmental intelligence

---

## Box 6.2 Circular bioeconomy examples of initiating reconfiguration pathway (P4)

As one of the biggest food retailers in Europe, the Aldi South group has set itself a science-based target (SBT) to reduce its overall operational emissions by more than a quarter by 2025. The group urges its suppliers, who are responsible for 75% of product-related emissions, to adopt the same SBT by the end of 2024 (ALDI, 2021). Therefore, the suppliers have received questionnaires on their current product environmental footprints (PEFs) and can expect to face mandatory reporting of environmental metrics in the coming years. The strict enforcement of, for example, barcode printing position standards for quick processing at checkout allows us to only guess at the power that this retailer has over its suppliers.

in the light of increasing climate change pressure. This concept refers to appointing specialists who can anticipate the potential impacts of pressure changes on and between economic, social, scientific/technical, and political/regulatory issues. Economic issues, such as changing market opportunities and financing possibilities as well as competitive advantages, have to be taken into consideration and be placed in relation to employees' motivation, image, and legitimacy (social issues) as well as subsidies, tax reductions, and changes in regulations (political and regulatory issues), complemented by a comprehensive but detailed overview over the dynamics of niche innovations, strategically directed research, development and demonstration, and the implementation of effective data management practices (scientific and technical issues).

## 3.2 High Pressure from Sociotechnical Landscape – De-alignment and Re-alignment (P2) & Technological Substitution (P3) Pathway

The incumbent regime may be destabilised by divergent, large, and sudden landscape-level changes such as the COVID-19 crisis. This crisis has exerted significant pressure on all countries to increase hygiene standards and introduce measures to minimise the spread of pathogens over borders and through daily routines. The fragility of many global supply chains, mostly seen in response to the need for medical equipment, opened the debate on stock availability and short supply chains to increase systemic resilience. Another important domain is the susceptible area of centralised food production and its long-distance transport via supply chains. Some cities faced food supply problems during lockdown, and a need for shorter producer-to-consumer models emerged. Further, mobility and transportation have also called for specific measures, which have already been taken in pilot cases – giving more space to pedestrians and cyclists and limiting the speed of motor vehicles across the city.

Sustainable solutions can become mainstream in such a dynamic environment that combines economic regeneration, better societal outcomes, and climate targets (Morone and Yilan, 2020). In these specific high-pressure cases, brand owners are either confronted with niche innovations already set up to be deployed and to substitute prevailing solutions and products (e.g., higher sanitary standards and adapted certification schemes to prevent the virus spreading in supermarkets (Carrefour, 2021), innovative solutions for hygiene-related waste streams) or experience a situation in which the niche level offers no alternative deployable solutions. Box 6.3 examines the efforts of the Recover Better campaign as an example of a possible indication of the initiation of a circular bioeconomy de-alignment and re-alignment pathway (high landscape pressure but underdeveloped niche innovations) in the wake of the current crisis.

High landscape pressure is an opportunity for developed niche innovations, the symbiotic co-development of innovations with low technological readiness levels, and the 'prepared' brand owners and retailers who have followed a proactive strategy during times of moderate or no pressure. However, most businesses

## Box 6.3 Possible circular bio-economy example of initiating de-alignment and re-alignment pathway (P2)

Under the Recover Better campaign, 155 companies – with a combined market capitalisation of over USD 2.4 trillion and representing over five million employees – have signed a statement urging governments around the world to *align* their COVID-19 economic aid and recovery efforts with the latest climate science (SBT, 2020). Some specific partners of this initiative prioritise evaluating the amount of single-use and other plastic waste created by increasing the consumption of essential goods and personal safety products due to the COVID-19 pandemic. The majority of the streams consist of personal protective equipment (PPE), single-use plastic bags, containers, and utensils for take-out food, and non-recyclable plastics to secure delivery packages of e-commerce purchases. Below are selected examples of the promotion of the transition to more circular bioeconomy practices in this campaign:

i   Mondelēz announced a packaging partnership with Philadelphia Packaging to utilise recyclable plastic containers in the European cream cheese market,

ii  SC Johnson announced a new Mr Muscle bottle made from 100% ocean-bound plastic through their global partnership with Plastic Bank,

iii Henkel declared its commitment to sustainability and set an ambitious goal for 2025 to use fully recyclable or reusable packaging materials and to reduce fossil-based virgin plastics by 50% in its consumer goods packaging, in turn also reducing the volume of packaging.

can be expected to 'tend to maintain the *status quo* and not react as long as they are not obliged to do so' (Boiral, 2006, p. 323). Heavy industries with slow renewable cycles for infrastructure and production facilities in particular are only likely to have reactive responses, followed by large investments for replacing existing production processes and respective sunk costs. Reactive responses are also associated with a command-and-control type of pressure, in contrast to economic pressure and self-regulation, making room for proactive responses (Demertzidis et al., 2015). Businesses that do not respond at all play an essential role in the incumbent regime. Engau and Hoffmann (2011) define these types of passive stakeholders as 'gamblers' who cannot cope with the prevailing uncertainty or maximising profits and dividends before the definite downfall of their enterprise.

Although the authors cannot provide circular bioeconomy examples involving brand owners and retailers for the P3 pathway (high landscape pressure, high developed niches), it is useful to look at a historical example of the phase-out of chlorofluorocarbons (CFCs) and the role of industry in discussing possibly relevant dynamics in the upcoming circular bioeconomy's P3 developments.

It took a decade to prove the Nobel prize-winning theory of Rowland and Molina that CFCs are causing a chain reaction in stratospheric ozone depletion. During this time, the use of CFCs sky-rocketed, led by the chemical companies Dow Chemical and DuPont, which mainly used then as a grain fumigant. Two years after proof was provided, the Montreal Protocol (1987) was signed, initiating the phasing-out of CFCs (Doherty, 2000). Although DuPont held the highest shares in CFC sales, it also 'acted as the industry leader in the global negotiations'. It influenced the primary negotiator, the US, to increase landscape pressure via bans (Rapid Transition Alliance, 2019). Environmental and health concerns had already much earlier resulted in policy action in the US (Doherty, 2000), forcing DuPont to develop alternatives which became an export hit once the Protocol was enacted.

Adoption and reaction strategies of companies include technical actions such as renewable energy investments, the design of and shift to environmentally friendly products and services, or investments in compensation measures and schemes (Boiral, 2006). In 2018, investments in renewable energy for power, heat, and transport (~USD 330 billion) and efficiency measures in industry, transport, and buildings (~USD 290 billion) significantly fell behind investments in fossil fuel supply and deployment (~USD 930 billion) (IEA, 2019). Thus, divestment strategies have to be considered next to governmental commitments to quit fossil fuel subsidies (~USD 430 billion in 2018) (IEA, 2021). Furthermore, companies such as Neste, which produce and retail fuel shifting to renewable and circular solutions, can be mentioned here (Il Bioeconomista, 2019), even though landscape pressure for renewable energy has only been significantly increasing since the last decade (Monk and Perkins, 2020).

Significant landscape pressure, in combination with low niche readiness levels, will leave brand owners and retailers, in addition to greening their supply chain, in a situation in which they have to buy into costly and readily deployable niche innovations. Even in this case, noteworthy market and policy uncertainties for the last development steps and market diffusion of these niche innovations have to be considered.

## 4 Conclusions

The transformation into a fair, just, sustainable, circular biobased economy relies heavily on the market introduction and market diffusion of technical, social, and organisational innovations. However, innovation processes take time, and the uptake of innovative solutions depends on several internal and external factors, especially correct timing and setting, represented as windows of opportunity for diffusing from niches to mass markets and eventually contributing to the incumbent regime of tomorrow. This discussion on the responsibilities, risks, and opportunities of brand owners and retailers in circular bioeconomy businesses was based on a theoretical typology of transition pathways describing the connection between the landscape pressure and readiness of existing innovative solutions. With brand owners representing secondary-sector and retailers tertiary-sector actors, this less-examined nexus accounts for significant shares of the energy and material flows of economic metabolism and thus deserves attention in the context of transition to a circular bioeconomy.

The COVID-19 crisis shows us, once again, what it means to be confronted with high landscape pressure. Even though the impacts of climate change and the demand of society for transition to sustainability are significantly growing, the landscape pressure regarding the transformation into a circular bioeconomy is still relatively moderate, resulting in an insufficiently funded innovation ecosystem and many opportunities for the brand owners and retailers of the incumbent regime. This fact is reflected in the various circular bioeconomy examples and strategies we collected concerning the low landscape pressure transformation (P1) and reconfiguration pathways (P4).

In the future, retailers could play a leading role in the bioeconomy transition process, especially if they set strict sustainability requirements for their suppliers, by determining product standards, communicating with consumers, and providing information on consumers' preferences back to the suppliers. The ability to transmit suppliers' brands, as in food retail, might render this process much more straightforward than the retail of longer-life products such as electronics and cars. Due to consumers' lack of awareness of the suppliers and brands of the built-in elements, the more important are top-down policies and regulation.

When landscape pressure becomes significant, we hope to be able to choose from a high diversity of readily deployable innovative solutions. Latecomers will then still be able to switch to sustainable practices: based, however, on higher costs and increased risks of not securing relevant market shares. Hitting the crisis with only a few readily deployable solutions and mostly underdeveloped innovations has to be avoided at all costs. High landscape pressure and the lack of deployable solutions can result in a power vacuum and even non-recoverable catastrophes if resources (financial, human, and organisational) become insufficient for a competitive co-evolution of niche innovations. As Hansen et al. discuss in this book (Chapter 11) 'a tsunami of innovations' is necessary against a high degree of pre-market mortality. Still, the consequences of inaction, in the case of high landscape pressure, depleted resources, and underdeveloped niche innovations, would stand in no relation to the risks and costs associated with financing this 'tsunami' and overcoming techno-economic lock-ins, including sunk and vested investments as well as the current commitments of the incumbent regime and its brand owners and retailers.

## References

ALDI (2021) 'ALDI south – responsibility'. https://cr.aldisouthgroup.com/en/responsibility/our-work-action/climate-protection (Accessed 10 March 2021).

Boiral, O. (2006) 'Global warming: Should companies adopt a proactive strategy?', *Long Range Planning*, 39, pp. 315–330. https://doi.org/10.1016/j.lrp.2006.07.002.

Carrefour (2021). 'Covid-19: Carrefour is awarded AFNOR certification in recognition of its sanitary practices' [WWW Document], Carrefour Group. https://www.carrefour.com/en/actuality/covid-19-carrefour-awarded-afnor-certification-recognition-its-sanitary-practices (Accessed 10 March 2021).

Demertzidis, N., Tsalis, T. A., Loupa, G. and Nikolaou, I. E. (2015) 'A benchmarking framework to evaluate business climate change risks: A practical tool suitable for investors decision-making process', *Climate Risk Management*, 10, pp. 95–105. https://doi.org/10.1016/j.crm.2015.09.002.

Doherty, R. E. (2000) 'A history of the production and use of carbon tetrachloride, tetrachloroethylene, trichloroethylene and 1,1,1-trichloroethane in the United States: Part 1–historical background; carbon tetrachloride and tetrachloroethylene', *Environmental Forensics*, 1, pp. 69–81. https://doi.org/10.1006/enfo.2000.0010.

EC (2014). 'Horizon 2020- Work programme 2014–2015. General Annex. G. Technology readiness levels (TRL)' [WWW Document]. https://ec.europa.eu/research/participants/data/ref/h2020/wp/2014_2015/annexes/h2020-wp1415-annex-g-trl_en.pdf (Accessed 10 March 2021).

EC (2018). 'Communication from the Commission to the European Parliament, the Council, the European Economic and Social Committee and the Committee of the Regions. A sustainable Bioeconomy for Europe: Strengthening the connection between economy, society and the environment', *COM*, 673.

EC (2020). Better Finance. Response to the consultation on the new consumer agenda.

Engau, C. and Hoffmann, V. H. (2011) 'Strategizing in an unpredictable climate: Exploring corporate strategies to cope with regulatory uncertainty', *Long Range Planning*, 44, pp. 42–63. https://doi.org/10.1016/j.lrp.2010.11.003.

Geels, F. and Raven, R. (2006) 'Non-linearity and expectations in niche-development trajectories: Ups and downs in Dutch biogas development (1973–2003)', *Technology Analysis & Strategic Management*, 18, pp. 375–392. https://doi.org/10.1080/09537320600777143.

Geels, F. W. (2004) 'From sectoral systems of innovation to socio-technical systems', *Research Policy*, 33, pp. 897–920. https://doi.org/10.1016/j.respol.2004.01.015

Geels, F. W. (2005) 'The dynamics of transitions in socio-technical systems: A multi-level analysis of the transition pathway from horse-drawn carriages to automobiles (1860–1930)', *Technology Analysis & Strategic Management*, 17, pp. 445–476. https://doi.org/10.1080/09537320500357319.

Geels, F. W. (2019) 'Socio-technical transitions to sustainability: A review of criticisms and elaborations of the multi-level perspective', *Current Opinion in Environmental Sustainability* 39, pp. 187–201. https://doi.org/10.1016/j.cosust.2019.06.009.

Geels, F. W. and Schot, J. (2007) 'Typology of sociotechnical transition pathways', *Research Policy*, 36, pp. 399–417. https://doi.org/10.1016/j.respol.2007.01.003.

Gleim, M. R., Smith, J. S., Andrews, D. and Cronin, J. J. (2013) 'Against the green: A multi-method examination of the barriers to green consumption', *Journal of Retailing*, 89, pp. 44–61. https://doi.org/10.1016/j.jretai.2012.10.001.

Gomes, L. A. de V., Facin, A. L. F., Salerno, M. S. and Ikenami, R. K. (2018) 'Unpacking the innovation ecosystem construct: Evolution, gaps and trends', *Technological Forecasting and Social Change*, 136, pp. 30–48. https://doi.org/10.1016/j.techfore.2016.11.009.

Gómez Martín, E., Giordano, R., Pagano, A., van der Keur, P. and Máñez Costa, M. (2020) 'Using a system thinking approach to assess the contribution of nature based solutions to sustainable development goals', *Science of the Total Environment*, 738, p. 139693. https://doi.org/10.1016/j.scitotenv.2020.139693.

GRI (2021) 'GRI standards English language' [WWW Document]. https://www.globalreporting.org/how-to-use-the-gri-standards/gri-standards-english-language/ (Accessed 10 March 2021).

Grubler, A. (2012) 'Energy transitions research: Insights and cautionary tales', *Energy Policy*, 50, pp. 8–16. https://doi.org/10.1016/j.enpol.2012.02.070.

Haller, K., Lee, J. and Cheung, J. (2020) 'IBM Institute for business value' [WWW Document]. IBM. https://www.ibm.com/thought-leadership/institute-business-value/report/consumer-2020 (Accessed 15 March 2021).

IEA (2019) 'World Energy Investment 2019'.

IEA (2021) 'IEA - Energy subsidies. Tracking the impact of fossil-fuel subsidies' [WWW Document]. IEA. https://www.iea.org/topics/energy-subsidies (Accessed 10 March 2021).

Il Bioeconomista (2019) 'Neste to divest its fuel retail business in Russia and sell it to PJSC Tafneft', *IL BIOECONOMISTA*. https://ilbioeconomista.com/2019/07/18/neste-to-divest-its-fuel-retail-business-in-russia-and-sell-it-to-pjsc-tafneft/ (Accessed 10 March 2021).

Istudor, L.-G. and Suciu, M.-C. (2020) 'Bioeconomy and circular economy in the European food retail sector', *EJSD*, 9, pp. 501–511. https://doi.org/10.14207/ejsd.2020.v9n2p501.

Jones, P. and Comfort, D. (2021) 'The circular economy: An exploratory case study from the paper and retail industry', *Athens Journal of Business and Economics*, 7, pp. 379–394. https://doi.org/10.30958/ajbe.7-4-5

Kemp, R., Schot, J. and Hoogma, R. (1998) 'Regime shifts to sustainability through processes of niche formation: The approach of strategic niche management', *Technology Analysis & Strategic Management*, 10, pp. 175–198. https://doi.org/10.1080/09537329808524310.

Klitkou, A., Bolwig, S., Hansen, T. and Wessberg, N. (2015) 'The role of lock-in mechanisms in transition processes: The case of energy for road transport', *Environmental Innovation and Societal Transitions*, 16, pp. 22–37. https://doi.org/10.1016/j.eist.2015.07.005.

Kuckertz, A. (2020) 'Bioeconomy transformation strategies worldwide require stronger focus on entrepreneurship', *Sustainability*, 12, 2911. https://doi.org/10.3390/su12072911.

Lai, K.-H., Cheng, T. C. E. and Tang, A. K. Y. (2010) 'Green retailing: Factors for success', *California Management Review*, 52, pp. 6–31. https://doi.org/10.1525/cmr.2010.52.2.6.

Lambin, E. F., Gibbs, H. K., Heilmayr, R., Carlson, K. M., Fleck, L. C., Garrett, R. D., le Polain de Waroux, Y., McDermott, C. L., McLaughlin, D., Newton, P., Nolte, C., Pacheco, P., Rausch, L. L., Streck, C., Thorlakson, T. and Walker, N. F. (2018) 'The role of supply-chain initiatives in reducing deforestation', *Nature Climate Change*, 8, pp. 109–116. https://doi.org/10.1038/s41558-017-0061-1.

Lee, N., Choi, Y. J., Youn, C. and Lee, Y. (2012) 'Does green fashion retailing make consumers more eco-friendly?: The influence of green fashion products and campaigns on green consciousness and behavior', *Clothing and Textiles Research Journal*, 30, pp. 67–82. https://doi.org/10.1177/0887302X12446065.

Macrae, N. (1976) 'The coming entrepreneurial revolution : A survey', *The Economist*, 261, pp. 41–65.

Markard, J., Suter, M. and Ingold, K. (2016) 'Socio-technical transitions and policy change – Advocacy coalitions in Swiss energy policy', *Environmental Innovation and Societal Transitions*, 18, pp. 215–237. https://doi.org/10.1016/j.eist.2015.05.003.

Markley, M. J. and Davis, L. (2007) 'Exploring future competitive advantage through sustainable supply chains', *International Journal of Physical Distribution & Logistics Management*, 37, pp. 763–774. https://doi.org/10.1108/09600030710840859.

Mathis, A. (2007) 'Corporate social responsibility and policy making: What role does communication play?', *Business Strategy and the Environment*, 16, pp. 366–385. https://doi.org/10.1002/bse.576.

McKinsey (2019) 'Five ways that ESG creates value'. http://ceros.mckinsey.com/the-next-normal-callout (Accessed 20 January 2021).

Meng, K. C. and Rode, A. (2019) 'The social cost of lobbying over climate policy', *Nature Climate Change*, 9, pp. 472–476. https://doi.org/10.1038/s41558-019-0489-6.

Monk, A. and Perkins, R. (2020) 'What explains the emergence and diffusion of green bonds?', *Energy Policy*, 145, 111641. https://doi.org/10.1016/j.enpol.2020.111641.

Morone, P. and Yilan, G. (2020) 'A paradigm shift in sustainability: From lines to circles', *Acta Innovations*, pp. 5–16. https://doi.org/10.32933/ActaInnovations.36.1.

Moyer, J. D. and Hedden, S. (2020) 'Are we on the right path to achieve the sustainable development goals?', *World Development*, 127. https://doi.org/10.1016/j.worlddev.2019.104749.

Naidoo, M. and Gasparatos, A. (2018) 'Corporate environmental sustainability in the retail sector: Drivers, strategies and performance measurement', *Journal of Cleaner Production*, 203, pp. 125–142. https://doi.org/10.1016/j.jclepro.2018.08.253.

Nakao, Y., Amano, A., Matsumura, K., Genba, K. and Nakano, M. (2007) 'Relationship between environmental performance and financial performance: An empirical analysis of Japanese corporations', *Business Strategy and the Environment*, 16, pp. 106–118. https://doi.org/10.1002/bse.476.

Papoutsi, A. and Sodhi, M. S. (2020) 'Does disclosure in sustainability reports indicate actual sustainability performance?', *Journal of Cleaner Production*, 260, 121049. https://doi.org/10.1016/j.jclepro.2020.121049.

Perez, C. (2009) 'Technological revolutions and techno-economic paradigms', *Cambridge Journal of Economics*, 34(1), pp.185–202.

Pohl, J., Hilty, L. M. and Finkbeiner, M. (2019) 'How LCA contributes to the environmental assessment of higher order effects of ICT application: A review of different approaches', *Journal of Cleaner Production*, 219, pp. 698–712. https://doi.org/10.1016/j.jclepro.2019.02.018.

Rapid Transition Alliance (2019) 'Back from the brink: How the world rapidly sealed a deal to save the ozone layer'. https://www.rapidtransition.org/stories/back-from-the-brink-how-the-world-rapidly-sealed-a-deal-to-save-the-ozone-layer/ (Accessed 30 December 2020).

Rotmans, J., Kemp, R. and van Asselt, M. (2001) 'More evolution than revolution: Transition management in public policy', *Foresight*, 3, pp. 15–31. https://doi.org/10.1108/14636680110803003

Ruiz-Real, J., Uribe-Toril, J., Gázquez-Abad, J. and de Pablo Valenciano, J. (2018) 'Sustainability and retail: Analysis of global research', *Sustainability*, 11, 14. https://doi.org/10.3390/su11010014.

Ruiz Sierra, A., Zika, E., Lange, L., Ruiz de Azúa, P. L., Canalis, A., Mallorquín Esteban, P., Paiano, P. and Mengal, P. (2021) 'The bio-based industries joint undertaking: A high impact initiative that is transforming the bio-based industries in Europe', *New Biotechnology*, 60, pp. 105–112. https://doi.org/10.1016/j.nbt.2020.09.003.

Sandén, B. A. and Azar, C. (2005) 'Near-term technology policies for long-term climate targets—economy wide versus technology specific approaches', *Energy Policy*, 33, pp. 1557–1576. https://doi.org/10.1016/j.enpol.2004.01.012.

SBT (2020) 'Over 150 global corporations urge world leaders for net-zero recovery from COVID-19' [WWW Document], Science Based Targets. https://sciencebasedtargets.org/news/over-150-global-corporations-urge-world-leaders-for-net-zero-recovery-from-covid-19 (Accessed 10 March 2021).

Schot, J. and Geels, F. W. (2008) 'Strategic niche management and sustainable innovation journeys: Theory, findings, research agenda, and policy', *Technology Analysis & Strategic Management*, 20, pp. 537–554. https://doi.org/10.1080/09537320802292651.

Sengers, F., Wieczorek, A. J. and Raven, R. (2019) 'Experimenting for sustainability transitions: A systematic literature review', *Technological Forecasting and Social Change*, 145, pp. 153–164. https://doi.org/10.1016/j.techfore.2016.08.031.

SGR (2020). *Scientists for Global Responsibility (SGR). The Enviornmental Impacts of the UK Military Sector*. ISBN: 978-0-9549406-9-0. Halton Mill, UK. https://www.sgr.org.uk/sites/default/files/2020-05/SGR-DUK_UK_Military_Env_Impacts.pdf (Accessed 17 June 2022).

UN/FCCC (2015) 'Conference of the parties, adoption of the Paris agreement', Paris, FR. 12 December 2015 U.N. Doc. FCCC/CP/2015/L.9/Rev/1. https://unfccc.int/resource/docs/2015/cop21/eng/l09r01.pdf (Accessed 17 June 2022).

United Nations Development Programme (2015) 'Transforming our world: The 2030 Agenda for sustainable development', A/RES/70/1, UNDP. New York, US. https://sustainabledevelopment.un.org/content/documents/21252030%20Agenda%20for%20Sustainable%20Development%20web.pdf (Accessed 17 June 2022).

Unruh, G. C. (2000) 'Understanding carbon lock-in', *Energy Policy*, 28, pp. 817–830. https://doi.org/10.1016/S0301-4215(00)00070-7.

van Vuuren, D. P., Kok, M., Lucas, P. L., Prins, A. G., Alkemade, R., van den Berg, M., Bouwman, L., van der Esch, S., Jeuken, M., Kram, T. and Stehfest, E. (2015) 'Pathways to achieve a set of ambitious global sustainability objectives by 2050: Explorations using the IMAGE integrated assessment model', *Technological Forecasting and Social Change*, 98, pp. 303–323. https://doi.org/10.1016/j.techfore.2015.03.005.

Vermeulen, W. J. V. and Ras, P. J. (2006) 'The challenge of greening global product chains: meeting both ends', *Sustainable Development*, 14, pp. 245–256. https://doi.org/10.1002/sd.270.

Youn, C., Kim, S., Lee, Y., Choo, H. J., Jang, S. and Jang, J. I. (2017) 'Measuring retailers' sustainable development', *Business Strategy and the Environment*, 26, pp. 385–398. https://doi.org/10.1002/bse.1924.

# 7

# SERVITISATION AND THE FUTURE OF BUSINESS DEVELOPMENT – INSIGHTS FROM THE FOREST INDUSTRY

*Katja Lähtinen and Liina Häyrinen*

## 1 Forest Industry Businesses and Services in Marketing Theories

Traditional product-based business models see customer value to be delivered by suppliers to customers, while services have typically been considered a separate value component for tangible products. Contrastingly to such product-based thinking, servitisation refers to a solution-seeking process and to the supply of comprehensive product–service systems, which enable value co-creation with customers and other actors (Box 7.1). This chapter presents the potential for servitisation development in the forest industry businesses with special focus on value chains connected to pulp and paper and sawn wood production.

The business environment of product-based industries has drastically changed in recent decades due to globalisation (Kindström, 2010). Forest industry businesses are not an exception, and to strengthen their competitiveness, companies, particularly those operating in higher production cost regions, have been pushed to seek new ways for value creation. Thus, by examining the development needs and opportunities in the production of pulp, paper, and sawn wood, this chapter provides broader insights on the business opportunities in any product-based industries during the era of global competition and circular bioeconomy.

In the forest industry, process and product innovations have traditionally gained most of the attention as sources for value creation (e.g., Hovgaard and Hansen, 2000; Stendahl and Roos, 2008; Nybakk et al., 2011). In addition, although services have been recognised as sources of business performance (Lähtinen and Toppinen, 2008), the role of developing comprehensive *product–service systems* through *business model innovations* (see Chapter 11 for an overview on innovation) has seldom been addressed. Even nowadays, forest industry businesses often follow product-based logic connected to processes and products, in which services are treated as a separate value component to market offerings

DOI: 10.4324/9781003003588-9

(Näyhä et al., 2015). From a marketing viewpoint, this means that customers are seen mostly as targets for sales instead of, for example, collaborators in value co-creation.

Following from product-based logic, views concerning business model implementation in forest industry have been more in line with the traditional understanding of economic exchange and the value creation of *goods-dominant logic*. According to such product-based marketing practices, value is embedded in the output of manufacturing processes delivered by the producers to customers through value-in-exchange (Vargo and Lusch, 2004, 2008; Grönroos and Voima, 2013; Heinonen and Strandvik, 2018). This approach holds neither acquiring profound knowledge of specific customer needs nor value co-creation with customers at the core of company actions (Kindström, 2010; Kindström and Kowalkovski, 2015; Kohtamäki and Rajala, 2016; Rabetino et al., 2017).

In contrast to product-based marketing practices, which are largely followed by forest industry businesses, marketing scholars have presented a fundamental paradigm shift in marketing over the last decades. As a result, increasing emphasis has been placed on intangible resources and value co-creation together with customers (e.g. Grönroos, 1994; Vargo and Lusch, 2004). Theoretically, those alternative service-based views have been specifically addressed by service-dominant logic, service logic, and customer-dominant logic, which are briefly described in Box 7.2.

---

**Box 7.1 Definition of servitisation and sustainable servitised business models**

*Servitisation* is employed in this chapter as a practical umbrella concept for service orientation. It is also used as a synonym for service-based views in relation to business models, which connects with 'the innovation of an organizations capabilities and processes to better create mutual value through a shift from selling product to selling product-service systems' (Baines et al., 2009, p. 555). In addition, a *sustainable servitised business model* is employed as a specific concept of those servitised business models emphasising the sustainability of actions.

---

**Box 7.2 Service-based views in marketing theories introduced especially in the 2000s**

*Service-dominant* logic evolved as an alternative marketing theory to goods-dominant logic. It holds the assumption that value is always co-created with multiple actors, who as beneficiaries define the value through their experiences (Vargo and Lusch, 2004, 2016; Lusch and Vargo, 2014). Thus, businesses acting as suppliers can only offer *value propositions*, while actual value creation is always defined by customers through *value-in-use* (Vargo and Lusch, 2008; Chandler and Lusch, 2015). To co-create value and achieve competitiveness, service-dominant logic emphasises the primacy of intangible resources, such as knowledge and skills, which act on tangible resources such as nature-based raw materials and products. Tangible resources are seen to have a secondary role in seeking for competitiveness, as their potential in value co-creation is dependent on the joint utilisation of tangible resources with appropriate intangible resources (Vargo and Lusch, 2004; Vargo and Akaka, 2009).

*Service logic* sees the possibilities for value co-creation to be dependent on collaboration between service providers and customers through interactive, collaborative, and dialogical processes in the *platform of value co-creation* (Grönroos, 2006; Grönroos et al., 2015; Heinonen and Strandvik, 2018). Service logic sees the platform of value creation as a pathway for businesses to gain opportunities for affecting customer value processes and value fulfillment (Grönroos, 2017). Compared to service-dominant logic, service logic additionally focuses more on recognising the strategic role of production-related actions and collaboration in service provision. This is a relevant issue, especially from the perspective of practical business models in the resource-dependent forest industry. In addition, while service-dominant logic conceptually focuses only on *value-in-use* emerging at the usage phase, service logic also acknowledges *value-in-exchange* as an operationalisation of provider opportunities to create value-in-use in the future (Pires et al., 2015; Grönroos, 2017).

*Consumer-dominant logic* argues that a need exists to shift away from provider-centricity represented both by service-dominant logic and service-logic (Heinonen et al., 2010). Instead of focusing merely on services, as accentuated by service-dominant logic, or interactions between suppliers and customers, as emphasised by service logic (Heinonen and Strandvik, 2015), consumer-dominant logic targets understanding how *value-in-use* accrues for customer and how *consumer experience on value* provided by the supplier is constructed in a customer's own context (Heinonen et al., 2010). Understanding consumer experience on value requires considering former and future experiences of customers with simultaneous consideration of their goals, resources, and objectives (Heinonen and Strandvik, 2018). Yet, most value-in-use accrues beyond the supplier's visibility in customer processes and practices through both product and service usage (Heinonen et al., 2010). Due to this, suppliers must pay attention to communication, to have information on customers' long-term value expectations and needs.

Compared to service-dominant logic, which emphasises the pure dominance of services in value co-creation, service logic and customer-dominant logic have stronger practical links with businesses in manufacturing industries. For example, they also address the potential of production-related actions and the usage of products and services in value co-creation with customers, as illustrated in Box 7.2. Thus, the views of service logic and customer-dominant logic on marketing are employed as a conceptual background in this book chapter to depict how the forest industry could servitise through innovations in processes, products, and business models (for innovation types, see Snihur and Viklund, 2019) that may also contribute to sustainability.

## 2 Sustainability and Servitised Business Models in Manufacturing Industries

The opportunities of companies to develop and uptake *servitised business models* is dependent on their industries and markets. For manufacturing companies, purely focusing on services may not even be a feasible option when seeking business success due to their strong dependency on tangible processes and products (Ulaga and Reinartz, 2011). As a difference from pure service providers, manufacturing companies with access to both tangible resources and capabilities have opportunities to develop their product–service systems. These systems may comprise combinations of one or more products and services, which meet the value expectations of various customer types, particularly in longer-term use, but also during the purchase phase.

From a managerial viewpoint, unique combinations of tangible resources (e.g., raw materials, machinery) and capabilities (e.g., management, collaboration relationships) in forest industry businesses may create sources of competitiveness for individual companies, which are not easily replicable by competitors (Lähtinen, 2007). Business models are employed as practical tools for defining the sources of competitiveness and value creation through product–service systems (e.g., DaSilva and Trkman, 2014), which may be based on the utilisation of both tangible resources and capabilities (Lähtinen, 2007).

Abreast with processes and products, innovations in business through servitisation are one way to seek competitiveness (Snihur and Viklund, 2019). The division of tangible and intangible resources (or capabilities) is not always unambiguous, as tangible resources may also have intangible properties. For example, forest industry customers may appreciate the origin of wood (e.g., domestic *vs.* imported), although the technological properties and even the environmental sustainability of wood materials of any origin may be similar due to standardisation and certification. Thus, wood material has both tangible and intangible properties, which are appreciated differently by various customer types. This is a practical example concerning the importance of communicating with customers to understand how they experience the various components of product–service systems, and how, for example, those components contribute to value-in-use also from the perspective of perceived sustainability.

Manufacturing industries are composed of heterogeneous businesses, and thus their motivation and possibilities to uptake the potential benefits of servitisation differ from each other (Luoto et al., 2017). From the business model perspective, adjusting product systems towards product–service systems and servitised business models is an innovation driven by the aim to fit a company's operations into a new competitive landscape (Kindström and Kowalkovski, 2015). Regarding service logic and customer-dominant logic, the adjustment relates to moving from production orientation and value delivery to customers at the purchase phase (i.e., value-in-exchange) towards service orientation and value co-creation through collaboration and understanding of customer needs (i.e., value-in-use).

At the interface of servitised business models and circular bioeconomy (see definition of and discussion on circular bioeconomy in Chapters 5 and 6 in this book), companies may try to gain competitiveness in the markets by including sustainability aspects in their comprehensive product–service systems. As explained in Box 7.1, these strategic actions are defined as *sustainable servitised business models* in this chapter. Table 7.1 shows examples of how the roles of services in value creation differ between product-based and servitised business models. In addition, Table 7.1 also illustrates how the development of services related to processes and products may contribute to uptaking innovative sustainable servitised business models, especially in manufacturing businesses (on the role of services in manufacturing industries, see Kindström, 2010).

Examples of integrating sustainability in servitised business models are formulated using Bakker et al. (2014); Toppinen et al. (2016); Parida et al. (2019); Ramsheva et al. (2019); Selvefors et al. (2019); Pelli et al. (2018); Ranta et al. (2020); Viholainen et al. (2021).

## 3 Forest Industry Value Chains as Sources for Multiple Businesses

Forest industry is composed of multiple businesses connected to various value chains through side streams, intermediate products, end products, and markets (Shmulsky and Jones, 2011). Especially in the 2000s, the biorefinery concept has emerged to describe forest industry value chains as a system of businesses, which, through the efficient use of all materials (e.g., side streams), manufacture high-value offerings to, for example, substitute fossil-based chemicals, fibres, plastics, and construction materials for a circular bioeconomy (Dessbesell et al., 2016).

Figure 7.1 is a simplified illustration of the linkages between pulp and paper, sawn wood, panel, and energy production, which can be considered the main value chains in the forest industry. Depending on their characteristics, businesses within the value chains connect to many types of markets composed of business customers and consumers (i.e., end users), as described later in this chapter. In all, considerable differences exist in the forest industry value chain structures.

**TABLE 7.1** Examples of illustration of forest industry value chains as a system of businesses, which may provide solutions for a circular bioeconomy through sustainable servitised business models

|  | Product-based business models | Servitised business models | Sustainable servitised business models |
|---|---|---|---|
| Services connected to processes | Services ensure proper functioning of processes and/or use of products<br>Focus in value-in-exchange | Services increase efficiency and value of processes connected to products<br>Focus in value-in-use | Services increase long-term resource efficiency and value of processes (e.g., waste management, material recycling, closing resource loops) |
| Services connected to products | Services add properties to products<br>Focus in value-in-exchange | Services add long-term usability of products<br>Focus in value-in-use | Services extend life cycle of products (e.g., repair, maintenance, refurbishment, and re-use of products) |
| Logic of value creation | Businesses focus on delivery of value to customers and value-in-exchange | Businesses focus on value co-creation with customers and value-in-use | Businesses focus on value co-creation with customers and sustainable value-in-use |

Side stream materials from pulp and paper production, sawn wood production, and panel production may be sold to business customers from other industries for further processing (e.g., resins from pulp production to chemical industries) or to business customers within the forest industries (e.g., chips from sawn wood production to pulp production).

Intermediate pulp and paper products, such as various paper qualities, are usually processed within forest industry businesses before they are sold to customers in other industries (e.g., printing and packaging industries) or to end users (e.g., drawing or packaging papers). Compared to pulp and paper products, the division between intermediate and final products is more ambiguous for sawn wood and panel products. Depending on the customers, the same products may be either intermediate products for business customers (e.g., sawn wood and panels are processed in carpentry industry businesses) or they may be final products for both business customers and consumers (e.g., sawn wood and panels used as such in construction industry businesses and by homebuilders).

Energy production in the forest industry comprises a vast diversity of products (e.g., heat, electricity, fuels). Energy offerings may be either intermediate products for business customers (e.g., pellets for energy plants) or end products for business customers and consumers (e.g., electricity and fuels for transportation).

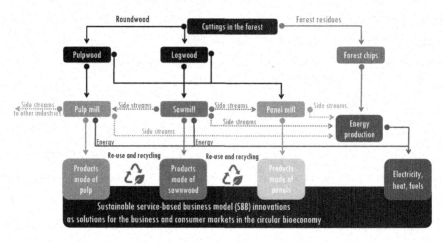

FIGURE 7.1  Simplified illustration of forest industry value chains as a system of businesses, which may provide solutions for a circular bioeconomy through sustainable servitised business models.

The external business environment and technologies of the forest industry affect the possibilities of businesses to develop and uptake sustainable servitised business models. In addition, changes in other industries (e.g., chemical, construction, energy, food, and textile) combined with business customer and consumer expectations affect the development paths of forest industry businesses. According to Näyhä et al. (2015), the current globalised business environment of the forest industry is characterised, for example, by digitalisation, climate change mitigation, and competition for raw materials. They all affect what new types of product–service systems are needed in the circular bioeconomy, and what types of sustainable servitised business models have value creation possibilities on the markets.

Prominent sustainable servitised business models especially connect with those offerings that are expected to face a demand increase in the global markets. Examples of such products include label papers used in smart packaging in the pulp and paper value chain and engineered wood products and modules used in industrial building in the sawn wood value chain (Hetemäki and Hurmekoski, 2020). These changes, which occurred in the forest industry during the past decades, particularly regarding the request for sustainability, are briefly addressed next, with special views on pulp and paper products and sawn wood products.

In addition, practical examples on how aspects of sustainable servitised business models may be addressed in the forest industry through service innovations linked with processes and products (see Table 7.1) are illustrated through two business cases: *label paper* related to the pulp and paper production value chain and *wood building* linked with the sawn wood production value chain.

# 4 Sustainability and Servitisation in the Forest Industry

## 4.1 Pulp and Paper Products – Label Paper

Products manufactured in the pulp and paper production value chain comprise, for example, graphic papers (e.g., qualities used for newspapers and writing), specialty papers (e.g., tissue paper used for hygiene products), and label paper (Bajpai, 2015). The pulp and paper production value chain has additionally integrated into material substitution through innovations in biorefinery operations (Pätäri et al., 2011; Toppinen et al., 2017), for example, with chemicals, polymers, and fibres, which traditionally have been made of fossil-based raw materials (Hetemäki and Hurmekoski, 2020).

Pulp is usually made from different softwood (e.g., spruce, pine) and hardwood (e.g., birch, eucalyptus) species and recycled paper fibres, which affect both its chemical and structural compositions and the properties of the products manufactured from it (e.g., various paper qualities; Simola et al., 2000; Gharehkhani et al., 2015; Danielewicz and Surma-Ślusarska, 2017). Businesses in pulp and paper production have traditionally caused adverse environmental impacts due to their water and energy usage and their effects on forest ecosystems (Toppinen et al., 2017).

Especially from the early 2000s onwards, businesses began recognising the importance of assessing and decreasing their effects on natural ecosystems as a part of corporate responsibility (Lähtinen et al., 2016), which paved the road for new sustainability innovations within companies (Kivimaa and Kautto, 2010). However, although pulp and paper businesses had made improvements in environmental sustainability starting from the late 1980s (e.g., reducing their use of chlorine due to the adverse impacts of dioxin in products and wastewater) (Popp et al., 2011), these improvements were targeted more at processes than products (Kivimaa and Kautto, 2010).

Especially in recent years, pulp and paper businesses have recognised a need for developing product–service systems that enable the uptake of servitised business models for the development of a circular bioeconomy (Brunnhofer et al., 2020). Label paper is one of the offerings in the pulp and paper value chain, with a strong potential for positive future market development (Hetemäki and Hurmekoski, 2020).

Label papers, used in various packaging purposes (e.g., cosmetic, medicine, food industries), are usually manufactured using bleached chemical kraft made of softwood and hardwood species (Määttänen, 2008; Vivek et al., 2016). Coatings, for example, affect the printability and opportunities to attach label papers to various surfaces (Kirwan, 2003). Self-adhesive label papers are usually covered with silicon-layered release paper, which protects the adhesive surface during transportation and storage, and which can be removed when attaching the label paper for its final use. Release paper waste circulation is a problem, as, for example, silicon in the material mix causes severe challenges for recycling (Belosinschi et al., 2012).

From the label paper businesses perspective, sustainability thinking in the production of pulp and paper products has been strongly connected to digitalised global value chains and the search for sustainable packaging solutions to meet the value expectations of business customers and consumers (Coles, 2013; Meherishi et al., 2019). Approximately 40% of packages in the world are made of pulp and paper products (Vivek et al., 2016). Development towards a circular bioeconomy may therefore bring a new, competitive edge for those pulp and paper businesses willing to and capable of renewing their business models to meet market expectations in the changing business environment (Hansen, 2016).

For example, label paper businesses can assist business customers in the packaging industries to design product–service systems that enhance sustainable consumption, and information in the packages may support consumers in making sustainable daily life choices (e.g., Nordin and Selke, 2010). In addition, label paper businesses are part of complex product–service systems through their connections, for example, with food industries (Fitzpatrick, 2012; Vivek et al., 2016). Thus, suppliers and customers in the label paper businesses have opportunities to co-create value through innovations, which connect, for example, with both process resource efficiency and product longevity.

The business case example in Box 7.3 illustrates what a change from a traditional product-based business model towards a sustainable servitised business model may mean in the **label paper** business. It also shows how the change from focusing on product systems to product–service systems may contribute to circular bioeconomy development.

## Box 7.3 A label paper business case – UPM Raflatac Ltd

The label paper business case of Raflatac Ltd, connected to RafCycle® solution, is a practical example of what implementing a sustainable servitised business model may mean in the pulp and paper products value chain from the perspective of packaging industry business customers. Raflatac Ltd belongs to the UPM-Kymmene corporation and UPM Group operating in 46 countries in the pulp, sawn wood, panel, and energy businesses. The company employs approximately 18,700 workers around the world.

Traditionally, packaging industry business customers have been responsible for managing the waste generated from the release paper attached to the label paper. As possibilities for release paper recycling are very limited, especially due to the material's silicon layer, large amounts of release paper waste have been landfilled. This has caused both adverse environmental impacts for ecosystems and costs for packaging industry businesses.

The Raflatac Ltd label paper business comprises the RafCycle® solution to collect release paper waste from packaging industry business customers. In reference to sustainable servitised business models, this is an example of implementing an innovation that improves the sustainability of customer processes by offering new services. However, Raflatac Ltd transitioning from a product-based business model towards a sustainable servitised business model has also led to the development of new product–service systems both for business customers and consumers in new markets.

Related to the development of new product–service systems, the recycled label paper waste is further processed into UPM ProFi® wood plastic composite in the next phase. The material is utilised for manufacturing new types of decking materials, which are suitable for a variety of purposes in gardens and public outdoor spaces. The decking materials may have various visual designs and colours, and they are recyclable. Thus, the release paper can be re-used through UPM ProFi® wood plastic composite.

The Raflatac Ltd business case example concretises how new services connected to processes and products has enabled not only an increase in value-in-use connected to label paper but also value-in-use connected to an entirely novel decking product made of UPM ProFi® wood plastic composite. From the perspectives of circular bioeconomy and sustainable servitised business models, the case also illustrates how environmental benefits, cost reductions, and new sustainable value-in-use may be simultaneously gained.

https://www.upm.com/investors/governance/

https://www.upmprofi.com/

https://www.upm.com/about-us/this-is-biofore/bioforecase/from-label-waste-into-a-new-product/

## 4.2 Sawn Wood Products – Wood Building

Sawn wood is made of softwood and hardwood species, which affect the technological and visual properties of the final solid products. Sawn wood made of softwood species is mostly used by the construction industry (e.g., building structures, doors, and windows), while sawn wood made of hardwood species is typically utilised for more decorative purposes (e.g., furniture, flooring, and cabinets) (Shmulsky and Jones, 2011). In addition, softwood species are used to manufacture engineered wood products such as glued laminated timber (glulam) and cross-laminated timber (CLT).

Engineered wood products in particular are utilised to substitute structural timber, especially in load-bearing structures (e.g., multistory wood buildings) (Schuler et al., 2001; Lam and Prion, 2003; Heräjärvi et al., 2004). Expectations for the global growth of sawn wood demand are especially grounded on societal aims towards sustainable building and housing, which in an urbanised society require industrialised solutions in the construction industry through engineered wood product and modular building solution usage (Hetemäki and Hurmekoski, 2020; Pelli and Lähtinen, 2020).

Especially since the early 2000s, interest towards the production of engineered wood products and wooden modular structures has increased among both forest and construction industry businesses around the globe (e.g., Toppinen et al., 2018; Tettey et al., 2019). The need to decrease energy use, greenhouse gas emissions, and dependence on extracted materials caused by the dominance of fossil-based material dependence in the construction industry (Toppinen et al., 2019a) are drivers behind this increase.

In the 2010s, pressures towards decreasing the environmental impacts of the construction industry, to enhance development towards a circular bioeconomy, have further supported business model development in businesses linked with engineered wood production businesses (Pelli and Lähtinen, 2020). As a result, instead of acting as merely building material suppliers for construction companies, engineered wood product manufacturers have begun exploiting their business potential for producing components and modules used in industrialised construction processes (Mahapatra and Gustavsson, 2008; Nordin et al., 2010; Höök et al., 2015; Hurmekoski et al., 2018). In addition, some companies manufacture their own modular wooden building solutions and are nowadays actively operating as builders and developers in the construction industry markets (Toppinen et al., 2019a; Stehn et al., 2021).

The business potential in sawn wood and engineered wood product manufacturing connects with the development in international building markets. Thus, to understand the circumstances for wood building businesses, a short description of the prevalent practices in the construction industry is needed. Traditionally, the production of multistory and public buildings has been dominated by concrete utilisation, which, compared to wooden structures, is a less prominent option for decreasing carbon dioxide emissions in the construction industry (Tettey et al., 2019; Hart et al., 2021). Combined with this, concrete is not well suited for modular prefabrication and transportation because of its heaviness (Urban, 2012). This has hindered the industrialisation of building processes, which, for decades, has been considered a prerequisite for increasing the efficiency and enhancing the competitiveness of construction industry businesses (Carter, 1967; Toole, 2001; Nadim and Goulding, 2011).

In recent years, global sustainability initiatives in particular have pushed the construction industries to decrease their usage of carbon-intensive materials (Toppinen et al., 2019b). Growing attention has concurrently been paid to increasing the energy efficiency of building processes and to the uptake possibilities of digitalisation, for example, to co-create value in actor networks (Holmström et al., 2015; Giesekam et al., 2016; Toppinen et al., 2018; Lähtinen et al., 2021). Compared with other materials, wood has many beneficial properties such as renewability, lightness, and strength. Compared to solid sawn wood, engineered wood products with homogeneous structural properties are better suited to be used in modules for industrialised construction practices, bringing benefits to suppliers, business customers, and consumers (Brege et al., 2014; Pelli and Lähtinen, 2020; Viholainen et al., 2020).

Sustainable construction initiatives connected to circular bioeconomy (Pelli and Lähtinen, 2020) have opened new opportunities for businesses in the sawn wood production value chains and for those companies also operating as builders and developers in construction industry markets (Toppinen et al., 2019a, 2019b). Recently, companies building wooden multistory residential buildings have gained a great deal of attention in their development efforts (e.g., Brege et al., 2014; Toppinen et al., 2019b; Lähtinen et al., 2021). As a result, wood building businesses are, to an increasing extent, becoming connected with housing markets, where business customers and consumers (i.e., residents) have various value expectations. In addition, regarding the life cycle of the buildings, business customers and consumers have different linkages with, for example, the construction and usage phases of residential buildings.

Business customers are mainly interested in the construction phase of residential buildings, which relates to processes and offerings through, for example, resource-efficient, on-time deliveries of building modules (Uusitalo and Lavikka, 2020). Consumers as residents mostly focus on the usage phase of the residential buildings (Viholainen et al., 2020; Lähtinen et al., 2022), which relates to the physical properties of the buildings, their locations, and to intangible resident expectations concerning the quality of their lives (Gram-Hanssen and Bech-Danielsen, 2004; Marsh and Gibb, 2011; Hasu et al., 2017; Lähtinen et al., 2021). Particularly, the physical properties of residential buildings are affected by choices made during the construction phase (e.g., Sirgy et al., 2005), and thus the expectations of business customers and consumers for product–service solutions supplied by businesses involved in wood building are not entirely disconnected. Business customers additionally include, for example, investors supplying apartments for rental markets, who are in a direct business relationship with end users as tenants.

Consumers interested in building design may drive service development in the construction industry (e.g., Nordin et al., 2010). In reference to sustainable servitised business models, this connects with value co-creation with customers and other actors through collaboration (Lessing and Brege, 2015; Toppinen et al., 2019b; Lähtinen et al., 2022), which are linked with service innovations related to processes and products. Resulting from this, the value-in-use of offerings can be increased, for example, by integrating future residents in the designing of apartment layout or selection of the materials (Lähtinen et al., 2022).

The business case example Box 7.4 illustrates the type of change possibly involved when transitioning from a traditional product-based business model towards a sustainable servitised business model in the context of wood building. In addition, it provides insights on how changes in business models connected with product–service systems instead of being linked solely with product systems may be aligned with circular bioeconomy development.

## Box 7.4 A wood building business case – Siklatilat Ltd

The wood building business case of Siklatilat Ltd is a practical example concerning the possibilities of uptaking sustainable servitised business models in the sawn wood and engineered wood products value chains. It also shows how both construction industry business customers and consumers may benefit from new service development. Siklatilat Ltd belongs to Sikla Corporation, which is a medium-sized company also operating in building development. Sikla Corporation is additionally involved in manufacturing modular wood building systems made of engineered wood products. The company employs approximately 160 workers in Finland.

Concrete-based multistory housing construction businesses have traditionally focused on the value-in-exchange connected to building processes, and a tangible product (i.e., residential building) has been their main market offering. Such regimes have largely bypassed the usage and end-of-life phases of buildings. This has resulted in superficial consideration of residents' housing value expectations linked with their lifestyles and in deficiencies when seeking for competitiveness through the value-in-use of residential buildings. In addition, concentrating on dominant building regimes has caused design deficiencies for material re-use and recycling and in lost opportunities for value co-creation through collaboration with customers and other actors.

Siklatilat Ltd aims for the value-in-use of buildings by seeking innovations in processes, which enables increasing the longevity of material and technological solutions in residential buildings and integration of consumer housing value expectations in building design. The company has also made up-stream investments for in-house fabrication of wooden building modules that connect with the development of resource-efficient (i.e., costs and ecological impacts) building processes by utilising renewable materials. Collaboration is at the business core to co-create value, for example, with consumers, other businesses, the public sector, and academic institutions.

The Siklatilat Ltd business case example concretises how service innovations connected to processes and products in wood buildings may enable the substitution of concrete-based materials with solutions originating from operations in sawn wood product value chains. It also shows how service innovations of products may change product orientation based on value-in-exchange (i.e., a residential building as the offering) towards service orientation (i.e., housing as the offering) and adding value-in-use for residents. Regarding circular bioeconomy and sustainable service-based business models, the case also shows how extended life-cycle thinking may both decrease environmental impacts and monetary costs combined with increased value co-creation with business customers and consumers.

https://www.sikla.fi/
https://www.sikla.fi/strategia/
https://www.sikla.fi/ratkaisu/yhtiomuotoiset-kodit/

# 5 Conclusions

The potential to uptake sustainable servitised business models in the forest industry were addressed in this chapter through service development for processes and products (i.e., product–service systems) that would lead to value co-creation with customers and sustainability benefits. The need for value co-creation with customers by understanding their needs has been emphasised in the marketing literature (e.g., service-dominant logic, service logic, and customer-dominant logic; e.g., Vargo and Lusch, 2004; Grönroos, 2006; Heinonen et al., 2010). Simultaneously, for manufacturing industries, such as forest industry businesses, value creation is a prerequisite to increase competitiveness and accelerate industry renewal in the globalised business environment (see also Chapter 11 published in this volume).

The importance of intangible capabilities and skills and the supply of services have gained increasing attention as a source of value creation and competitiveness also for manufacturing industries, especially in the recent past. However, while developing comprehensive and sustainable product–service systems, forest industry businesses will also, in the future, be dependent on tangible resources and manufacturing processes. Due to this, it may not be a feasible option for them to purely focus on services, which are sometimes emphasised in the marketing literature (e.g., service-dominant logic), when seeking business solutions, even in the era of a circular bioeconomy.

For manufacturing companies, the development of product–service systems has been found to be an avenue for strengthening competitiveness (Ulaga and Reinarz, 2011). Compared to pure service providers, manufacturing businesses have skills in technological manufacturing processes that enable the synergic development of products and services for achieving the best possible fit in offerings. For example, services related to tangible processes and products may bring environmental, social, and economic benefits (e.g., services for material recycling and re-use of products) to forest industry businesses. These benefits contribute not only to value-in-exchange at the purchase phase but also value-in-use experienced by customers in the long term. In addition, the development of sustainable servitised business models in the forest industry also supports achieving the aims of a circular bioeconomy.

This chapter addressed practical opportunities for moving towards sustainable servitised business models in the forest industry in relation to value chains in pulp and paper production and sawn wood production. As a result of changes in the global business environment caused by digitalisation, climate change mitigation, and raw material competition, both value chains contain businesses with high possibilities to contribute to the circular economy. The uptake of sustainable servitised business models may not only lead to benefits for society but also for individual businesses. For example, through the development of comprehensive product–service systems, businesses may not only be able to increase their income as a result of the value increase of their offerings but also reduce their costs due to increases in resource efficiency.

We introduced two business cases related to label paper (UPM Raflatac Ltd) and wood building (Siklatilat Ltd), which provided views on what sustainable servitised business models may mean in the forest industry. In the label paper case, new services connected to processes have not only resulted in cost reductions for customers through a new waste management system but also enabled an extension in the life cycle of materials and introduced new innovative products for construction industry markets. In the wood building case, an introduction of new services connected to products has created opportunities to lengthen the life cycle of residential buildings through sustainability thinking. Additionally, it has extended the building business logic from product-based thinking and from considering housing to be the final market offering towards service-based thinking, in which housing is a service for consumers that comprises both tangible and intangible qualities.

Overall, businesses connected with forest industry value chains have strong potential to benefit from and contribute to circular bioeconomy development through the uptake of sustainable servitised business models. To be truly successful, businesses must be able to integrate life cycle thinking in their product–service systems by considering environmental, social, and economic views of sustainability that enable value co-creation through relationships with other businesses and consumers (i.e., end users).

Forest industry businesses are dependent on tangible resources and thus these will remain sources for competitiveness also in the future. However, recognising what service innovations are the most prominent sources of value, appreciated not only by customers but also by other actors in society, is a focal point from the perspective of developing towards a circular bioeconomy and enhancing competitiveness in the global markets.

## References

Baines, T. S., Lightfoot, H. W., Benedettini, O. and Kay, J. M. (2009) 'The servitization of manufacturing – A review of literature and reflection on future challenges', *Journal of Manufacturing Technology Management*, 20, pp. 547–567.

Bajpai, P. (2015) *Green Chemistry and Sustainability in Pulp and Paper Industry*. Cham: Springer, p. 258.

Bakker, C., Wang, F., Huisman, J. and den Hollander, M. (2014) 'Products that go round: Exploring product life extension through design', *Journal of Cleaner Production*, 69, pp. 10–16.

Belosinschi, D., Chabot, B. and Brouillette, F. (2012) 'Release-paper: Can phosphate esters be an alternative to silicone?', *BioResources*, 7, pp. 902–912.

Brege, S., Stehn, L. and Nord, T. (2014) 'Business models in industrialized building of multi-storey houses', *Construction Management and Economics*, 32, pp. 208–226.

Brunnhofer, M., Gabriella, N., Schöggl, J.-P., Stern, T. and Posch, A. (2020) 'The biorefinery transition in the European pulp and paper industry – A three-phase Delphi study including a SWOT-AHP analysis', *Forest Policy and Economics*, 110, 101882.

Carter, J. (1967) 'Components and architect', *RIBA Journal*, 74, pp. 476–477.

Chandler, J. D. and Lusch, R. F. (2015) 'Service systems: A broadened framework and research agenda on value propositions, engagement, and service experience', *Journal of Service Research*, 18, pp. 6–22.

Coles, R. (2013) 'Paper and paperboard innovations and developments for the packaging of food, beverages and other fast-moving consumer goods', in N. Farmer (ed.), *Trends in Packaging of Food, Beverages and Other Fast-Moving Consumer Goods (FMCG): Markets, Materials and Technologies*. Elsevier Science & Technology, Cambridge: Woodhead Publishing, pp. 187–220.

Danielewicz, D. and Surma-Ślusarska, B. (2017) 'Properties and fibre characterisation of bleached hemp, birch and pine pulps: A comparison', *Cellulose*, 24, pp. 5173–5186.

DaSilva, C. M. and Trkman, P. (2014) 'Business model: What it is and what it is not', *Long Range Planning*, 47, pp. 379–389.

Dessbesell, L., Xu, C., Pulkki, R., Leitch, M. and Mahmood, N. (2016) 'Forest biomass supply chain optimization for a biorefinery aiming to produce high-value bio-based materials and chemicals from lignin and forestry residues: A review of literature', *Canadian Journal of Forest Research*, 47, pp. 277–288.

Fitzpatrick, L. (2012) 'Developing the strategy', in L. Fitzpatrick, K. Verghese and H. Lewis (eds.), *Packaging for Sustainability*. London: Springer-Verlag Limited, pp. 1–39.

Gharehkhani, S., Sadeghinezhad, E., Kazi, S. N., Yarmanda, H., Badarudin, A., Safaei, M. R. and Zubir, M. N. M. (2015) 'Basic effects of pulp refining on fiber properties— A review', *Carbohydrate Polymers*, 115, pp. 785–803.

Giesekam, J., Barrett, J. R. and Taylor, P. (2016) 'Construction sector views on lowcarbon building materials', *Building Research and Information*, 44, pp. 423–444.

Gram-Hanssen, K. and Bech-Danielsen, C. (2004) 'House, home and identity from a consumption perspective', *Housing, Theory and Society*, 21, pp. 17–26.

Grönroos, C. (1994) 'From marketing mix to relationship marketing: Towards a paradigm shift in marketing', *Asia-Australia Marketing Journal*, 32, 4–20.

Grönroos, C. (2006) 'Adopting a service logic for marketing', *Marketing Theory*, 6, pp. 317–333.

Grönroos, C. (2017) 'On value and value creation in service: A Management perspective', *Journal of Creating Value*, 3, pp. 125–141.

Grönroos, C., Strandvik, T. and Heinonen, K. (2015) 'Value co-creation: Critical reflections', in J. Gummerus and C. Von Koskull (eds.), *The Nordic School – Service Marketing and Management for the Future*. Helsinki: CERS, Hanken School of Economics, pp. 69–81.

Grönroos, C. and Voima, P. (2013) 'Critical service logic: Making sense of value creation and co-creation', *Journal of the Academy of Marketing Science*, 41, pp. 133–150.

Hansen, E. (2016) 'Responding to the bioeconomy: Business model innovation in the forest sector', in A. Kutnar and S. S. Muthu (eds.), *Environmental Impacts of Traditional and Innovative Forest-Based Bioproducts*. Singapore: Springer Science+Business Media, pp. 227–248.

Hart, J., D'Amico, B. and Pomponi, F. (2021) 'Whole-life embodied carbon in multistory buildings: Steel, concrete and timber structures', *Journal of Industrial Ecology*, 25, pp. 403–418.

Hasu, E., Tervo, A. and Hirvonen, J. (2017) 'Lifestyles and housing design: Case Finnish townhouse', *Nordic Journal of Architectural Research*, 29, pp. 35–57.

Heinonen, K. and Strandvik, T. (2015) 'Customer-dominant logic: Foundations and implications', *Journal of Services Marketing*, 29, pp. 472–484.

Heinonen, K. and Strandvik, T. (2018) 'Reflections on customers' primary role in markets', *European Management Journal*, 36, pp. 1–11.

Heinonen, K., Strandvik, T., Mickelsson, K.-J., Edvardsson, B., Sundström, E., Andersson, P. (2010) 'A customer-dominant logic of service', *Journal of Service Management*, 21, pp. 531–548.

Heräjärvi, H., Jouhiaho, A., Tammiruusu, V. and Verkasalo, E. (2004). 'Small-diameter scots pine and birch timber as raw materials for engineered wood products', *International Journal of Forest Engineering*, 15, pp. 23–34.

Hetemäki, L. and Hurmekoski, E. (2020) 'Forest bioeconomy development: Markets and industry structures', in W. Nikolakis (ed.), *The Wicked Problem of Forest Policy*. Cambridge: Cambridge University Press. https://doi.org/10.1017/9781108684439.

Holmström, J., Singh, V. and Främling, K. (2015) 'BIM as infrastructure in a Finnish HVAC actor network: Enabling adoption, reuse, and recombination over a building life cycle and between projects', *Journal of Management Engineering*, 31(1), pp. 1–12.

Höök, M., Stehn, L. and Brege, S. (2015). 'The development of a portfolio of business models: A longitudinal case study of a building material company', *Construction Management and Economics*, 33, pp. 334–348.

Hovgaard, A. and Hansen, E. 2004. 'Innovativeness in the forest products industry', *Forest Products Journal*, 54, pp. 26–33.

Hurmekoski, E., Pykäläinen, J. and Hetemäki, L. (2018) 'Long-term targets for green building: Explorative Delphi backcasting study on wood-frame multi-story construction in Finland', *Journal of Cleaner Production*, 172, pp. 3644–3654.

Kindström, D. (2010) 'Towards a service-based business model – Key aspects for future competitive advantage', *European Management Journal*, 28, pp. 479–490.

Kindstörm, D. and Kowalkowski, C. (2015) 'Service driven business model innovation: Organizing the shift from a product-based to a service-centric business model', in N. Foss and T. Saebi (eds.), *Business Model Innovation: The Organizational Dimension*. Oxford: Oxford University Press, pp. 191–216.

Kirwan, M. J. (2003). 'Paper and paperboard packaging', in R. Coles, D. McDowell and M. J. Kirwan (eds.), *Food Packaging Technology*. London: Blackwell Publishing CRC Press, pp. 241–281.

Kivimaa, P. and Kautto, P. (2010). 'Making or breaking environmental innovation? Technological change and innovation markets in the pulp and paper industry', *Management Research Review*, 33, pp. 289–305.

Kohtamäki, M. and Rajala, R. (2016). 'Theory and practice of value co-creation in B2B systems', *Industrial Marketing Management*, 56, pp. 4–13.

Lähtinen, K. (2007). 'Linking resource-based view with business economics of woodworking industry: Earlier findings and future insights', *Silva Fennica*, 41, pp. 149–165.

Lähtinen, K., Häyrinen, L., Jussila, J., Harju, C., Toppinen, R. and Toivonen, R. (2022) 'Branding wooden multi-storey construction – Real-estate agents as gatekeepers for enhancing consumer value in housing', *Journal of Forest Economics*, 37. http://dx.doi.org/10.1561/112.00000538.

Lähtinen, K., Häyrinen, L., Roos, A., Toppinen, A., Aguilar Cabezas, F. X., Thorsen, B. J., Hujala, T., Nyrud, A. Q. and Hoen, H. F. (2021). 'Consumer housing values and prejudices against living in wooden homes in the Nordic region', *Silva Fennica*, 55, pp. 1–27.

Lähtinen, K. and Toppinen, A. (2008) 'Financial performance in Finnish large and medium-sized sawmills: The effects of value-added creation and cost-efficiency seeking', *Journal of Forest Economics*, 14, pp. 289–305.

Lähtinen, K., Yucong, G., Li, N. and Toppinen, A. (2016) 'Biodiversity and ecosystem services in supply chain management in the global forest industry', *Ecosystem Services*, 21, pp. 130–140.

Lam, F. and Prion, H. G. L. (2003) 'Engineered wood products for structural purposes', in S. Thelandersson and A. J. Larssen (eds.), *Timber Engineering*. Chichester, England: John Wiley & Sons, Ltd, pp. 15–22.

Lessing, J. and Brege, S. (2015) 'Business models for product-oriented house-building companies – Experience from two Swedish case studies', *Construction Innovation*, 15, pp. 449–472.

Luoto, S., Brax, S. A. and Kohtamäki, M. (2017). 'Critical meta-analysis of servitization research: Constructing a model-narrative to reveal paradigmatic assumptions', *Industrial Marketing Management*, 60, pp. 89–100.

Lusch, R. F. and Vargo, S. L. (2014) *Service-Dominant Logic: Premises, Perspectives, Possibilities*. Cambridge: Cambridge University Press.

Määttänen, M. (2008) *Die Cutting of a Self Adhesive Laminate and Removing the Waste Matrix*. Final Thesis. Tampere Polytechnic, University of Applied Sciences. 111 pages + 12 appendices.

Mahapatra, K. and Gustavsson, L. (2008) 'Multi-storey wood buildings – breaking industry path dependency', *Building Research Information*, 36, pp. 638–648.

Marsh, A. and Gibb, K. (2011) 'Uncertainty, expectations and behavioural aspects of housing market choices', *Housing, Theory and Society*, 28, pp. 215–235.

Meherishi, L., Narayana, S. A. and Ranjani, K. S. (2019) 'Sustainable packaging for supply chain management in the circular economy: A review', *Journal of Cleaner Production*, 537, 117582.

Nadim, W. and Goulding, J. S. (2011) 'Offsite production: A model for building down barriers: A European construction perspective', *Engineering, Construction and Architectural Management*, 18, pp. 82–101.

Näyhä, A., Pelli, P. and Hetemäki, L. (2015) 'Services in the forest-based sector – unexplored futures', *Foresight*, 17, pp. 378–398.

Nordin, F., Öberg, C., Kollberg, B. and Nord, T. (2010) 'Building a new supply chain position: An exploratory study of companies in the timber housing industry', *Construction Management and Economics*, 28, pp. 1071–1083.

Nordin, N. and Selke, S. (2010) 'Social aspect of sustainable packaging', *Packaging Technology and Science*, 23, pp. 317–326.

Nybakk, E., Crespell, P. and Hansen, E. (2011) 'Climate for innovation and innovation strategy as drivers for success in the wood industry: Moderation effects of firm size, industry sector, and country of operation', *Silva Fennica*, 45, pp. 415–430.

Parida, V., Burström, T., Visnjic, I. and Wincenta, J. (2019). 'Orchestrating industrial ecosystem in circular economy: A two-stage transformation model for large manufacturing companies', *Journal of Business Research*, 101, pp. 715–725.

Pätäri, S., Kyläheiko, K. and Sandström, J. (2011) 'Opening up new strategic options in the pulp and paper industry: Case biorefineries', *Forest Policy and Economics*, 13, pp. 456–464.

Pelli, P. and Lähtinen, K. (2020, January) 'Servitization and bioeconomy transitions: Insights on prefabricated wooden elements supply networks', *Journal of Cleaner Production*, 244, 118711.

Pires, G. D., Dean, A. and Rehman, M. (2015). 'Using service logic to redefine exchange in terms of customer and supplier participation', *Journal of Business Research*, 68, pp. 925–932.

Popp, D., Hafner, T. and Johnstone, N. (2011). 'Environmental policy vs. public pressure: Innovation and diffusion of alternative bleaching technologies in the pulp industry', *Research Policy*, 40, pp. 1253–1268.

Rabetino, R., Kohtamäki, M. and Gebauer, H. (2017). 'Strategy map of servitization', *International Journal of Production Economics*, 192, pp. 144–156.

Ramsheva, Y. K., Prosman, E. J. and Wæhrens, B. V. (2019). 'Dare to make investments in industrial symbiosis? A conceptual framework and research agenda for developing trust', *Journal of Cleaner Production*, 223, pp. 989–997.

Ranta, V., Keränen, J. and Aarikka-Stenroos, L. (2020) 'How B2B suppliers articulate customer value propositions in the circular economy: Four innovation-driven value creation logics', *Industrial Marketing Management*, 87, pp. 291–305.

Schuler, A., Adair, C. and Elias, E. (2001) 'Engineered lumber products taking their place in the global market', *Journal of Forestry*, 99, pp. 28–35.

Selvefors, A., Rexfelt, O., Renström, S. and Strömberg, H. (2019) 'Use to use e A user perspective on product circularity', *Journal of Cleaner Production*, 223, pp. 1014–1028.

Shmulsky, R. and Jones, P. D. (2011) *Forest Products and Wood Science - An Introduction.* West Sussex: Wiley-Blackwell, A John Wiley & Sons, Inc., Publication, 477 p.

Simola, J., Malkavaara, P., Alén, R. and Peltonen, J. (2000) 'Scanning probe microscopy of pine and birch kraft pulp fibres', *Polymer*, 41, pp. 2121–2126.

Sirgy, M. J., Grzeskowiak, S. and Su, C. (2005) 'Explaining housing preference and choice: The role of self-873 congruity and functional congruity', *Journal of Housing and the Built Environment*, 20, pp. 329–347.

Snihur, Y. and Viklund, J. (2016) 'Searching for innovation: Product, process, and business model innovations and search behavior in established firms', *Long Range Planning*, 52, pp. 305–325.

Stehn, L., Engström, S., Uusitalo, P. and Lavikka, R. (2021) 'Understanding industrialized house building as a company's dynamic capabilities', *Construction Innovation*, 21, pp. 5–21.

Stendahl, M. and Roos, A. (2008). 'Antecedents and barriers to product innovation – a comparison between innovating and non-innovating strategic business units in the wood industry', *Silva Fennica*, 42, pp. 659–681.

Tettey, U. Y. A., Dodoo, A. and Gustavsson, L. (2019). 'Effect of different frame materials on the primary energy use of a multi storey residential building in a life cycle perspective', *Energy and Buildings*, 185, pp. 259–271.

Toole, T. M. (2001). 'Technological trajectories of construction innovation', *Journal of Architectural Engineering*, 7, pp. 107–114.

Toppinen, A., Pätäri, S., Tuppura, A. and Jantunen, A. (2017) 'Futures. The European pulp and paper industry in transition to a bio-economy: A Delphi study', *Futures*, 88, pp. 1–14.

Toppinen, A., Miilumäki, N., Vihemäki, H., Toivonen, R. and Lähtinen, K. (2019a) 'Collaboration and shared logic for creating value-added in three Finnish wooden multi-storey building projects', *Wood Material Science and Engineering*, 14, pp. 269–279.

Toppinen, A., Sauru, M., Pätäri, S., Lähtinen, K. and Tuppura, A. (2018) 'Internal and external factors of competitiveness shaping the future of wooden multistorey construction in Finland and Sweden', *Construction Management and Economics*, 37, pp. 1–16.

Toppinen, A., Sauru, M., Pätäri, S., Lähtinen, K. and Tuppura, A. (2019b) 'Internal and external factors of competitiveness shaping the future of wooden multistorey construction in Finland and Sweden', *Construction Management and Economics*, 37, pp. 1–16.

Ulaga, W. and Reinartz, W. J. (2011). 'Hybrid offerings: How manufacturing firms combine goods and services successfully', *Journal of Marketing*, 75, pp. 5–23.

Urban, F. (2012) 'Social reform, state control, and the origins of mass housing', in F. Urban (ed.), *Tower and Slab: Histories of Global Mass Housing.* London: Routledge, Taylor & Francis Group, pp. 7–18.

Uusitalo, P. and Lavikka, R. (2020). 'Overcoming path dependency in an industrialized house building company through entrepreneurial orientation', *Buildings*, 10, pp. 1–22.

Vargo, S. L. and Lusch, R. F. (2004) 'Evolving to a new dominant logic for marketing', *Journal of Marketing*, 68, pp. 1–17.

Vargo, S. L. and Lusch, R. F. (2008) 'Service-dominant logic: Continuing the evolution', *Journal of the Academy of Marketing Science*, 36, pp. 1–10.

Vargo, S. L. and Akaka, M. A. (2009) 'Service-dominant logic as a foundation for service science: Clarifications', *Service Science*, 1, pp. 32–41.

Vargo, S. L. and Lusch, R. F. (2016) 'Institutions and axioms: An extension and update of service-dominant logic', *Journal of the Academy of Marketing Science*, 44, pp. 5–23.

Viholainen, N., Kylkilahti, E., Autio, M. and Toppinen, A. (2020) 'A home made of wood: Consumer experiences of wooden building materials', *International Journal of Consumer Studies*, 44, pp. 542–551.

Viholainen, N., Kylkilahti, E., Autio, M., Pöyhönen, J. and Toppinen, A. (2021) 'Bringing ecosystem thinking to sustainability-driven wooden construction business', *Journal of Cleaner Production*, 292, pp. 1–13.

Vivek, S. M. and Kumar, S. (2016) 'A review: Papers in packaging', *International Journal of Science, Engineering and Computer Technology*, 6, pp. 14–16.

# PART 3

# Governance and Policy Mechanisms

# 8

# THE PRIVATE SECTOR ENGAGEMENT PARADOX

## The Proliferation of Finance and Market Driven Sustainability Tools Alongside the Acceleration of Environmental Degradation

*Benjamin Cashore*

## 1 Introduction

Over 30 years ago, students and practitioners of global sustainability began to turn to the private sector in the hopes of advancing more efficient and effective policy innovations. The result has been the promotion of a range of public and private finance and market driven (FMD) policy interventions including the United Nation's Agenda 2030, the proliferation of domestic circular and bioeconomy national strategies, the EU Green Deal, the US Green New Deal, and the EU taxonomy for sustainable activities (Hrabanski, 2017; Ladu and Blind, 2017; Dietz et al., 2018; D'amato and Korhonen, 2021). Three decades later, we have witnessed two paradoxical trends: widespread engagement of the private sector in the development and implementation of FMD innovations, and the alarming acceleration of critical environmental challenges impacting the planet – notably the climate crisis and the mass species extinction crisis. This evidence, in turn, has led applied scholars and practitioners to understand better the motivations for private sector engagement, and the 'enabling conditions' through which improved designs might be developed and applied. Meanwhile, the constant redesign, and proliferation, of novel FMD initiatives has coincided with the climate and species extinction crises becoming more acute (IPBES, 2019; IPCC, 2019).

This chapter reviews the plausibility of a counterintuitive explanation for these trends: that the correlations between the proliferation of private sector engagement in and reinforcing of FMD solutions alongside the acceleration of environmental crises are not owing to poor policy design and implementation challenges (Scheyvens et al., 2016; Lambin et al., 2018), but rather to highly successful, but competing, sustainability transformation projects (Visseren-Hamakers et al., 2021). I explore the potential of this argument by reviewing Cashore's

DOI: 10.4324/9781003003588-11

four sustainability problem conceptions (Cashore, 2021; Cashore and Bernstein, 2022), each of which is reinforced by four distinct schools: commons (Type 1), optimisation (Type 2), compromise (Type 3), and prioritisation (Type 4). I argue, drawing on Cashore and Bernstein (2022), that transitions conforming to Type 4 conceptions have given way, over the last 30 years, to fostering Type 3, 2, and 1 transformations all of which champion human material interests – despite overwhelming evidence that these motivations are largely the cause of environmental degradation.

This chapter assesses the plausibility of the explanation in the following steps. First, it reviews the proliferation of private sector engagement in innovations over the last 30 years designed to ameliorate a range of 'real world' sustainability policy challenges, most recently articulated through the UN's Sustainable Development Goals (SDGs). For analytical traction, the chapter draws on select examples developed to ameliorate forest sector sustainability challenges. This section reveals an 'accordion' approach in which narrow and firm-level private sector engagement initiatives were first advanced beginning in the 1980s but, following evidence about environmental degradation, more comprehensive global initiatives were advanced. Resulting evidence of lack of uptake of these amidst ongoing environmental degradation, the accordion returned to narrower and firm-level commitments. Second, I review how the four schools of sustainability (Cashore, 2013, 2019) that I have elaborated individually and with collaborators (Cashore, 2013, 2021; Cashore et al., 2019), championed very distinct sustainability transformation projects (Visseren-Hamakers et al., 2021). Each of these, in turn, carries subtly distinct approaches for adjudicating internal and external 'whack-a-mole' effects: i.e., those cases in which solving one problem makes another worse. Third, I apply this framework to offer a reinterpretation of the emergence, design, and competing ideas of sustainability transformations within the Forest Stewardship Council, Reduced Emissions from Deforestation and Forest Degradation (REDD+), legality verification (LV), and today's heavy emphasis on corporate 'no-deforestation' and 'net zero' commitments. Fourth, I conclude by discussing strategies through which the private sector might help achieve, rather than exacerbate, Type 4 environmental transformations.

## 2 The Private Sector Engagement Paradox: Acceleration of Policy Innovations and Environmental Degradation

### 2.1 Private Sector Engagement in Sustainability Policy Innovations

Since the early 1980s, national and transnational actors have designed a range of private governance and private/public initiatives under the umbrella of FMD policy tools. The overall aim was to promote sustainable forestry in ways that continued to foster economic advances, but that better reflect the needs of forest-dependent peoples and environmental degradation (Cashore and Nathan, 2020).

Many of these emerged following two related intergovernmental efforts: the International Tropical Timber Agreement (Gale, 1998), which endeavoured to foster economic growth, social responsibility, and environmental stewardship through trade liberalisation and which was ultimately criticised by environmental groups as a 'logging charter' (Humphreys, 2006); and failed efforts to achieve a global forest convention at 1992 Rio Earth Summit that environmental groups had hoped would achieve meaningful 'on the ground' reforms.

It was in these contexts that a range of businesses, business associations, and non-governmental organisations turned to promoting private governance initiatives as potentially more efficient, and effective, than asserted truculent governmental processes. Initial efforts were placed on firms seeking to expand their own 'corporate social responsibility' (Auld et al., 2008) initiatives with which to improve their 'social license to operate' (Herrmann, 2004). This would lead firms to commit to avoid purchasing products whose production contributed to deforestation, especially in the global south (Brody, 1987; Rainforest Alliance, 2001), as well as engaging stakeholders (Sharma, 1998). These efforts were subsequently reinforced, and followed, by firms seeking outside certification of their internal 'environmental management systems' that were put in place to help achieve organisational sustainability goals (Potoski and Prakash, 2005). However, following concerns that firms may not be best placed to develop the standards to ameliorate the environmental challenges their operations were causing, and similar concerns that extractive businesses had 'watered down' intergovernmental processes, a range of NGOs, led by the WWF and likeminded private sector interests, came together to create the Forest Stewardship Council (FSC) global certification system (Cashore et al., 2004b). The idea was to turn to market incentives to foster the world's first global 'non-state market driven' NSMD governance institutions (Cashore, 2002) that sought to champion a range of 'on the ground' sustainable forestry practices. The main tool was to provide an eco-label to those firms who auditing as being in compliance with a set of pre-established forestry standards, and then to use this recognition to improve their overall image, gain market access, and potentially earn a 'price premium'. The overall mission, which subsequently proliferated to a range of other sectors (Bernstein and Cashore, 2007), was that these systems of private governance could either help replace or fill governance gaps, within domestic settings around the world (Elliott and Donovan, 1996; Bernstein and Cashore, 2004; Gulbrandsen, 2004; Börzel and Risse, 2010).

By the 2000s, however, many applied scholars and practitioners were frustrated over what they perceived as mixed results (van der Ven et al., 2018). While support for FSC certification and its competitor, the 'Program for the Endorsement of Forest Certification' (PEFC) had increased over time (Figures 8.1 and 8.2), its uptake was relatively weak in developing and emerging economy countries (Figure 8.3), with relatively limited uptake in the tropics compared to boreal and temperate forests (Figure 8.4). They also noted that the majority of productive forest land remained uncertified (Figure 8.5).

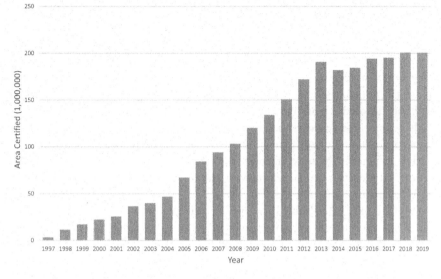

**FIGURE 8.1** Total certified land under the Forest Stewardship Council (FSC).

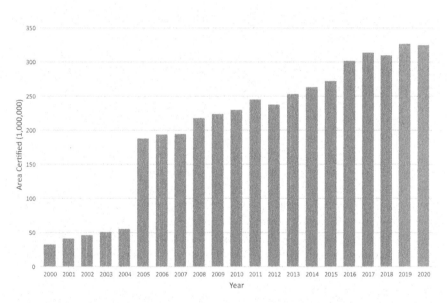

**FIGURE 8.2** Total certified land under the Programme for the Endorsement of Forest Certification (PEFC).

These unexpected trends would lead many forest activists to engage with the private sector to champion the narrower goal of promoting 'legality compliance' to domestic forest policies (Glastra, 1999; Lehman, 2000; FAO, 2005; Lawson, 2014; Mendlewicz, 2017). The overall tool focused on reducing 'illegal

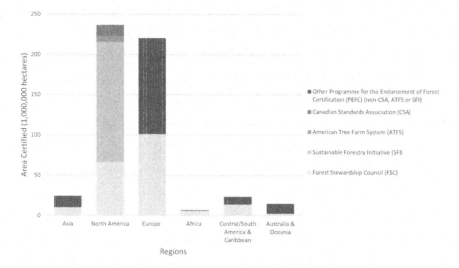

**FIGURE 8.3** Land certified by region.

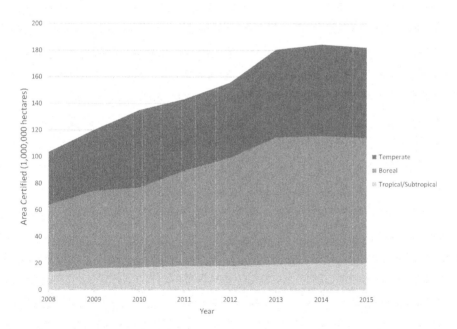

**FIGURE 8.4** Certification support by biome.

trade' in forest products by showing some type of proof that the wood products they were selling conformed to legal requirements of the country in which they were extracted. Private sector engagement in these types of FMD tools was important for reinforcing domestic sovereignty rather than imposing 'top down'

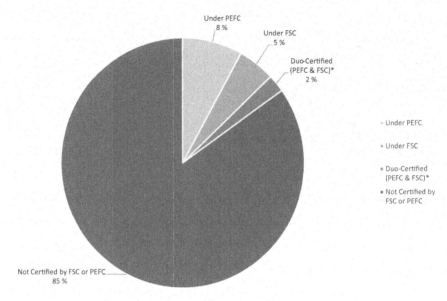

Under PEFC
8 %

Under FSC
5 %

Duo-Certified
(PEFC & FSC)*
2 %

- Under PEFC

- Under FSC

- Duo-Certified
(PEFC & FSC)*

- Not Certified by
FSC or PEFC

Not Certified by FSC or PEFC
85 %

**FIGURE 8.5** Share of productive forest land certified by the Forest Stewardship Council (FSC) and/or the Programme for the Endorsement of Forest Certification (PEFC).

behavioural requirements (Buckrell, 2005; Canby, 2005). Some argued that this showed promise in fostering sustainability in those domestic settings that while lacking enforcement capacity, did have, on their books, fairly stringent domestic policy requirements (McDermott et al., 2010).

The emphasis on legality compliance resulted in two ways in which the private sector was engaged. The first was an emphasis on passing domestic legislation in the United States, the European Union, Australia, and Japan, requiring that importers show 'due care' or 'due diligence' that they were not importing illegal forest products.[1] The result was strong signals to the private sector that they would need to find ways to provide due diligence when engaging in, and benefiting from, global forest products trade. The second form was the approach advanced by the European Union 'Forest Law Enforcement, Governance and Trade' (FLEGT) that combined financial incentives and capacity building support with which to entice a developing country to sign a bilateral Voluntary Partnership Agreements (VPA) aimed at improving its domestic forest policy and governance. The EU also promised preferential markets to signatory countries (Cashore et al., 2016; Wodschow et al., 2016; Carodenuto and Cashore, 2019).

Initial excitement, however, has been subdued as negotiations have taken much longer than expected and support has largely flatlined (Figure 8.6) leading EU policy officials to become frustrated over a 'slow and very costly processes' that has, after 20 years, resulted in 'only one country (out of 15)' 'with operating licensing system in place' (Brown, 2021), leading some to conclude that there is 'No evidence that VPAs have contributed to reducing illegal logging in the partner countries and the consumption of illegally-harvested wood in the EU' (Figure 8.7).

Similar dynamics were at play in the mid-2000s with the use of public and private 'financing' tools, sparked during COP 2005, and coalesced at the Bali 2007 COP meeting (Pistorius, 2012), under the banner of REDD+. These efforts would be designed and championed, by a range of companies and private sector organisations, as well as the UNFCCC secretariat, the World Bank, the United Nations Environment Program, a number of NGOs and bilateral development agencies, as well as individual countries such as oil-rich Norway (Dimitrov, 2005; Zhu et al., 2010; Nathan and Pasgaard, 2017). The original idea was sparked by scientific evidence that forest degradation and deforestation were contributing to climate change – especially in the tropics (Santilli et al., 2005). The tool itself focused on creating economic incentives to avoid deforestation and manage forests to sequester carbon. It has leveraged both public and private sources of funding and is being used by many countries to help address their Paris Climate Accord commitments.

Like the FSC and legality verification cases, initial euphoria over REDD+ led to frustration over the decade-plus delay – especially among the largest funders – in pledges, deposits, and approvals (Figure 8.8), and, like the VPA case, recognition that even if fully funded, such financing was a 'drop in the bucket' compared to the private sector financing of those extractive industries that caused the deforestation in the first place (Kill, 2019).

This historical context is important for three reasons. First, it allows us to understand the rationale for the private sector engagement in FMD innovations. Second, and partly as a result, it helps explain the ineffectiveness of these solutions to date in reversing ongoing deforestation, species extinctions, and climate-related forest emissions (Figures 8.9–8.11). Third, it helps place in context how the private sector responses to these trends that returned to firm-level corporate social responsibility and corporate sustainability initiatives (Barnett et al., 2021) – albeit with a fresh new 'environmental, social, governance' (ESG) acronym to

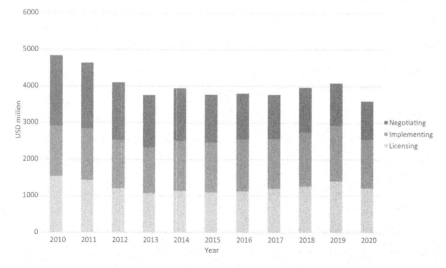

**FIGURE 8.6**   Import value to EU27+UK by Voluntary Partnership Agreements (VPA) status.

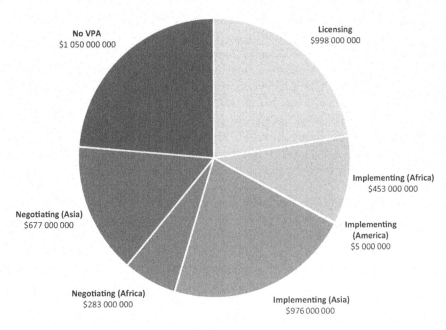

**FIGURE 8.7** Voluntary Partnership Agreements (VPA) share of forest products imports.

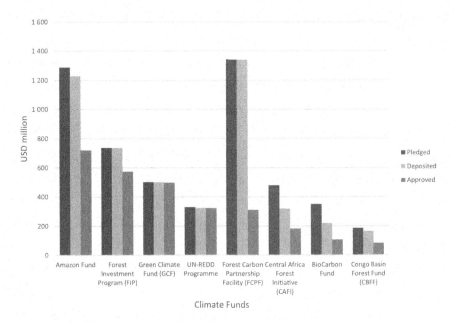

**FIGURE 8.8** Reducing Emissions from Deforestation and forest Degradation (REDD+) Climate Fund pledges, deposits, and approvals.

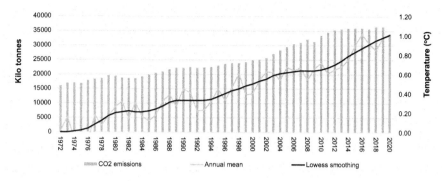

**FIGURE 8.9**  Increase in $CO_2$ emission and global temperatures.

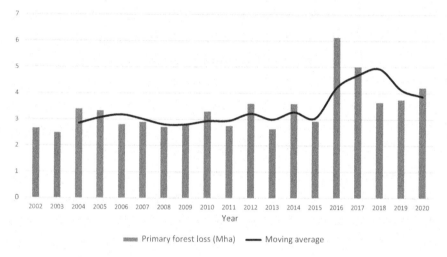

**FIGURE 8.10**  Tropical forest loss.

replace the old CSR label (Table 8.1). This return to the 1980s accordion place-ment is now playing out in the forest sector through a range of firm-level com-mitments to reform their supply chains including 'no deforestation' and 'net zero' climate commitments (Ou et al., 2021; Panwar, 2021).

## 3  The Four Faces of Sustainability

What then explains the ongoing emphasis on policy designs for improving pri-vate sector engagement, despite three decades of empirical evidence that these efforts have coincided with continued if not worsening environmental deg-radation? Cashore (2020) and Cashore and Nathan (2020) argue that a 'good governance norm complex' permeates a range of private sector, governmental

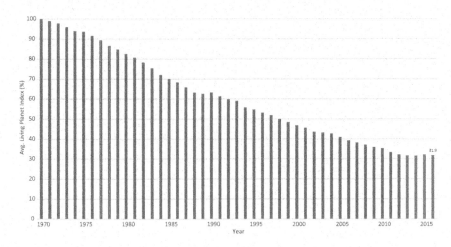

**FIGURE 8.11** Decline in species abundance.

**TABLE 8.1** The accordion of private sector engagement in finance and market driven policy initiatives

|  | *Emergence* |
| --- | --- |
| Firm-level forest sustainability initiatives<br>- Corporate social responsibility (CSR)<br>- Corporate sustainability (CS)<br>- Social license to operate (SLO) | Late 1980s |
| Certification of a firm's internal sustainability procedures<br>- Environmental Management Systems (EMS) | Late 1980s |
| Certification of prescriptive environmental and social standards<br>- NGO backed Forest Stewardship Council (FSC) | 1993 |
| Industry backed certification programs<br>- Program for the Endorsement of Forest Certification<br>- Greater emphasis on procedures and business-friendly standards) | 1999 |
| Legality verification<br>- EUTR/VPA process<br>- Domestic import requirements | Circa 2001 |
| Reduced Emissions from Deforestation and degradation (REDD+) | 2005 (formalised at Bali 2007 UNFCC COP) |
| Firm-level Environmental and Social Governance (ESG)<br>- No deforestation commitments<br>- Net-zero climate pledges | Circa 2012 |

and non-governmental organisations that advances a strongly held causal belief, despite empirical evidence to the contrary, that policy tools, if well designed, can foster synergies across a range of governance components from capacity building to accountability to transparency to inclusion and balance among environmental, social, and economic goals. This chapter reviews a complementary but distinct approach that Cashore has advanced through individual and collaborative assessments, which posits that there are not one, but four competing faces of sustainability – reinforced by four leading schools of thought – all of which identify competing ideas about what, exactly, is to be transformed. I draw on this framework to advance the argument that far from being ineffective, the myriad of private sector engagements with FMD tools have been highly effective in ameliorating some problems over others. Recognition of these carries profound implications about how to address each school's distinct 'whack-a-mole' effects, i.e., the phenomenon in which solving one problem makes another worse.

The *commons* (Type 1 reinforcing) school is motivated by the ethical obligations to promote meaningful 'collective action' institutions capable of avoiding 'tragedies of the commons' in which short-term resource depletion causes catastrophic of collapse economic sustainability. Ostrom and her students contributed to this school by identifying a subclass of commons tragedies, known and 'common pool resources', that she argued were best served by local governance solutions rather than privatisation (Ostrom, 1990). The application of school's institutional design recommendations has been highly *transformational* in helping local communities manage resources, including forests, for their long-term economic benefits (Ostrom, 1999; Gibson et al., 2000). Somewhat ironically, this school has advocated 'polycentric governance' as a way to 'scale up' decentralised processes to promote global economic sustainability of a particular resource.

*Moles*: This schools' focus on a particular resource problem – such as limiting harvesting of economically beneficial, utility enhancing fish and timber to levels in line with their rates of biological rates of reproduction – means that questions about whether converting the marine or land resources into other potentially higher economically beneficially uses – such as what occurs when marine ecosystems are converted to fish farms, forests into palm oil or agriculture or plantations – fall outside of its theoretical and prescriptive underpinnings. More important for this chapter, this school is silent about what to do about overwhelming evidence that managing for long-term sustained yields that, by degrading the natural ecosystems, render extinct, or endangers, forest-dependent species (Cashore and Bernstein, 2022)

In contrast, the *optimisation* (Type 2 reinforcing) school incorporates as many synergistic and whack-a-mole effects as possible when adjudicating whether, and how, to address any sustainability problem that might come along. For these reasons, adherents to this school devote much time and analytic attention to finding ways to systematically *comparing* the range of impacts of policy tools or institutional arrangements against their 'utility' enhancing or reinforcing outcomes (Pinchot, 1987). The preoccupation with minimising utility and undermining unintended 'whack-a-mole' effects of a behaviour, for example, industrialisation processes that enhance wages, incomes, and profits, while undermining local cultural practices and environmental conservation, is a process that this school refers to as 'internalising externalities'.

A leading strand of this school accomplishes this task by applying 'cost-benefit' analysis to calculate and identify the most economically 'optimal' approach to address any given problem. This approach achieves this task by systematically comparing the direct economic benefits of a policy tool, approach, or activity – such as palm oil production that increases incomes, wages, and profits, with potentially negative utility undermining effects that might occur to humans through loss of nature, cultural traditions. The commensurability of all types of utility to their economic utility equivalents is often conducted through 'willing to pay' calculations (Salles, 2011; Thomas and Chindarkar, 2019). This approach has led the US EPA, for instance, as Cashore and Bernstein have noted (Cashore and Bernstein, 2022, p. 7), to value a human life at $9.47 million USD (Environmental Protection Agency, 2020).

A second strand of this school within international relations assesses support for global policies and/or institutions against whether, and how, they might convey relative (Waltz, 1959) or absolute utility enhancing gains for states (Keohane, 1984) and recently, private actors and organisations. Both strands are motivated by the ethical imperative, reinforced by widespread empirical evidence (Loayza and Raddatz, 2010) that efforts to improve aggregate economic utility have lifted millions out of poverty (Sachs, 2006; Liu et al., 2020).

Within sustainability studies, this strand of international relations has produced the 'Oslo-Potsdam' (Hovi et al., 2003) solution for assessing the effectiveness of global governance and international agreements not on their ability to ameliorate a climate and species extinctions problems in line with that scientists indicate are required to avoid catastrophic ecological outcomes (Kütting, 2000), but on the most optimal solution for maintaining utility enhancing benefits (Young, 2003). When faced with such criticism that this school's approach undermines environmental concerns, they usually 'double down' on their rationalist project by assigning utility values with which to incorporate, through a process known as 'internalising externalities', environmental moles (Sukhdev et al., 2011; Thomas and Chindarkar, 2019). These frames explain why, for instance, Nobel Prize-winning economist William Nordhaus has found that – in contrast to the ecological scientists finding that anything over 1.5°C warming risks catastrophic environmental outcomes –the most optimal or 'economically rational' reduction possible is 3.2°C (Nordhaus, 2017).

This school's thinking permeates World Bank projects across the world and has been taken up by governments across the world (Cashore and Nathan, 2020). In China alone, this approach, including the way it has engaged forest management (Hyde et al., 2008), has lifted 100s of millions out of poverty. Overall, there have been undisputed correlations (Figure 8.12) between advancing economic growth and the massive reduction in poverty when defined, and measured, as

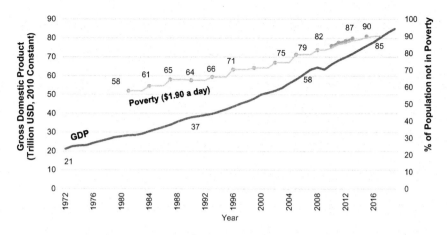

**FIGURE 8.12** World economic growth and poverty alleviation.

increased in income (Thomas and Chindarkar, 2019). This school has also been prominent, since the 1990s, in shaping the global sustainability agenda in general (Bernstein, 2001) and on forests in particular (Humphreys, 2006). This school has been highly transformational in fostering a particular approach to sustainability that champions massive growth in forest exports (Figure 8.13) and the preference for utility-enhancing FMD tools as a means to reduce deforestation (UN Environment, 2020).

*Moles*: As this school is focused on society-wide moles, it necessarily incorporates an effort to incorporate a range of outcomes, including environmental and social challenges (Cashore and Bernstein, 2022). However, this school is silent on what to do about the outcomes that are exacerbated by championing utility-enhancing outcomes – such as species losses that are caused by utility-enhancing activities (Lippke et al., 1990; Spies et al., 2018). It also narrows the treatment of the climate crisis to policy designs that target the utility undermining impacts of the climate crisis (Nordhaus, 2017).

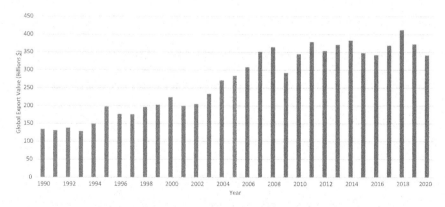

**FIGURE 8.13** Export value of global forest products.

*The compromise* (Type 3 reinforcing school) is motivated by strong ethical foundations aimed at empowering a range of voices and stakeholders within policy-making processes and to treating social and environmental outcomes as distinct from, and needing balance with, economic goals. Within sustainability studies, this school has thought about and advanced ways to achieve consensus and compromise-based solutions through stakeholder dialogue and negotiations between contesting ideas and interests (Cashore and Bernstein, 2022). These ideas have been prominent in the creation of a range of private governance innovations, especially thinking about the most appropriate and effective way to include a range of environmental, social, and economic stakeholders in deliberating over tools design and standards (Tollefson et al., 2008). Researchers from this school have found that if designed well, such inclusionary approaches can help foster political legitimacy and authority (Dryzek, 1990; Eckersley, 1992) including with private governance (Cashore, 2002; Risse, 2011) in general and forest arrangements in particular (Overdevest and Zeitlin, 2016).

Indeed, this school is also behind the long history of UN-inspired efforts to advance the 'three-legged stool' of sustainability (WCED, 1987) that attempts to compromise, or find synergies, across economic, environmental, and social problems (Bernstein, 2001). In sum, this school has been *highly transformative* in engaging conversation across a range of values and for fostering stakeholder dialogues to achieve consensus. Its latest transformative impact includes seeing the UN adopt the SDGs framework (Bernstein, 2017), which replaced the Millennium Development Goals (MDB Joint Statement, 2021).

*Moles*: While this school also incorporates moles by advocating a compromise approach in which no single problem or set of interests dominates, it can, for the same reasons, produce decisions that are inconsistent with the science of what is required to address a particular problem (Cashore et al., 2019). For instance, Victor (2015), in acknowledging the Paris Accord as 'transformative' event sparked by the compromise school that achieved consensus by dropping mandatory requirements, has also acknowledged that the Accord's problem-oriented 1.5°C and 2°C objectives were 'ridiculous'. Similarly, when the Canadian province of Newfoundland invoked a Type 3 compromise dialogue to address biologists warning that they were overharvesting cod, the stakeholders adopted a policy that chose higher catch levels that what was projected to be required to save the fisheries (McKenna, 1992). The result was that the fisheries collapsed, undermining Type 1 fisheries and Type 4 ocean ecosystems (Cashore and Bernstein, 2022).

The *prioritisation* (Type 4 reinforcing school) rejects Types 2 and 3 'commensurability' biases (Tribe, 1972) to instead ranking problems according to their importance through a lexical ordering orientation (Cashore and Bernstein, 2022). Adherents to this school apply a 'sequentialist' analysis in which the policy design being offered is consistent with what is required to ameliorate the problem at hand. The most often cited example of a globally diffused sequentialist approach concerns the eradication of slavery in which the very application of

**TABLE 8.2** Four sustainability schools and their reinforcing types

| | | *Utility Rationale Dominates* | |
|---|---|---|---|
| | | *Yes* | *No* |
| Application to a specific type of problem structure? | **YES (contingent)** Generalises only to the problem at hand) | **THE COMMONS SCHOOL (TYPE 1 REINFORCING)**<br><br>• **Problem specification**<br>- resource depletion 'tragedies of the commons'<br>- e.g., harvesting resources such as fish and timber beyond the reproduction yield rate<br>- subclass includes 'common pool resources' (CPR)<br><br>• **Problem orientation**<br>- Producing collectively optimal institutions for the resource in question | **THE PRIORTISATION SCHOOL (TYPE 4 REINFORCING)**<br><br>• **Problem specification**<br>- irreversible environmental tragedies<br>- e.g., species extinctions, catastrophic ecological effects of climate change<br>- Subclass includes 'super wicked' problems<br><br>• **Problem orientation**<br>- utility/economic motivations are the cause, not the solution |
| | **NO (universal)** Generalises to all problems | **THE OPTIMISATION SCHOOL (TYPE 2 REINFORCING)**<br><br>• **Problem specification**<br>- all<br><br>• Problem orientation<br>- Aggregate utility | **THE COMPROMISE SCHOOL (TYPE 3 REINFORCING)**<br><br>• **Problem specification**<br>- all<br><br>• Problem orientation<br>- Economic utility shares stage with, rather than subsumes underneath, social, cultural, and environmental goals |

*Source*: Cashore and Bernstein (2022).

the compromise school to adjudicate who could or could not own slaves, or the optimisation school to adjudicate the utility enhancing benefits of owning slaves, would undermine the problem itself: i.e., no one, for any reason, ought to be allowed to own another human being. The same logic applies to efforts to address species extinction crises: i.e., policymakers and designers have no choice but to grant Type 4 status to endangered species because they face two choices: either conserve habitat protections consistent with what scientists' project is required to maintain the viability of the species or do not undertake these provisions and risk species extinction.

Likewise, the prioritisation school addresses the climate crisis by finding solutions – in contrast to Nordhaus – that are consistent with climate scientists finding that we must be limiting warming to 1.5 degrees to avoid catastrophic ecological impacts or risk newfound outcomes. While the Prioritisation school was initially prominent in the 1970s in advocating for strong domestic environmental regulations and promoting international organisations such as UNPE, it has failed to achieve its transformative agenda, in part because of the dominance of the optimisation and compromise schools (McAfee, 1999)

*Moles:* The most important implication for our review is that, taken together, each school adjudicates how to address 'whack-a-mole' problems that fall outside their preferred type: the commons, economic optimisation, and compromise schools narrow an ability to address Type 4 problems that are synergistic with their preferred type. In contrast to Types 3 and 2, but consistent with Type 1, the prioritisation school advances its analytical approach first based on the key features of the problem at hand and then addresses second- and third-order problems only in ways that do not undermine, but reinforce an ability to ameliorate the Type 4 problem

## 4 Case Illustrations

Application of this framework permits the weaving of a novel historical narrative with which to review and assess the argument that it is the success of the transformational projects of the commons, optimisation, and compromise school, rather than poorly designed Type 4 solutions, that explains the Private Sector Engagement Paradox

### 4.1 Forest Stewardship Council

The creation of the Forest Stewardship Council is illustrative of the implicit and explicit ways in which the four faces of sustainability are championed by different actors and coalitions both in the original design of, and revisions to, its institutional arena and standard setting. As Nikolakis and Wood's chapter on the FSC as an example of NGO-Business collaboration general, and IFLs engagement in particular, the very design was owing to efforts to embed environmental and social norms within market-based initiatives. It did so with the expressed purpose of creating synergies with the optimisation school's Type 2 reinforcing approach and the prioritisation schools 'on the ground' Type 4 problems. However, there was an uneasy and unresolved tension between those that sought to understand how these might be fostered to have enough authority to address Type 4 problems, from those that were content in letting the FSC design and its uptake determine whether these problems could be solved. In other words, one approach saw private governance as doing a better job than governments to ameliorate Type 4 problems, while the other saw private governance as the more 'economically rational' governance approach with which to foster economic utility while assessing possible synergies with environmental and social moles.

In addition, at the very outset, the FSC concerns about deforestation coalesced and created an uneasy tension with those environmental activists who were concerned about the decline of Type 4 ecosystems and those Type 1 forest management practitioners and resource scholars. The FSC also was explicitly appealing to Type 2 post-WWII development agencies, such as the World Bank, who were increasingly looking for innovative ways to minimise environmental degradation from their development projects. Somewhat ironically, it also brought together Type 1 and Type 4 'community forestry' advocates, despite their very different ideas about what kinds of practices to emphasise within these decentralised arenas.

Likewise, Type 4 prioritisation school initially advocated for a Type 4 proposal in which 70% of the votes would be granted to a single environmental and social chamber, while a second business chamber would be granted 30% of the voting weight (Auld, 2014). This would have had the effect of giving voice to business interests, without them ever being able to trump Type 4-oriented stakeholders.

Ultimately these tensions and contradictions led to a Type 3 compromise approach to stakeholder governance in which three equally weighted environmental, social, and economic chambers would themselves be divided equally to weight North and South members equally (Tickell, 1997). The FSC also embraced 'bottom up' inclusionary stakeholder deliberations with which to develop locally appropriate standards (Elliott, 2005; Conroy, 2007). We also know that initially the range of principles and goals the FSC identified were not viewed as need of 'balance', but rather in finding economic incentives to achieve *all* of them.[2] This meant that the FSC implicitly 'punted' into the future about what to do when inevitable moles appeared between economic development, deforestation, and even community engagement in supply chains.

However, as a market-based mechanism that could only be effective in addressing Type 4 problems to the extent that it either drew on, or became embedded in, global markets (Cashore, 2002; Bernstein and Cashore, 2007), the FSC face an initial dilemma: lower standards would lead to high support among firms but low impacts, while high standards would lead to low support and low impact (Cashore et al., 2007). This meant that strategists were required to navigate the 'chicken and egg' challenges in which increasing market support for the certification program would allow them to increase standards in line with that benefit – but not at such a high level initially that they undermined required support for a later stage (Cashore et al., 2007; Judge-Lord et al., 2020). The FSC was aware that whereas some Type 4 prioritisation school activists demanded strong standards initially, this might, ironically, undermine impacts at a later time by kneecapping support before it had a chance to institutionalise (Cashore et al., 2004b; Auld and Cashore, 2012). We also know that whenever the FSC initiated standards that targeted, in some way, Type 4 improving practices (Cashore et al., 2004a), it would be met by strong competition from industry 'competitors' offering Type 1 and 2 'business friendly' regulations (Judge-Lord et al., 2020). Meanwhile, the FSC was well aware that much of its funding – which came from donations from US-based foundations and some development agencies – could not last forever (Conroy, 2007).

While far from preordained, what we now know is that the FSC's efforts to gain market uptake have ended up, a quarter century later, being criticised by Type 4 environmental activists as fostering Type 2, 3, and 1 conceptions that have contributed to environmental degradation (Greenpeace International, 2018). We also know that its efforts to wean itself from foundation and government funding to a reproducing model have also been criticised for implicitly empowering Type 1 business interests. This turn, some argue, was reinforced, in part, to a decision to impose a tax on the amount of land certified, which meant that removing or not granting certification to a particular company, and/or increasing Type 4 rules, would undermine the FSC's operating budget (Auld and Cashore, 2012). By 2029, the new tax would constitute 81% of the FSC operating budget, while donations fell to 1% (FSC-AC, 2021).

These design changes also coincided with the ongoing expansion of FSC-certified tropical plantations in developing countries that social activists criticised as fostering (Type 1 and 2) motivations over Type 4 indigenous and environmental concerns (Auld, 2014; Bartley, 2018). In response, and to be sure, the FSC devoted developed proactive principles governing indigenous people's rights and launched a governance review, but many were unsatisfied with what they perceived as a compromise approach. Meanwhile, and in part for these reasons, deforestation continues to expand in those countries in which the FSC has made inroads, rendering the broader question as to whether this private governance innovation ever had the ability – given enormous hurdles – to achieve Type 4 impacts (van der Ven and Cashore, 2018; van der Ven et al., 2018).

Moreover, part of the lack of uptake can be traced to the emergence of the PEFC, which decidedly advanced Type 1, 2, and 3 conceptions against Type 4 futures. Origins of PEFC programs can be traced back to industrial and private owners who sought to offer a more flexible, Type 2 and 1 business-friendly approach to sustainable forestry that better respected individual firm autonomy and often longstanding partnerships between governance agencies and the private sector (Cashore et al., 2004b). In fact, its US program – the Sustainable Forestry Initiative – was originally designed by the US timber lobby following the Type 2 and 1 losses following Type 4 rules aimed at conservation old-growth forest ecosystems in order to maintain the viability of the Northern Spotted Owl (Cashore, 1997).

### 4.2 Legality Compliance

Application of the four faces of sustainability framework to legality compliance reveals a largely undisputed role for Type 3 and 2 conceptions of sustainability.

Indeed, whereas rhetorically and substantively the FSC included Type 4 in its original design, LV was about 'weeding out' the worst forms of illegal activity, that many argued were culprits in unregulated deforestation. This resulted initially in a 'bootleggers and Baptists' coalition of Type 2 businesses – many of whom supported the PEFC over the FSC – and Type 4 environmental activists – who saw LV as an opportunity to quickly reverse the most egregious forest degradation practices – especially given the limited uptake of the FSC (Cashore and Stone, 2012). This, in turn, led sustainability scholars to argue that legality verification might eventually have a stronger impact if it first tended to Type 2 interests which, once institutionalised, might better advance Type 4 problems (Cashore and Stone, 2014). However, LV efforts have largely stayed in the first phase. In fact, Type 1 community forestry advocates were concerned that legality might also undermine their problems, especially since so many indigenous communities did not have legal title to their lands (Seymour, 2008) and did lead to a number of reforms and proposals to minimise this impact (Humphreys et al., 2017). Likewise, the requirement that VPAs engage local stakeholders in developing approaches to legality compliance has been celebrated by Type 3 sustainability scholars for its ability to incorporate local peoples and indigenous communities into national conversations (Overdevest and Zeitlin, 2016), even in the face of ongoing deforestation.

## 4.3 REDD+

Similarly, REDD+ was initially informed by those advancing Type 4, 3, 2, and 1 transformations. Many biologists and activists saw REDD+ as finally providing enough financial incentives to meet, rather than undermine Type 4 concerns about the loss of species and forest ecosystems, especially in the tropics (Stickler et al., 2009). However, there is also no question that as a financing mechanism that turned to converting material interests into conservation, its Type 4 impact would be limited to those synergistic with Type 2 transformations. Indeed, the idea was that REDD+ could promote Type 1 community forestry and Type 2 notions of sustainable development that would be more effective than previous policy designs in conserving nature. The result was significant interest in the private sector in turning to forest finance as a way to generate strong Type 2 returns that might, in some way, curb Type 4 deforestation. Over time, Type 3 conceptions led to a strong emphasis on stakeholder deliberations in 'REDDiness' projects and a range of non-carbon value including (Types 3 and 1) conceptions of indigenous rights (Ebeling and Tippmann, 2008; Stickler et al., 2009; Ricketts et al., 2010). Over a decade, Type 2 financing for REDD+ would become the dominant transformative agenda, while its supporters engaged in a range of policy design changes to incorporate Type 4, 3, and 1 forest sustainability challenges. (Chhatre and Agrawal, 2009; Peskett et al., 2011; Bernard et al., 2012; Visseren-Hamakers et al., 2012; Danielsen et al., 2013; Lawlor et al., 2013; Reytar and Veit, 2016). Experimentation with this type of financing, in which designers believed that synergies were indeed possible through creative thinking, would also entrench the UN's continued emphasis on Green Economy (Sukhdev et al., 2011) championed at Rio +20 (Clémençon, 2012) along with the parallel Consumer Goods Forum. However, the evidence to date is that these Type 2 transformations have come at the expense of Type 4 impacts. As Milne et al have found (2018) that REDD+ was a 'blunt tool for [Type 4] change', as it contained inherent and fundamental 'dissonance between …objectives and outcomes' rendering it unlikely to provide a solution to the global climate crisis. And yet despite these trends, the 2021 Glasgow COP meeting again doubled down on private sector financing as a means to reverse climate-related deforestation (*The Guardian*, 2021)

### 4.4 Net Zero and No Deforestation Pledges

The impact of the commons, optimisation and compromise schools in shaping certification, legality compliance, and financing for carbon tools helps place in context the accordion being squeezed back into firm-level sustainability efforts, albeit under a new ESG label. On the surface, the latest flurry of activity, including the latest announcement at Glasgow to 'this time' to find adequate (Type 2) funding to reverse (Type 4) deforestation (*The Guardian*, 2021) and the climate crisis (Hare and Höhne, 2021), seems to imply that the private sector has finally reached the type of commitments necessary to address Type 4 environmental challenges (Lambin et al., 2018). However, those advocating addressing the climate crisis as Type 4 problems have already projected that even if public and private sector pledges were all realised, the cumulative impacts would not be consistent with what is needed to avoid catastrophic ecological collapse (Hare and Höhne, 2021). Indeed, some of those working on corporate pledges – including sustainability experts – have concluded that their (Type 2) organisational missions render them poorly placed to adopt policies in line with Type 4 climate and biodiversity crises (Fancy, 2021; Kishan, 2021). This may be why less attention has been placed on this history of failed pledges in the past and, instead, on the opportunity to advance Type 4 problems by designing Type 2 policies tools in ways that might create synergies with Type 4 problems (Bos and Wu; Kreibich and Hermwille, 2021). It is for these reasons that many companies have expressed concerns that while they have made pledges on deforestation and climate, they are not fully aware of what this means in practice and what they might do to foster such a process.

### 5 Towards a Type 4 Role for the Private Sector

Several important conclusions emerge through the application of the four problem conception types and their four reinforcing schools, to make sense of private sector's role in advancing the proliferation of FMD sustainability tools that have coincided with the acceleration of environmental degradation.

First, as all four schools of sustainability are motivated by strong moral foundations, any appeal to 'ethical' behaviours is as likely to reinforce the commons, optimisation, and compromise schools as it is the prioritisation schools' transformative project. Second, there is little doubt that the private sector has played an important role in fostering Type 2 sustainability transformations that have helped lift millions out of poverty. Third, the evidence from the last 50 years is that Type 2 transformations are largely responsible for, and have coincided with, the degradation of Type 4 problems. Fourth, it is critically important that sustainability scholars assess whether and how businesses might be part of a Type 4 solution not because they happen to be employed in places that advance business sustainability (Panwar, 2021), but rather because of their potential role in transforming, rather than undermining, Type 4 transformations.

Fifth, and somewhat counterintuitively, it does appear that the private sector can play a role in Type 4 transformations if policy designers simultaneously avoid pressures to drift towards Type 3 and 2 solutions. For example, the private sector in general, and their Type 2 chasing interests in particular, played a supporting role in advancing innovative and less costly 'cap and trade' policy tools with which to meet Type 4 regulations to reduce acid rain pollution in the Canadian Great Lakes (Burtraw and Swift, 1996). Recognition of this means guarding against those promoting 'cap and trade' and finance tools that makes solving the Type 4 climate problem conditional upon maintaining Type 2 transformations (Carney, 2016). Sixth, it does not follow that an emphasis on changing finance and markets towards Type 4 problems requires beginning, and ending, with finance and climate policy tools. Indeed, traditional Type 4 regulations – such as those that were sparked to ameliorate acid rain in North America's great lakes (Burtraw and Swift, 1996) – triggered cost-effective 'cap and trade' program designs to meet, rather than avoid, Type 4 behaviours.

This contrasts with today's narrative in that we simply need to find additional private sector funding, and more commitments, to address the climate crisis, when there is little empirical evidence for this rhetoric, or approach, for Type 4 transformations. On the other hand, there is widespread evidence that such an orientation will maintain the Type 2 transformative project.

For all these reasons it behooves all of those seeking to understand the private sector's role in sustainability transformations is that they have been highly transformational – creating meaningful and lasting impacts on poverty alleviation through economic development. This means that those advancing private sector solutions to addressing Type 4 problems need to be guarded against 'lessons learned' exercises that reinforce Type 1 collective action (1990) (Ostrom, 1986), Type 2 institutional analysis (Hovi et al., 2003), and even Type 3 stakeholder collaborations (Díaz-Reviriego et al., 2019; Barnett et al., 2021) that are 'ill fit for purpose' for ameliorating Type 4 environment problems. For all these reasons those championing the private sector to advance policy tools and designs have a duty to be clear as to why their efforts might prioritise, rather than undermine, Type 4 transformations.

## Acknowledgements

Cashore thanks two reviewers for their helpful comments on a previous draft. He thanks Petrina Gee, Mehtab Ahmed Jagil, Ashwath Dasarathy, and Christopher Skelto for the production of graphs and research assistance. He is grateful to collaborators on related projects including Iben Nathan, Ingrid Visseren-Hamakers, Yixian Sun, Hamish van der Ven, David Humphreys, Graeme Auld, Steven Bernstein, and Michael Stone.

## Notes

1 The reason why legislation gained domestic support is that it would also provide economic relief for producers in the North, whose prices were being deflating owing to cheaper, illegally produced products from foreign competitors. Policy designers therefore worked to ban illegal imports, which resulted from, and entrenched, a number of Bootleggers and Baptists coalitions (Cashore and Stone, 2014). The relevant development agencies also indirectly supported these efforts by assisting producer countries and companies in meeting the new requirements.
2 To be, there were voices at the time who were concerned that failure to distinguish Type 4 ecosystem management principle with the emphasis on green consumerism was bound to create an immediate drift toward ecology degradation outcomes. (Reeve, 1993)

## References

Auld, G. (2014) *Constructing Private Governance: The Rise and Evolution of Forest, Coffee, and Fisheries Certification*. New Haven, CT: Yale University Press.

Auld, G., Bernstein, S. and Cashore, B. (2008) 'The new corporate social responsibility', *The Annual Review of Environment and Resources*, 33(1), pp. 413–435.

Auld, G. and Cashore, B. (2012) 'Appendix F: Forestry review', in Steering Committee on the State-of-Knowledge Assessment of Standards and Certification (ed.), *Toward Sustainability: The Roles and Limitations of Certification*. Washington, DC: Resolve, pp. 73–89.

Barnett, M. L., Henriques, I. and Husted, B. W. (2021) *Salvaging Corporate Sustainability*. Cheltenham: Elgar.

Bartley, T. (2018) *Rules without Rights: Land, Labor and Private Authority in the Global Economy*. New Haven, CT: Oxford University Press.

Bernard, F., McFatridge, S. and Minang, P. A. (2012) 'The private sector in the Redd+ Supply Chain: Trends, challenges and opportunities', *ASB Partnership for the Tropical Forest Margins and International Institute for Sustainable Development*. https://www.iisd.org/publications/report/private-sector-redd-supply-chain-trends-challenges-and-opportunities-key.

Bernstein, S. (2001) *The Compromise of Liberal Environmentalism*. New York: Columbia University Press.

Bernstein, S. (2017) 'The United Nations and the governance of sustainable development goals', in N. Kanie and F. Biermann (eds.), *Governance through Goals: New Strategies for Global Sustainability*. Cambridge, MA: MIT Press, pp. 213–239.

Bernstein, S. and Cashore, B. (2004) 'Non-state global governance: Is forest certification a legitimate alternative to a global forest convention?', in J. Kirton and M. Trebilcock (eds.), *Hard Choices, Soft Law: Combining Trade, Environment, and Social Cohesion in Global Governance*. Aldershot: Ashgate Press, pp. 33–63.

Bernstein, S. and Cashore, B. (2007) 'Can non-state global governance be legitimate? An analytical framework', *Regulation and Governance*, 1(4), pp. 347–371.

Börzel, T. A. and Risse, T. (2010) 'Governance without a state: Can it work? Governance without a State', *Regulation & Governance*, 4(2), pp. 113–134.

Bos, J. and Wu, Y. (2021) 'How banks can accelerate net-zero emissions commitments', https://www.wri.org/insights/banks-paris-alignment-net-zero-finance.

Brody, J. E. (2007) *Concern for Rain Forest Has Begun to Blossom* [Section C; Page 1, Column 1; Science Desk]. The New York Times, 13 October 1987 [cited 10 August 2007]. http://www.lexisnexis.com.

Brown, S. (2021) *Ngo's Fear Eu Weakening Illegal Logging Regulations*. Organized Crime and Corruption Reporting Index. https://www.occrp.org/en/daily/14328-ngo-s-fear-eu-weakening-illegal-logging-regulations.

Buckrell, J. (2005) *Global Witness Ena Fleg Ministerial Declaration Comments*. Global Witness.

Burtraw, D. and Swift, B. (1996) 'A new standard of performance: An analysis of the clean air act's acid rain program', *Environmental Law. Reporter*, 26, 10411.

Canby, K. (2005) 'Comparison of multi-stakeholder statements on illegal logging and associated trade', Paper read at The Forests Dialogue, 2–3 November, at St. Petersburg, Russia.

Carney, M. (2016) 'Resolving the climate paradox', *Arthur Burns Memorial Lecture, Berlin*, 22.

Carodenuto, S. and Cashore, B. (2019) 'Can non-state regulatory authority improve domestic forest sustainability? Assessing interactive pathways of influence in Cameroon', in S. Wood, R. Schmidt, K. W. Abbott, B. Eberlein and E. Meidinger (eds.), *Transnational Business Governance Interactions: Enhancing Regulatory Capacity, Ratcheting up Standards and Empowering Marginalized Actors*. Northampton, MA: Edward Elgar Publishing Cheltenham, UK.

Cashore, B. (1997) 'Governing forestry: Environmental group influence in British Columbia and the US Pacific Northwest', PhD, Political Science, University of Toronto, Toronto.

Cashore, B. (2002) 'Legitimacy and the privatization of environmental governance: How Non-state market driven (Nsmd) governance systems gain rule‚Äìmaking authority', *Governance*, 15(4), pp. 503–529.

Cashore, B. (2013) 'Building a problem focused architecture for landscapes', Paper read at Governance and Legal Frameworks for Sustainable Landscapes, Global Landscapes Day 8 March, at Warsaw Poland Sunday, 17 November.

Cashore, B. (2019, Spring) 'A growing disconnect between environmental problems and solutions', *Distilled*, pp. 6–7.

Cashore, B. (2020) 'Good governance gone bad: Towards effective implementation of the global sustainable development agenda', Paper read at Revised version of paper presented to the 'Interactions between Private and Public Authority in Global (Business) Governance: Comparative and Inter-Disciplinary Perspectives', Melbourne, Australia, 2–3 December 2019, 4 September.

Cashore, B. (2021) 'Strategies for triggering transformative climate change pathways: Towards "Fit for Purpose" philanthropic and donor engagement', in Prepared as a contribution to Climate and Land Use 2030: Resources for Funders (CLU2030), Policy Input Paper. Washington, DC: Meridien Institute.

Cashore, B. and Bernstein, S. (2022) 'Bringing the environment back in: Overcoming the tragedy of the diffusion of the commons metaphor', *Perspectives on Politics*, pp. 1–24. https://doi.org/10.1017/S1537592721002553.

Cashore, B. and Nathan, I. (2020) 'Can Finance and Market Driven (FMD) interventions make "weak" states stronger? Lessons from the good governance norm complex in Cambodia', *Ecological Economics*, 177, 106689.

Cashore, B. and Stone, M. W. (2012) 'Can legality verification rescue global forest governance? Analyzing the potential of public and private policy intersection to Ameliorate forest challenges in Southeast Asia', *Forest Policy and Economics*, 18, pp. 13–22.

Cashore, B. and Stone, M. (2014) 'Does California need delaware? Explaining Indonesian, Chinese, and United States support for legality compliance of internationally traded products', *Regulation and Governance*, 8, pp. 49–73.

Cashore, B., Auld, G. and Newsom, D. (2004a) 'The United States' race to certify sustainable forestry: Non-state environmental governance and the competition for policy-making authority', *Business and Politics*, 5(3), pp. 219–259.

Cashore, B., Auld, G., Bernstein, S. and McDermott, C. L. (2007) 'Can non-state governance 'ratchet up' global environmental standards? Lessons from the forest sector', *Review of European Community and International Environmental Law*, 16(2), pp. 158–172.

Cashore, B., Leipold, S., Cerutti, P. O., Bueno, G., Carodenuto, S., Chen, X., de Jong, W., Denvir, A., Hansen, C., Humphreys, D. and McGinley, K. (2016) 'Global governance approaches to addressing illegal logging: Uptake and lessons learnt', in D. Kleinschmit, S. Mansourian, C. Wildburger and A. Purret (eds.), *Illegal Logging and Related Timber Trade – Dimensions, Drivers, Impacts and Responses a Global Scientific Rapid Response Assessment Report*. Vienna: International Union of Forest Research Orgnizations, pp. 119–131.

Cashore, B. W., Auld, G. and Newsom, D. (2004b) *Governing through Markets: Forest Certification and the Emergence of Non-State Authority*. New Haven, CT: Yale University Press.

Chhatre, A. and Agrawal, A. (2009) 'Trade-offs and synergies between carbon storage and livelihood benefits from forest commons', *Proceedings of the National Academy of Sciences*, 106(42), pp. 17667–17670.

Clémençon, R. (2012) 'Welcome to the anthropocene: Rio+20 and the meaning of sustainable development', *Journal of Environment & Development*, 21(3), pp. 311–338.

Conroy, M. E. (2007) *Branded! How the 'Certification Revolution' Is Transforming Global Corporations*. Gabriola Island: New Society Publishers.

D'amato, D. and Korhonen, J. (2021) 'Integrating the green economy, circular economy and bioeconomy in a strategic sustainability framework', *Ecological Economics*, 188, p. 107143.

Danielsen, F., Adrian, T., Brofeldt, S., Van Noordwijk, M., Poulsen, M. K., Rahayu, S., Rutishauser, E., Theilade, I., Widayati, A., An, N. T. and Bang, T.N. (2013) 'Community monitoring for Redd + : International promises and field realities', *Ecology and Society*, 18(3), 41.

Díaz-Reviriego, I., Turnhout, E. and Beck, S. (2019) 'Participation and inclusiveness in the intergovernmental science–policy platform on biodiversity and ecosystem services', *Nature Sustainability*, 2(6), pp. 457–464.

Dietz, T., Börner, J., Förster, J. J. and Von Braun, J. (2018). 'Governance of the bioeconomy: A global comparative study of national bioeconomy strategies', *Sustainability*, 10(9), 3190.

Dimitrov, R. S. (2005) 'Hostage to norms: States, institutions and global forest politics', *Global Environmental Politics*, 5(4), pp. 1–24.

Dryzek, J. S. 1990. *Discursive Democracy: Politics, Policy, and Political Science*. Cambridge, New York: Cambridge University Press.

Ebeling, J. and Tippmann, R. (2008) 'International policy for avoided deforestation – Reaching synergies for environment & development', in ISTF (ed.), *Drivers of Land Use Change in the Tropics: Bioenergy and Avoided Deforestation*. New Haven, CT: Yale University.

Eckersley, R. (1992) *Environmentalism and Political Theory: Toward an Ecocentric Approach*. Albany: State University of New York Press.

Elliott, C. (2005) 'From the tropical timber boycott to forest certification', in D. Burger, J. Hess and B. Lang (eds.), *Forest Certification: An Innovative Instrument in the Service of Sustainable Development?* Eschborn, Germany: GTZ, Programme Office for Social and Ecological Standards, pp. 79–90.

Elliott, C. and Donovan, R. (1996). 'Introduction', in V. M. Viana, J. Ervin, R. Donovan, C. Elliott and H. Gholz (eds.), *Certification of Forest Products: Issues and Perspectives*, 1–10. Washington, DC, Covelo, CA: Island Press.

Environmental Protection Agency (2020) *Mortality Risk Valuation*. U.S. EPA 2020. https://www.epa.gov/environmental-economics/mortality-risk-valuation#whatvalue.

Fancy, T. (2021) 'Blackrock hired me to make sustainable investing mainstream. Now i realize it's a deadly distraction from the climate-change threat', *The Globe and Mail*, 15 April.

FAO (2005) 'Potential implications for the forest industry of corporate zero-deforestation commitments', in *58th Session of the FAO Advisory Committee on Sustainable Forest-Based Industries*. Rome: FAO, ITTO.

FSC-AC (2021) *Consolidated Financial Statements*. Abstoss & Wolters.

Gale, F. P. (1998) *The Tropical Timber Trade Regime*. New York: St. Martin's Press.

Gibson, C. C., McKean, M. A. and Ostrom, E., eds. (2000) *People and Forests: Communities, Institutions and Governance*. Cambridge, MA: MIT Press.

Glastra, R., ed. (1999) *Cut and Run: Illegal Logging and Timber Trade in the Tropics*. Ottawa: International Development Rearch Centre.

Greenpeace International (2018) *Greenpeace International to Not Renew Fsc Membership*. Amsterdam: Greenpeace.

Gulbrandsen, L. H. (2004) 'Overlapping public and private governance: Can forest certification fill the gaps in the global forest regime?' *Global Environmental Politics*, 4(2), pp. 75–99.

Hare, B. and Höhne, N. (2021) 'Cop26 is creating false hope for a 1.5c rise – The stark reality is very different', *The Guardian* (London) 2021]. https://www.theguardian.com/commentisfree/2021/nov/09/cop26-false-hope-climate-analysis-targets.

Herrmann, K. K. (2004) 'Corporate social responsibility and sustainable development', *Indiana Journal of Global Legal Studies*, 11(2), pp. 204–232.

Hovi, J., Sprinz, D. F. and Underdal, A. (2003) 'Regime effectiveness and the oslopotsdam solution: A rejoinder to oran young', *Global Environmental Politics*, 3(3), pp. 105–107.

Hrabanski, M. (2017) 'Private sector involvement in the millennium ecosystem assessment: Using a un platform to promote market-based instruments for ecosystem services', *Environmental Policy and Governance*, 27(6), pp. 605–618.

Humphreys, D. (2006) *Logjam: Deforestation and the Crisis of Global Governance*. London: Earthscan.

Humphreys, D., Cashore, B., Visseren-Hamakers, I. J., De Jong, W., McGinley, K., Denvir, A., Torres, P. C. and Lupberger, S. (2017) 'Towards durable multistakeholder-generated solutions: The pilot application of a problem-oriented policy learning protocol to legality verification and community rights in peru', *International Forestry Review*, 19(3), pp. 278–293.

Hyde, W. F., Wei, J. and Xu, J. (2008) 'Economic growth and the natural environment: The example of China and its forests since 1978', Environment for Development Discussion Paper Series EfD DP 08-11. https://media.rff.org/documents/EfD-DP-08-11.pdf.

IPBES (2019) *Global Assessment Report on Biodiversity and Ecosystem Services*. Bonn: Intergovernmental Science-Policy Platform on Biodiversity and Ecosystem Services.

IPCC (2019) *Ar6 Synthesis Report: Climate Change 2022*. New York: United Nations.

Judge-Lord, D., McDermott, C. L. and Cashore, B. (2020) 'Do private regulations ratchet up? How to distinguish types of regulatory stringency and patterns of change', *Organization & Environment*, 33(1), pp. 96–125.

Keohane, R. O. (1984) *After Hegemony: Cooperation and Discord in World Political Economy*. Princeton, NJ: Princeton University Press.

Kill, J. (2019) *Redd+: A Lost Decade for International Forest Conservation*. Heinrich Boll Stiftung: The Green Political Foundation.

Kishan, S. (2021) 'Corporate climate efforts lack impact, say former sustainability executives: They're speaking out, pushing for more aggressive government policies to address societal problems', *Bloomberg*, June 3.

Kreibich, N. and Hermwille, L. (2021) 'Caught in between: Credibility and feasibility of the voluntary carbon market post-2020', *Climate Policy*, 21(7), pp. 939–957.

Kütting, G. (2000). *Environment, Society, and International Relations: Towards More Effective International Environmental Agreements*. London: Routledge.

Ladu, L. and Blind, K. (2017). 'Overview of policies, standards and certifications supporting the european bio-based economy', *Current Opinion in Green and Sustainable Chemistry*, 8, pp. 30–35.

Lambin, E. F., Gibbs, H. K., Heilmayr, R., Carlson, K. M., Fleck, L. C., Garrett, R. D., le Polain de Waroux, Y., McDermott, C. L., McLaughlin, D., Newton, P. and Nolte, C. (2018) 'The role of supply-chain initiatives in reducing deforestation', *Nature Climate Change*, 8(2), pp. 109–116.

Myers Madeira, E., Blockhus, J. and Ganz, D. J. (2013) 'Community participation and benefits in Redd+: A review of initial outcomes and lessons', *Forests*, 4(2), pp. 296–318.

Lawson, S. (2014) 'Consumer goods and deforestation: An analysis of the extent and nature of illegality in forest conversion for agriculture and timber plantations', in *Forest Trends Report Series, Forest Trade and Finance*. https://www.forest-trends.org/wp-content/uploads/imported/for168-consumer-goods-and-deforestation-letter-14-0916-hr-no-crops_web-pdf.pdf.

Lehman, S. (2008) *Environmentalists Turn to Consumers for Help in Curbing Amazon Forest Devastation*. Worldstream: Associated Press, 11 April 2000 [cited 21 July 2008]. http://www.lexisnexis.com/

Lippke, B. R., Gilles, J. K., Lee, R. G. and Sommers, P. E. (1990) 'Three-state impact of spotted owl conservation and other timber harvest reductions: A cooperative evaluation of the economic and social impacts', University of Washington, University of California, Oregon State Univeristy Institute of Forest Resources.

Liu, M., Feng, X., Wang, S. and Qiu, H. (2020) 'China's poverty alleviation over the last 40 years: Successes and challenges', *Australian Journal of Agricultural and Resource Economics*, 64(1), pp. 209–228.

Loayza, N. V. and Raddatz, C. (2010). 'The composition of growth matters for poverty alleviation', *Journal of Development Economics*, 93(1), pp. 137–151.

McAfee, K. 1999. 'Selling nature to save it? Biodiversity and green developmentaiism', *Environment and Planning D: Society and Space*, 17, 22.

McDermott, C., Cashore, B. W. and Kanowski, P. (2010) *Global Environmental Forest Policies: An International Comparison*. London: England Earthscan.

McKenna, B. (1992) 'Cod shutdown casts doubt on newfoundland economy', *The Toronto Star*, 4 July.

MDB Joint Statement (2021) *Joint Statement by the Multilateral Development Banks: Nature, People and Planet*. https://ukcop26.org/mdb-joint-statement/.

Mendlewicz, M. (2017) *An Assessment of No-Deforestation Commitments in the Brazilian Amazon: The Case of Soy and Cattle in Mato Grosso*. New Haven, CT: Yale School of Forestry & Environmental Studies.

Milne, S., Mahanty, S., To, P., Dressler, W., Kanowski, P. and Thavat, M. (2018) 'Learning from 'Actually Existing' Redd+: A synthesis of ethnographic findings', *Conservation and Society*, 1, pp. 84–95.

Nathan, I. and Pasgaard, M. (2017) 'Is Redd+ Effective, Efficient, and Equitable? Learning from a Redd+ Project in Northern Cambodia', *Geoforum*, 83, pp. 26–38.

Nordhaus, W. D. (2017) 'Revisiting the social cost of carbon', *Proceedings of the National Academy of Sciences*, 114(7), pp. 1518–1523.

Ostrom, E. (1986). 'An agenda for the study of institutions', *Public Choice*, 48, pp. 3–25.

Ostrom, E. (1990) *Governing the Commons: The Evolution of Institutions for Collective Action*. Cambridge: Cambridge University Press.

Ostrom, E. (1999) 'Coping with tragedies of the commons', *Annual Review of Political Science*, 2, pp. 493–535.

Ou, Y., Iyer, G., Clarke, L., Edmonds, J., Fawcett, A. A., Hultman, N., McFarland, J. R., Binsted, M., Cui, R., Fyson, C. and Geiges, A. (2021) 'Can updated climate pledges limit warming well below 2°C?' *Science*, 374(6568), pp. 693–695.

Overdevest, C. and Zeitlin, J. (2016) 'Experimentalism in transnational forest governance: Implementing Eu Forest Law Enforcement Governance and Trade (FLEGT) voluntary partnership agreements in Indonesia and Ghana', The Amsterdam Centre for Contemporary European Studies SSRN Research Paper 2016/02.

Panwar, R. (2021) 'Optimism amid despair: How to avoid a net-zero debacle', *Business & Society*: 00076503211053816.

Peskett, L., Schreckenberg, K. and Brown, J. (2011) 'Institutional approaches for carbon financing in the forest sector: Learning lessons for Redd+ from forest carbon projects in Uganda', *Environmental Science & Policy*, 14(2), pp. 216–229.

Pinchot, G. (1987) *Breaking New Ground*. Washington, DC: Island Press.

Pistorius, T. (2012) 'From red to Redd+: The evolution of a forest-based mitigation approach for developing countries', *Current Opinion in Environmental Sustainability*, 4(6), pp. 638–645.

Potoski, M. and Prakash, A. (2005) 'Covenants with weak swords: Iso 14001 and facilities' environmental performance', *Journal of Policy Analysis and Management*, 24(4), pp. 745–769.

Rainforest Alliance (2007) *About the Rainforest Alliance: Our History Timeline* [Archived webpage]. Rainforest Alliance, 31 October 2001 [cited 15 March 2007]. http://web.archive.org/web/20010627082518/www.rainforestalliance.org/about/history2.html#1986.

Reeve, R. (2006) *The Forest Stewardship Council Aims, Principles and Criteria: A Critical Examination Predicting Failure* [Resolution]. Rettet den Regenwald e. V, 30 September 1993 [cited 5 December 2006]. http://forests.org/archive/general/fsc.htm.

Reytar, K. and Veit, P. (2016) 'Indigenous peoples and local communities are the world's secret weapon in curbing climate change', World Resources Institute.

Ricketts, T. H., Soares-Filho, B., da Fonseca, G. A., Nepstad, D., Pfaff, A., Petsonk, A., Anderson, A., Boucher, D., Cattaneo, A., Conte, M. and Creighton, K. (2010) 'Indigenous lands, protected areas, and slowing climate change', *PLoS Biology*, 8(3), e1000331.

Risse, T. (2011) 'Governance in areas of limited statehood: Introduction and overview', in T. Risse (ed.), *Governance without a State: Policies and Politics in Areas of Limited Statehood*. New York: Columbia University Press, pp. 1–38.

Sachs, J. D. (2006) *The End of Poverty: Economic Possibilities for Our Time*. New York: Penguin.

Salles, J.-M. (2011) 'Valuing biodiversity and ecosystem services: Why put economic values on nature?', *Comptes Rendus Biologies*, 334(5–6), pp. 469–482.

Santilli, M., Moutinho, P., Schwartzman, S., Nepstad, D., Curran, L. and Nobre, C. (2005) 'Tropical deforestation and the kyoto protocol', *Climatic Change*, 71, pp. 267–276.

Scheyvens, R., Banks, G. and Hughes, E. (2016) 'The private sector and the SDGS: The need to move beyond 'Business as Usual', *Sustainable Development*, 24(6), pp. 371–382.

Seymour, F. (2008) 'Forests, climate change, and human rights: managing risk and trade-offs', Center for International Forestry Research.

Sharma, S. (1998) *A Theory of Corporate Environmental Responsiveness*. London: St. Mary's University.

Spies, T. A., Stine, P. A., Gravenmier, R. A., Long, J. W. and Reilly, M. J. (2018) 'Synthesis of science to inform land management within the northwest forest plan area', in *General Technical Report PNW-GTR-966*. Portland, OR: US Department of Agriculture, Forest Service, Pacific Northwest Research Station.

Stickler, C. M., Nepstad, D. C., Coe, M. T., McGrath, D. G., Rodrigues, H. O., Walker, W. S., SOARES-FILHO, B. S. and Davidson, E. A. (2009) 'The potential ecological costs and cobenefits of Redd: A critical review and case study from the amazon region', *Global Change Biology*, 15(12), pp. 2803–2824.

Sukhdev, P., Prabhu, R., Kumar, P., Bassi, A., Patwa-Shah, W., Enters, T., Labbate, G. and Greenwalt, J., (2011) 'Redd+ and a green economy: Opportunities for a mutually supportive relationship', *UN-REDD Programme Policy Brief Issue#01*. https://www.uncclearn. org/resources/library/redd-and-a-green-economy-opportunities-for-a-mutually-supportive-relationship/.

*The Guardian* (2021) 'World leaders have agreed a deal that aims to halt and reverse global deforestation over the next decade as part of a multibillion-dollar package to tackle human-caused greenhouse gas emissions', *The Guardian* (London) 2021 [cited 3 November 2021]. https://www.theguardian.com/environment/2021/nov/01/biden-bolsonaro-and-xi-among-leaders-agreeing-to-end-deforestation-aoe.

Thomas, V. and Chindarkar, N. (2019) *Economic Evaluation of Sustainable Development*. New York: Palgrave Macmillan.

Tickell, O. (2008) *Part-Certified Products May Carry Fsc Logo*. Timber Trades Journal, 18 January 1997 [cited 20 July 2008]. http://www.lexisnexis.com/.

Tollefson, C., Gale, F. and Haley, D. (2008) *Setting the Standard: Certification, Governance, and the Forest Stewardship Council*. Vancouver: UBC Press.

Tribe, L. H. (1972) 'Policy science: Analysis or ideology?', *Philosophy & Public Affairs*, 2(1), pp. 66–110.

UN Environment (2020) 'The UN environment programme and nature-based solutions', in U. Environment (ed.), *UNEP at 75th Session of the UN General Assembly Our Positions*.

van der Ven, H. and Cashore, B. (2018) 'Forest certification: The challenge of measuring impacts', *Current Opinion in Environmental Sustainability*, 32, pp. 104–111.

Van der Ven, H., Rothacker, C. and Cashore, B. (2018, September) 'Do eco-labels prevent deforestation? Lessons from non-state market driven governance in the soy, palm
oil, and cocoa sectors', *Global Environment Change*, 52, pp. 141–151.

Victor, D. (2015) 'Why paris worked: A different approach to climate diplomacy', *Yale
Environment 360*, December 15.

Visseren-Hamakers, I. J., Cashore, B., Loorbach, D., Kok, M. T. J., Koning, S. D., Vull-
ers, P. and van Veen, A.C. (2021) 'How to save a million species? Transformative
governance through prioritization', in I. Visseren-Hamakers and M. Kok (eds.), *Transforming Biodiversity Governance*. Cambridge: Cambridge University Press, pp. 67–90.

Visseren-Hamakers, I. J., McDermott, C., Vijge, M. J. and Cashore, B. (2012) 'Trade-
offs, co-benefits and safeguards: Current debates on the breadth of Redd+', *Current
Opinion in Environmental Sustainability*, 4(6), pp. 646–653.

Waltz, K. N. (1959) *Man, the State and War: A Theoretical Analysis*. New York: Columbia
University Press.

WCED (1987) *Our Common Future*. Oxford: Oxford University Press.

Wodschow, A., Nathan, I. and Cerutti, P. (2016) 'Participation, public policy-making,
and legitimacy in the EU voluntary partnership agreement process: The cameroon
case', *Forest Policy and Economics*, 63(1), pp. 1–10.

Young, O. R. (2003) 'Determining regime effectiveness: A commentary on the oslo-potsdam solution', *Global Environmental Politics*, 3(3), pp. 97–104.

Zhu, X., Ravnkilde Moeller, L., De Lopez, T. and Romero, M. Z. (2010). 'Pathways for
implementing Redd +. Experiences from carbon markets and communities', UNEP
Riso Centre.

# 9

# INTACT FOREST LANDSCAPES AND THE FOREST STEWARDSHIP COUNCIL

## Lessons for NGO–Business Cooperation

*William Nikolakis and Peter Wood*

## 1 Introduction

Businesses and non-government organisations (NGOs) are powerful actors who produce rules and norms that affect socio-ecological systems (Cashore, 2002; Yaziji and Doh, 2009). Both have access to unique resources, capabilities, and networks to influence change on local to global scales. Because of this, partnerships between NGOs and businesses are viewed as critical for achieving sustainable development goals (Hartman et al., 1999), as already identified in Chapter 2. Drawing on distinct sectoral resources, networks and capabilities can, in theory, facilitate knowledge sharing to solve complex problems (Laasonen et al., 2012). However, there are some obvious challenges to NGO and business partnerships for sustainable development: they have distinct and often conflicting interests and values, with businesses generating profits for shareholders (though this is changing) and NGOs aiming to achieve a public good (Nikolakis and Innes, 2020). This can lead to different goals, objectives, and timeframes. All these interactions and relationships exist within the broader political economy and the market forces that inform the relative position actors who are entering into partnership (Moog et al., 2015; Ferns and Amaeshi, 2019; Broad et al., 2020).

Indeed, the differences between NGOs and business may be difficult to bridge, and result in competition (and conflict) rather than cooperation. Nevertheless, NGOs and business do cooperate: but under what conditions does this emerge, and can it be sustained? The literature provides insights into how inter-organisational cooperation is enabled, taking culture into consideration. Chen et al. (1998) theorised six enabling conditions for cooperation: a superordinate goal, group identity, trust, accountability, communication, and reward distribution. The unique nature of each context and the dynamic socio-institutional conditions in which cooperation is embedded makes general 'enabling conditions' problematic.

DOI: 10.4324/9781003003588-12

We note a significant body of literature on NGO–business cooperation, but this is largely divided into *collaboration* (or bringing dynamic capabilities together) *and adversarialism* (strategies for competing) (Laasonen et al., 2012), and there is little scholarly literature on what enables cooperation.

Drawing on the case of the Forest Stewardship Council (FSC), this chapter discusses the six enabling conditions for cooperation between NGOs and business. The FSC is a non-state market-based certification system with strong NGO and business involvement (Cashore, 2002; Schepers, 2010; Moog et al., 2015). When it emerged in 1993, NGOs and Indigenous Peoples were optimistic that the FSC's unique governance structure would level the playing field with business, drawing upon market forces and eco-labelling to reward companies that meet the FSC's standards (Cashore, 2002). The FSC sought to certify forests that are managed 'responsibly'. However, what this ultimately means, and therefore which forests are eligible for certification, has been debated ever since.

This chapter focuses on the contentious concept of Intact Forest Landscapes (IFLs), an 'unbroken expanse of natural ecosystems within the zone of current forest extent, showing no signs of significant human activity, and large enough that all native biodiversity, including viable populations of wide-ranging species, could be maintained' (Potapov et al., 2008, p. 2). IFLs are critically important for mitigating climate change, maintaining water supplies, safeguarding biodiversity, and protecting human health (Watson et al., 2018).

Restricting IFLs from the FSC is challenging and leads to the question of whether NGOs and business truly have 'shared goals, or whether they are simply 'strange bedfellows', brought together, but with fundamentally different goals that preclude true cooperation. As some scholars suggest, NGO–business collaboration need not be about reaching consensus and agreement, but conflict and tension is critical for sustainability (Laasonen et al., 2012; Brand et al., 2020). Using a theoretical framework to evaluate cooperation and the contextual hegemonic factors, this chapter provides an overview of current thinking on NGO–business cooperation and, focusing on the FSC case, examines the dynamics of NGO–business competition and cooperation related to IFLs.

## 2 NGOs and Business Cooperation

The literature on NGO–business cooperation is interdisciplinary, spanning management, psychology, and planning disciplines. One body of literature is positive about the potential for NGO–business cooperation to address a range of complex problems such as sustainable development. Under this perspective, both parties bring unique resources together, that is, typically, firms bring resources and NGOs bring legitimacy (*a resource dependency perspective*) (see Murphy and Bendell, 1999; Linton, 2005; Yaziji and Doh, 2009; Eden and Bear, 2010; Bendell, 2017). However, another body of literature is cynical about whether the goals and interests of NGOs and businesses can ever be truly aligned, let alone solve deeply rooted systemic issues such as sustainable development (*adversarial perspective*) (see Schepers, 2006; Murphy and Bendell, 1999; Hussain and Moriarty, 2018). Scholars from the adversarial perspective argue that NGOs offer an important disciplinary and regulatory role for firms on sustainable development and should maintain this independence (Hussain and Moriarty, 2018; Brand et al., 2020).

There is little literature on the role of conflict in NGO–business collaborations – a major gap according to Laasonen et al. (2012), who suggest that conflict is important for cooperation. Indeed, Brand et al. (2020) argue that seeking consensus in NGO–business collaborations is misguided and imposes unnecessary limitations on engagement. Moog et al. (2015) observed that in the multi-stakeholder FSC governance system, seeking consensus among member excludes opposing and radical views – this has undermined the FSC's legitimacy and limited broader cooperation among diverse actors.

A number of studies have documented resource dependency and conflict perspectives. Nahi (2018) observed that the sustainable development agenda is driving cross-sectoral collaboration and concluded that NGOs and business generate shared value (social outcomes for NGOs, and profits for business). For successful cross-sectoral partnerships in the Marine Stewardship Council, Fowler and Heap (1998) found that sufficient resources, shared goals, and skilled and sensitive management were essential conditions. They noted that it is easier to translate environmental goals into business goals than it is to translate business goals into environmental goals.

De Lange et al. (2016) applied complexity theory to illuminate how NGOs and business change from foes to friends. They conceptualised a process of 'mutual adaptation', in which cooperation enables future gazing and communication and joint strategic responses to future trends. They documented that, although sharing capabilities enables mutual adaptation and cooperation, there must also be shared strategic objectives. Creating shared objectives is a challenge, given the distinct institutional logics of NGOs and business and their distinct cultures (Crane, 1998).

Laasonen et al. (2012) and Joutsenvirta (2011) argued that discourse between NGOs and business is critical for implementing sustainability, with literature emphasising a 'discourse legitimation struggle'. Discourse encompasses ideas, beliefs, and assertions, and Humphreys (2009) articulates a distinction between *discourse as knowledge* and *discourse as ideology*. He noted the growth of neoliberalism in forest policy and governance through a *discourse of ideology*, which emphasises and legitimates private regulation (like the FSC). Joutsenvirta (2011) observed the '…rational and moral struggles around contested issues – and the linguistic patterns and moves they contained – acted as a mechanism that (re) defined what [corporate social responsibility] CSR and its boundaries were in a specific setting at a given point of time' (p. 71). Forestry companies frame themselves as socially and environmentally conscious, whereas NGOs challenge this moral status and define CSR. Forestry companies can collaborate with NGOs to define these CSR standards, guided and influenced by social norms and trends; but co-opting CSR standards by business interests involves a risk (Hussain and Moriarty, 2018). As Ferns and Amaeshi (2019) concluded, hegemonic processes are at play in NGO–business cooperation, as one coalition attempts to prevail over the other, typically through discourse interactions. They conceptualised a spectrum of discourse interaction from maintaining the *status quo*, to reforms, through to transformative change.

## 2.1 Cooperation Framework

Inter-organisational cooperation involves commitments (binding and non-binding, formal or non-formal) to work towards common goals, through structured or unstructured processes. Often resources and capabilities are combined to pursue these common goals (Morrow et al., 2004; Nikolakis and Guðjónsson, 2021). Chen et al. (1998) conceptualised six mechanisms that positively influence inter-organisational cooperation and are shaped by the culture in which the cooperation is embedded (be it individualist or collectivist). Cultural dynamics influence cooperation in different ways, as norms and values enable (or constrain) cooperative interactions. Figure 9.1 illustrates the dynamics of this cooperation framework, shaped by cultural dynamics.

- First, a *superordinate goal*, or a goal that is perceived as interdependent in individualist cultures (where individual goal achievement is dependent on another achieving their goal), or as a shared goal in collective cultures.

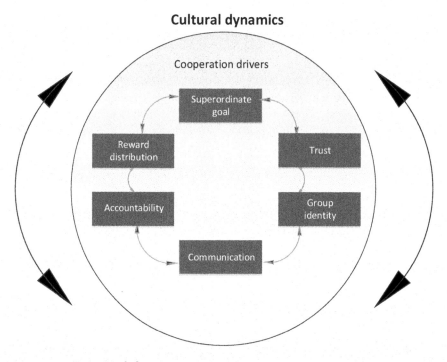

**FIGURE 9.1** Framework for cooperation.

- Second, the level of importance of *group identity* enhancement in a culture (enhancing standing in the group).
- Third, whether *trust* is based on cognition (rational) or affect (emotional).
- Fourth, whether *accountability* mechanisms are more individualised (that is, when the individual internalises accountability and responsibility to perform commitments), or whether group accountability and social pressures are more determinative.
- Fifth, whether partial *communication* or full communication channels are used. Partial communication involves more socially distant forms of communication, such as email or phone, which is favoured in more individualist cultures, whereas in collectivist cultures, the preference is of full communication channels, or face-to-face communication.
- Sixth, whether *reward distribution* is based on equity (contribution) or equality.

## 3 The FSC and the Exclusion of IFLs

This section examines the stakeholder dynamics within the FSC, and the deep divisions that emerged from an NGO proposal to exclude large IFLs from the FSC system. The issue of IFLs exacerbated existing tensions, exposing the vastly different interests of each.

### 3.1 Origin, Structure, and Power Dynamics of the FSC

FSC governance is based on a cooperative, consensus-based approach, attempting to balance the interests of environmental, social, and economic actors, organised into distinct 'chambers', with membership and voting rights distributed accordingly, and balanced for global North and South representation. For most jurisdictions, this represents a departure from the power imbalance experienced by environmental, social, and Indigenous actors outside this forum, who are normally outmatched by government-industry interests.

The FSC's collaborative approach to establishing forestry certification standards is unique. Although the core principles and criteria of certification standards are globally established, they are further developed and tailored to local contexts by national and sub-national working groups. This power-sharing governance structure comes with built-in tension: the FSC relies on the support and endorsement of NGOs and Indigenous Peoples for its credibility and legitimacy (Nikolakis et al., 2012, 2014), but it also relies on business participation and membership for its operational budget and market presence (Schepers, 2010).

The process of developing FSC's standards has been intense and political, at both the international and local levels, because much is at stake for each chamber, FSC offices and staff, and accredited certifying bodies. NGOs and Indigenous groups are potentially at a reputational risk associated with weak standards (or weak application). Standards higher than regulations can pose a risk to forestry firms' profitability and timber access (Sharma and Henriques, 2005). Accredited certification bodies, which, as members of the Economic Chamber also hold voting rights, have an interest in ensuring that as much forest area as possible is eligible for certification, to maximise demand for their auditing services (Schepers, 2010). Certifying bodies compete for business, and critics argue that this encourages a 'race to the bottom', as companies hire certifiers that are perceived as less stringent in the application of standards (Tollefson et al., 2009). Consequently, NGOs have pushed for more pre-scriptive standards that are less open to interpretation (McDermott, 2012).

Moreover, the chambers are far from homogeneous in composition, often resulting in conflicting positions among actors with seemingly similar goals. For example, firms addressing an eco-conscious market are likely to be more concerned about having the FSC brand tarnished by controversies than standards being set too high. Similarly, certification bodies that believe they hold a 'higher bar' than others have an interest in ensuring more prescriptive standards. Finally, the budgets of FSC International and national offices are largely supported by membership dues and certification fees, resulting in constant pressure to increase the number of participating companies and areas certified.

Legitimacy issues have called into question whether FSC deserves its rep-utation as a model multi-stakeholder governance forum (Moog et al., 2015). Increasingly frequent scandals and a resulting decline in consumer confidence in its integrity have prompted high-profile defections by founding NGOs.

One of the main factors undermining the position of NGOs is a lack of alternative channels through which to achieve their goals, given the failures of international governmental efforts to address deforestation (e.g., the sustainable management of forests was defined loosely enough that industrial plantations were conflated with primary and intact forests) (Mackey et al., 2015) and the lack of an alternative certification system for the FSC.

Business, on the other hand, successfully established an alternative to the FSC – the Programme for the Endorsement of Forest Certification (PEFC) and its national affiliates, often with the support of national governments interested in minimising the FSC's market power. The proliferation of competing sys-tems confused the marketplace and consumers; and despite attempts by NGOs to discredit these industry-led systems (e.g., FERN, 2001), the lack of strong consumer/market preference for the FSC weakened the position of the NGOs (as well as that of the FSC) and strengthened that of business.

The increasing complexity of the FSC system imposed a significant burden on NGO resources, and over time, this outpaced their ability to meaningfully engage in standards and policy development and play an on-the-ground watch-dog role (Moog et al., 2015). Thus, business came to dominate the policy and standards discussions (Hussain and Moriarty, 2018), having more resources to engage in lengthy technical processes, greater financial power (FSC offices were financially dependent on business to pay for operations), and a tight relationship with large NGOs (most notably WWF and their Global Forest and Trade Net-work) that supported business interests.

### *3.2 Relaxed Rules, Rapid Expansion*

One of the most contentious issues in the FSC has been the certification of primary forest logging (Poore, 2003). The protection of these forests was one of the main motivating factors for NGOs and Indigenous Peoples to support the creation of FSC in the first place.

In its early days (1995), the FSC restricted products originating from primary forests (Principle 9), simply stating that: *'Primary forests, well-developed secondary forests, and sites of major environmental, social or cultural significance shall be conserved'* (FSC, 2010). In 1999, following the outcome of a working group, this principle was amended to allow logging in primary forests, but only if high conservation values were protected. This allowed for expansion of the area eligible for certification, and rapid growth of the FSC system. However, critics contested that a loose interpretation of this concept by certifying bodies resulted in a 'slippery slope' and that logging should not have been certified in primary forests (Greenpeace, 2008). As certifications began to proliferate, monitoring became difficult, as proving the loss of specific high conservation values of a primary forest required significantly more resources and technical expertise than simply excluding primary forests from the system.

In 2004, following pressure from Economic Chamber members, the 'FSC Mixed' system was introduced, allowing non-certified material to be included in FSC-labelled products, resulting in the rapid expansion of the FSC. A new 'Controlled Wood' policy was intended to coarsely screen for 'unacceptable' sources (e.g., from illegal logging, logging that violated civil rights, and High Conservation Value Forests). However, the processes and standards established to oversee this system were very complicated and time consuming, favouring the participation of better-resourced Economic Chamber members and limiting the capacity of Environmental and Social Chamber members. The system allowed companies to source from massive areas of non-certified forest, making monitoring difficult. NGOs repeatedly brought to light controversial sources of wood that had been certified (Hance, 2011; Greenpeace, 2013).

Due to many of the controversial issues assigned to working groups and technical committees, reaching consensus took years. Attempts by the FSC to address these problems exacerbated this dynamic (Greenpeace, 2010). Environmental and social groups were able to offset business' advantage in these processes to some degree, thanks to their ability to bring media attention to bad conduct (Conniff, 2018). Several founding NGOs quit the FSC in protest of what they saw as a variety of failings, including Robinwood (2009), the Swedish Society for Nature Conservation (2010), and FERN (2011).

NGOs that continued to belong to the FSC despite these findings, including Greenpeace and the Rainforest Action Network, faced criticism and public campaigns for lending the FSC their credibility and enabling the 'greenwashing' of primary forest logging (Hance, 2010). These groups justified their continued participation by claiming that by remaining members, they were better able to hold FSC to account and make efforts to change the system from within. They continued to do so for several more years.

## 3.3 Business Resists IFL Exclusion, NGOs Compromise

A growing awareness was evolving in the scientific community of the unique characteristics associated with IFLs, and their rapid decline in area worldwide (Box 9.1).

NGOs quickly adopted the IFL framing to prioritise their conservation, also within the FSC. The binary nature of the IFL's concept contrasted with the more malleable concept of High Conservation Value Forest (HCVF), which resulted in protracted debates over whether forest management had, in fact, impacted the conservation values of primary forests. The surface area of (and threats to) IFLs is more easily monitored than the maintenance of high conservation values, as remote sensing can quickly detect the appearance of logging roads and skid trails (de Wasseige and Defourny, 2004). The notion of IFLs also bypassed the quagmire of defining 'sustainable forest management', which inevitably favoured business interests with greater resources and capacity. Primary forest logging is also known to follow a pattern of boom-and-bust, in which an initial spike in economic activity is followed by a sharp decline once the resource is depleted (e.g., Rodrigues, 2009); NGOs' push to restrict IFL logging within the FSC reflected their wariness of certifying the 'boom' phase.

In 2011, Greenpeace released a report calling for the protection of IFLs but was careful to emphasise that this was due to industrial exploitation, and not traditional/Indigenous use, and that Indigenous Peoples' rights must be respected in the process (Greenpeace, 2011). Some members of the Economic Chamber cautioned that excluding IFLs from logging would severely constrain firms. However, this was precisely the goal of NGOs or others seeking to spare IFLs. Success for NGOs was a loss for firms. Moreover, excluding IFLs from the FSC would not necessarily result in protection, as IFLs excluded from the FSC would still be available for non-FSC-certified companies to log.[1]

Greenpeace tabled a motion (Motion 65) at the FSC General Assembly in 2014, to restrict IFL logging in FSC-certified forests, but softened on some points (Greenpeace, 2011). For example, IFL logging would be allowed if 'a comprehensive and representative protected area network has been established', if 'priority has been given to small-scale and low-impact community forest use wherever appropriate', and if 'the buffer around the core road-building and other fragmentation impacts are avoided or minimized' (FSC Watch, 2014). However, following significant pushback from business interests, even this language was further watered down, and several more loopholes were introduced, allowing more logging in IFLs. In the end, the motion deferred to local standards development groups to determine specific levels of protection. If these were not in place by 2016, a default 80% 'core IFL' protection per forest management unit (FMU) would be applied (FSC, 2014). In the end, the motion was passed

---

## Box 9.1 Intact forest landscapes

Only 36% of Earth's remaining forests are considered primary forests (Mackey et al., 2014), and 18% qualifies as 'intact' (more than 500 km$^2$ contiguous square kilometres, according to Potapov et al.). The fact that Earth has lost around 35% of its pre-industrial forest cover means that IFLs have been reduced to 11.7% of what once was forested. Only 12% of remaining IFL (or 1.4% of all pre-industrial forest cover) is protected (Potapov et al., 2017). More than 70% of the remaining IFL is in five countries (Russia, Canada, Brazil, the Democratic Republic of the Congo, and Indonesia), with 50% of this located in boreal forest, 46% in equatorial, and 3% in temperate (Mackey et al., 2014).

Since the inception of the FSC, much has been learned about what drives forest loss, and a greater appreciation of the impacts of forest *degradation*, as opposed to outright deforestation. Processes such as REDD+ have placed greater emphasis on the role of other sectors, namely agriculture, in converting forests to other uses.

Although logging may not cause immediate deforestation (tropical forest logging is done selectively, as marketable species are found at low densities), it causes widespread degradation (Pearson et al., 2017) and plays a facilitating role in the eventual conversion of forest to other uses. Forestry infrastructure, most notably road building, is known to be responsible for introducing illegal logging, poaching, and development pressures, particularly in areas with poor governance (Laurance et al., 2009), with increased human immigration and degradation of natural resources following in its wake (Morgan et al., 2019).

---

by a substantial majority (99% support from Environmental and Social chambers, including Indigenous Peoples' organisations, and 73% from the Economic Chamber; Greenpeace, 2015). One critic lamented that 'Greenpeace's endorsement of Motion 65 means that it has driven a bulldozer and logging truck over its former demands to protect intact forests' (FSC-Watch, 2014).

Canada, Brazil, Russia, and the Congo Basin were priorities for the implementation of Motion 65, as they contained the vast majority of the remaining IFLs. This took the form of creating additional, complex processes for considering whether/how the policy should be implemented at the national/regional level, including complex formulas for logging in IFLs. The FSC received considerable pushback from business interests in these countries, often with the support of local FSC staff.[2] Business interests in the Congo Basin were successful in reducing the exclusion of 'core' IFL areas to 50% in this region. In 2016, the FSC International Board of Directors backtracked on Motion 65, citing the potential for 'significant undesired side effects' in IFL countries, and issued an 'advice note' allowing logging within IFLs to continue, as long as this did not impact more than 20% of the IFLs within the FMU, and did not reduce any IFLs below the 50,000 ha threshold in the landscape (FSC, 2017).

A major rift between business and NGOs became visible at the 2017 General Assembly in Vancouver, Canada. The Economic Chamber took an unprecedented hard line and voted as a block, opposing several motions put forward by the Environmental and Social Chambers (Rossoman, 2017), and passed a motion calling for regional studies of the impact of excluding IFLs (emphasising business impacts). Shortly after, in March 2018, Greenpeace International resigned from the FSC, 'due to inconsistent implementation and failures to protect forests', leaving it to national offices to decide whether to continue to engage with local initiatives (Greenpeace, 2018).

Now in 2021, certain members of the Economic Chamber are continuing to push back on excluding IFLs from the FSC. One industry association wrote that there is 'still work to do to achieve consensus', ignoring the high level of approval the original motion had received. This calls for the IFL policy to be re-opened for discussion at the next General Assembly, and notes industry's preference for conserving only 20% of IFLs (European Sustainable Timber Coalition, republished by FSC International, 2020).

## 3.4 The Future of IFL in the FSC and Other Policy Venues

Given the strong influence of business over national and regional FSC offices, such as in Canada and the Congo Basin, it is likely that the percentage of IFLs excluded from logging will be significantly less than the 80% protection recommended in Motion 65. At the next General Assembly, members will consider the results of the Motion 65 impact assessments, heavily geared towards business interests. For example, a Congo Basin study recommends capping IFL protection at 20%, cautioning that greater protection will cause companies to give up their FSC certificates, despite also noting that only 1.4% of all Congo Basin IFL area is located within FSC concessions (Form International, 2020).

Instead of the relatively straightforward approach of excluding IFLs completely, what instead was developed were complex mathematical formulas for determining what percentage of each IFL per FMU can be logged, making it very difficult to ensure compliance and introducing room for interpretation by certifying bodies. This created a very complicated and protracted series of processes favouring well-resourced business members. In doing so, businesses successfully neutralise the threat posed by the simple-yet-powerful binary framing (intact/non-intact) initially proposed by NGOs.

While the IFL concept was being deliberated within the FSC, alternative policy venues for pursuing the protection of forests emerged. The most notable was REDD+[3] (within the UNFCCC), promising financial incentives to reduce deforestation and forest degradation. REDD+ surpassed forest certification in terms of its importance to NGOs in the international forest regime (at least in the tropics). However, REDD+ presented its own risks and limitations for NGOs, such as including primary forest logging in the sustainable management of forests (and qualifying for REDD+ funding and credits) (Griscom et al., 2014).

## 4 Examining Enabling Conditions in FSC's NGO–Business Cooperation

The six cooperation levers in Figure 9.1 can be used to examine the enabling conditions in the FSC for NGO–business cooperation. First, the **superordinate goal** of encouraging 'responsible' forest management catalysed NGO–business cooperation in the FSC. This vague term allowed different actors to come together and held much promise – NGOs could achieve their conservation goals, and firms could obtain social licences and market access (a resource dependency perspective). However, as goal specificity increased over time (through principles, criteria, and indicators), and the rapid expansion of FSC brought larger industrial operations into the mix, the distance in positions between NGOs and business became starkly apparent. The binary nature of IFLs in particular brought long-simmering differences to a head. For NGOs focused on stopping deforestation, IFLs were home to the 'best of the last' remaining primary forest, and the Indigenous populations that depended upon them. Excluding IFLs from FSC-certified logging was far from a radical idea, compared to FSC's original standard that excluded all primary forest logging, whether intact or not. Many NGOs considered it a bare minimum first step towards achieving sustainability (restricting FSC-certified logging to the 90% of the world's original forest cover already logged). Meanwhile, business (though not all Economic Chamber members) maintained that all forests should be eligible for 'sustainable management'. Thus, the IFL issue revealed that there was no longer a shared superordinate goal, if indeed there ever had been one.

Second, in terms of **group identity**, while FSC promotes a pluralistic form of governance within the three chambers, the IFL issue exposed deep divisions and an in- and out group identity between and within chambers. The fact that some FSC Economic Chamber members actively supported and worked with the competing PEFC system indicated this lack of shared 'group identity'. Indeed, even in the Environmental Chamber, the scope of IFL caused rifts, with some Environmental Chamber members supporting members in the Economic Chamber who supported limiting the IFL standard. Cultural differences between NGOs and business (Crane, 1998), and among the different actors from across the world, also contributed to the lack of shared group identity between NGOs and business – which was likely to have negative trust implications.

The third lever of cooperation was **trust**: rational or emotional forms of trust can promote and sustain cooperation towards a superordinate goal. Trust was slowly built across the different chambers. However, trust is eroded through conflict, particularly when positions are binary and competitive. Increased complexity and the scale of the FSC system made it difficult for NGOs to engage with the system and monitor implementation, though specific controversial certifications gave them cause to distrust. The IFL issue (particularly business' and FSC's attempts to undermine Motion 65) exposed competing interests and mitigated trust, which had negative implications for cooperation (and even participation in the system).

Another factor, and the fourth lever of cooperation, was **accountability**: when NGOs and business are accountable to different and oft-competing interests. While some group accountability was produced within the FSC mechanisms, businesses remained accountable to their shareholders and NGOs to their members (to deliver on their goals; e.g., to stop deforestation). This situation limited cooperation, particularly when consensus was an important precondition for action.

The fifth lever of cooperation was **communication**. Dialogue is central to NGO–business collaborations (Laasonen et al., 2012), and critical for NGOs and businesses when defining sustainability in the forest sector (Joutsenvirta, 2011). The FSC created a mechanism for face-to-face communication in the form of a series of meetings (the IFL Solutions Forum), which in theory had positive effects on trust and enabled cooperation (Chen et al., 1998). However, much of this focused on mitigating the impact of Motion 65 on business and eventually led to the FSC further relaxing restrictions. It is difficult to know whether this additional communication resulted in reciprocal cooperation on the part of business.

The sixth lever of cooperation was **reward distribution**. The FSC rewards certified businesses with the social licence to sell their products (something that is more important when sourcing from controversial areas), and sometimes (but not always) a market premium. The reward for participating NGOs was less tangible – it allowed them to be able to direct market demand to a type of forest management that they did support, and to report to their members that they were making the industry's practices more sustainable. Although not directly relevant to this study, the norm differences in the benefits of cooperation, and how these benefits should be distributed, were distinct and compete for IFLs, with binary positions and outcomes that likely frustrate cooperation.

Figure 9.2 illustrates that larger forces provided business interests with more power to achieve their own goals; and several factors mitigated NGOs from insisting on tougher FSC standards (Moog et al., 2015), including restricting logging in IFLs. In applying the cooperation framework, we note this framework neglects broader power dynamics – that is, differences in resources and power, or what Ferns and Amaeshi (2019) refer to as 'hegemonic processes', which can shape (or constrain) cooperation. In the case of IFLs, NGOs were faced with either going along with business or quitting, and many did the latter. The 'double compromise' outcome reflected this imbalance and produced yet another series of complicated processes and possible loopholes for business. The present difficulty NGOs face in trying to stop logging in IFLs, a small subset of the larger 'primary forest' areas, shows how far things have slid towards industry interests over the lifetime of the FSC.

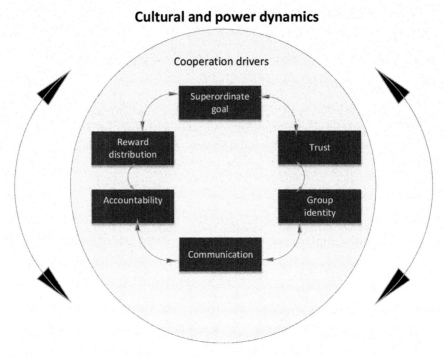

FIGURE 9.2 Framework for cooperation and power in NGO–Business collaboration in the FSC.

## 5 Conclusions

The case of IFLs highlights the questions that should be asked in NGO–business cooperation: whose cooperation and on whose terms? Indeed, this case demonstrates the hegemonic processes in which forestry is embedded and reflected in a legitimation struggle – the case of IFLs puts a spotlight on this struggle, which at heart is a struggle over the control of forests and the benefits, played out in discourse and coalition building. While the FSC was developed as a mechanism to incentivise responsible forest management, incorporate diverse voices and seek consensus, scholars have argued that in collaborations, *all voices* should be heard, and that consensus is a constraint to supporting more transformative change. They also theorise that conflict is critical to change and should be accommodated. But, in the case of the FSC and IFLs, we note that conflict can also limit cooperation and entrench the status quo of unsustainable logging and the depletion of IFLs.

The FSC has an ambitious task – to accommodate distinct voices to solve deforestation and forest degradation. However, the FSC has been undermined by a downward pressure on standards and market forces that have not delivered the premium anticipated for more sustainable products. We document that forestry businesses have actively frustrated the FSC, particularly around the issue of logging primary forests and IFLs, creating alternative certification schemes to challenge the FSC's legitimacy and influence. In analysing cooperation between NGOs and business, the lesson of the FSC and IFLs brings attention to the potent influence of power in both enabling and undermining cooperation and the mechanisms enabling cooperation – in this case, not simply strange bedfellows with different goals, but unequal bedfellows with competing goals.

The case of the FSC and IFLs calls into question whether business should have a say in setting the parameters of sustainability. Given the current lack of a superordinate goal within the FSC, it could be that NGOs wishing to protect the remaining primary forest, particularly IFLs, begin to pursue alternative channels of influence that are less complex and not subject to the same power imbalance. What this would mean for the FSC and forest certification, and for relationships between NGOs and industry more generally, is unclear, but will no doubt be the subject of much debate in the years to come.

## Notes

1  See Wood (2018) for a review of literature on the sustainability of tropical forest management.
2  Notably Canada, which boasts one quarter of all FSC-certified forests.
3  Originally launched as 'REDD' at UNFCCC COP15- reducing emissions from deforestation and forest degradation, this was later amended (Bali Action Plan, 2007) to include 'the role of conservation, sustainable management of forests, and enhancement of forest carbon stocks', which came to be known as 'REDD+'.

## References

Bendell, J., ed. (2017) *Terms for Endearment: Business, NGOs and Sustainable Development.* London: Routledge.

Brand, T., Blok, V. and Verweij, M. (2020) 'Stakeholder dialogue as agonistic deliberation: Exploring the role of conflict and self-interest in business–NGO interaction', *Business Ethics Quarterly*, 30(1), pp. 3–30.

Cashore, B. (2002) 'Legitimacy and the privatization of environmental governance: How non–state market–driven (NSMD) governance systems gain rule–making authority', *Governance*, 15(4), pp. 503–529.

Chen, C. C., Chen, X. P. and Meindl, J. R. (1998). 'How can cooperation be fostered? The cultural effects of individualism-collectivism', *Academy of Management Review*, 23(2), pp. 285–304.

Conniff, R. (2018) 'Greenwashed timber: How sustainable forest certification has failed', *Yale Environment*, 360. https://e360.yale.edu/features/greenwashed-timber-how-sustainable-forest-certification-has-failed.

Crane, A. (1998) 'Culture clash and mediation: Exploring the cultural dynamics of business-NGO collaboration', *Greener Management International*, 24, pp. 61–76.

de Lange, D. E., Armanios, D., Delgado-Ceballos, J. and Sandhu, S. (2016) 'From foe to friend: Complex mutual adaptation of multinational corporations and nongovernmental organizations', *Business & Society*, 55(8), pp. 1197–1228.

de Wasseige, C. and Defourny, P. (2004) 'Remote sensing of selective logging impact for tropical forest management', *Forest Ecology and Management*, 188(1–3), pp. 161–173.

Eden, S. and Bear, C. (2010) 'Third-sector global environmental governance, space and science: comparing fishery and forestry certification', *Journal of Environmental Policy & Planning*, 12(1), pp. 83–106.

European Sustainable Timber Coalition (2020) 'Debate on FSC intact forest landscape protection continues', Republished May 12, 2020 on FSC International's website: https://fsc.org/en/newsfeed/debate-on-fsc-intact-forest-landscape-protection-continues.

FERN (2001) *Behind the Logo: An Environmental and Social Assessment of Forest Certification Schemes*. Moreton-in-Marsh: FERN.

Ferns, G. and Amaeshi, K. (2019) 'Struggles at the summits: Discourse coalitions, field boundaries, and the shifting role of business in sustainable development', *Business & Society*, 58(8), pp. 1533–1571.

Forest Stewardship Council (FSC) (2017) 'History of a motion: Intact forest landscapes'. https://ga2017.fsc.org/history-of-a-motion-intact-forest-landscapes-ifls/

Forest Stewardship Council (FSC) (2020) 'Debate on IFL protection continues'. https://fsc.org/en/newsfeed/debate-on-fsc-intact-forest-landscape-protection-continues.

Form International (2020) 'Assessment of the impact of the implementation of intact forest landscapes related management and protection measures in the Congo Basin'. http://ppecf-comifac.com.w011c3fd.kasserver.com/files/documentation/conseils_lecture/Report%20Impact%20Assesment%20motion%2065%20Congo%20Basin%20V5.2%20FINAL.pdf.

Fowler, P. and Heap, S. (1998). 'Learning from the marine stewardship council: A business--NGO partnership for sustainable marine fisheries', *Greener Management International*, 98(24), pp. 77–90. https://web.s.ebscohost.com/ehost/detail/detail?vid=0&sid=b3f0c39d-0eef-46d7-b330-39c3e878591a%40redis&bdata=JnNpdGU9ZWhvc3QtGl2ZSZzY29wZT1zaXRl#db=a9h&AN=2259393.

FSC Watch (2014) 'Greenpeace loses the plot: Motion 65 shambles, and an ugly failure to protect 'intact forests'. https://fsc-watch.com/2014/09/18/greenpeace-loses-the-plot-motion-65-shambles-and-an-ugly-failure-to-keep-the-fsc-strong/

Global Witness (2009) 'Trick or treat: REDD, development and sustainable forest management'. https://cdn.globalwitness.org/archive/files/pdfs/trick_or_treat.pdf.

Greenpeace (2008) 'Holding the line: Recommendations and progress to date on Certification Body and FSC performance following a critical analysis of a range of "controversial" certificates'. http://archivo-es.greenpeace.org/espana/Global/espana/report/other/holding-the-line-with-fsc-vol-2.pdf.

Greenpeace (2010) 'Holding the line with FSC, reloaded'. https://wayback.archive-it.org/9650/20200504144104/http://p3-raw.greenpeace.org/international/Global/international/publications/forests/2011/Holding%20the%20Line%20Reloaded%20-%20Nov%202010.pdf.

Greenpeace (2011) 'Intact forest landscapes: Why it is crucial to protect them from industrial exploitation'. http://www.intactforests.org/pdf.publications/Intact.Forest.Landscapes.Greenpeace.2011.pdf.

Greenpeace (2013) 'Resolute's flawed "controlled wood" threatens FSC's credibility'. https://wayback.archive-it.org/9650/20200425062749/http://p3-raw.greenpeace.org/international/en/news/Blogs/makingwaves/resolutes-flawed-controlled-wood-threatens-fs/blog/46425/

Greenpeace (2015) 'Protecting intact forests & FSC's motion 65: Getting the facts straight'. https://www.greenpeace.org/canada/en/story/644/protecting-intact-forests-fscs-motion-65-getting-the-facts-straight/

Greenpeace (2018) 'Statement on forest certification and guidance for companies and consumers'. https://fscwatchdotcom.files.wordpress.com/2018/03/6b3d1c70-greenpeace-statement-on-forest-certification-and-guidance-for-companies-and-consumers_final1.pdf.

Griscom, B., Ellis, P. and Putz, F. E. (2014) 'Carbon emission performance of commercial logging in East Kalimantan, Indonesia', *Global Change Biology*, 20, 3. https://doi.org/10.1111/gcb.12386.

Hance, J. (2010) 'A total ban on primary forest logging needed to save the world, an interview with activist Glen Barry', *MongaBay.* https://news.mongabay.com/2010/06/a-total-ban-on-primary-forest-logging-needed-to-save-the-world-an-interview-with-activist-glen-barry/

Hance, J. (2011, May 22) 'Locals clash with "sustainable" FSC logging company in the Congo',*MongaBay.*https://news.mongabay.com/2011/05/locals-clash-with-sustainable-fsc-logging-company-in-the-congo/

Hartman, C. L., Hofman, P. S. and Stafford, E. R. (1999) 'Partnerships: A path to sustainability', *Business Strategy and the Environment*, 8(5), pp. 255–266.

Humphreys, D. (2009) 'Discourse as ideology: Neoliberalism and the limits of international forest policy', *Forest Policy and Economics*, 11(5–6), pp. 319–325.

Hussain, W. and Moriarty, J. (2018) 'Accountable to whom? Rethinking the role of corporations in political CSR', *Journal of Business Ethics*, 149(3), pp. 519–534.

IISD (2019) 'Five organizations launch partnership to protect intact forests'. https://sdg.iisd.org/news/five-organizations-launch-partnership-to-protect-intact-forests/

Joutsenvirta, M. (2011) 'Setting boundaries for corporate social responsibility: Firm–NGO relationship as discursive legitimation struggle', *Journal of Business Ethics*, 102(1), pp. 57–75.

Laasonen, S., Fougère, M. and Kourula, A. (2012). 'Dominant articulations in academic business and society discourse on NGO–business relations: A critical assessment', *Journal of Business Ethics*, 109(4), pp. 521–545.

Laurance, W.F., Goosem, M. and Laurance, S. G. (2009) 'Impacts of roads and linear clearings on tropical forests', *Trends in Ecology & Evolution*, 24(12), pp. 659–669.

Linton, A. (2005) 'Partnering for sustainability: Business–NGO alliances in the coffee industry', *Development in Practice*, 15(3), pp. 600–614.

Mackey, B., DellaSala, D. A., Kormos, C., Lindenmayer, D., Kumpel, N., Zimmerman, B., Hugh, S., Young, V., Foley, S., Arsenis, K. and Watson, J. E. (2014, March/April). 'Policy options for the world's primary forests in multilateral environmental agreements', *Conservation Letters*, 8(2), pp. 139–147.

McDermott, C. (2012). 'Trust, legitimacy and power in forest certification: A case study of the FSC in British Columbia', *Geoforum*, 43(3), pp. 634–644.

Moog, S., Spicer, A. and Böhm, S. (2015) 'The politics of multi-stakeholder initiatives: The crisis of the Forest Stewardship Council', *Journal of Business Ethics*, 128(3), pp. 469–493.

Morgan, D., Strindberg, S., Winston, W., Stephens, C. R., Traub, C., Ayina, C. E., Ndolo Ebika, S. T., Mayoukou, W., Koni, D., Iyenguet, F. and Sanz, C. M. (2019). 'Impacts of selective logging and associated anthropogenic disturbance on intact forest landscapes and apes of Northern Congo', *Frontiers in Forests and Global Change*, 2. https://doi.org/10.3389/ffgc.2019.00028.

Murphy, D. F. and Bendell, J. (1999). 'Partners in time? Business, NGOs and sustainable development'. http://insight.cumbria.ac.uk/id/eprint/3365/1/Murphy_PartnersInTime.pdf.

Nahi, T. (2018) 'Co-creation for sustainable development: The bounds of NGO contributions to inclusive business', *Business Strategy & Development*, 1(2), pp. 88–102.

Nikolakis, W., Cohen, D. H. and Nelson, H. W. (2012) 'What matters for socially responsible investment (SRI) in the natural resources sectors? SRI mutual funds and forestry in North America', *Journal of Sustainable Finance & Investment*, 2(2), pp. 136–151.

Nikolakis, W. and Guðjónsson, G. (2021) 'Building voluntary partnerships for climate action: An exploratory study from Iceland', *Cleaner and Responsible Consumption*, 3, 100023.

Nikolakis, W. and Innes, J. L. (eds.) (2020) *The Wicked Problem of Forest Policy: A Multidisciplinary Approach to Sustainability in Forest Landscapes*. Cambridge: Cambridge University Press.

Nikolakis, W., Nelson, H. W. and Cohen, D. H. (2014) 'Who pays attention to indigenous peoples in sustainable development and why? Evidence from socially responsible investment mutual funds in North America', *Organization & Environment*, 27(4), pp. 368–382.

Pearson, T. R., Brown, S., Murray, L. and Sidman, G. (2017) 'Greenhouse gas emissions from tropical forest degradation: An underestimated source', *Carbon Balance and Management*, 12(1), 3.

Poore, D. (2003) *Changing Landscapes: The Development of the International Tropical Timber Organization and Its Influence on Tropical Forest Management*. Oxon: Routledge.

Rossoman, G. (2017). 'Is the forest stewardship council going to stay "fit for purpose" for this century?', *Monga Bay*, 31 October, 2017. https://news.mongabay.com/2017/10/is-the-forest-stewardship-council-going-to-stay-fit-for-purpose-for-this-century-commentary/

Schepers, D. H. (2006) 'The impact of NGO network conflict on the corporate social responsibility strategies of multinational corporations', *Business & Society*, 45(3), pp. 282–299.

Schepers, D. H. (2010). 'Challenges to legitimacy at the Forest Stewardship Council', *Journal of Business Ethics*, 92(2), pp. 279–290.

Sharma, S. and Henriques, I. (2005) 'Stakeholder influences on sustainability practices in the Canadian forest products industry', *Strategic Management Journal*, 26(2), pp. 159–180.

Tollefson, C., Gale, F. and Haley, D. (2009) *Setting the Standard: Certification, Governance, and the Forest Stewardship Council*. Vancouver, BC: UBC Press.

Watson, J. E., Evans, T., Venter, O., Williams, B., Tulloch, A., Stewart, C., Thompson, I., Ray, J. C., Murray, K., Salazar, A. and McAlpine, C. (2018) 'The exceptional value of intact forest ecosystems', *Nature Ecology & Evolution*, 2, pp. 599–610.

Wood, P. (2018) 'The sustainability of commercial forest management in tropical forest. A report prepared for Rainforest Foundation Norway'. https://d5i6is0eze552.cloudfront.net/documents/RF_report_0919_print.pdf?mtime=20190920102251.

Yaziji, M. and Doh, J. (2009) *NGOs and Corporations: Conflict and Collaboration*. New York: Cambridge University Press.

# 10

# THE INTERNET OF TREES AND NETWORKED SURVEILLANCE

## A Multi-Stakeholder Effort to Protect the Resilience of Ecosystems

*Mario D. Schultz and Peter Seele*

## 1 Introduction

Humanity is currently facing numerous grand challenges. Grand challenges are large-scale problems that society, and consequently businesses, face that accompany profound societal and environmental impacts (Helbing, 2013; Ferraro et al., 2015; Alford and Head, 2017). Climate change and poverty are among the most well-known examples. Insect-borne diseases can also be perceived as a large-scale challenge given the threat they pose to ecosystems worldwide. Due to their complexity, uncertainty, and multiple actor involvement, grand challenges are difficult to address. Consequently, new ways of thinking are required for tackling and governing them (more about governance in Chapters 8 and 9).

Against this backdrop, increasing digitalisation provides new opportunities to address and monitor grand challenges at scale. In this chapter, we focus on the role of digital surveillance, referring to 'the focused, systematic and routine attention to personal details for the purposes of influence, management, protection or direction' (Lyon, 2007, p. 14). Digital data and data analytic techniques may provide new insights into society and the ecosystems surrounding us, helping us govern grand challenges. Thus, the purpose of this chapter is to explore different surveillance forms, such as top-down, bottom-up, and networked surveillance, and their potential for tackling grand challenges.

Central to the chapter is a single-case study of an extreme case: the grand challenge of an invasive alien species in the form of the Asian long-horned beetle, which threatens public and private tree populations worldwide. In this chapter, we focus on the context of Bavaria in Germany. Our case promotes a thorough understanding of the context and generates novel theoretical insights into surveillance and grand challenges (Eisenhardt, 1989; Eisenhardt and Graebner, 2007; Yin, 2009). We apply an inductive approach to theorising and

DOI: 10.4324/9781003003588-13

normative reasoning about the roles of corporations, governmental institutions, and environmental organisations when addressing grand challenges (Barzelay, 1993; Brigley, 1995). The findings of our single case study show that different forms of surveillance, such as top-down and bottom-up surveillance, are used by governmental but also private actors to address the critical threat posed by the beetle. Although these approaches aim to resolve the same challenge of the invasive beetle, they remain largely disconnected. Thus, we identify networked surveillance as a potential approach of networked governance to address the grand challenge of the Asian long-horned beetle, as it holds potential to link the efforts of previously disconnected actors. Networked surveillance can create new benefits and insights that help manage grand challenges and overcome power concentrations and authority issues. In this way, networked surveillance may be perceived as a pro-social surveillance approach that links multiple societal actors to better govern large-scale environmental challenges by utilising modern digital technologies.

## 2 Theoretical Background

### 2.1 Grand Challenges and Governance Networks

Grand challenges, sometimes also referred to as wicked problems, are multifaceted, unresolved issues with large-scale societal impacts (Helbing, 2013; Ferraro et al., 2015; Alford and Head, 2017). Recent business and sustainability research (Banks et al., 2016; Eisenhardt et al., 2016; George, 2016) is increasingly engaging in the study of grand challenges, striving to uncover how these 'specific critical barriers' can be removed or at least mitigated (George et al., 2016, p. 1881). Grand challenges are particularly difficult to tackle due to their complexity, uncertainty, evaluative nature, and multiple actor involvement, which raises the following authority issues.

### 2.1.1 Complexity, Uncertainty, Evaluation

Grand challenges are generally highly complex challenges that stretch across various borders and are therefore encountered by a wide public. Their complexity arises from multiple interactions and relations and non-linear dynamics (Ferraro et al., 2015). This makes them unclear and difficult to grasp in the present and assess if their future development is also challenging. As grand challenges cut across societies and jurisdictions, different actors evaluate them differently, which means that 'their definition, stakes, and consequences are caught up in processes of continual reconfiguration, depending on whom and what becomes associated with them' (Ferraro et al., 2015, p. 5). Consequently, grand challenges often cannot be approached in conventional ways, such as via top-down governmental intervention (Helbing, 2013; Blok et al., 2016).

## 2.1.2 Authority Issue

One of the typical characteristics of grand challenges is the lack of a central authority to tackle them (Levin et al., 2012). In fact, the scale of grand challenges (e.g., climate change) means that they stretch across multiple countries, and thus no single higher authority exists to allocate responsibilities. This calls for governance networks, which can be understood as new inter-organisational networks aiming for collective goals, such as earth system governance and dealing with the protection of global public goods (Albareda and Waddock, 2018). This means that attempts to tackle grand challenges vary and involve governments, businesses, and society on multiple levels (Blok et al., 2016). Thus, governments increasingly become stakeholders within a more extensive governance network instead of being a single central authority (Sorensen and Torfing, 2009; Lievens, 2015; Albareda and Waddock, 2018). Overall, grand challenges require multiple stakeholders' enduring efforts and need 'novel ideas and unconventional approaches to tackle their complex and evolving mix of technical and social elements' (Eisenhardt et al., 2016, p. 1113). Against this background, digitalisation provides new opportunities to address grand challenges, as is discussed next.

## 2.2 Approaches to Theorising Digitalisation: Liquid Surveillance and Open Data

Society has entered a novel digital era in which smart devices and sensors are ubiquitous and continuously collecting, tracing, sorting, and recording vast amounts of data (Ball et al., 2012). Digitalisation has become the buzzword that summarises this transformational shift, impacting economies and governments, as well as broader society worldwide (Kronblad, 2020). Digitalisation refers to the pervasive implementation and usage of information and communication technology (ICT), which includes the internet of things, blockchain technology, and artificial intelligence (Kagermann, 2015). Digital technologies have changed and are continuing to reshape various sectors, leading to new business opportunities and possibly offering enhanced value creation to multiple stakeholders (Kagermann, 2015; Kronblad, 2020). Nature conservation and grand environmental challenges are no exception to this digital trend, given the vast potential and possible opportunities that rest in the new technologies (Arts et al., 2015; van der Wal and Arts, 2015).

Digitalisation can be conceptualised in different ways. In this chapter, we follow the approach of Zygmunt Bauman and David Lyon, who coined the term liquid surveillance, which is a combination of the two themes of liquid modernity (Bauman, 2001) and surveillance (Lyon, 2007, 2010). Zygmunt Bauman describes the current state of the world as 'liquid modernity' a condition in which the transitory (liquid) rather than the permanent (solid) prevails (Bauman, 2001). Thus, the state of the world is characterised by its fluid rather than permanent structures, in which conventional institutional and power structures melt or split (Bauman and Lyon, 2013). In addition, Lyon (2007, p. 14) defines surveillance as 'the focused, systematic and routine attention to personal details for the purposes of influence, management, protection or direction'. As the merger of these themes, liquid surveillance represents a concept that 'captures the reduction of the body to data and the creation of data-doubles', indicating a shift from the analogue to the digital, and thus, a merging of the physical and the digital spheres (Lyon, 2010, p. 325).

Perceiving surveillance as a liquid stream evokes associations with the natural environment (Bauman and Lyon, 2013). Yet, thus far, few studies have explored how surveillance relates to the way in which digital technologies may assist in monitoring and governing our natural surroundings (Saito et al., 2015; van der Wal and Arts, 2015). Whereas surveilling human actors often carries negative connotations and raises concerns over privacy and the abuse of power and control, the opposite may hold when it comes to the natural environment and gaining deeper insights into grand challenges (Bernstein, 2017; Lyon, 2018; Zuboff, 2019). Detailed insights and information about the natural environment can be beneficial for conserving habitats and preventing adverse societal outcomes (van der Wal and Arts, 2015; Bernstein, 2017). Thus, the surveillance concept can provide valuable insights into grand challenges and control them in a pro-social fashion. In this regard, it is important to differentiate between three different types of surveillance, as outlined by Whelan (2019): (1) top-down (2), bottom-up (3), and networked.

### 2.2.1 Top-Down Surveillance

This type of surveillance refers to a central intermediary, such as the government or an organisation, which surveils others. General surveillance perceptions are often associated with this panopticon-style monitoring that is accompanied by a disciplining, big-brother governance model (Seele, 2016; Hong, 2017). Thus, this surveillance type allows a corporation to, for example, control or secure its trademark, product, or service, such as in the case of sharing economy platforms, when users' compliance with platform regulations is monitored (Whelan, 2019).

### 2.2.2 Bottom-Up surveillance

Bottom-up surveillance, sometimes referred to as sousveillance or watching from below, represents an inversion of the top-down approach (Ganascia, 2011; Fernback, 2013). Thus, this surveillance type refers to individuals engaging in surveillance to protect themselves and hold other key players, such as the state or organisations, accountable (Whelan, 2019). It encourages reflection on surveillance. It may arise from distrust and is directed at self-interest or collective interest against an organisational observer (Mann et al., 2002).

### 2.2.3 Blockchain-Based Networked Surveillance

The third surveillance type can be seen as one of its most recent forms, as it is associated with blockchain or Distributed Ledger Technology (Whelan, 2019). As such, it represents a decentralised, typically non-hierarchical form of surveillance, with a blockchain enabling the monitoring and irreversible recording of all kinds of information and interactions based on a majority approval (Kewell et al., 2017). Whereas in a top-down surveillance system, the central actor is the state, and in the bottom-up approach, the individual, in networked surveillance, the records are on a decentralised public ledger (Whelan, 2019). Thus, in contrast to the previous surveillance types, blockchain-based surveillance has a distributed and decentralised power and governance structure (Albareda and Waddock, 2018; Dierksmeier and Seele, 2020). Consequently, this third type of surveillance stands out from traditional surveillance approaches.

### 2.2.4 Open Data

Surveillance entails that digital data are derived from the surveillance process (Ball et al., 2012). The collected information thereby represents a valuable resource, which may be monetised or used as an instrument to wield power, as is often the case for top-down and bottom-up surveillance forms (Zuboff, 2019). In contrast, blockchain-based surveillance is an approach in which data can benefit all actors in a broader society network (Helbing and Pournaras, 2015; Kewell et al., 2017; Helbing, 2019). Thus, it can be seen as a transparency approach that entails new opportunities for learning and control (Bernstein, 2017). The knowledge gained from surveillance in the form of digital data can benefit all involved actors, which makes networked surveillance valuable when it comes to managing grand challenges (Baru, 2018).

### 2.3 Linking Networked Governance of Grand Challenges, Open-Data, and Surveillance

As grand challenges are increasingly tackled by governance networks, including public, semi-public, and private entities, digitalisation may become an increasingly important connector and facilitator. Thus, the previously described effects that accompany surveillance and open data indicate fundamental transformations that can have new impacts on the way in which governance networks address grand challenges. Consequently, new forms of meta-governance may arise which link multiple actors and aim to address challenges to global commons (Sorensen and Torfing, 2009; Albareda and Waddock, 2018). However, Sorensen and Torfing (2009) underline that novel forms of network governance may not be inherently effective and may lead to deadlocks as well as transparency and accountability issues. Thus, their performance should not be taken for granted and may hinge on the context (Sorensen and Torfing, 2009). Consequently, this chapter will draw on empirical data from the environmental threat posed by the Asian long-horned beetle to explore how, in the form of surveillance, digitalisation can provide new insights into tackling grand challenges via a network of actors that strive to protect global commons in the form of tree populations. In this regard, we discuss surveillance and open data and a single-case study to expand our understandings of networked governance in the digital age.

## 3 Surveillance to Track and Trace the Asian Long-Horned Beetle in Bavaria, Germany

The Asian long-horned beetle (or starry sky beetle) is a woodboring insect that spreads via international trade and attacks healthy hardwood trees in temperate climate zones (Bulletin OEPP/EPPO, 1999). The beetle is a severe threat to tree populations worldwide, as it can cause tremendous economic and ecological harm (Nowak et al., 2001). As it killed millions of trees in China in the 1980s, the insect is considered a quarantine pest and features among the most dangerous invasive alien species (Haack et al., 2010). Consequently, the Asian long-horned beetle can be categorised as a grand challenge (Ferraro et al., 2015; Gross and De Dreu, 2019). In this section, we adopt a single case-study approach (Box 10.1) to present insights into the role and potential of surveillance for tracking and tracing pests, focusing on the Asian long-horned beetle infestation in Bavaria (Germany).

### 3.1 Asian Long-Horned Beetle Infestations and Top-Down Surveillance

Currently, authorities in Bavaria are handling the Asian long-horned beetle in five infestation areas, using what could be termed top-down surveillance (two previous infestations have been declared eradicated). The LfL Bayern (plant health services of the federal government) uses a unique ICT system to manage the established Asian long-horned beetle quarantine zones in Bavaria. Whenever an Asian long-horned beetle infestation requires felling measures, the LfL Bayern runs a routine data collection process. Within a radius of 100 m around each infested tree, a digital tree registry is created, featuring the beetle's host plants. As small as 1 cm in diameter, trees are recorded in the field via rugged tablets and a user-interface based on the open-source software QGIS. The data collection process is carried out by trained staff members of LfL Bayern.

The top-down surveillance system of quarantine zones enables the authorities to understand the extent of an infestation and make an evidence-based decision regarding all future measures. The data are stored in the authority's database and include information on the tree species, its precise location, and a description of all data collected during the monitoring/mapping process. Usually, information about the tree's condition, Asian long-horned beetle symptoms or findings, and the type of control measures (visual monitoring, tree climbers, or sniffing dogs) are documented. The collected data can be updated, and information about following monitoring procedures is added at any given time. In this way, the surveillance measures help the authorities control and track an Asian long-horned beetle outbreak over time and thus prevent the beetle's spread to other regions. Control measures are strict and involve the monitoring of private properties and the disposal of any plant clippings. Thus, to succeed in the control measures, the plant health services and governmental authorities depend on the support of citizens and private businesses. This appears to be particularly relevant when detecting new Asian long-horned beetle infestations.

## Box 10.1 Data and methods of single-case study

An inductive research approach based on a single-case study is particularly appropriate for examining extreme cases, which are characterised by their complexity and non-linear dynamics. Extreme cases can be highly relevant for probing unexplored terrain and creating novel theoretical insights into tackling the underlying issues (Eisenhardt et al., 2016). The data for this study stem from multiple sources, in line with the criteria for rigorous case studies (following Gibbert et al., 2008). The material includes primary data from archives and interviews, as well as secondary data from existing research on the Asian long-horned beetle.

An advantage of 'extreme cases' is their broad media coverage, which enriches the collected data (Eisenhardt et al., 2016). Our study profits from Asian long-horned beetle-related news reports, press releases, publications of national and international organisations, the website content of authorities and the plant health agency, and legal guidelines and regulations. Semi-structured interviews were conducted of business firms and authorities. The interviewed companies were identified and contacted according to their location in an Asian long-horned beetle infested (or formerly infested) area in 2017.

The company interviews elicited information about: (i) the experiences of the companies with the Asian long-horned beetle, (ii) corporate conduct that could be considered a form of surveillance, and (iii) the companies' perceptions of future infestation risks and their firm's role in countering such challenges. The interviews of the authorities followed a similar structure, but with a focus on surveillance in relation to the administrative and regulatory management of outbreak sites and in contrast to the corporate and governmental views on the issue. The interviews lasted between 20 and 120 minutes, were conducted in German, and recorded pursuant to the approval of the interviewee.

The analysis followed an iterative process of exploring the literature and data to identify recurring and meaningful elements in the focal data sources and to separate them from irrelevant aspects (Gibbert et al., 2008). To strengthen the analysis, the interview data were compared with archival data sources, such as official reports, press releases, and news reports (Gibbert et al., 2008). The analysis focused on the following central categories: the kind of company, government, and environmental organisation involvement; explicit or implicit financial losses due to the Asian long-horned beetle; perceptions of the Asian long-horned beetle's risk; business' relations with governmental controls and business-government interplay; involvement in resolving current infestations and future outbreaks; and potential engagement in surveillance processes aimed at countering the Asian long-horned beetle.

### 3.2 The Asian Long-Horned Beetle and Bottom-Up Surveillance

Companies have reported two outbreaks in Bavaria, although this may directly impact their business conduct. Companies are generally not compensated if trees located on their premises have to be felled. Currently, no government support or insurance covers such losses. Moreover, implicit financial damage occurs when regulatory measures impinge upon specific companies' business conduct within a quarantine zone. For example, nurseries and other firms are involved in recycling horticultural waste and are particularly affected by governmental restrictions. This leads to indirect revenue losses, as the interviews revealed:

> 'They [the governmental measures] have the disadvantage that we are no longer allowed to use our traditional, contractual buyer, and now we drive to another company. Our transport there is more expensive because we don't have a return shipment. This impinges on our freight volume, which is not available for other transport. ...In the case of individual self-commitment, we carry this obligation because we are close to the subject [of the beetle]. ...The quarantine zone can be lifted, and then, things are fine again. The fastest action is for me [as a company] to work actively together with the municipality so that the issue can be resolved in a timely manner'.
>
> *(Interview with the CEO, undisclosed SME, 2017)*

One can conclude that public quarantine measures do not, in general, favour companies. Surprisingly, although the measures were sometimes described as 'very stringent', most businesses considered them appropriate, given the risk that the beetle represents to the broader natural environment:

> 'At first – of course – we were sad that the maple trees had to be felled. But these view trees are not a big loss compared to the nearby deciduous forests that are at risk. It's dreadful to imagine what kind of damage it [the beetle] could cause if it spread there'.
>
> *(CEO, domestic harbour Kehlheim, 2017)*

The biggest advantage of individual companies carrying out surveillance themselves is the (early) detection of the beetle and the protection of local tree populations. Bottom-up surveillance can provide learning opportunities for the individual organisation to detect potential threats and identify risky shipments. It is crucial for the control of the Asian long-horned beetle that companies share knowledge of a possible outbreak or risky cargo that might carry a beetle:

> Yes, we have reported suspicious pallets, which turned out to be infested with Asian long-horned beetles. Yet, to be fair, we do not have the resources or trained personnel to check constantly for symptoms of the

beetle. Of course, we support the authorities where we can, but one should note that the container quantities in a harbour are vast and the amount of time we have to discharge is limited.

*(Interview with the CEO Fichtl Logistics, 2017)*

Importers or companies that might be a source of Asian long-horned beetle introduction are not viewed as the 'black sheep' or the 'ones to blame', but as a final link in the supply chain – a link that is confronted with a form of negligence or carelessness that happened several steps earlier. Thus, bottom-up surveillance could help individual organisations keep track of their supplier network and protect both their businesses and the environment in which they are embedded from the threat of the Asian long-horned beetle.

### 3.3 The Need for Networked Surveillance

As shown above, the actors involved in the Asian long-horned beetle case are engaging in different forms of surveillance. Plant health services carry out top-down surveillance following governmental regulations. A key advantage of the LfL's surveillance system is that it creates a tree registry that enables the storage of precise information, even about a single tree. This centralised approach helps monitor and control specific quarantine zones. However, it is limited to detecting new Asian long-horned beetle infestations. Here, businesses' bottom-up surveillance comes into play, as it helps identify not only infested trees but also risky Asian long-horned beetle shipments, such as infested tree logs or wood packaging material carrying the beetle. However, as indicated by the quote by the CEO of Fichtl Logistics (above), corporate efforts to counter the Asian long-horned beetle depend on the successful interplay of multiple actors, involving businesses, the government, and environmental organisations. Thus, a decentralised surveillance approach would help share and exchange information more efficiently between different actors of a more comprehensive network, even stretching across countries.

## 4 The Role of Networked Surveillance in Tackling Grand Challenges

### 4.1 Pro-Social Networked Surveillance System

Networked surveillance systems refer to a pro-social approach based on a post-panoptic[1] surveillance notion (see, e.g., Lyon, 2006 Exploring new avenues to theorise surveillance). What is central to this surveillance notion is not a single actor but a collective network that strives to use open data to address grand challenges such as the Asian long-horned beetle (Bauman and Lyon, 2013; Baru, 2018; Whelan, 2019). A network can be generally seen as a group of more than three actors or organisations that are 'linked through multilateral ties and connected in ways that facilitate the achievement of a common goal' (Provan et al., 2007, p. 482). Thus, networked surveillance may be perceived as a pro-social form of surveillance aimed at linking multiple societal actors to better govern a common concern in the form of a grand challenge. In the case of the Asian long-horned beetle, such a basic networked approach (Table 10.1) would link all actors with the common goal of protecting the existing public and private tree populations and consist of at least three main elements: (1) a methodology that allows for the unequivocal *identification/digitalisation* of an object such as a tree, which may include a marking or tagging technique, (2) a *decentralised public ledger information system*, providing all network members with the surveillance data, and (3) human- or technology-assisted networked *surveillance*.

### 4.1.1 Identification/Digitalisation

The digital identification of an object can be ensured on the basis of the desired accuracy. Concerning trees, mass detection of large-scale forest areas can be achieved using drones or other aerial identification methods (see, e.g., Bluesky International, 2015). Another even more precise methodology is the use of radio

**TABLE 10.1** Role of networked surveillance in tackling grand challenges

*Main elements of networked surveillance system*

1 Identification/digitalisation
  Method that enables unequivocal identification/digitalisation of an object (e.g., tree)
2 Decentralised public ledger information system
  Providing surveillance data to all network members
3 Human and technology-assisted surveillance
  Manual and automated data collection and storage on public ledger information system

Opportunities and limitations for better addressing grand challenges
- Open surveillance data from multiple actors:
  - Enables better understanding of grand challenges and how they evolve over time
  - Connects previously isolated data sources for a holistic understanding of challenges
- Decentralised approach:
  - Linking previously disconnected actors and resolving authority issues
  - Irreversible, majority-approved blockchain prevents power concentrations of single actors
- Governance network:
  - Grand challenges require a global approach and cross-country collaboration
  - Public ledger information can enable cross-border information exchange
- Accountability and transparency
  - Requires accountability framework
  - Inbuilt transparency and instruments to safeguard from misuse

frequency identification (RFID) tags. These tags are composed of an electro-magnetic circuit and a memory unit with a unique identifier that can be read from a distance using a distinct frequency (Ngai et al., 2008). RFID tags have the advantage that they can be used for tracking not only static but also dynamic entities. If a tree is cut, the object identifier, such as an RFID tag or nail, can remain in the log, providing basic information. Thus, it links to the digital data entry or digital tree with all associated information (Tzoulis et al., 2014).

### 4.1.2 Decentralised Public Ledger Information System

Once the object is tagged or marked with a unique identifier (e.g., via an ID based on the exact location or an RFID tag), it is digitalised and can become part of an information system such as a public ledger (Kewell et al., 2017). This database can consist of what Lyon (2010, 2014) calls 'data doubles' or digitally mirrored images of real objects (in this case, trees). Such virtual images can be extended as further information is attached to them (Ball et al., 2012). Storing the information in a unified open standard, such as the eXtensible Markup Language (XML), would help connect corporations with governmental institutions and other relevant groups and allow the exchange of information across organisational borders (Seele, 2016a).

### 4.1.3 Human and Technology-Assisted Surveillance

The public ledger information system can serve as the core infrastructure that enables the involved actors to store and exchange data through surveillance. This data collection process can take various shapes: it may be automated via sensors or interfaces such as drones or aeroplanes, or it can be done manually by human operators that use smart devices, or a combination of manual and automated data gathering methods. Thus, a simple smartphone interaction with an RFID tag of a living tree could warn authorities about a potential beetle infestation. Ultimately, as the surveillance data become available as open data on a blockchain, it can prove valuable for all actors in the network and in broader society (Helbing and Pournaras, 2015; Helbing, 2019), thereby enabling new opportunities for learning and control (Bernstein, 2017).

## 4.2 Opportunities and Limitations of a Networked Surveillance System

### 4.2.1 New Learning and Control Opportunities for Addressing Grand Challenges

The overall network surveillance system can offer the involved actors several options for learning and control and may thus assist in addressing the grand challenge of the Asian long-horned beetle (Ferraro et al., 2015; Bernstein, 2017). Due to their complexity, uncertainty, and evaluative nature, addressing grand challenges is particularly problematic. Open surveillance data may represent part of the solution, helping us better understand complex grand challenges and how they evolve over time. In this regard, a networked surveillance approach can provide valuable new data and insights from various actors and perspectives to illuminate the core of the challenge. In addition, increased information can reduce uncertainties about the development of the grand challenge. With the data stored on an irreversible blockchain, evaluative differences may be countered effectively, as they have the same evidence base (Ferraro et al., 2015). When it comes to grand challenges, authority issues are often a crucial barrier (Levin et al., 2012). The crucial aspect of the networked surveillance approach is the storage of data in a decentralised open or public ledger.

In contrast to top-down and bottom-up surveillance, a networked approach enables the distribution of information (Ganascia, 2011; Whelan, 2019). Thus, with a networked surveillance approach, businesses, governments, and environmental organisations can become members of a more extensive governance network, allowing all members access to information (Lievens, 2015; Albareda and Waddock, 2018). In other words, digital technologies are used to collect, process, store, and distribute information so that the entire network benefits. These benefits may even go beyond a single context and help connect actors across countries, as grand challenges require cross-border cooperation.

Overall, via a networked approach, governments may become increasingly able to control the beetle via enhanced information and data from multiple sources. For example, governments may identify or intercept risky shipments based on the trade date shared by corporations (Schultz and Seele, 2020), or backtrack the origin of an infested tree or wood packaging material through a supply chain and identify potential undiscovered outbreaks. Meanwhile, corporations can increase processes' efficiency and productivity through seamless data exchange between all the involved actors. As the previous examples show, a commercially used tree can be tracked throughout its entire lifecycle, up to the final product, which may also be of particular interest to the timber industry, automating commercial processes and providing transparent insights into their supply chains, as well as quality control (Fraunhofer Press, 2010). Thus, trees and forests at large may be better managed as a natural resource, and most importantly, better protected as a public good. A downside of this networked approach is the requirement of certain basic information and communication infrastructure, and the energy consumption associated with blockchain mining (Dierksmeier and Seele, 2020).

### 4.2.2 Accountability and Transparency

As depicted above, networked surveillance may help address grand challenges. However, it is important to keep in mind that no form of surveillance should ever be considered either neutral or something categorically dangerous or harmful (Bennett et al., 2014):

> 'I have never regarded surveillance as somehow intrinsically negative or malign. It seems to me there are plenty of opportunities for setting up surveillance that is appropriate and this [the Asian long-horned beetle] seems to be a case in point'.
>
> *(Interview with David Lyon, 2017)*

As the depicted approach aims to govern a grand challenge via a networked approach, it requires an accountability framework (Sorensen and Torfing, 2009; Albareda and Waddock, 2018). Given that the Asian long-horned beetle threatens public and private tree populations, all the involved actors have the same public good, namely protecting the natural environment at the core. However, even a pro-social form of surveillance such as the outlined networked approach, requires accountability mechanisms and instruments that safeguard potential misuse.

> It's possible to think of ways it could be used that went beyond the beetle. … So function creep into some other area. Even mission creep, where you use the same system for something completely different. …Accountability, responsibility, transparency – openness to transparency in the sense of how the agent of surveillance is transparent about what they are doing.
>
> *(Interview with David Lyon, 2017)*

As previous research has highlighted, a networked surveillance approach comes with the risk of anonymity or pseudonymity, which needs to be addressed to account for potential misuse (Whelan, 2019). Consequently, a networked surveillance system also requires inherent accountability and transparency structures to hold actors accountable and prevent misconduct (Albareda and Waddock, 2018).

## 5 Conclusions and Outlook

In this chapter, we have addressed the surveillance concept from a pro-social perspective and aimed to address grand challenges and protecting ecosystems in the form of tree populations. Our rationale for choosing an inductive single case study approach was to critically test and expand current understandings of surveillance regarding the governance of grand (natural) challenges (Lyon, 2006). Using the case study, we outlined networked surveillance as a communicational approach that can link multiple stakeholders to better govern underlying grand challenges. This blockchain-based networked approach may help deliver socially and environmentally beneficial outcomes (Kewell et al., 2017) but needs to be further developed in terms of what specific tasks and responsibilities business firms, governmental bodies, and environmental organisations take on, especially when addressing issues of legitimacy and accountability.

What goes beyond this chapter and provides fruitful avenues for future research is the study of other forms of pro-social surveillance aiming for the digital conservation of the natural environment (Saito et al., 2015; van der Wal and Arts, 2015). As forests are threatened not only by invasive alien species but also other global risk factors such as forest fires, illegal logging, and climate change, novel networked approaches to addressing these issues are in demand (Helbing, 2013; White, 2019). Once an element of the natural environment is digitally identified and connected to a broader network, several new possibilities arise. As real-time monitoring of ecosystems, even in the most remote locations (including the oceans, see, e.g., the sail drone project in Staff et al., 2014; Meinig et al., 2019) of the planet, become not only technically possible but also reliably available at low cost, surveillance will be much more widespread in the future (Sethi et al., 2018). Thus, tree populations may become part of a wider global network, like the planetary nervous net outlined by Helbing (2015). These developments may also strengthen the status of the natural environment as a crucial stakeholder in an interconnected planet (Starik, 1995; Laine, 2010). Referring to the threat of accelerating degradation of global ecological systems, Sama, Welcomer and Gerde (2004) asked some years ago, 'Who speaks for the trees?' Growing digitalisation may provide a somewhat peculiar answer: as some authors and internet pioneers suggest, in a not too distant future, we might see the development of an 'interspecies internet', as an extended communication platform that includes not only humans (Simmelink, 2017; Jones, 2019). Thus, with technological advancements and sensory data, evolving trees may be increasingly able to 'speak' for themselves via the data they provide.

## Note

1 Post-panoptic surveillance theory refers to research that goes beyond the dominant panopticon metaphor for analysing surveillance (Lyon, 2006). Whereas panoptic frameworks typically invoke oppressive or disciplinary interpretations, post-panoptic theorising also considers overlooked qualities and processes of surveillance.

## References

Albareda, L. and Waddock, S. (2018) 'Networked CSR governance: A whole network approach to meta-governance', *Business and Society*, 57(4), pp. 636–675. https://doi.org/10.1177/0007650315624205.

Alford, J. and Head, B. W. (2017) 'Wicked and less wicked problems: A typology and a contingency framework', *Policy and Society*, 36(3), pp. 397–413. https://doi.org/10.1080/14494035.2017.1361634.

Arts, K., van der Wal, R. and Adams, W. M. (2015) 'Digital technology and the conservation of nature', *Ambio*, 44(S4), pp. 661–673. https://doi.org/10.1007/s13280-015-0705-1.

Ball, K., Haggerty, K. and Lyon, D. (2012) *Routledge Handbook of Surveillance Studies*. New York: Routledge.

Banks, G. C., Pollack, J. M., Bochantin, J. E., Kirkman, B. L., Whelpley, C. E. and O'Boyle, E. H. (2016) 'Management's science-practice gap: A grand challenge for all stakeholders', *Academy of Management Journal*, 59(6), pp. 2205–2231. https://doi.org/10.5465/amj.2015.0728.

Baru, C. (2018) 'How to deliver translational data-science benefits to science and society', *Nature*, 561(7724), pp. 464–464. https://doi.org/10.1038/d41586-018-06804-4.

Barzelay, M. (1993) 'The single case study as intellectually ambitious inquiry', *Journal of Public Administration Research and Theory*, 3(3), pp. 305–318. https://doi.org/10.2307/1181786.

Bauman, Z. (2001) *Liquid Modernity, Contemporary Sociology*. Malden: Polity Press.

Bauman, Z. and Lyon, D. (2013) *Liquid Surveillance: A Conversation*. Cambridge: Polity Press.

Bennett, C. J., Haggerty, K. D., Lyon, D. and Steeves, V. (2014) *Transparent Lives : Surveillance in Canada*. Edmonton: Athabasca University Press. https://doi.org/10.15212/aupress/9781927356777.01.

Bernstein, E. S. (2017) 'Making transparency transparent: The evolution of observation in management theory', *Academy of Management Annals*, 11(1), pp. 217–266. https://doi.org/10.5465/annals.2014.0076.

Blok, V., Gremmen, B. and Wesselink, R. (2016) 'Dealing with the wicked problem of sustainability in advance', *Business and Professional Ethics Journal*. https://doi.org/10.5840/bpej201621737.

Bluesky International (2015) *National Tree Map from Bluesky*. http://www.bluesky-world.com/national-tree-map.

Brigley, S. (1995) 'Business ethics in context: Researching with case studies', *Journal of Business Ethics*, 14(3), pp. 219–226. https://doi.org/10.1007/BF00881436.

Bulletin OEPP/EPPO (1999) 'EPPO data sheets on quarantine pests', *EPPO Bulletin*, 29(74), pp. 497–501.

Dierksmeier, C. and Seele, P. (2020) 'Blockchain and business ethics', *Business Ethics: A European Review*, 29(2), pp. 348–359. https://doi.org/10.1111/beer.12259.

Eisenhardt, K. M. (1989) 'Building theories from case study research', *Academy of Management Review*, 14(4), pp. 532–550. https://doi.org/10.2307/258557.

Eisenhardt, K. M. and Graebner, M. E. (2007) 'Theory building from cases: Opportunities and challenges', *The Academy of Management Journal*, 50(1), pp. 25–32.

Eisenhardt, K. M., Graebner, M. E. and Sonenshein, S. (2016) 'Grand challenges and inductive methods: Rigor without rigor mortis', *Academy of Management Journal*, 59(4), pp. 1113–1123. https://doi.org/10.5465/amj.2016.4004.

Fernback, J. (2013) 'Sousveillance: Communities of resistance to the surveillance environment', *Telematics and Informatics*, 30(1), pp. 11–21. https://doi.org/10.1016/j.tele.2012.03.003.

Ferraro, F., Etzion, D. and Gehman, J. (2015) 'Tackling grand challenges pragmatically: Robust action revisited', *Organization Studies*, 36(3), pp. 363–390. https://doi.org/10.1177/0170840614563742.

Fraunhofer Press. (2010) 'Research news', *Fraunhofer Press*, 37(3), pp. 153–167.

Ganascia, J. G. (2011) 'The new ethical trilemma: Security, privacy and transparency', *Comptes Rendus Physique*, 12(7), pp. 684–692. https://doi.org/10.1016/j.crhy.2011.07.002.

George, G. (2016) 'From the editors: Management research in AMJ: Celebrating impact while striving for more', *Academy of Management Journal*, 59(6), pp. 1869–1877. https://doi.org/10.5465/amj.2016.4006.

George, G., Howard-Grenville, J., Joshi, A. and Tihanyi, L. (2016) 'Understanding and tackling societal grand challenges through management research', *Academy of Management Journal*, 59(6), pp. 1880–1895. https://doi.org/10.5465/amj.2016.4007.

Gibbert, M., Ruigrok, W. and Wicki, B. (2008) 'What passes as a rigorous case study?', *Strategic Management Journal*, 29(13), pp. 1465–1474.

Gross, J. and De Dreu, C. K. W. (2019) 'Individual solutions to shared problems create a modern tragedy of the commons', *Science Advances*, 5(4), pp. 1–7. https://doi.org/10.1126/sciadv.aau7296.

Haack, R. A., Hérard, F., Sun, J. and Turgeon, J. J. (2010) 'Managing invasive populations of asian longhorned beetle and citrus longhorned beetle: A worldwide perspective', *Annual Review of Entomology*, 55(1), pp. 521–546. https://doi.org/10.1146/annurev-ento-112408-085427.

Helbing, D. (2013) 'Globally networked risks and how to respond', *Nature*, 497(7447), pp. 51–59. https://doi.org/10.1038/nature12047.

Helbing, D. (2015) 'Creating ("making") a planetary nervous system as citizen web', in *Thinking Ahead - Essays on Big Data, Digital Revolution, and Participatory Market Society*. Cham: Springer International Publishing, pp. 189–194. https://doi.org/10.1007/978-3-319-15078-9_13.

Helbing, D. (ed.) (2019) *Towards Digital Enlightenment, Towards Digital Enlightenment*. Cham: Springer International Publishing. https://doi.org/10.1007/978-3-319-90869-4.

Helbing, D. and Pournaras, E. (2015) 'Build digital democracy', *Nature*, 527(7576), pp. 33–34. https://doi.org/10.1038/527033a.

Hong, S. (2017) 'Criticising surveillance and surveillance critique: Why privacy and humanism are necessary but insufficient', *Surveillance & Society*, 15(2), pp. 187–203. https://doi.org/10.24908/ss.v15i2.5441.

Jones, R. (2019) 'An interspecies internet? Thinking and acting feminist - Animal rights discourse online', *for(e)dialogue*, 3(1), pp. 1–20. https://doi.org/10.29311/for(e)dialogue.v3i1.3142.

Kagermann, H. (2015) 'Change through digitization—Value creation in the age of industry 4.0', in *Management of Permanent Change*. Wiesbaden: Springer Fachmedien Wiesbaden, pp. 23–45. https://doi.org/10.1007/978-3-658-05014-6_2.

Kewell, B., Adams, R. and Parry, G. (2017) 'Blockchain for good?', *Strategic Change*, 26(5), pp. 429–437. https://doi.org/10.1002/jsc.2143.

Kronblad, C. (2020) 'How digitalization changes our understanding of professional service firms', *Academy of Management Discoveries*, p. amd.2019.0027. https://doi.org/10.5465/amd.2019.0027.

Laine, M. (2010) 'The nature of nature as a stakeholder', *Journal of Business Ethics*, 96(S1), pp. 73–78. https://doi.org/10.1007/s10551-011-0936-4.

Levin, K., Cashore, B., Bernstein, S. and Auld, G. (2012) 'Overcoming the tragedy of super wicked problems: Constraining our future selves to ameliorate global climate change', *Policy Sciences*, 45(2), pp. 123–152. https://doi.org/10.1007/s11077-012-9151-0.

Lievens, M. (2015) 'From government to governance: A symbolic mutation and its repercussions for democracy', *Political Studies*, 63(1_suppl), pp. 2–17. https://doi.org/10.1111/1467-9248.12171.

Lyon, D. (ed.) (2006) *Theorizing Surveillance: The Panopticon and Beyond*. Cullompton, Devon: Willan Publishing.

Lyon, D. (2007) *Surveillance Studies: An Overview*. Cambridge: Polity Press.

Lyon, D. (2010) 'Liquid surveillance: The contribution of zygmunt bauman to surveillance studies', *International Political Sociology*, 4(4), pp. 325–338. https://doi.org/10.1111/j.1749-5687.2010.00109.x.

Lyon, D. (2014) 'Surveillance, snowden, and big data: Capacities, consequences, critique', *Big Data & Society*, 1(2), pp. 1–13. https://doi.org/10.1177/2053951714541861.

Lyon, D. (2018) *The Culture of Surveillance: Watching as a Way of Life*. Cambridge: Polity Press.

Mann, S., Nolan, J. and Wellman, B. (2002) 'Sousveillance: Inventing and using wearable computing devices for data collection in surveillance environments', *Surveillance & Society*, 1(3), pp. 331–355.

Meinig, C., Burger, E. F., Cohen, N., Cokelet, E. D., Cronin, M. F., Cross, J. N., De Halleux, S., Jenkins, R., Jessup, A. T., Mordy, C. W. and Lawrence-Slavas, N. (2019) 'Public–private partnerships to advance regional ocean-observing capabilities: A saildrone and NOAA-PMEL case study and future considerations to expand to global scale observing', *Frontiers in Marine Science*, 6(JUL), pp. 1–15. https://doi.org/10.3389/fmars.2019.00448.

Ngai, E. W. T., Moon, K. K., Riggins, F. J. and Candace, Y. Y. (2008) 'RFID research: An academic literature review (1995–2005) and future research directions', *International Journal of Production Economics*, 112(2), pp. 510–520. https://doi.org/10.1016/j.ijpe.2007.05.004.

Nowak, D. J., Pasek, J. E., Sequeira, R. A., Crane, D. E. and Mastro, V. C. (2001) 'Potential effect of anoplophora glabripennis (coleoptera: cerambycidae) on urban trees in the United States', *Journal of Economic Entomology*, 94(1), pp. 116–122.

Provan, K. G., Fish, A. and Sydow, J. (2007) 'Interorganizational networks at the network level: A review of the empirical literature on whole networks', *Journal of Management*, 33(3), pp. 479–516. https://doi.org/10.1177/0149206307302554.

Saito, K., Nakamura, K., Ueta, M., Kurosawa, R., Fujiwara, A., Kobayashi, H. H., Nakayama, M., Toko, A. and Nagahama, K. (2015) 'Utilizing the cyberforest live sound system with social media to remotely conduct woodland bird censuses in Central Japan', *Ambio*, 44(4), pp. 572–583. https://doi.org/10.1007/s13280-015-0708-y.

Sama, L. M., Welcomer, S. A. and Gerde, V. W. (2004) 'Who speaks for the trees? Invoking an ethic of care to give voice to the silent stakeholder', in S. Sharma and M. Starik (eds.), *Stakeholders, the Environment and Society*. Massachusetts: Edward Elgar Publishing, Inc., pp. 140–165.

Schultz, M. D. and Seele, P. (2020) 'Conceptualizing data-deliberation: The starry sky beetle, environmental system risk, and Habermasian CSR in the digital age', *Business Ethics: A European Review*, 29(2), pp. 303–313. https://doi.org/10.1111/beer.12256.

Seele, P. (2016) 'Envisioning the digital sustainability panopticon: A thought experiment of how big data may help advancing sustainability in the digital age', *Sustainability Science*, 11(5), pp. 845–854. https://doi.org/10.1007/s11625-016-0381-5.

Sethi, S. S., Ewers, R. M., Jones, N. S., Orme, C. D. L. and Picinali, L. (2018) 'Robust, real-time and autonomous monitoring of ecosystems with an open, low-cost, networked device', *Methods in Ecology and Evolution*, 9(12), pp. 2383–2387. https://doi.org/10.1111/2041-210X.13089.

Simmelink, A. (2017) *Interspecies Internet, The Parliament of Things*. https://theparliamentofthings.org/article/interspecies-internet/.

Sorensen, E. and Torfing, J. (2009) 'Making governance networks effective and democratic through metagovernance', *Public Administration*, 87(2), pp. 234–258. https://doi.org/10.1111/j.1467-9299.2009.01753.x.

Staff, W. *et al.* (2014) *The Drone That Will Sail Itself Around the World*. https://www.wired.com/2014/02/saildrone/#.

Starik, M. (1995) 'Should trees have managerial standing? Toward stakeholder status for non-human nature', *Journal of Business Ethics*, 14(3), pp. 207–217. https://doi.org/10.1007/BF00881435.

Tzoulis, I. K., Andreopoulou, Z. S. and Voulgaridis, E. (2014) 'Wood tracking information systems to confront illegal logging', *Journal of Agricultural Informatics*, 5(1), pp. 9–17.

van der Wal, R. and Arts, K. (2015) 'Digital conservation: An introduction', *Ambio*, 44, pp. 517–521. https://doi.org/10.1007/s13280-015-0701-5.

Whelan, G. (2019) 'Trust in surveillance: A reply to Etzioni', *Journal of Business Ethics*, 156(1), pp. 15–19. https://doi.org/10.1007/s10551-018-3779-4.

White, T. (2019) *Topher Whiteelectronic 'Ears' Listen to World's Rainforests*, Rolex. https://www.rolex.org/rolex-awards/applied-technology/topher-white (Accessed 26 March 2020).

Yin, R. K. (2009) *Case Study Research: Design and Methods*. London: Sage Publications.

Zuboff, S. (2019) *The Age of Surveillance Capitalism: The Fight for a Human Future at the New Frontier of Power*. London: Profile Books Ltd.

**PART 4**

# Business Sustainability Tomorrow?

# 11

# THE QUANDARY OF SUSTAINABILITY-ORIENTED INNOVATIONS

*Eric Hansen, Jaana Korhonen, Rajat Panwar, and Marko Hakovirta*

## 1 Introduction

Contemporary academic and policy discourses on sustainability quickly converge around innovation. Why? Because the power of innovation is time tested: innovations have enabled seven billion of us to meet our existential needs and live longer than the people in any other period in recorded history. By defying Malthusian predictions of collapse, innovation has taken centre stage in the Western worldview to such an extent that it is often the foremost, if not the sole, source of hope for humanity as it faces a crisis. It is worth noting here that we are writing this chapter in the hope that the breakthrough vaccines against COVID-19 will end the pandemic and normalise our lives. In this technology-dominated or rather technology-defined period of human history, it is not surprising that we so heavily rely on technological innovations to resolve environmental problems, including climate change. What is surprising, however, is that despite over half-a-century-long experimentation with sustainability-oriented innovations, the state of the environment has only deteriorated. The reader will have heard countless times that climate change has now become an emergency. It is time to examine the disconnect between innovation and sustainability. This is the broad aim of this chapter.

Innovation is defined in myriad ways. Here, we refer to innovation as new products, processes, and businesses systems, including new business models and new value creation systems. Innovation is typically viewed as a tool for economic growth and so it underpins unrestricted material consumption. As long as this expansionist paradigm prevails, profitability-oriented companies will innovate to encourage us to consume more so that they can generate higher profits (see Chapter 12). This paradigm needs scrutiny – and disciplining – as the unsustainability of

DOI: 10.4324/9781003003588-15

our production and consumption systems becomes increasingly obvious and their perilous effects on planetary boundaries become scientifically validated.

We facilitate this scrutiny in this chapter. Fundamentally, our contention is that, while innovation is typically considered a firm-level phenomenon, a complex multi-layered system actually governs the ultimate effectiveness of innovations in addressing sustainability concerns (Geels, 2018). The dynamic between firm-level innovation activities and system-level environmental outcomes results from complex interactions among multiple technical, social, political, economic, ecological, and interactional actors (Smith et al., 2005). In other words, the professed power of technological innovations to solve societal and environmental problems is curtailed by a host of non-technical factors over which an individual firm – or even a collective of firms – does not have much control. The dominant thinking, that innovations can lead to desired environmental outcomes, appears to assume that environmental problems are contained within a small homogenous geography, economic systems are localised or selectively global, political will is focused on problem solving, and human behaviour is not rationally bounded. In other words, the notion that innovation can address environmental problems makes numerous unrealistic assumptions, which must be illuminated. In the rest of this chapter, we clarify the disconnect between sustainability-oriented innovations and sustainability, identify the underlying hurdles, and propose a way forward.

## 2 The Labyrinth of Innovation-Driven Sustainability

There are numerous building blocks and obstacles between the emergence of an innovation and the macro-outcome of sustainability. In his widely acknowledged conceptualisation, Geels (2018) captured the multi-layered turns and dead-ends of this complex journey in what he calls a *socio-technical transition* (see Chapter 6). Geels argues that the process of large-scale transitions can be decomposed into three mutually related but hierarchically distinct phenomena: socio-technical landscape, socio-technical regime, and niche-level innovations. The *socio-technical landscape* is the bedrock on which innovations rest and is shaped by both slow-changing trends (e.g., demographics, geopolitics) and exogenous shocks (e.g., wars, economic crises, major events). A changed landscape requires compensatory interventions to maintain landscape stability. The onset of COVID-19 is an illustrative example of how changes in the socio-technical landscape necessitate innovation; in this case, the development of a vaccine. A vaccine is a *niche-level* innovation that involves activities of individual firms (or entrepreneurs). For niche-level innovations to function as a landscape-level intervention, they must pass through the *socio-technical regime*. The regime comprises numerous actors (e.g., consumers, regulators) and their actions (consumer willingness to change behaviour, regulators enacting conducive policies) – essentially an infrastructure of actors that exist in alignment (or not) with each other. Geels (2018) does not explicitly state so, but essentially the socio-technical regime is a market-level phenomenon and the alignment is essentially what economists would call a well-functioning market, which has suppliers, buyers, and intermediary entities to facilitate transactions between the two. Project Warp Speed, the Centers for Disease Control, the healthcare system, and the public are all elements that coalesce to form the socio-technical regime (US context). With this as a backdrop, illustrating that innovations and broader societal outcomes are tied within a complex milieu, we now turn to explain the disconnection between sustainability-oriented innovations and sustainability.

## 3 A Tripartite Framework of the Disconnect Between Innovation and Sustainability

Here, we use a tripartite conceptualisation (Figure 11.1) to depict three settings in which innovations struggle. Our contention is that these settings act similarly to a multi-layered barricade restraining firm-level innovations from realising macro-level sustainability outcomes. Myriad challenges face an innovation on its journey from idea to adoption/use. We call these firm-level hurdles, system-level hurdles, and the system-sustainability chasm.

### 3.1 Firm-Level Hurdles

### 3.1.1 Shareholder Orientation

Despite the prominence that stakeholder management has gained in the business lexicon over several decades, most firms' primary guiding philosophy remains shareholder-centric. The prominence of shareholder centralism is so deeply entrenched in corporate thinking that sustainability is embraced to the extent that it is aligned with shareholder interests. In some cases, striking this 'win–win' is possible, but often, sustainability and business benefits pose trade-offs, which firms almost invariably settle in favour of financial considerations. In the literature, multiple compelling arguments have claimed (e.g., Pinkse and Kolk, 2010; Barnett, 2019) that a win–win focused stakeholder orientation in fact prioritises the firm, but not society or the environment. Societal and environmental interests are, at best optimised, but optimisation occurs within such a large, complex set of constraints that very few firms are able to strike a meaningful balance between producing environmental good and making financial gains.

Consider this: our instances of environmentally exemplar companies have remained more or less the same for the last two decades. As educators in the field, we are constantly searching for more examples to share with students about how companies can strike a win–win. We are rarely able to go beyond the Patagonias and Interfaces of the world. Every time we hear of their innovative practices (which have been an ongoing saga for the 20 years), we feel like screaming. How can one ignore the fact that most business sectors usually only have one or two environmentally sound companies, while we have been thumping our chests about mainstreaming stakeholder orientation? Is this extremely niche

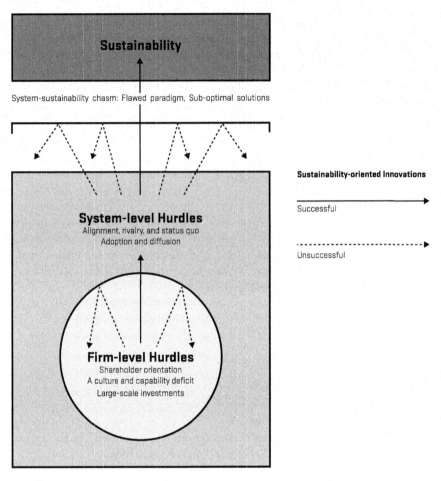

**FIGURE 11.1** Tripartite framework of disconnect between innovation and sustainability.

phenomenon really mainstreaming? How long can we afford to celebrate the best without truly moving the rest; how long can we remain wishful? Panwar et al. (2017) claimed that the win–win argument was an academic necessity in the 1970s, to shield corporate sustainability/social responsibility from the brutal arsenal of Friedman and his ardent coterie. Now, win–win is a liability; it prevents us from seeing things as they really are. Escaping its clutches is an absolute necessity.

Given that the prioritisation of profitability is essential for firms operating within capitalist economic systems (which now also dominate traditionally socialistic societies), the firm-level win–win paradox can only be overcome through changes in structural and governance architectures that can buffer firms against their primary duties to shareholders (see Chapters 12 and 13). B Corps (https://bcorporation.net/), for example, could be one alternative, but their slow growth makes us apprehensive about the veracity of the claim that they can supplant traditional corporations. Despite growth in recent years, B Corps still remains restricted to a narrow niche. In any case, we need to recognise the smokescreen of stakeholderism: because it is no more than a disguised shareholderism. In their acerbic critique, Doane and Abasta-Vilaplana (2005) described this smokescreening as charming the corporate psychopath. The point is that shareholder orientation often reigns over stakeholder orientation, and for most companies this is a fundamental barrier to pursuing sustainability-oriented innovations. As a way forward, we need new forms of organisations that have higher degrees of freedom to prioritise sustainability.

### 3.1.2 A Culture and Capability Deficit

The strategic management literature has explored many theoretical approaches to explain why some firms are more competitive than others. Dynamic capabilities, being able to adapt, orchestrate, and innovate (Teece, 2014), are especially relevant in our context. A full exploration of dynamic capabilities is not possible here, but two cultural characteristics of a firm may be especially relevant for formulating sustainability-oriented innovations, innovativeness, and collaborative(ness).

An innovative firm possesses a strong propensity to create and/or adopt new products, processes, or business systems. Innovativeness can characterise entire industry sectors: software is seen as inherently innovative, whereas the forest sector, in contrast, is seen as traditional, conservative, and risk averse (Guerrero and Hansen, 2020); in other words, suffering from an innovativeness deficit. This is important, because innovativeness leads to successful innovation as well as social, environmental, and economic performance (Kuzma et al., 2020).

Like innovativeness, the inclination to collaborate is also a cultural phenomenon. Effective sustainability-oriented innovation may require rethinking competition and collaboration among the actors involved in evolving innovation networks (Boons and Lüdeke-Freund, 2013). The agency and behaviour of actors and their interactions and relationships have been an emerging area of sustainability-oriented innovation literature (Avelino et al., 2016; Savaget et al., 2019). Sustainability-oriented innovations are inherently complex and require multiple bodies of knowledge, something that may only be accomplished via collaboration across industry sectors, in order to obtain the diversified expertise and knowledge necessary for success.

Collaboration between large and small players sharing complementary resources and knowledge helps develop entire value networks (Geels, 2014). Small firms may, for example, lack the resources to push their products or services in the markets and benefit from a large firm's supplier and customer networks, financial assets, and interdisciplinary knowhow. Biotechnology and other rapidly changing fields are particularly attractive for developing entrepreneurial partnerships between large and small companies and we can see this in the bioeconomy transition; for example, in Metsä Fibre's Äänekoski bioproducts mill in Finland, where small firms are co-located and rely on the mill for supply.

To produce the volume of sustainability-oriented innovations necessary to move the sustainability needle requires firms across the economy to develop more innovative and collaborative cultures. Centuries of effort have honed the skills and tools necessary for effective competition. However, what remains highly underdeveloped are the skills and tools necessary to collaborate, an ingredient essential for creating next-generation innovations that benefit environmental sustainability.

### 3.1.3 Large-Scale Investments

Innovation requires significant capital investments, which are not easy to obtain given the fact that the majority of new products introduced to the market are ill-fated. The failure rate depends on the industry and the nature of the product or service, but in some cases it can be as high as 90% of all newly introduced products (Christensen et al., 2005). Thus, to develop a large enough number of sustainability-oriented innovations – whether related to products or processes – which are ultimately accepted in the market requires a tsunami of innovations, given the very high degree of pre-market mortality. This clearly entails colossal risk capital which in today's economically constrained and volatile times remains a major challenge in most countries.

Innovation projects can be financed through external sources (e.g., debt, grants, crowd sourcing) or internal sources, which mainly consist of retained profits or (new) equity (Hottenrott and Peters, 2012). The intangible nature of innovation projects renders them more costly for external financing than alternative projects (Alderson and Betker, 1996). Hence, raising capital for innovation projects becomes even more difficult for a company: investments are risky due to high rates of failure, and investments are more costly. Moreover, innovation projects often have considerably long gestation periods, which means that returns are not immediate and hence internal investments in innovation projects may cause short-term cash flow problems (Hall, 2002). What is a rather ironic situation is that companies with higher innovativeness face greater fundraising challenges (Hottenrott and Peters, 2012), which makes innovation a rarer occurrence than we need to be able to make a dent in environmental degradation.

A key proposal, then, is to strengthen private and public financing programmes to foster sustainability-oriented innovations. Cecere et al. (2020) argue that focusing on small and medium-sized enterprises through public financing can provide the needed impetus. Channelling green finance through public lending programmes to small companies in developing and the least developed countries is important. More importantly, such finance should prioritise innovations leading to business model changes rather than bolt-on sustainability initiatives that tend to wither away during financially volatile periods (Panwar et al., 2015).

## 3.2 System-Level Hurdles

### 3.2.1 Misalignment, Rivalry, and Status Quo

Beyond firm borders, sustainability-oriented innovation faces a complex system of actors and interactions. Perhaps the most immediate challenge comes from competing firms (inter-firm rivalry). Incumbent firms, of course, defend their position in the marketplace against start-up innovations and can squash sustainability-oriented innovations before they even get off the ground. Large firms that are heavily invested in a particular product and its manufacturing systems are partially locked into a pathway of continuation (path dependency). Kodak's failure to react to developments in digital photography is a good example of the results of path dependency. Traditional steel companies with large, integrated mills, in turn, were slow to react to the introduction of mini-mills (Verespej, 2004), a different, small-scale production technology.

In addition to inter-firm rivalry, a host of other system actors impact the viability of an innovation. Regulations and codes, for example, can be key hurdles and are typically slow to change. North American building codes have been a key impediment to the adoption of mass timber in multi-storey buildings. Code changes take place at a glacial pace and vested interests often fight against change. The inclusion of multi-storey wooden buildings in building codes was clearly not embraced by, for example, the cement industry. While the above examples are only a sampling of the actors and dynamics in the complex system, they illustrate the labyrinth that innovations must successfully navigate from the domain of the firm to market acceptance. It is only when the right set of actors is aligned correctly that an innovation can successfully break through to market success.

### 3.2.2 Adoption and Diffusion

Final consumers are the ultimate arbiters for the destiny of many products. As most humans are averse to change, this creates long time lags between the introduction of an innovation and eventual large-scale adoption. Complex interdependencies underlie the process of innovation diffusion, including key factors influencing how innovations are taken up in the marketplace. Early sustainability-oriented innovations in consumer goods, such as household cleaning products based on 'natural' ingredients, often performed poorly compared to their chemically based cousins. Lacking a relative advantage, they were relegated to a small market segment of especially environmentally oriented consumers. The adoption of electric vehicles (EVs) is constrained on multiple fronts. First, high cost means they are accessible to only an extremely thin slice of society. Beyond this, they are not compatible with the existing, petroleum-based infrastructure. Limited range and recharging station availability hinder larger-scale adoption.

Even in an ideal situation, with an attractive innovation and close compatibility with existing systems, innovations take time to diffuse into the marketplace.

In terms of sustainability-oriented innovations, this means that positive environmental contributions remain unrealised. In a world where the metrics of environmental degradations are trending in the wrong direction, we can ill afford slow diffusion of sustainability-oriented innovations.

### 3.3 The System-Sustainability Chasm

Unfortunately, humans desire 'stuff'. Society and economies rest on a flawed foundation of ever-increasing consumption. Beyond the firm and the system are macro phenomena that impact sustainability-oriented innovation and may thus mitigate contributions to greater sustainability. At its more fundamental level, the challenge to sustainability rests on these disconnects.

#### 3.3.1 Flawed Paradigm

The foundations of our economic systems are tied to continuous, unlimited growth. The primary macro measures of the health of an economy are gross domestic product (GDP) and GDP growth. The shortcomings of GDP as a metric are numerous and well documented, as it 'ignores social costs, environmental impacts and income inequality' (Costanza et al., 2014, p. 283). A common management mantra refers to being able to manage only what is measured. As there is no simple measure of sustainability, it is often ignored or approached in an insufficiently holistic fashion.

A harsh reality facing sustainability efforts is the rapidly expanding global population, accompanied by advancing affluence. Global population growth and imitation of Western lifestyles and consumption levels by consumers in developing economies make sustainability outcomes practically unattainable. Innovation, combined with globalisation, makes new products universally available in the world and fuels consumerism. The European Commission (2019) estimates that middle-class spending will grow from about USD 37 trillion in 2017 to USD 64 trillion by 2030. The consumer paradigm of 'more is better' is eating away at the earth's resources. Busy lifestyles based on the availability of disposable 'take-away' products and services, faster cycles of fashion, and the shortening lifespans of products cause massive amounts of waste. Innovation is not sustainable if it fosters overconsumption. As we progress to an anticipated population of over ten billion in 2100 (UN, 2020) and the affluence of all people increases, the planetary deficit will multiply. In fact, it is claimed that current levels of resource consumption require 1.77 planet earths (The World Counts, 2020).

#### 3.3.2 Sub-Optimal Solutions

An often ignored yet important disconnect between innovation and sustainability is the unintended consequences of technology and the rebound effect, in which increased eco-efficiency translates into greater consumption (Herring and

Sorrell, 2009). It must also be recognised that efficiency is generally a strategy for cost reduction rather than an idealistic philosophy of conserving resources (York and McGee, 2015). Sustainability gains from technological improvements are often cancelled out by distortions in human behaviour. For example, automobile fuel efficiency gains tend to be nullified by increased driving. This phenomenon (Jevon's Paradox) is said to be the result of price reductions, in this case making fuel and driving less expensive. Closer examination of the phenomenon reveals it to be multifaceted, with both direct and indirect effects increasing resource use (York and McGee, 2015).

Solar and wind energy are changing the global energy sector, providing distinct environmental benefits. However, these energy sources also have negative impacts. Sulphur hexafluoride is a synthetic gas used in electrical installations. It is nearly 24,000 times as warming as carbon dioxide and persists in the atmosphere for at least 1,000 years. Unfortunately, power grids that facilitate the distribution of solar- and wind-generated electricity also leak sulphur hexafluoride (BBC, 2019). Therefore, the very technology designed to combat global warming is in effect contributing to the problem. Added to this are other environmental impacts such as the production of solar panels and their end-of-life disposal, whether through dumping, recycling or refurbishing. We are not suggesting that wind and solar power are worse for the environment than fossil-based energy; we are merely pointing out that sustainability-oriented innovations are riddled with inherent limitations of their own which can generate problems that must be monitored. At the minimum, it is important to recognise the likelihood of a considerable gap between the stated and realised potential of a given technological breakthrough in addressing a given environmental problem.

Consider the example of EVs that are often touted as a solution to excessive emissions caused by an ever-growing automobile sector. EVs are also mired in unintended consequences: although battery-driven EVs help in cutting carbon emissions, several studies show that battery production and disposal processes result in increased soil toxicity. We are essentially playing 'whack-a-mole' with sustainability solutions (Cashore et al., 2019), as we address one problem only to find out that another has raised its head (see also Chapter 8).

In addition to such unintended consequences, technological advances also produce undesirable social implications, which may translate into environmental degradation. First, technological breakthroughs produce goods and services that can be accessed by privileged countries or sections of society, at least in the early phases. One of the co-authors has seen more Teslas parked outside a few dozen houses on Marine Drive in Point Grey, Vancouver than in the entire city of New Delhi. When anecdotes speak, they speak loudly. The haves and the have-nots that technological breakthroughs produce in the world is a critical divide. As long as there is a Sweden and there is a Somalia, technological solutions will continue to provide benefits that only a portion of the humanity will derive. Prahalad (2012), we feel, was a bit too enthused in seeing the *fortune at the bottom of the pyramid.* When it comes to the distribution of the gains of environmentally friendly technologies, we see more *misfortune.* The world, as it is!

Reliance on innovation and technology is essentially rooted in Robert Solow's paradigm that sees resource exhaustion as an opportunity for innovation-based growth, not a catastrophe. It pushes to the margin the constraint-based philosophy that Malthus advanced through his scholarly work and has formed the very basis of life in many Eastern societies, among Indigenous People in particular. The domination of the Western worldview, which underpins the *technology-as-panacea* philosophy has led to an expansionist paradigm that all problems can be resolved through human ingenuity and innovations. At times, this has proven to be the case, but environmental problems are wicked problems which, we believe, require a trans-paradigmatic therapy that combines elements from collective human wisdom developed here and there, and beyond here and there.

## 4 How Can the Promise of Sustainability-Oriented Innovations Be Realised?

It should be clear at this point that sustainability-oriented innovation is complicated. Many actors play a role in successful innovation. In the case of sustainability-oriented innovations, especially influential actors are policymakers, firms, and consumers. We address the potential roles of each below, while acknowledging that myriad other actors are involved.

### 4.1 Innovation-Friendly Policies

Policymakers have many touchpoints in a complex system of carrots and sticks. In an intricate network of interactions among actors, it is essential that policy considers the bigger picture. For example, systems-level competition rather than materials competition is likely to provide more optimal sustainability solutions.

Thoughtful and effective legislation is required to move society towards improved sustainability. Legislation may be more effective when developed in concert with other key actors, such as firms. Columbia Forest Products, a major producer of hardwood plywood in the US, worked with the California Air Resources Board to adjust standards for allowable VOC (volatile organic compound) off-gassing from wood panel products destined for indoor environments. This corresponded to an innovation in adhesives technology that allowed Columbia to meet the standard, thus benefitting the firm as well as the air quality in the built environment. Legislation that impacts consumer behaviour is equally important. If consumers are forced to pay the full price, including externalities, this will have a concrete impact on purchase decisions. It is this idea that motivates carbon tax advocates. Mechanisms exist to convert efficiency improvement into conservation instead of increased production and consumption, such as taxes on natural resources (York and McGee, 2015).

Equally important are incentives that drive both firms and consumers towards sustainability-oriented innovations, incentives safe from unintended consequences. Government procurement policies are the low-hanging fruit in this realm. The EU's Green Public Procurement programme is an example of this, and most EU Member States have a National Action Plan associated with Green Public Procurement. Companies should participate in policymaking, such as establishing procurement rules and protocols. The approach should utilise a holistic, systems-level mentality, creating designs that benefit society first and their own operations second.

Policymakers also play a key role in education systems. Appropriate education, at all levels, is needed not only for the average citizen in terms of intelligent consumption, but sustainability-savvy managers, government servants, and other professionals are required across the economy. This suggests a deeper and broader coverage of the topic 'from the cradle to the grave'. Children influence purchase decisions by their parents, so early education is needed. As sustainability issues and knowledge are constantly evolving, lifelong learning is critical.

Although this chapter has been critical of the sustainability performance of innovation, we acknowledge that more (not less), and better innovation is needed. Accordingly, policymakers must make wise investments in science and in research and development. Investments are needed across the board to improve sustainability, but there is a special need for more holistic systems for quantifying environmental impact, enabling comparisons across systems and approaches. As recent research shows, the Scope 3 carbon impacts of a company can represent the vast majority of a firm's overall impact (Panwar, 2020). Accordingly, tools such as life-cycle analysis based on a limited cradle-to-gate approach provide an exceptionally narrow picture of system impacts. Given these unintended consequences and this narrowness, we have a long way to go before arriving at a more holistic understanding of our actions. In a similar vein, improved approaches are need for understanding and then influencing consumer purchase decisions.

Visionary public procurement policies have great potential for driving sustainability-oriented innovations (Pellegrino and Savona, 2017). British Columbia's 'Wood First' policy requires consideration of wood products in government building projects. The US established the BioPreferred® Programme in 2002 and reauthorised it in 2018, with the goal of increasing the use of renewable materials. Transparency and labelling efforts influence consumer demand, such as the ENERGY STAR® programme that facilitates informed purchasing by appliance consumers via easy-to-understand labelling depicting energy use. The Tesla story in Norway shows what reduced taxes and other perks such as avoidance of road tolls and congestion charges can do for adoption in the marketplace.

## 4.2 More Capable Firms

It has long been argued that the primary reason for the existence of a firm is to increase profits for shareholders (Friedman, 1970). Clearly, a firm must be profitable before it can invest in sustainability-oriented innovations. A modern view of the firm suggests it has a broader set of responsibilities to a wide set of stakeholders, and a responsibility for strong environmental performance. As previously emphasised, more, not less innovation is needed – and better innovation. Fundamentally, most firms need to be better at innovating. Innovative companies tend to be more competitive, which places them in a position to make more meaningful contributions to sustainability.

Firms must carefully consider the environmental impacts of an innovation as well as its profit potential. The unintended consequences of well-intentioned actions are too significant to ignore. In reality, firms require enhanced assessment tools in order to properly estimate the environmental impacts of their designs. It is important that companies instil cultures that are not only consistently and systematically sustainability oriented, but which are also watchful of the sustainability impacts that innovations can and cannot produce.

Firms should become more adept at managing consumer demand. Much remains to be learned about why and how consumers' behaviour can be aligned with sustainable consumption. Breaking free of incumbent firms, industries, and systems is not a trivial task, and innovation fails to promote sustainability if it does not serve the needs and practices of consumers. Alternative approaches, such as sufficiency/sharing economy innovations may provide preventive mechanisms to consumption, yet their ultimate sustainability contribution remains largely untested (e.g., Bocken and Short, 2016; Curtis and Mont, 2020). Recent evidence suggests that sharing economy approaches increase overall consumption (Laukkanen and Tura, 2020) as they evolve towards the separation of users and producers and more 'professional' business models which then translate into an increased focus on consumption (Geissinger et al., 2019). Consumption practices and innovations are co-dependent, meaning businesses must renew themselves along with changing consumer practices (McMeekin and Southerton, 2012).

## 4.3 Intelligent Consumption Required

As purchasing behaviour drives supply chain decisions, it can be said that consumers have the ultimate currency in sustainability progress. Intelligent consumption is a necessary ingredient for future sustainability, yet the authors are not overly optimistic. Given how society is susceptible to consuming misinformation, believing conspiracy theories, and thus engaging in outright idiocy, as became evident in the US for much of 2020 and the beginning of 2021, it is naive to assume that there is a critical mass of consumers who are informed and conscientious enough to make planet-friendly purchase decisions. Regardless of its currency in literature, ultimately, conscious consumerism is a niche phenomenon. Still, the importance of guiding consumers towards more meaningful involvement in environmentally friendly purchasing is undeniable. Environmental non-governmental organisations (ENGO) play a major role in increasing consumer awareness and driving sustainability-oriented innovation through pressuring corporations to change practices. Greenpeace has a long history and a deserved reputation for battling large corporations and at the same time promoting stories to final consumers. An ongoing palm oil campaign now claims that multiple companies that committed to stop buying from 'rainforest destroyers' have failed to keep their promise and are buying 'dirty palm oil' (Greenpeace, 2020). Of course, in order to make its supply chains more sustainable, a firm needs to adopt innovative technologies and practices (Murcia et al., 2020).

As emphasised above, it is critical that policymakers and firms help lead consumers in the right direction. However, evidence suggests that the exact opposite is the norm – policies encourage green consumerism rather than address the structural changes needed to truly address sustainability (Akenji, 2014). Ultimately, individual consumers must take it upon themselves to become sufficiently informed to make sustainability-oriented decisions. This includes both less and smarter consumption. Consumers must play a larger role for sustainability to become reality (Martek et al., 2019). They must be engaged in innovation processes to integrate more sustainable products and services into everyday practices (Köhler et al., 2019). Similarly, involvement in policy creation can help build policy portfolios with greater consumer participation and greater impact.

Given the combined growth of population and affluence, intelligent consumption is unlikely to be sufficient. It is not just about consuming more smartly, it is also about consuming less. Ironically, approaches such as green consumerism may fuel consumption. If a product is 'green' then consumers feel freer to consume than they perhaps otherwise might. Various studies and organisations have segmented consumers based on their 'greenness'. A small segment of consumers have true green attitudes. Unfortunately, this segment also tends to be the most affluent, with a larger consuming profile. It is entirely possible that the overall environmental impact of the average 'brown' consumer is less than the average 'green' consumer. Often the most environmentally friendly action may be to simply use an existing product, even one not so environmentally friendly (old automobile), rather than purchasing something new with its associated resource requirements. A rather informative adage often circulates in the green building community: *the greenest building is the one that already exists*. The 'brown' consumer driving the same gas guzzler for a decade may possibly do less damage to the environment than the 'green' consumer who purchases three different environmentally friendly models in the same period.

## 5 Conclusions

Innovation has proven to be an effective approach to resolving numerous problems, yet it has so far been utterly ineffective in holistically addressing the environmental crisis. This chapter argued that the path from sustainability-oriented innovations to sustainability is not seamless, but riddled with complex dependencies and contingencies. Sustainability entails system-level changes on a global scale, which, we argue, are unattainable if we focus on innovations alone.

For a secure and sustainable future, it is critical that we shake the expansionist paradigm. To do so, it would be important to give up the deeply held assumption that we can simply innovate our way out of pending environmental disasters. Work on sustainability-oriented innovations has evolved from a focus primarily on individual technologies or products to entire production and consumption systems. This evolution must continue, but more quickly. Meaningful advances in sustainability require multiple actors working in concert to destabilise existing regimes, moving towards more sustainable ways of living. Collective problems, without a central redressal authority, require an 'all-feasible-tools' and 'all-hands-on-deck' approach. There is no single solution, and there is certainly no easy solution. Critical analyses are needed to develop a finer-grained understanding of the potential and the limits of innovation. Answers to questions such as when, how, to what degree, and under what conditions can innovation help the environment are important; as are the answers to questions such as how and when can innovation actually hurt the pursuit of sustainability, and which alternative approaches would be more suitable. Taking an inclusive approach is important: there is much to be learned from Indigenous communities and Eastern civilisation to make the planet more sustainable. Innovation certainly has a place in the transition to sustainability, but it is not a panacea.

George Bernard Shaw was not referring to innovations when he said 'there are two tragedies in life. One is to lose your heart's desire. The other is to gain it'. But if he had been, he would have been right. Sustainability-oriented innovations abound, but sustainability continues to elude us. Here is our final message: innovations need to be gauged against impact, not simply their promise. If they are not impactful on a global level, which is evident, alternative approaches must be explored. We must stop giving technological innovations undue glorification as the solution for achieving sustainability.

## References

Alderson, M. and Betker, B. (1996) 'Liquidation costs and accounting data', *Financial Management*, 25(2), pp. 25–36.

Akenji, L. (2014) 'Consumer scapegoatism and limits to green consumerism', *Journal of Cleaner Production*, 63, pp. 13–23.

Avelino, F., Grin, J., Pel, B. and Jhagroe, S. (2016) 'The politics of sustainability transitions', *Journal of Environmental Policy & Planning*, 18(5), pp. 557–567.

Barnett, M. L. (2019) 'The business case for corporate social responsibility: A critique and an indirect path forward', *Business & Society*, 58(1), pp. 167–190.

BBC. (2019) 'Climate change: Electrical industry's 'dirty secret' boosts warming'. https://www.bbc.com/news/science-environment-49567197.

Bocken, N. M. and Short, S. W. (2016) 'Towards a sufficiency-driven business model: Experiences and opportunities', *Environmental Innovation and Societal Transitions*, 18, pp. 41–61.

Boons, F. and Lüdeke-Freund, F. (2013) 'Business models for sustainable innovation: State of the art and steps towards a research agenda', *Journal of Cleaner Production*, 45, pp. 9–19.

Cashore, B., Bernstein, S., Humphreys, D., Visseren-Hamakers, I. and Rietig, K. (2019) 'Designing stakeholder learning dialogues for effective global governance', *Policy and Society*, 38(1), pp. 118–147.

Cecere, G., Corrocher, N. and Mancusi, M. L. (2020) 'Financial constraints and public funding of eco-innovation: Empirical evidence from European SMEs', *Small Business Economics*, 54(1), pp. 285–302.

Christensen, C. M., Cook, S. and Hall, T. (2005) *Marketing Malpractice. Make Sure All Your Products Are Profitable*. 2nd ed. Harvard Business Review. https://hbr.org/2005/12/marketing-malpractice-the-cause-and-the-cure.

Costanza, R., Kubiszewski, I., Giovannini, E., Lovins, H., McGlade, J., Pickett, K. E., Ragnarsdóttir, K.V., Roberts, D., De Vogli, R. and Wilkinson, R. (2014) 'Development: Time to leave GDP behind', *Nature News*, 505(7483), pp. 283–285.

Curtis, S. K. and Mont, O. (2020) 'Sharing economy business models for sustainability', *Journal of Cleaner Production*, 266, 121519.

Doane, D. and Abasta-Vilaplana, N. (2005) 'The myth of CSR', *Stanford Social Innovation Review*, 3(3), pp. 22–29.

European Commission (2019) https://ec.europa.eu/knowledge4policy/foresight/topic/growing-consumerism/more-developments-relevant-growing-consumerism_en.

Friedman, M. (1970) 'A friedman doctrine: The social responsibility of business is to increase its profits', *The New York Times Magazine*, September 13.

Geels, F. W. (2014) 'Reconceptualising the co-evolution of firms-in-industries and their environments: Developing an inter-disciplinary Triple Embeddedness Framework', *Research Policy*, 43(2), pp. 261–277.

Geels, F. W. (2018) 'Disruption and low-carbon system transformation: Progress and new challenges in socio-technical transitions research and the multi-level perspective', *Energy Research & Social Science*, 37, pp. 224–231.

Geissinger, A., Laurell, C., Öberg, C. and Sandström, C. (2019) 'How sustainable is the sharing economy? On the sustainability connotations of sharing economy platforms', *Journal of Cleaner Production*, 206, pp. 419–429.

Greenpeace (2020) 'Tell big companies to drop dirty palm oil, The time is up for forest-destroying products'. https://www.greenpeace.org/canada/en/tell-big-companies-to-drop-dirty-palm-oil/

Guerrero, J. E. and Hansen, E. (2020) 'Company-level cross-sector collaborations in transition to the bioeconomy: A multi-case study', *Forest Policy and Economics*, 123, 102355.

Hall, B. (2002) 'The financing of research and development', *Oxford Review of Economic Policy*, 18(1), pp. 35–51.

Herring, H. and Sorrell, S., (2009) 'Energy efficiency and sustainable consumption', *The Rebound Effect*. Hampshire: Palgrave Macmillan.

Hottenrott, H. and Peters, B. (2012) 'Innovative capability and financing constraints for innovation: more money, more innovation?', *Review of Economics and Statistics*, 94(4), pp. 1126–1142.

Köhler, J., Geels, F. W., Kern, F., Köhler, J., Geels, F. W., Kern, F., Markard, J., Wieczorek, A., Alkemade, F., Avelino, F., Bergek, A., Boons, F., Fünfschilling, L., Hess, D., Holtz, G., Hyysalo, S., Luhas, J., Mikkilä, M., Uusitalo, V. and Linnanen, L. (2019) 'An agenda for sustainability transitions research: State of the art and future directions', *Environmental Innovation and Societal Transitions*, 31, pp. 1–32.

Kuzma, E., Padilha, L. S., Sehnem, S., Julkovski, D. J. and Roman, D. J. (2020) 'The relationship between innovation and sustainability: A meta-analytic study', *Journal of Cleaner Production*, 259, 120745.

Laukkanen, M. and Tura, N. (2020) 'The potential of sharing economy business models for sustainable value creation', *Journal of Cleaner Production*, 253, 120004.

Martek, I., Hosseini, M. R., Shrestha, A., Edwards, D. J. and Durdyev, S. (2019) 'Barriers inhibiting the transition to sustainability within the Australian construction industry: An investigation of technical and social interactions', *Journal of Cleaner Production*, 211, pp. 281–292.

McMeekin, A. and Southerton, D. (2012) 'Sustainability transitions and final consumption: Practices and socio-technical systems', *Technology Analysis and Strategic Management*, 24, pp. 345–361.

Murcia, M. J., Panwar, R. and Tarzijan, J. (2020) 'Socially responsible firms outsource less', *Business & Society*, 60, pp. 1507–1545.

Panwar, R. (2020) 'Corporate sustainability needs a paradigm shift', A lecture (virtually) delivered at the Energy Summit Speaker Series', Appalachian State University, Boone, NC. October 1.

Panwar, R., Nybakk, E., Hansen, E. and Pinkse, J. (2017) 'Does the business case matter? The effect of a perceived business case on small firms' social engagement', *Journal of Business Ethics*, 144(3), pp. 597–608.

Panwar, R., Nybakk, E., Pinkse, J. and Hansen, E. (2015) 'Being good when not doing well: Examining the effect of the economic downturn on small manufacturing firms' ongoing sustainability-oriented initiatives', *Organization & Environment*, 28(2), pp. 204–222.

Pellegrino, G. and Savona, M. (2017) 'No money, no honey? Financial versus knowledge and demand constraints on innovation', *Research Policy*, 46(2), pp. 510–521.

Pinkse, J. and Kolk, A. (2010) 'Challenges and trade-offs in corporate innovation for climate change', *Business Strategy and the Environment*, 19(4), pp. 261–272.

Prahalad, C. K. (2012) 'Bottom of the pyramid as a source of breakthrough innovations', *Journal of Product Innovation Management*, 29(1), pp. 6–12.

Savaget, P., Geissdoerfer, M., Kharrazi, A. and Evans, S. (2019) 'The theoretical foundations of sociotechnical systems change for sustainability: A systematic literature review', *Journal of Cleaner Production*, 206, pp. 878–892.

Smith, A., Stirling, A. and Berkhout, F. (2005) 'The governance of sustainable sociotechnical transitions', *Research Policy*, 34, pp. 1491–1510.

Teece, D. J. (2014) 'The foundations of enterprise performance: Dynamic and ordinary capabilities in an (economic) theory of firms', *Academy of Management Perspectives*, 28(4), pp. 328–352.

The World Counts (2020) 'We are consuming the future'. https://www.theworldcounts.com/challenges/planet-earth/state-of-the-planet/overuse-of-resources-on-earth/story (Accessed 13 December 2020).

UN (2020) 'Department of economic and social affairs population dynamics'. https://population.un.org/wpp/DataQuery/ (Accessed 21 December 2020).

Verespej, M. A. (2004) 'Steel's dilemma, import complaints and bankruptcies mask structural problems that integrated steelmakers must address to survive'. https://www.industryweek.com/the-economy/article/21952950/steels-dilemma. (Accessed 13 December 2020).

York, R. and McGee, J. A. (2016) 'Understanding the Jevons paradox', *Environmental Sociology*, 2(1), pp. 77–87.

# 12

# BUSINESS IN A STRONGLY SUSTAINABLE SOCIETY?

*Iana Nesterova and Ben Robra*

## 1 Introduction

The current historic moment is characterised by unsustainability, manifested in the unfolding global ecological collapse and overall societal degradation. For many decades, various scholars have been questioning the socio-economic foundations of this dire state of affairs, i.e., the constant, unrestricted pursuit of economic growth (Daly, 1968; Georgescu-Roegen, 1975; Bonnedahl and Heikkurinen, 2019). In recent times, approaches critiquing economic growth as the goal of the economy and society have become even more frequent. An ever-increasing number of scholars see the imperative of economic growth as the driver of ecological and societal degradation (see, e.g., Foster et al., 2010; Jackson, 2017). Such scholars maintain that to achieve a sustainable society, economies need to undergo a substantial transformation and abandon the pursuit of economic growth.

Despite the call for a fundamental transformation, the dominant approach to addressing the issue of degradation remains merely reformative, i.e., aligned with weak sustainability. Theories of weak sustainability are exemplified in the way in which natural and human-made 'capital' is seen as substitutable and the default orientation towards economic growth is maintained (Goodland and Daly, 1996). The main issue of this approach is that it does not go far enough, i.e., it does not question the very foundations of unsustainability. It aims to adjust the economy by incorporating environmental and social considerations while continuing to rely on mainstream economic practice and theorising (Eskelinen and Wilén, 2019). Such environmental adjustment is evident in, for instance, the focus on efficiency (Hopwood et al., 2005), i.e., aiming to reduce the resources and energy used per unit produced (Dyllick and Hockerts, 2002) while failing to address the need to reduce production overall, including the use of resources and

DOI: 10.4324/9781003003588-16

energy (Bonnedahl and Heikkurinen, 2019). Moreover, the weak sustainability discourse does not reflect on the means and ends of societies' existence.

Economic growth remains not only unquestioned by the weak sustainability discourse; it is also viewed as the solution to both ecological and societal problems. For instance, the United Nations' Sustainable Development Goals simultaneously promote economic growth and social and environmental sustainability (Robra and Heikkurinen, 2019; UN, 2020; see also Chapter 2 in this book). It appears absurd that severe ecological and societal problems would be solved using the means by which they were originally created. Ketola et al. (2019, p. 24) appropriately maintain that weak sustainability is 'unsustainability in progressive disguise'. Rather than addressing the underlying mechanisms of the unfolding crises, weak sustainability represents a continuation of business as usual.

Advocates of strong sustainability have challenged and criticised the foundations of the weak sustainability approach (Bonnedahl and Heikkurinen, 2019). The strong sustainability discourse argues that the substitutability of natural and human-made 'capital' is at best very limited (Goodland and Daly, 1996). It acknowledges the inevitable openness of an economic system that derives resources from its environment, while the waste produced by economies returns to the environment (Boulding, 1966; Melgar-Melgar and Hall, 2020). As the capacity of the planet to provide resources and to absorb waste is limited, the imposing of restrictions on economic activities and their growth is unavoidable. Thus, strong sustainability requires adopting a position beyond economic growth, beyond endless increases in production and consumption. One such position is degrowth. Degrowth is a comprehensive vision that imagines a society that is radically different to the current norm. Such a vision is useful for strong sustainability to become a reality, as it represents an ideal towards which societies can strive. To achieve a strongly sustainable society, degrowth proposes intentionally making economies simultaneously smaller and better (Nesterova, 2020a). The smaller size of economies refers to reduced production and consumption and thus reduced matter-energy throughput and returning the scale of economies to within the planet's boundaries. The betterment of economies means reorientating away from the current culture that revolves around material wealth (Fromm, 2002a) towards pursuing wellbeing in a broader sense; that of humans, non-humans, and nature. To pursue wellbeing, degrowth implies shifting away from capitalism and its focus on capital accumulation and expansion (Foster, 2011; Koch and Buch-Hansen, 2020; Buch-Hansen and Carstensen, 2021). Capitalism is a complex phenomenon that includes various agents, the relationships between them, structures, and the dictatorship of a particular class (see, e.g., Lefebvre, 1991, p. 10). Capitalism exploits nature and society (Foster et al., 2010; Surak, 2016) and does not benefit the majority of people (Russell, 1994), whereas degrowth aims for a good life for all.

To enable a strongly sustainable, degrowth society and economy, structures and agents need to undergo a substantial transformation (Nesterova, 2020a, 2021b). This would have implications for everything in the economy, including businesses, as businesses reproduce capitalism via profit-seeking and capital accumulation. By intentionally transforming themselves and participating in making the current socio-economic system more strongly sustainable, businesses can become part of the societal efforts to achieve a strongly sustainable society rather than continue working against this goal by reproducing existing capitalist structures.

Investigating the role of businesses in achieving a strongly sustainable society is a complex matter. It involves theorising about the approaches that should be avoided and those that should be welcomed. It also involves envisioning what change should entail on the level of business and how moving towards a strongly sustainable society could be enacted. To show the contrast between an unhelpful and a desirable approach, this chapter compares a mere reformation (Section 2) and a radical transformation of business (Section 3), while equating weak sustainability with a reformative and strong sustainability with a transformative approach to sustainability. It emphasises how, as part of the socio-economic transformation, businesses need to be transformed rather than merely reformed, thus creating space for more adventurous theorising (Section 4). Section 5 outlines the significant challenges encountered when transforming a business, and Section 6 summarises the arguments and offers a way forward.

## 2 Why Does the Reformation of Business Not Suffice?

Social structures can be reproduced or transformed by agents (Bhaskar, 1998). Reformation largely falls within the premise of the reproduction of structures while making an improvement. Transformation, on the other hand, signifies a complete change. The weak sustainability approach is that of reformation. Central to weak sustainability are the inter-related notions of decoupling, efficiency, and technicism. Weak sustainability aims to maintain economic growth while maintaining belief in and pursuing decoupling. Decoupling postulates that economic growth can continue while resource use is declining and ecological impact diminishing (Jackson, 2017). In other words, economic activity is aimed to be separated from its ecological foundations and impacts. Decoupling is problematic as a concept, as the kind of decoupling that is required (absolute, global, permanent, fast, and large) has not been evidenced (Jackson, 2017; Parrique et al., 2019). The impossibility of absolute decoupling arises from the realisation that something cannot be produced from nothing. Producing anything, either goods or services, presupposes a transformation of nature. Economic growth signifies and increases in the production of goods and services, thus more transformation of nature, even if such production is carried out more efficiently by using better technology.

Improvements in efficiency via the utilisation of technology are the focus of the weak sustainability approach in its attempt to address environmental degradation in practice (Bonnedahl and Heikkurinen, 2019). The pursuit of efficiency is not bad in itself. However, on its own, this approach is problematic, as although rightly focusing on qualitative improvement, it ignores the question of quantity (Heikkurinen and Bonnedahl, 2019). Moreover, it can be counter-productive and lead to increased rather than decreased (as would be expected) use of resources and a higher ecological impact through the rebound effect (Alcott, 2005; Parrique et al., 2019). The rebound effect arises when savings gained from the use of a seemingly more efficient product are negated by even larger expenditure elsewhere or increased use of the given product or resource. This is particularly true in the context of capitalism, in which firms reinvest savings in pursuit of further capital accumulation and consumers spend such savings on the seemingly unlimited products constantly offered via the mechanism of wants creation.

Another issue associated with the focus on efficiency is related to technology. Since efficiency gains are hoped for through technological innovations (see Chapter 11), weak sustainability encourages solutions to the ecological crisis that are based on techno-optimism. Like efficiency, technology is not necessarily bad. However, the problem lies in blind, uncritical and unrestricted techno-optimism (see Heikkurinen and Ruuska, 2021). Such techno-optimism does not account for, or acknowledge, the validity of other alternatives (Grunwald, 2018; Nesterova, 2021a) and leaves very little space for other ways of being in and relating to the world.

Examples of reformative approaches to business are business models that are in line with economic visions based on weak sustainability, such as green growth economy and circular economy (Zink and Geyer, 2017; Spash, 2020). A green growth economy focuses on decoupling economic growth from environmental impact through an increase in efficiency. Likewise, the currently popular in sustainability circles concept of a circular economy focuses on technological advancements to enable decoupling and the continuation of economic growth (Ellen MacArhtur Foundation, 2015; Kirchherr et al., 2017; Schröder et al., 2019). Such conceptualisations of the circular economy fail to take the real, biophysical limits of the planet into account (Giampietro, 2019). Moreover, the circular economy can in fact increase overall production, which partially or even fully counteracts the benefits gained from its implementation (see Zink and Geyer, 2017). This does not mean that the circular economy concept has nothing to offer the sustainability discourse. Indeed, closing material loops as much as possible is compatible with degrowth. However, this aspiration should recognise the irreversibility of the degradation of materials and the necessity of seeing better processes as part of producing enough rather than more. The same major pitfalls of relying solely on improving processes, technological innovation, and the rebound effect affect the visions of the economy when a larger socio-economic transformation and reconsideration of humanity's goals are not pursued. For instance, efficiency can only help achieve sustainability if the rebound effect is counteracted by supplementing efficiency with sufficiency (Robra et al., 2020) and when the overall goal of production is reflected upon. In this case, production processes become qualitatively better and quantitatively in line with the limits imposed by the planet and are carried out with the worthwhile goal of providing a good life for all.

The reformation of business fails because it remains largely superficial. It fails to question the *raison d'être* of business itself and the guiding principle of business, i.e., profit maximisation stemming from the pursuit to accumulate capital. This is exemplified in various attempts to supplement profit with other considerations, as is done in accreditation schemes such as B Corp and Future-Fit. For instance, B Lab, which designed the B Corp certification scheme, aims to 'balance profit and purpose' (B Lab, 2020a), thus leaving the profit motive itself unquestioned. It states that 'B Corps use profits and growth as a means to a greater end: positive impact for their employees, communities, and the environment' (B Lab, 2020a). This attempts to achieve greater ends, precisely via the means that ultimately destroy these ends. Likewise, the Future-Fit scheme attempts to balance 'environmental, social and financial success' (Future-Fit Foundation, 2020). The weak sustainability approach can also be exemplified in the attempt to balance profit with people and the planet, as made by Elkington (1998). Such balancing is counterproductive, as striving for increasing profits, albeit supplemented with social and environmental considerations, leads inevitably to the exploitation of people and the destruction of nature (Foster et al., 2010). If profit remains the goal, which it inevitably does in a capitalist economy, business activity will aim for the valorisation of capital, i.e., constantly increasing its value. This is achieved by seeing human labour and nature as mere inputs into the process of production (Gorz, 1989, 2012).

While such powerful mechanisms as the need and drive to accumulate capital exist and dictate the manner in which businesses operate, initiatives such as recycling should be viewed as insufficient and potentially as greenwashing and distraction from the significant change needed. Such radical change requires leaving whole sectors behind. For instance, B Lab (2020b) states that any company, including an oil company, can obtain their certification, thus become a B Corp, if it is able to demonstrate its commitment to making a social and environmental impact. Considering the urgent need to change to renewable energy for a truly sustainable economy and society (Melgar-Melgar and Hall, 2020), it becomes evident that the ambiguous positive actions that accompany the core, destructive activity of an oil company will not replace the concrete need for such companies to cease to exist in a strongly sustainable society.

## 3 What Does Transformation of Business Mean and Entail?

The weak sustainability approach causes our attention and effort to deviate from much-needed radical alternatives that fundamentally question the *status quo*. Considering the ever-deteriorating state of the environment and of society, time should be considered. A much more radical approach needs to be outlined and adopted (Trainer, 2020). The practices and values at the core of weak sustainability are only relatively enduring. They are not laws of nature, but a result of historical development, and can thus be challenged and changed (Ketola et al., 2019). Hence, transformation is possible.

Contrary to weak sustainability, which remains within the remit of economic activities, strong sustainability goes as far as questioning not only the economic domain itself but also the prevailing capitalist structures and our ways of being in the world and relating to it. It acknowledges the need to move from materialistic wealth to wellbeing in co-existence (Bonnedahl and Heikkurinen, 2019). In this case, sustainability does not refer to sustaining economic growth (Foster et al., 2010). Rather, it has a deeper and more philosophical connotation and contemplates sustaining the life of humans and non-humans into the future. While weak sustainability remains reformative towards *economies* and the processes within them, strong sustainability signifies a transformative approach to *societies*.

The need for transformation starts with the obvious desirability of flourishing rather than the suffering (Sayer, 2011) of many (Russell, 1994 [1935]), and the recognition of the value of the non-human world, independent of humans (Collier, 1999; Ketola et al., 2019). It aims to achieve a strongly sustainable society, a society that maintains ecological sustainability via producing and consuming less and that can provide a good life for all (Jackson, 2017; Maxton, 2018; Trainer, 2020). Aiming to reduce production and consumption as well as the required transformation has fundamental implications on all levels and in all aspects of the economy, which are inter-related. These go from rethinking the economy as a whole (e.g., limits to resource use, the means and ends of economic activities, desirable sectors, vital needs), to the producers themselves (e.g., organisational forms, motives for production), which includes businesses.

The required transformation of business is best seen and understood as part of the transformation of the socio-economic system. It involves asking deep questions about the nature and the aims of business and allows us to escape the premises, convictions, and neoliberal ideology of business and mainstream organisational studies. Such mainstream studies rely on neoclassical economic theorising, which maintains that business is a profit-maximising entity. Transdisciplinary and heterodox approaches such as social-ecological economics (Spash, 2012) and philosophy (Bhaskar, 2012; Ruuska et al., 2020) are used instead. The transformation of business is a radical and adventurous approach, which sees business as a social entity and asks a retroductive question about what business should be for a strongly sustainable society to be possible (Nesterova, 2020a), starting from the inevitability and primacy of the acceptance of the necessary change in society as a whole.

In a strongly sustainable society, production activities need to put as little strain on the earth's limited resources as possible; thus, emphasis is placed on reducing production in a way that is conducive to good life. Production must satisfy genuine, but not excessive or hedonic human needs (Spash, 2012). This becomes the ultimate aim of production in a strongly sustainable society. In other words, producing for use-value needs to replace production for exchange-value (Eskelinen and Wilén, 2019). It signifies a fundamental rethinking of production, which in a strongly sustainable society completely deviates from the pursuit of capital accumulation through profit maximisation. The transformation of business goes far beyond the improvement of processes and entails a radically different approach altogether. An *overall* reduction in businesses' use of resources is needed, not merely their efficient use or a reduction in use *per unit* (Heikkurinen and Bonnedahl, 2019). Sufficient satisfaction of needs concerns all members of society; thus beyond efficiency, production should be characterised by effectiveness (i.e., satisfying the needs of all) and sufficiency (so that everyone has enough) (Heikkurinen and Bonnedahl, 2019).

The concept of degrowth has direct implications for businesses and can be used to outline how business can be transformed, i.e., the direction in which businesses need to move to become suitable for a strongly sustainable society. This can be done by translating the key premises of degrowth, i.e., matter-energy throughput reduction, consideration of people and non-humans, and deviation from the profit maximisation imperative, to the microeconomic level of businesses (Nesterova, 2020a, 2021b). Such considerations concern all business operations, the reasons of production, and the ends to which production is carried out. The implications of degrowth for business are comprehensive because they relate to all levels of reality, including physical (e.g., matter-energy throughput reduction) and social (i.e., consideration of people, including the self) reality. Moreover, they include ethical arguments, such as considering non-humans and deviation from the self-serving profit maximisation imperative. The implications of degrowth are that the balancing of profit, people, and the planet is replaced by the pursuit of the wellbeing of people and non-humans, while respecting the limits of the planet. In other words, in a strongly sustainable society, the centrality of profit should be replaced with the centrality of ethics, which implies satisfaction of everyone's genuine needs, and the need to eventually abandon the profit motive altogether (Nesterova, 2020a). Clearly, such abandonment of the profit motive is not an easy undertaking. Neither is it immediately possible, considering the need in the capitalist system to make a profit to survive. Thus, abandonment of the profit motive can be seen not as a step or an event, but as an intentional journey from making profits sufficient (rather than maximising profit) to deviating from the idea of profit completely in a society that has left capitalism and its mechanisms behind. However, the question arises of whether the transformation of business that needs to occur is so profound that it means the end of business itself.

## 4 From Business to Strongly Sustainable Organisations and Beyond

The required transformation of business as part of societal transformation towards a strongly sustainable society is profound. Businesses need to actively participate in reshaping the socio-economic system and subsequently sustaining it in its new form. As a strongly sustainable society does not aim for growth in the number of businesses or growth in their turnover and other quantitative indicators, this offers new opportunities to abandon the focus on business in its common forms of corporation and limited company (Lawson, 2014). This, in turn, means directing human creative efforts towards alternatives, considering a much wider variety of alternative organisational forms (Parker et al., 2014), and highlighting the validity of other possible ways of organising production rather than viewing other organisational forms and ways of production as radical, marginal, or niche. Thinking in terms of economic organisations rather than in terms of business does not mean that businesses will disappear as social entities. Viewed as communities of people (Lawson, 2014), businesses can change their forms, i.e., intentionally *trans*-form themselves and continue to use their capacities in terms of existing equipment, materials, and skills to produce, albeit radically differently and for altogether different ends.

Various alternative organisational forms can co-exist in the same economy and include a multitude of options. Such new forms should be more conducive to aims that transcend profit maximisation and the mechanisms associated with this, such as the creation of wants. In terms of the principles of operation, such organisations may include the principles of anarchism and democracy. In terms of ownership, alternative organisations may include community- and worker-owned organisations and independently owned small-scale artisanal and craft producers. Community energy projects, community-supported agriculture, hobby and amateur production, and peer production are but a few examples of possibilities that can be considered. Moreover, some production may be organised informally, and likewise include a variety of options, from foraging to household production and production by communities for their own use or for sharing with others.

Thus, businesses can assume multiple forms on their journey to become suitable for a strongly sustainable society, but what should remain central despite the nature of the chosen organisational form is sufficient production to satisfy needs, not production for capital accumulation. Placing needs satisfaction rather than profit at the core of transformation requires a fundamental change in values (Nesterova, 2020a). This is an essential part of a larger cultural transformation towards non-material sources of life satisfaction and cooperation (Trainer, 2020), a different conception of productive life, and being in and relating to the world (Fromm, 2002b; Bhaskar, 2012). Thus, an important part of the transition towards a strongly sustainable society is indeed the required change in ourselves, which includes raising awareness of embodied energy, adjusting one's expectations, developing an ethic of respect for living beings (Melgar-Melgar and Hall, 2020), and nurturing love towards the self, others, and nature, which in turn implies care, concern, responsibility, and knowledge (Fromm, 2002b; Sayer, 2011; Bhaskar, 2012). In other words, it is not the discovery of ideal organisational forms, but the development of radically different worldviews and ways of relating with the world that is at the very core of transformation (Nesterova, 2021a). Without such profound psychological and philosophical changes,

changes in the choices of organisational forms will not occur; and even if they do occur, they would not be sustained.

The all-encompassing transformation of attitudes to business and of businesses that is required for a strongly sustainable society may indicate that a more fruitful and liberating pathway of theorising on production for such societies could go down the path of post-business or what we refer to as 'beyond business'. If a business internalised strong sustainability, the nature of the transformed business would clash with the notion of business as an entity to which the mechanism of capital valorisation is inherent. This may indicate that such a transformed business can no longer be described as a business. Does this mean that private firms will cease to exist? Trainer (2020) and Nesterova (2020a, 2021a, 2021b) argue that *small* firms can still play a role in a transformed, strongly sustainable society. Thus, a firm's existence may depend on the scale and degree to which it influences the socio-economic system. For instance, a small-scale firm specialising in artisanal production, using low technology, and serving the local market is more compatible with a strongly sustainable society than a multinational corporation (see Nesterova, 2021a). However, it should be noted that such small-scale firms will operate in markets, which play a much smaller role than the markets in modern society (Trainer, 2020) and which may disappear altogether as a strongly sustainable society advances on the emerging path of strong sustainability. It is also essential that such firms remain small and are not forced to borrow and repay interest, as is the case in the capitalist economy. Moreover, it is important not to romanticise small firms and see them uncritically as *the* business form for a strongly sustainable society. For instance, Russell (1994 [1935]) offered the example of innumerable and unnecessary small shops in London that operated for the leisure of the idle rich, not for the purpose of satisfying genuine needs. Although Russell's example is from over 80 years ago, the critique still stands more than ever.

## 5 Transformation of Business: Systemic and Agential Constraints

The transformation of business is challenging, as businesses are not isolated from the world around them. They face both systemic constraints (constraining socio-economic structures) and agential constraints (those relating to individual humans, agents). Hence, the transformation of business should not be seen independently from the transformation of the socio-economic system or the change in individuals involved in business.

The transformation of businesses is constrained by the evident fact that businesses exist within the system of capitalism, which imposes its logics and rules on individual humans and businesses. Considering the inter-relation between agents and structures (Bhaskar, 1989, 1998), businesses exist as agents in the economy within structures that constrain their transformation. For instance, one of the key implications of thinking in terms of strong sustainability is the deviation from profit maximisation (Nesterova, 2020a). However, capitalism, with its inherent drive for capital accumulation, necessitates and dictates profit-seeking, making, and maximisation (Foster et al., 2010). Thus, even businesses that attempt to operate differently cannot be regarded as operating fully in line with a strongly sustainable society as long as they remain embedded within capitalist structures. In a capitalist system, even starting an alternative economic organisation may be prohibitive without borrowing, which necessitates repayment with interest, ultimately awakening a profit motive and encouraging growth and participation in capitalism. This is not to say that businesses should stop striving for a better world. Firms should challenge capitalist structures by operating in a radically different manner. For instance, by sharing knowledge free of charge, a firm can provide others with the opportunity to not pay for knowledge elsewhere, thus allowing them to withdraw from participation in a capitalist system on a certain occasion (Nesterova, 2020b). Yet, a full transformative potential can be exercised only if businesses are liberated from capitalism, its culture, and its competitive environment, so they can transform into economic organisations that are fully compatible with a strongly sustainable society.

For a strongly sustainable society that allows businesses to exist as strongly sustainable, alternative economic organisations, a post-capitalist socio-economic system is essential. Such a system would take the biophysical basis of societies and economies into consideration, pursue a good life for all, and manifest an entirely different culture. Without envisioning and striving for the transformation of society as a whole, efforts to outline what businesses should be transformed into and what actions individual businesses should take would remain insufficient. This is because capitalist forces and tendencies such as competition operate at a systemic level (Wigger and Buch-Hansen, 2013). The actions of individual businesses, no matter how radical they may seem or indeed be, are not enough. Envisioning the new system should, however, not be the domain of experts, and participation should be encouraged. In the words of Bhaskar (2002, p. 70), '[w]e don't need mediators, or authorities, or political or any other kind of leaders'. This is because every human being has a capacity for freedom, imagination, and creativity (Tuan, 1998; Bhaskar, 2012), for thought and reflection (Tuan, 1976). Thus, while sharing knowledge is useful, no actors should be seen as 'key'.

Shifting the socio-economic system away from capitalism requires transform- ing culture towards cooperation and away from affluence, and our economies towards self-sufficiency and localised production where possible. It also involves creating cooperative and participatory governance systems (Trainer, 2020). Such governance and decision-making will have implications for production, as eco- nomic decisions regarding employment and needs satisfaction could become a more cooperative and democratic effort, not dictated by firms' pursuits to max- imise profits. Communities should be able to decide what needs to be produced, when, how, by whom and to what ends, as well as how the end product could become accessible to everyone who needs it.

Agential constraints refer to the individuals involved in business and the prevailing values and beliefs that individual humans hold. Transformation necessitates a fundamental change in values. At its core, strong sustainability holds the notion of harmonious and respectful co-existence between humans and nature. It recognises the value of nature in itself and, therefore, rejects the view that nature is subservient to human needs and wants (Collier, 1999; Ketola et al., 2019). Thus, strong sustainability thinking is grounded not only in evidence-based scepticism towards weak sustainability solutions, but also in philosophy, ethics, and morality (Ruuska et al., 2020). One implication of such thinking is the recognition that the purpose of nature and non-humans is not merely to be used by humans. Humans share the planet with other beings, which signifies the need to consider and respect them and to identify ways of relating to them (see e.g., Bhaskar, 2012). This applies to the socio-economic system as a whole, including the process of production and each organisation involved in this process, as well as to individual humans who hold certain worldviews and manifest them through their actions.

To facilitate such a change in values, we need to completely deviate from teaching neoclassical economics (Nesterova, 2021b). As heterodox economics (such as ecological economics) is increasingly being taught, the theoretical foundation of weak sustainability itself, i.e., neoclassical economics also continues to be taught while remaining oblivious towards human nature, co-existence with others (Nancy, 2000), and the way in which the economy is embedded within larger systems, i.e., society and the environment (Melgar-Melgar and Hall, 2020). Neoclassical economics justifies economic growth and capital accumulation, the possibility of which arises precisely due to its lack of recognition of the environment that houses society and hence the economy (Gills and Morgan, 2020). Moreover, neoclassical economics fails to include ethics in its theorising; thus, weak approaches to sustainability do not hold an axiological position, which would place value on nature and non-human life (Spash, 2020). This results in a situation in which the sustainability discourse is advised by the school of economics entirely unsuitable to advise on matters of nature, life, morality, and ethics.

The required transformation of education has profound implications for business education specifically, as well as for how business should be taught. We cannot expect that business education, based on neoclassical economics and its disregard for the inevitable embeddedness of economies in nature and society and its ignorance towards other relevant sciences (e.g., sociology, psychology, geography) and humanities (e.g., history, anthropology, philosophy), will produce business managers and employees with any attitudes other than those compliant with capitalism. A new kind of social-ecological microeconomics needs to be established (Nesterova, 2021b), which recognises not only the implications of biophysical and ecological economics on the microeconomic level, but also includes ethics, a realistic conception of human beings and their relationships and organisations; a deeper understanding of the space within which humans and their organisations exist and with which they interact (Lefebvre, 1991). Apart from business education, the importance of educating the wider population on biophysical matters cannot be underestimated (Melgar–Melgar and Hall, 2020). This may have implications for consumers intentionally making choices in line with strong sustainability. However, it may also be the case that the flaws of the education system cannot be transformed until the economic system is transformed (Russell, 1994 [1935]). This is to say that the capitalist system itself has no incentive to educate the workforce and consumers on alternatives that would undermine it and provide tools for people to deviate from the very mechanisms and ideology that sustain it (Ruuska, 2019). The transformation of society and its multiple systems and the transformation of business should thus be seen as a complex, interrelated process. It is essential to highlight that better policies will not suffice to address the constraints discussed in this section. These constraints are structural, not legislative (Surak, 2016). Developing better policies is merely one aspect of the integrated vision of a desirable change.

## 6 Conclusion

In this chapter, we have investigated the relationship between business and a strongly sustainable society. The relationship was framed as a question, because this connection is far from straightforward. Our answer to the question of whether these two aspects can coexist, in simple yes and no terms, is 'no'. This is because business as a capitalist mode of production, existing for the purpose of capital accumulation is not compatible with a truly strongly sustainable society which opposes growth and capital accumulation. Thus, not only is business as usual impossible in a strongly sustainable society; a reformed business that retains the imperative of profit-making and maximisation while attempting to supplement it with considerations of the environment and people, is also impossible. Only after undergoing a radical, all-encompassing transformation will businesses become suitable for a strongly sustainable society. However, this leads us to propose that a more fruitful theoretical path should go beyond business and focus on alternative economic organisations instead. The end of business as we know it should be seen as liberating, as an opportunity for creativity and participation. It does not mean that economic organisations will cease to exist, or that production will stop altogether. Production in a strongly sustainable society will continue, without a doubt, but it will be carried out by individuals, households, and communities themselves, as well as organisations such as cooperatives, micro-agricultural initiatives, peer production organisations, and others. Businesses can become part of this process in a strongly sustainable society if they transform into degrowth-compatible organisations. Businesses are inherently social entities (Lawson, 2014; Nesterova, 2020a), and individuals involved in a business can intentionally work to transform business operations. A few small, private firms may remain. However, they will have to operate according to degrowth principles, and importantly, deviate from profit maximisation as an imperative. These businesses would become a niche in a strongly sustainable socio-economic system.

The transformation of business should be seen as a challenging undertaking. As businesses are embedded within powerful capitalist structures, these structures must be radically and intentionally transformed to provide ground for the existence of a patchwork of new economic organisations. The transformation of the existing socio-economic system and agents, including the transformation of business, signifies a transformation of the way in which we relate to the world. This concerns both culture and individual worldviews. A completely different way of being in the world becomes necessary, manifested by recognising that we share this planet with other beings, both human and non-human. Ultimately, this requires developing love, care, and deep respect towards them (Bhaskar, 2012; Nesterova, 2021b). Without such serious philosophical work on challenging our current ideologies, attitudes, values, beliefs, worldviews, and behaviours, which often result in utilitarianism and the exploitation of nature, humans, and non-humans, seemingly concrete proposals regarding business models, organisational forms, and practices remain insufficient.

## References

Alcott, B. (2005) 'Jevons' paradox', *Ecological Economics*, 54(1), pp. 9–21.

B Lab (2020a) 'About B Corps', www.bcorporation.net/about-b-corps (Accessed 24 April 2020).

B Lab (2020b) 'Could an oil company become a B Corp?', www.bcorporation.uk/faq-item/could-oil-company-become-b-corp (Accessed 12 May 2020).

Bhaskar, R. (1989) *Reclaiming Reality: A Critical Introduction to Contemporary Philosophy.* London: Verso.

Bhaskar, R. (1998) *The Possibility of Naturalism: A Philosophical Critique of the Contemporary Human Sciences.* 3rd ed. London: Routledge.

Bhaskar, R. (2002) 'The philosophy of meta-reality', *Journal of Critical Realism*, 1(1), pp. 67–93.

Bhaskar, R. (2012) *The Philosophy of MetaReality: Creativity, Love and Freedom.* London: Routledge.

Bonnedahl, K. J. and Heikkurinen, P. (2019) 'The case for strong sustainability', in K. J. Bonnedahl and P. Heikkurinen (eds.), *Strongly Sustainable Societies: Organising Human Activities on a Hot and Full Earth.* London: Routledge, pp. 1–20.

Boulding, K. E. (1966) 'The economics of the coming spaceship Earth', in H. Jarrett (ed.), *Environmental Quality in a Growing Economy.* Baltimore, MD: Johns Hopkins University Press, pp. 3–14.

Buch-Hansen, H. and Carstensen, M. B. (2021) 'Paradigms and the political economy of ecopolitical projects: Green growth and degrowth compared', *Competition & Change.* https://doi.org/10.1177/1024529420987528.

Collier, A. (1999) *Being and Worth.* Abingdon: Routledge.

Dyllick, T. and Hockerts, K. (2002) 'Beyond the business case for corporate sustainability', *Business Strategy and the Environment*, 11(2), pp. 130–141.

Elkington, J. (1998) *Cannibals with Forks: The Triple Bottom Line of 21st Century Business.* Gabriola: New Society Publishers.

Ellen MacArthur Foundation (2015) 'Towards a circular economy: Business rationale for an accelerated transition'. https://www.ellenmacarthurfoundation.org/assets/downloads/TCE_Ellen-MacArthur-Foundation_9-Dec-2015.pdf.

Eskelinen, T. and Wilén, K. (2019) 'Rethinking economic ontologies: From scarcity and market subjects to strong sustainability', in K. J. Bonnedahl and P. Heikkurinen (eds.), *Strongly Sustainable Societies: Organising Human Activities on a Hot and Full Earth*. London: Routledge, pp. 40–57.

Foster, J. B. (2011) 'Capitalism and degrowth - An impossibility Theorem', *Monthly Review*, 62(8), pp. 28–33.

Foster, J. B., Clark, B. and York, R. (2010) *The Ecological Rift: Capitalism's War on the Earth*. New York: Monthly Review Press.

Fromm, E. (2002a) *The Sane Society*. Abingdon: Routledge.

Fromm, E. (2002b) *Man for Himself: An Inquiry into the Psychology of Ethics*. Abingdon: Routledge.

Future-Fit Foundation (2020) 'What you need to know'. www.futurefitbusiness.org/what-you-need-to-know/ (Accessed 24 April 2020).

Georgescu-Roegen, N. (1975) 'Energy and economic myths', *Southern Economic Journal*, 41(3), pp. 347–381.

Giampietro, M. (2019) 'On the circular bioeconomy and decoupling: Implications for sustainable growth', *Ecological Economics*, 162, pp. 143–156.

Gills, B. and Morgan. J. (2020) 'Teaching climate complacency: Mainstream economics textbooks and the need for transformation in economics education', *Globalizations*. https://doi.org/10.1080/14747731.2020.1808413.

Goodland, R. and Daly, H. (1996) 'Environmental sustainability: Universal and non-negotiable', *Ecological Applications*, 6(4), pp. 1002–1017.

Gorz, A. (1989) *Critique of Economic Reason*. London: Verso.

Gorz, A. (2012) *Capitalism, Socialism, Ecology*. London: Verso.

Grunwald, A. (2018) 'Diverging pathways to overcoming the environmental crisis: A critique of eco-modernism from a technology assessment perspective', *Journal of Cleaner Production*, 197, pp. 1854–1862.

Heikkurinen, P. (2019) 'Degrowth: A metamorphosis in being', *Nature and Space*, 2(3), pp. 528–547.

Heikkurinen, P. and Bonnedahl, K. J. (2019) 'Dead ends and liveable futures: A framework for sustainable change', in K. J. Bonnedahl and P. Heikkurinen (eds.), *Strongly Sustainable Societies: Organising Human Activities on a Hot and Full Earth*. London: Routledge, pp. 289–301.

Heikkurinen, P. and Ruuska, T., eds. (2021) *Sustainability Beyond Technology: Philosophy, Critique and Implications for Human Organization*. Oxford: Oxford University Press.

Hopwood, B., Mellor, M. and O'brien, G. (2005) 'Sustainable development: Mapping different approaches', *Sustainable Development*, 13(1), pp. 38–52.

Jackson, T. (2017) *Prosperity Without Growth: Foundations for the Economy of Tomorrow*. 2nd ed. Abingdon: Routledge.

Ketola, T., Räsänen, T. and Syrjämaa, T. (2019) 'The long history of unsustainability: Inter-species relations since the 1850s', in K. J. Bonnedahl and P. Heikkurinen (eds.), *Strongly Sustainable Societies: Organising Human Activities on a Hot and Full Earth*. Abingdon: Routledge, pp. 23–39.

Kirchherr, J., Reike, D. and Hekkert, M. (2017) 'Conceptualizing the circular economy: An analysis of 114 definitions', *Resources, Conservation and Recycling*, 127, pp. 221–232.

Koch, M. and Buch-Hansen, H. (2020) 'In search of a political economy of the post-growth era', *Globalizations*. https://doi.org/10.1080/14747731.2020.1807837.

Lawson T (2014) 'The nature of the firm and peculiarities of the corporation'. www.repository.cam.ac.uk/bitstream/handle/1810/245884/The-Nature-of-the-Firm-and-Peculiarities-of-the-Corporation.pdf?sequence=1 (Accessed 02 July 2018).

Lefebvre, H. (1991) *The Production of Space*. Oxford: Basil Blackwell.

Maxton, G. (2018) *Change!: Warum Wir Eine Radikale Wende Brauchen*. München: Komplett Media.

Melgar-Melgar, R. E. and Hall, C. A. S. (2020) 'Why ecological economics needs to return to its roots: The biophysical foundation of socio-economic systems', *Ecological Economics*, 169, 106567.

Nancy, J-L. (2000) *Being Singular Plural*. Stanford, CA: Stanford University Press.

Nesterova, I. (2020a) 'Degrowth business framework: Implications for sustainable development', *Journal of Cleaner Production*, 262, 121382.

Nesterova, I. (2020b) 'Small business transition towards degrowth', PhD thesis, University of Derby, UK.

Nesterova, I. (2021a) 'Small, local, and low-tech firms as agents of sustainable change', in P. Heikkurinen and T. Ruuska (eds.), *Sustainability Beyond Technology: Philosophy, Critique, and Implications for Human Organization*. Oxford: Oxford University Press, pp. 230–253.

Nesterova, I. (2021b) 'Small firms as agents of sustainable change', *Futures*, 127, 102705.

Parker, M., Cheney, G., Fournier, V. and Land, C. (2014) *The Routledge Companion to Alternative Organization*. Abingdon: Routledge.

Parrique, T., Barth, J., Briens, F., Kerschner, C., Kraus-Polk, A., Kuokkanen A. and Spangenberg, J. H. (2019) 'Decoupling debunked: Evidence and arguments against green growth as a sole strategy for sustainability'. European Environmental Bureau.

Robra, B. and Heikkurinen, P. (2019) 'Degrowth and the sustainable development goals', in L. Filho et al. (eds.), *Decent Work and Economic Growth. Encyclopedia of the UN Sustainable Development Goals*. Springer, Cham, pp. 1–10. https://doi.org/10.1007/978-3-319-71058-7_37-1

Robra, B., Heikkurinen, P. and Nesterova, I. (2020) 'Commons-based peer production for degrowth? – The case for eco-sufficiency in economic organisations', *Sustainable Futures*, 2, 100035.

Russell, B. (1994 [1935]) *In Praise of Idleness*. London: Routledge.

Ruuska, T. (2019) *Reproduction Revisited: Capitalism, Higher Education and Ecological Crisis*. MayFlyBooks, www.mayflybooks.org.

Ruuska, T., Heikkurinen, P. and Wilen, K. (2020) 'Domination, power, supremacy: Confronting anthropolitics with ecological realism', *Sustainability*, 12(7), 2617.

Sayer, A. (2011) *Why Things Matter to People: Social Science, Values and Ethical Life*. Cambridge: Cambridge University Press.

Schröder, P., Bengtsson, M., Cohen, M., Dewick, P., Hofstetter, J. and Sarkis, J. (2019) 'Degrowth within – Aligning circular economy and strong sustainability narratives', *Resources Conservation and Recycling*, 146, pp. 190–191.

Spash (2012) 'New foundations for ecological economics', *Ecological Economics*, 77, pp. 36–47.

Surak, S. M. (2016) 'Capitalist logics, pollution management, and the regulation of harm: Economic responses to the problem of waste electronics', *Capitalism Nature Socialism*, 27(1), pp. 106–122.

Trainer, T. (2020) 'De-growth: Some suggestions from the simpler way perspective', *Ecological Economics*, 167, 106436.

Tuan, Y-F. (1976) 'Humanistic geography', *Annals of the Association of American Geographers*, 66(2), pp. 266–276.

Tuan, Y-F. (1998) *Escapism*. Baltimore, MD: Johns Hopkins University Press.

UN. (2020) 'Sustainable development goals'. www.sustainabledevelopment.un.org/?menu=1300 (Accessed 11 April 2020).

Wigger, A. and Buch-Hansen, H. (2013) 'Competition, the global crisis, and alternatives to neoliberal capitalism: A critical engagement with anarchism', *New Political Science*, 35(4), pp. 604–626.

Zink, T. and Geyer, R. (2017) 'Circular economy rebound', *Journal of Industrial Ecology*, 21(3), pp. 593–602.

# 13

# THE QUEST FOR A SUSTAINABLE HYBRID BUSINESS

*Ellen Stenslie*

## 1 Introduction

Multiple global reports are painting an alarming picture of the state of our planet and are confirming the need to transform our way of living. We have been given a 'code red' and are urged to reduce GHG emissions (IPCC, 2021), stop the rapid decline of nature (IPBES, 2019), and radically reduce overconsumption and unsustainable economic growth in order to ensure sustainability and stay within planetary boundaries (O'Neill, Fanning, Lamb, & Steinberger, 2018). Yet, our desire for material goods seems endless and the consumption of key materials such as fossil fuels, metals, minerals, and biomass is projected to double by 2060 (OECD, 2018). How do we build a sustainable economy that addresses this unabated growth?

The above crises are all manifestations of an economy that has failed to fully internalise the environmental costs of production and continuous economic growth. Resolving these crises means the business sector will have to adapt and innovate in an economy with very different conditions from now. The rules are changing, and we are now witnessing an emerging business paradigm in which many businesses seek to be part of the solution rather than the problem; a paradigm that includes a shift away from deep-rooted institutions such as shareholder primacy and profit maximisation by integrating a broad set of environmental and social values into the core of the organisation. Redefining the purpose of corporations as that of creating shared value and not merely financial profit will drive innovation and reshape capitalism's relationship with society (Porter and Kramer, 2019, p. 4). A group of businesses that does exactly this are those explored in this chapter. By rejecting the neoclassical model of enterprise, they show how one of the most fundamental institutions of our economy can be changed to address the aforementioned challenges facing our planet.

DOI: 10.4324/9781003003588-17

Although most organisations belong to one of the three sectors, public, private, or non-profit (Schröer and Jäger, 2015), for a long time the boundaries between them have become increasingly blurred (Dees and Anderson, 2003; Billis, 2010). Hybrid organisations are organisations that go beyond one organisational form, and often operate across traditional sectors boundaries. Hybrid businesses working with environmental issues, which we here focus on, are both market orientated and mission centred, meaning that they use private-sector approaches and market forces for solving environmental and social issues traditionally associated with the public and non-profit sector. They represent a development in which business organisations have become less commercial, and more like non-profit organisations (Battilana et al., 2012), but also one where non-profit organisations have become more business-like and take on previously public tasks, as for example seen in the UK National Health Service. In doing so, they represent innovation that challenges the traditional ways of economic organising and distinguish themselves from traditional for-profit and non-profit organisations (Boyd, 2009; Wilson and Post, 2013). Hybrid businesses set out to resolve environmental and social issues and are different from traditional businesses in how they grow, prioritise profit, value social/ecological systems, compete, and integrate sustainability (Haigh and Hoffman, 2014). The sustainability-oriented hybrid businesses thus represents a shift in the way that environmental and social responsibility is integrated into the organisation and thereby redefine what a sustainable business can look like.

Environmentally oriented businesses have received significant attention from researchers. Hestad et al. (2020) have identified as many as 60 terms and concepts related to sustainability and hybrid organisations. Examples include ecopreneurship, sustainability-driven entrepreneurship, and environmental ventures. For the sake of readability, this text uses the term 'sustainability hybrids'. This chapter is based on the relevant literature and empirical work on environmental social enterprises in the United Kingdom. It first provides a general overview of sustainability-oriented hybrid businesses and their core characteristics and subsequently discusses their potential role in the transformation towards a sustainable economy.

## 2 Organisations in Flux – A Gradual Shift towards Hybridity and Sustainability

While mainstream business has received significant criticism for its inability and/or unwillingness to internalise social and environmental responsibilities into its business models and value chains, hybrid businesses have been lauded by many for their emphasis on social and environmental responsibility. Indeed, the world has changed since the turn of the millennium, when business critique heightened, diagnosing the modern corporation as a psychopath (Bakan, 2005). Around this same time, the ideas of corporate social responsibility (CSR) seeped into the mainstream (Herrera et al., 2011). CSR and sustainability reporting are now, to a large extent, formalised activities, resulting in a shift in our expectations towards businesses. Today, businesses proudly proclaim how responsible they are. However, the extent to which environmental/social responsibility is integrated into the core of the business, or whether it is mere window dressing and greenwashing still varies tremendously (Jørgensen and Pedersen, 2011). A recent international sweep of 500 company websites showed that as much as 40% of the environmental claims made by these companies may be misleading (CMA, 2021). Gamble et al. (2020) analysed the extent to which a social/environmental mission was integrated in 256 North American-certified B Corps,[1] a group of companies that have voluntarily sought certification for their environmental and social responsibility, and found that only a quarter had a business model where these missions were well integrated. Those who had high environmental scores were more likely to have integrated models, but the most important factor was age; younger firms were far more likely to have an integrated model. This confirms a trend where innovative and young green firms are challenging older and more traditional firms on sustainability in a number of industries (Hockerts and Wüstenhagen, 2010) and that a new generation of socially and environmentally conscious entrepreneurs is emerging.

Still, in the mainstream, economic value creation comes first, and CSR is primarily motivated by risk management and increased financial value (Albuquerque et al., 2019). Research on multinational corporations working with the UN's Sustainable Development Goals demonstrates how corporations tend to focus on internally actionable targets to avoid negative impacts and externalities. They focus much less on targets that are more external, generally 'doing good' or those related to public goods, taking a narrow and passive role (Van Zanten and Van Tulder, 2018). This tendency is also discussed in Chapter 2.

Many businesses are currently working on gradually integrating environmental and social responsibilities, but some not at all. In contrast, sustainability hybrids can be seen to enact a meaning of sustainability that goes further than CSR (Page and Katz, 2010). They go further by assuming – at their core – some environmental and social responsibility as the purpose of their existence. They set themselves apart by wanting to make a net positive value contribution to society and sustainability. This is achieved through the way in which they create and share value. Such spill-over value creation is rare in traditional companies, beyond maximising the value for paying consumers, and is generally not undertaken unless it is aligned with profitmaking activities (Santos et al., 2015). Hybrid businesses aim to create social and environmental value spill-over as a default, for example by providing benefits to other groups than customers, despite facing obstacles when doing so (ibid.). Just exactly how different they are will be shown in the next section.

## 3 Defining Sustainability-Oriented Hybrid Businesses

The complex nature of these organisations makes generalisations and the building of comprehensive typologies difficult. Doherty et al. (2014, pp. 417–418) define hybrid organisations as 'structures and practices that allow the coexistence of values and artefacts from two or more categories'. This means they organise by mixing and matching elements in innovative ways. Hybridity occurs across different dimensions and can be identified in the business model, the legal structure, how the organisation is financed (public or private) and managed, the value orientation, and more (see Karré, 2020). Hybrid businesses operate in a space between government organisations, traditional charities, and traditional corporations. Some examples are non-profit businesses with income-generating activities, social enterprises, and social businesses (Alter, 2007). Many of the hybrid forms stem from long-standing traditional organisations such as cooperatives, mutual societies, or community businesses, trading while integrating some sort of wider societal benefit.[2]

One leading kind of hybrid business is the so-called social enterprise. Hybridity is the defining characteristic of social enterprise (see Grassl, 2012; Battilana and Lee, 2014) and can help explain its emergence, management, and performance (Doherty et al., 2014). A social enterprise uses commercial strategies to maximise improvements in human and environmental well-being rather than profits for external shareholders and can be both for-profit and not-for-profit (Ridley-Duff and Bull, 2011). Whether hybrids such as social enterprises are part of the social economy[3] or the private sector varies (Vickers and Lyon, 2014), some lean more towards the business sector, others the charity sector. Social enterprises have increased rapidly all over the world over the last decade and many work with environmental issues. Examples are consulting services, ecosystem preservation, and management of nature areas. They are engaged in sustainable food production, recycling, renewable energy, sustainable clothing production, transportation, environmental consultancy, or educational services (Kirkwood and Walton, 2014; Vickers and Lyon, 2014). Box 13.1 presents one example of this.

---

**Box 13.1 An example of a sustainability hybrid and social enterprise**

Belu is a bottled water and water filtration system company based in the UK. It is fully owned by the NGO WaterAid and all profits from the social enterprise are reinvested in clean water, toilet infrastructure, and hygiene primarily in developing countries. Their environmental and social purpose is manifested throughout the organisation, reflected in how they make decisions and structure their business. Belu describes itself as a

> 'business that puts people and the environment first. Launched in 2007, our purpose is to change the way the world sees water. In pursuit of this purpose, we invest our profits into saving carbon emissions from entering the atmosphere, championing a circular economy and ending water poverty.'

> (Belu, 2021)

Social enterprises and other hybrids represent a contrast to traditional corporations as their success is measured by positive impact, their income is reinvested to generate a more positive societal effect (Defourny and Nyssens, 2006). They go further than adopting a triple bottom line (Elkington, 1998) or CSR (Dyllick and Hockerts, 2002) in the way they balance their different aims, and specifically do not prioritise the financial mission. Success in hybrids is the value captured not only for the business owners, but the impact, and the value created for society, for example, environmental benefits or social gains (Santos et al., 2015). For sustainability-oriented entrepreneurs, income is a means to improve the environment (Jolink and Niesten, 2015). Although profit is important for making an impact, it is not the primary goal (Stubbs, 2017). However, one may envisage a divide between entrepreneurs pursuing the win–win of maximising profits while doing good, and those who see money purely as a means of reinvesting in their societal and/or environmental mission, reflecting different positions on the hybridity continuum.

Sustainability hybrids are typically set up by sustainability entrepreneurs, described as entrepreneurs 'focused on the preservation of nature, life support and community in the pursuit of perceived opportunities to bring into existence future products, processes and services for gain, where gain is broadly construed to include economic and non-economic gains to individuals, the economy and society' (Shepherd and Patzelt, 2011, p.137). Many 'ecopreneurs' who start value-based hybrids see themselves as system transforming and agents of innovative change (Pastakia, 1998; Isaak, 2002; Schaper, 2002). They tend to have prior experience or a personal engagement with their environmental mission and to be deeply committed to sustainability (Lee and Battilana, 2013). This manifests in how they build their organisation, and according to Haigh and Hoffman (2014, p. 230), hybrid organisations are 'more likely to strive to understand the value of nature beyond its utility resource value than are companies practicing mainstream corporate sustainability'. Their view of nature is not an endless pool of resources; they consider it something to be protected and preserved. The leading role of green entrepreneurs setting up hybrids should thus not be underestimated in the pursuit of sustainability (Isaak, 2002; Parrish and Foxon, 2006; Schaltegger and Wagner, 2011; Wilson and Post, 2013).

## 4 The Logics of Hybrids

Most of these hybrids are deeply oriented towards sustainability and seek to contribute to net-positive sustainability by combining 'commercial, social, and environmental logics, beliefs, and practices simultaneously', making them a particularly interesting group in regard to sustainability transformation (Hestad et al., 2020, p. 647). In this section, we focus on institutional logics, a lens often used to analyse different forms of hybrid organisations in order to understand their uniqueness (Battilana and Lee, 2014). Institutional logics are socially constructed assumptions, values, beliefs, and rules that provide our social reality with meaning, they 'provide a link between individual agency and cognition and socially constructed institutional practices and rule structures' (Thornton and Ocasio, 1999 in Thornton and Ocasio, 2008, p. 101). Such logics are shared understandings of how things should be done in the organisation, and institutions act as rationality contexts, motivating human agency (Vatn, 2005), impacting what becomes the right way to act and the legitimate goals of the organisation (Scott, 2001). These institutions and logics are highly resilient social structures, giving important meaning and stability to social life within an organisation (Scott, 2001). By pursuing financial as well as social and/or environmental aims, hybrids like social enterprises demonstrate the pursuit of multiple logics and the combination of different institutions (Parrish, 2010; Pache and Santos, 2013; Doherty et al., 2014). A distinct feature of sustainability-oriented hybrid organisations is their combination of social, environmental, *and* commercial logic; not only two of these, which is common in many hybrid forms (Hestad et al., 2020). Figure 13.1 provides a framework for the application of all three logics and the potential sustainability impact, showing how the scale and time considered is also a factor in terms of sustainability. While in practice many traditional enterprises take steps to increase sustainability and are not only concerned with the commercial logic, the framework demonstrates the significant steps necessary in order to achieve net positive sustainability impact.

One way to understand business models is to see them as reflections of different logics (Teece, 2010; Laasch, 2018). Research on sustainable business models (SBM) has provided much insight into how social and environmental value is integrated in the creation, capture, and delivery of value in businesses (Boons and Lüdeke-Freund, 2013; Schaltegger et al., 2016; see also Chapter 3). What characterises the choices of businesses that apply SBMs is a combination of different institutional logics, a prioritisation of their social and ecological mission, their determination to be consistent, and partnerships with similar actors to obtain support from their community (Schneider and Clauß, 2020, p. 392). Organising as a hybrid can be considered a business model (Bocken et al., 2014), but having an SBM does not necessarily make an organisation a hybrid. Interviews with sustainability-oriented social enterprises interviewed in the UK found a full integration and prioritisation of environmental value into the business model, echoing a sustainability logic throughout. However, they also demonstrated challenges.

Being a hybrid business is a constant balancing act. Hybrid businesses have been characterised as having 'two masters' (Tyler, 2010) or 'bowing before dual gods' (Smith and Besharov, 2019). A well-recognised challenge for hybrids is dealing with conflicting institutional logics (Jay, 2013; Doherty et al., 2014). For example, as hybrids operate in both private and public markets, as well as in the spaces in-between, they need to manoeuvre both competitive market logic and civil society cooperative logic. Balancing the three logics explained earlier increases the risk of trade-offs not only between the commercial and the social or environmental but also between the environmental and the social. The different

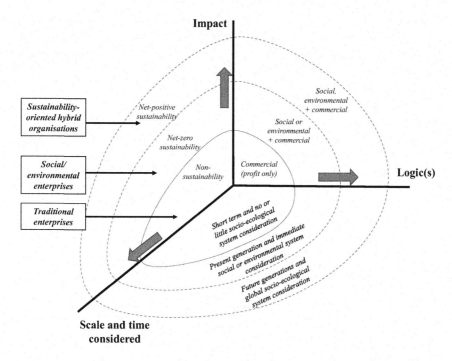

**FIGURE 13.1**   Framework for understanding the sustainability impact of different levels of institutional logics (Hestad et al., 2020, p. 657).

logics create tension in management and decision-making (Pache and Santos, 2013; Laasch, 2018), businesses that add social/ecological objectives to their business model often find that this creates complexities, making it more challenging than being a traditional business (Schneider and Clauß, 2020). This is not only because they need to deal with multiple stakeholders (Stubbs and Cocklin, 2008), but also because of the potential conflicts between institutional logics (Jay, 2013; Pache and Santos, 2013). Research indicates that tensions between different logics are particularly prevalent between social/environmental objectives and commercial ones (Smith et al., 2013; Jolink and Niesten, 2015). In many environmental hybrids, however, the sustainability logic becomes the dominant logic, and conflicts are thereby avoided (Smith and Besharov, 2019).

Balancing the delicate line between a social and/or environmental mission and financial viability makes the hybrids fragile to external pressures and expectations. Management issues arise when trying to maximise both financial and social performance (Zahra et al., 2009), and when figuring out their identity in the face of conflicting demands from various stakeholders (Pache and Santos, 2013). The success of the hybrid thus depends on the abilities of the leaders to balance opposing logics (Jay, 2013; Schröer and Jäger, 2015). According to Smith and Besharov (2019), leaders need to develop 'guardrails', i.e. formal structures, leadership and stakeholder relationships, as well as 'paradoxical frames', i.e. for leaders to understand hybridity in order to influence the business and enable an ongoing adaptation and creation of meaning that reduces tension and sustains the business over time. Managers who are deeply committed to the mission find it less problematic to adhere to the principles (Schneider and Clauß, 2020), and the risk of mission drift[4] and conflicts between institutional logics decreases when broader aims are systematically integrated into the business model (Stenslie, forthcoming; Täuscher and Abdelkafi, 2018).

Many hybrid businesses struggle to be financially sustainable (Hahn and Ince, 2016), a well-known challenge to social economy organisations and social enterprises. Regardless of profit orientation, in many cases, surviving economically becomes even more challenging because hybrids tend to reject business opportunities not aligned with their values (Schneider and Clauß, 2020; Stenslie, forthcoming). Whereas traditional companies are free to accept any income within legal and perhaps moral limitations, hybrids need to carefully choose whom they interact with and what their activities are. They need to ensure that their value chains are aligned with their own values to safeguard their legitimacy. They are also selective about whom they accept finance from as investors (Choi and Gray, 2008). Many sustainable hybrids experience financial conflicts and trade-offs between their economic and environmental aims, and their social and environmental aims, but not all. Stubbs (2017) interviewed B Corp entrepreneurs and found no dilemma between profits and social purpose; however, Stenslie (forthcoming) found that this was a continuous quandary for a majority of environmental social enterprises that faced decisions in which the environmentally optimal choice would entail a significant economic loss, sometimes even threatening the organisation's existence. Although all B Corp entrepreneurs saw their businesses as tools for change to create a better world, they had a predominantly commercial business model, albeit 'underpinned by a sustainability mindset... or set of values that we didn't want to compromise on' (Stubbs, 2017, p. 338). Those interviewed by Stenslie tended to be non-profit and less commercially oriented, with a strong dominance of environmental logic. This illustrates how different hybrids operate along the various dimensions of hybridity and the differences in the extent to which entrepreneurs lead with a commercial or environmental/social logic.

The real challenge for hybrids then lies in creating business models and institutions that align different logics and goals in order to create synergies rather than conflicts (Haigh and Hoffman, 2014). The level of conflict is dependent on the extent to which the organisation works to integrate the social or environmental mission; whether the commercial activity is actively combined with a social activity, or whether the social activity is less integrated into commercial activities. Some hybrids serve the customers/clients and the beneficiaries separately, thus removing the direct link between payment and benefits. Keeping both groups happy makes such hybrids more difficult to manage, and to keep from mission drift (Santos et al., 2015). Hybrids need to balance the value they capture and create systematically, to face competing demands, and to avoid some dominating others (ibid.). Managing three different logics generates an institutional complexity that can become a barrier to achieving aims (Jay, 2013). Nevertheless, it is also in the combination of these three logics (i.e. financial and both social and environmental) that the real potential for a significant sustainability contribution lies (Hestad et al., 2020).

## 5 Legal Institutions

It is not only the business model that echoes the underlying logics of the hybrid, but also the choice of legal structure. For many decades, the basics of corporate legal structures have remained the same, often poorly matching the needs of hybrid organisations. A small, family-run business in a village is very different from a multinational company, yet most businesses are organised as sole proprietorship or limited companies. The emergence of hybrid businesses has led to the development of novel legal structures that may be defined as 'a corporate entity that embodies legal tools which require and/or encourage the pursuit of dual economic and social mandates within businesses' (Liao, 2014, p. 67). One example is the *Community Interest Company* (CIC), a British legal structure created in 2005 for social enterprises. CICs serve a stated community interest and must annually report on this. Their activities can vary from sustainable food production, to recycling or healthcare (within the NHS). Although CICs can be limited by shares or guarantees, they are companies regulated by company law and taxed in the same way as any other (CIC-Regulator, 2017). Structurally, a CIC resembles both a non-profit commercial charity and a traditional business, but its most important traits are an asset lock and a cap on dividends, ensuring that surplus is reinvested into the community interest as opposed to transferred outside of the company.

Conversely, the *Benefit Corporation* (BC) is an American legal structure first passed in 2010. It is a for-profit business but has a legally stated purpose to consider public benefit and an obligation to annually report on its social and environmental performance using a third party standard (B Lab, 2021). Reformed legal structures for cooperatives and other social-purpose businesses are also growing across Europe and other parts of the world. The adoption of the above structures remains low, albeit increasing and causing significant interest.

These structures are still far from the norm, but they represent a willingness amongst lawmakers to reform the law to offer hybrids options. These structures are a tool for change (Stubbs, 2017) that allow disruptive innovation by meeting societal needs in a way that traditional corporations do not, and without the financial pressure on directors (Liao, 2014). Empirical research by Stenslie (forthcoming) shows that entrepreneurs of sustainability-oriented social enterprises carefully choose legal institutions that provide them with legitimacy, help them achieve their missions (environmental, social, and financial), and enable them to attract funding. Legal institutions aid hybrid businesses in their balancing act by providing structural limitations but also opportunities for demonstrating their uniqueness and accountability over standard forms. The measures towards transparency and accountability provided by these structures, although not perfect, offer some reassurance to the public, government agencies, and investors that this is a business that takes its commitment towards social and/or environmental value creation seriously. Further development of hybrid legal structures is thus important for the strengthening and growth of hybrid businesses (Hysa et al., 2018).

## 6 Can Sustainable Hybrid Businesses Lead the Way Towards Sustainability?

The discussion on business and sustainability relates to a larger political debate on how environmental issues should be addressed and the economy structured. Much of the positivity towards both CSR and commercial hybrid models is based on their potential role of applying market forces to solve societal issues. The belief remains that under certain conditions, 'the invisible hand of capitalism' will ensure that the profit-seeking behaviour of self-interested actors is aligned with their values in terms of societal welfare and ensuring good solutions for all. The current CSR and sustainability paradigm is largely founded upon arguments for the business case for sustainability (Schaltegger et al., 2019), i.e. making money *and* 'saving the planet'. Thus, although not legal requirements for businesses, shareholder primacy and profit maximisation remain extremely influential institutions, challenging the pursuit for sustainability (Sjåfjell et al., 2015). However, the neoliberal 'win–win' rhetoric much like the 'shared value' rhetoric (Porter and Kramer, 2019) is still about increasing overall value production, and not about, for example, redistribution. The outcome is rarely fair for people (Santos et al., 2015, p. 40), or the planet.

How society conceptualises and integrates economic growth is fundamental to how businesses can operate. In a world in which economic growth is pursued as the holy grail, unsustainable growth remains an object of critique (Daly, 1977; Jackson, 2009). As mentioned at the beginning of this chapter, we need to significantly reduce overconsumption and unsustainable economic growth to progress towards sustainability. Business organisations can play a vital role in this process if they can change their approach towards environmental resources, e.g., by implementing circularity in production and consumption, or reducing and changing consumption patterns altogether, which many hybrids work to achieve. Approaches to reduce economic growth and growth in consumption include the green economy, degrowth, and post-growth, however, they all reflect very different ideological foundations of sustainability and growth. The green economy is system preserving, relying on technological fixes and emphasising the use of markets and benefits for the private sector to achieve sustainability (see Chapter 4 for a further discussion on the green economy). Degrowth, on the other hand, calls for 'an equitable downscaling of production and consumption that increases human well-being and enhances ecological conditions at the local and global level' (Schneider et al., 2010, p. 512) and seeks a systemic change on multiple levels, in particular, in social justice. Finally, postgrowth advocates aim to define how we can organise an economy and make it less growth oriented, yet still focused on well-being and prosperity within planetary limits, minimising resource use and satisfying sufficient needs (Jackson, 2009, 2017; Koch, 2020).

The institutionas of a capitalist green economy would probably be very different from that in a degrowth economy, in particular in terms of how success is measured and how growth is enacted. Many social enterprises and hybrid organisations see growth as a way in which to increase their impact, and green entrepreneurs tend to prefer moderate growth (Haigh and Hoffman, 2014; Vickers and Lyon, 2014; Hahn and Ince, 2016, p. 42). For many hybrid entrepreneurs, growth should not compromise values such as transparency, independence, and mission orientation, and being 'deep green', many of these enterprises actively reject business language and traditional forms of economic growth (Vickers and Lyon, 2014). An example of this is the social enterprise Belu (see Box 13.1), which has stated that in order to minimise its carbon footprint, it will not export its products outside the country, making an active choice to grow less in order to remain sustainable (Belu, 2021). A degrowth economy would furthermore entail a radically hybrid form of enterprise, most likely a type of social enterprise or eco-social enterprise (Johanisova et al., 2013; Johanisova and Fraňková, 2017). Yet others argue that the not-for-profit enterprise model is a necessary step towards sustainability (Hinton, 2021), challenging the way in which most business and a major share of hybrids operate today.

Sustainability in business, including hybrids, is complicated because there is no unified idea of what a sustainable enterprise should look like and because the underlying assumptions about economic and environmental systems and growth have implications for what is considered viable. While some might say a sustainable hybrid is one that produces green bamboo straws as opposed to plastic straws, others may see straws as a waste of natural resources, based on convenience rather than necessity (unless needed, for example, in healthcare). In a deeply sustainable economy, many of today's businesses would probably not exist, as they are fundamentally unsustainable, even when applying circular economy solutions. The debate on hybrids and sustainability thus relates to larger value-based political discussions that rarely make it to the mainstream. Chapter 12 argues that the current enterprise's aim will never be to be sustainable. Others yet claim that social, hybrid businesses are the way forward to make capitalism more sustainable (Hysa et al., 2018) and can change capitalism itself (Wilson and Post, 2013; Santos et al., 2015). The question of whether hybrids can fix a failing economic system and inspire a new, more responsible form of capitalism, however, remains unanswered (Santos et al., 2015).

One part of the fix would require a set of new policies. But the current emphasis on a green, growth-based economy acts as a barrier to state action, as environmental policies cannot reduce growth (Koch, 2020). Still, an active government can take the lead by building networks with actors from all sectors in order to build the transformation towards sustainability (ibid.). Sustainability-oriented hybrid organisations are well positioned for such a transition, as they are embedded in related active networks and are already integrating many sustainability dimensions and combining logics from different sectors to achieve change. But although they have long been put forth as a panacea for societal issues (Hall et al., 2010), more research is needed to understand the nature of hybrid organisations, the role they play in the economy, and how mainstream companies can move towards sustainability (Haigh and Hoffman, 2014). Research on sustainable hybrids has long lacked understanding of socio-ecological interactions, as well as of the environmental impact of economic activities, and these need to be better understood to assess the true potential of hybrids to create change (Muñoz and Cohen, 2017). Specifically, more empirical research, as well as improved frameworks for understanding the complexities and outcomes on sustainability-oriented hybrids, is needed in order to assess their potential to transform the economy (Hestad et al., 2020). While a significant amount of research shows that hybrid businesses are succeeding in providing value beyond the financial bottom line (Hahn and Ince, 2016), measuring not only the direct environmental impact but also the role of hybrids in transforming the economy is a complex task. Haigh and Hoffman (2014, p. 227) have developed several propositions to guide research on hybrid organisations, including challenging '*beliefs* about social, ecological and economic systems'; '*competitive practices*'; and 'how sustainability is *enacted*'. These propositions illustrate how it is essential to keep exploring how hybrids and their particular approach to sustainability not only can lead to societal transformation but also how the wider system around them would need to change in order to accommodate these particular types of economic institutions.

## 7 Conclusion

This chapter has explored hybrid enterprises from a sustainability perspective. Sustainability-oriented hybrid businesses exist in a variety of forms, all demonstrating institutional change in how businesses can define success, value nature, grow, and enact sustainability. By emphasising their environmental and/or social mission above their financial, they redefine the norms, conventions, and formal rules for what being a business means, This implies placing weight on cooperation, compassion, and value-based leadership, nurturing a sustainable economy less obsessed with financial capital and growth (Schröer and Jäger, 2015).

However, working to integrate these changes and prioritising environmental and social aims is inherently complex and entails constantly weighing up sometimes conflicting priorities, becoming a constant challenge especially for management. Furthermore, the end result for sustainability depends on what type of hybridity is being prioritised and how sustainability is enacted. If the commercial logic is allowed to dominate, this likely reduces the prospects of a significant contribution towards sustainability. The distinction remains between mainstream businesses integrating social and environmental concerns versus radical change-making sustainability hybrids seeking to reform the economy and redefine what a business is.

Changing the way in which business organisations are institutionally structured can have far-reaching effects on the broader economic system. However, while these hybrids attempt to address the challenges we face, the ones they face attempting to survive within an economic system that does not favour them are significant. To support sustainable hybrids, governments could enact novel policies to shift certain system dynamics, and e.g. the investment sector could alter the criteria for their investments. This entails redirecting economic growth towards a broader set of value creation. Finally, further research on developing more sophisticated hybrid legal structures and empirical data from these can offer valuable insights. The opportunities and innovation that expanding hybrid organisational forms present are significant and should not be ignored in the transition towards a sustainable economy.

## Notes

1  The B Corp certification is an international certification system of the NGO B Lab. It is connected to, although not the same as, the Benefit Corporation, a legal corporate form restricted to the US.
2  Cooperatives are a membership form of social economy organisation and may not always be defined as hybrids, depending on their characteristics.
3  The social economy includes cooperatives, mutual societies, non-profit associations, foundations, etc. They operate in a broad number of commercial activities within many sectors, and are governed by values such as solidarity, participation, and primacy of people over capital.
4  For more information on mission drift, see (Battilana et al., 2012; Ben-Ner, 2002).

## References

Albuquerque, R., Koskinen, Y. and Zhang, C. (2019) 'Corporate social responsibility and firm risk: Theory and empirical evidence', *Management Science*, 65(10), pp. 4451–4469.
Alter, K. (2007) 'Social enterprise typology', *Virtue Ventures LLC*, 12, pp. 1–124.
B Lab (2021) 'Benefit corporation FAQ'. https://benefitcorp.net/faq.
Bakan, J. (2005) *The Corporation: The Pathological Pursuit of Profit and Power*. New York: Simon and Schuster.
Battilana, J. and Lee, M. (2014) 'Advancing research on hybrid organizing–Insights from the study of social enterprises', *Academy of Management Annals*, 8(1), pp. 397–441.
Battilana, J., Lee, M., Walker, J. and Dorsey, C. (2012, Summer) '*In search of the hybrid ideal*. Stanford Social Innovation Review', *Stanford Social Innovation Review*, 51, 55.
Belu. (2021) 'Belu homepage'. https://belu.org/
Ben-Ner, A. (2002) 'The shifting boundaries of the mixed economy and the future of the nonprofit sector', *Annals of Public and Cooperative Economics*, 73(1), pp. 5–40.
Billis, D. (2010) *Hybrid Organizations and the Third Sector: Challenges for Practice, Theory and Policy*. Basingstoke: Macmillan International Higher Education.
Bocken, N., Short, S. W., Rana, P. and Evans, S. (2014) 'A literature and practice review to develop sustainable business model archetypes', *Journal of Cleaner Production*, 65, pp. 42–56.

Boons, F. and Lüdeke-Freund, F. (2013) 'Business models for sustainable innovation: state-of-the-art and steps towards a research agenda', *Journal of Cleaner Production*, 45, pp. 9–19.

Boyd, B. (2009) *Hybrid Organizations: New Business Models for Environmental Leadership.* Sheffield: Greenleaf Publishing.

Choi, D. Y. and Gray, E. R. (2008) 'Socially responsible entrepreneurs: What do they do to create and build their companies?', *Business Horizons*, 51(4), pp. 341–352. https://doi.org/10.1016/j.bushor.2008.02.010.

CIC-Regulator (2017) *Frequently Asked Questions.* Office of the Regulator of Community Interest Companies: Crown. https://assets.publishing.service.gov.uk/government/uploads/system/uploads/attachment_data/file/641412/13-786-community-interest-companies-frequently-asked-questions.pdf.

CMA (2021) 'Global sweep finds 40% of firms' green claims could be misleading' [Press release]. https://www.gov.uk/government/news/global-sweep-finds-40-of-firms-green-claims-could-be-misleading.

Daly, H. E. (1977) *Steady-State Economics.* San Francisco: W.H. Freeman.

Dees, J. G. and Anderson, B. B. (2003) 'Sector-bending: Blurring lines between non-profit and for-profit', *Society*, 40(4), pp. 16–27.

Defourny, J. and Nyssens, M. (2006) 'Defining social enterprise', *Social Enterprise: At the Crossroads of Market, Public Policies and Civil Society*, 7, pp. 3–27.

Doherty, B., Haugh, H. and Lyon, F. (2014) 'Social enterprises as hybrid organizations: A review and research agenda', *International Journal of Management Reviews*, 16(4), pp. 417–436.

Dyllick, T. and Hockerts, K. (2002) 'Beyond the business case for corporate sustainability', *Business Strategy and the Environment*, 11(2), pp. 130–141.

Elkington, J. (1998) *Cannibals with Forks: The Triple Bottom Line of 21st Century Business*: Stony Creek, CT: New Society Publishers.

Gamble, E. N., Parker, S. C. and Moroz, P. W. (2020) 'Measuring the integration of social and environmental missions in hybrid organizations', *Journal of Business Ethics*, 167(2), pp. 271–284.

Grassl, W. (2012) 'Business models of social enterprise: A design approach to hybridity', *ACRN Journal of Entrepreneurship Perspectives*, 1(1), pp. 37–60.

Hahn, R. and Ince, I. (2016) 'Constituents and characteristics of hybrid businesses: A qualitative, empirical framework', *Journal of Small Business Management*, 54, pp. 33–52.

Haigh, N. and Hoffman, A. J. (2014) 'The new heretics: Hybrid organizations and the challenges they present to corporate sustainability', *Organization & Environment*, 27(3), pp. 223–241.

Hall, J. K., Daneke, G. A. and Lenox, M. J. (2010) 'Sustainable development and entrepreneurship: Past contributions and future directions', *Journal of Business Venturing*, 25(5), pp. 439–448. https://doi.org/10.1016/j.jbusvent.2010.01.002.

Herrera, A. A., Alcañiz, E. B., Pérez, R. C. and Garcia, I. S. (2011) 'Epistemological evolution of corporate social responsibility in management: An empirical analysis of 35 years of research', *African Journal of Business Management*, 5(6), pp. 2055–2064.

Hestad, D., Tàbara, J. D. and Thornton, T. F. (2020) 'The three logics of sustainability-oriented hybrid organisations: A multi-disciplinary review', *Sustainability Science*, 16(2), pp. 647–661.

Hinton, J. (2021) 'Five key dimensions of post-growth business: Putting the pieces together', *Futures*, 131, 102761.

Hockerts, K. and Wüstenhagen, R. (2010) 'Greening Goliaths versus emerging Davids—Theorizing about the role of incumbents and new entrants in sustainable entrepreneurship', *Journal of Business Venturing*, 25(5), pp. 481–492.

Hysa, X., Zerba, E., Calabrese, M. and Bassano, C. (2018) 'Social business as a sustainable business model: making capitalism anti-fragile', *Sustainability Science*, 13(5), pp. 1345–1356.

IPBES (2019) 'Global assessment report on biodiversity and ecosystem services of the Intergovernmental Science-Policy Platform on Biodiversity and Ecosystem Services'. https://ipbes.net/sites/default/files/inline/files/ipbes_global_assessment_report_summary_for_policymakers.pdf:

IPCC (2021) 'Summary for policymakers', in *Climate Change 2021: The Physical Science Basis. Contribution of Working Group I to the Sixth Assessment Report of the Intergovernmental Panel on Climate Change*. Cambridge University Press. https://www.un.org/press/en/2021/sgsm20847.doc.htm.

Isaak, R. (2002) 'The making of the Ecopreneur', *Greener Management International*, 2002(38), pp. 81–91. https://doi.org/10.9774/GLEAF.3062.2002.su.00009.

Jackson, T. (2009) *Prosperity without Growth: Economics for a Finite Planet*. Earthscan, London, New York: Routledge.

Jackson, T. (2017) *Prosperity without Growth: Foundations for the Economy of Tomorrow*. 2nd ed. Abingdon: Routledge.

Jay, J. (2013) 'Navigating paradox as a mechanism of change and innovation in hybrid organizations', *Academy of Management Journal*, 56(1), pp. 137–159.

Johanisova, N., Crabtree, T. and Fraňková, E. (2013) 'Social enterprises and non-market capitals: a path to degrowth?', *Journal of Cleaner Production*, 38, pp. 7–16.

Johanisova, N. and Fraňková, E. (2017) 'Eco-social enterprises', in C. L. Spash (ed.) *Routledge Handbook of Ecological Economics: Nature and Society*. Abingdon, UK: Routledge, pp. 507–516.

Jolink, A. and Niesten, E. (2015) 'Sustainable development and business models of entrepreneurs in the organic food industry', *Business Strategy and the Environment*, 24(6), pp. 386–401.

Jørgensen, S. and Pedersen, L. J. T. (2011) 'The why and how of corporate social responsibility', *Beta: Scandinavian Journal of Business Research*, 25(2), pp. 121–137.

Karré, P. M. (2020) 'Hybrid organisations: between state and market', in D. Billis and C. Rochester (eds.) *Handbook on Hybrid Organisations*. Cheltenham, UK: Edward Elgar Publishing, pp. 31–47.

Kirkwood, J. and Walton, S. (2014) 'How green is green? Ecopreneurs balancing environmental concerns and business goals', *Australasian Journal of Environmental Management*, 21(1), pp. 37–51. https://doi.org/10.1080/14486563.2014.880384.

Koch, M. (2020) 'The state in the transformation to a sustainable postgrowth economy', *Environmental Politics*, 29(1), pp. 115–133.

Laasch, O. (2018) 'Beyond the purely commercial business model: Organizational value logics and the heterogeneity of sustainability business models', *Long Range Planning*, 51(1), pp. 158–183.

Lee, M. and Battilana, J. (2013) 'How the zebra got its stripes: Impringing of individuals and hybrid social ventures', *Harvard Business School Organizational Behavior Unit Working Paper* (No. 14–005).

Liao, C. (2014) 'Disruptive innovation and the global emergence of hybrid corporate legal structures', *European Company Law*, 11(2), pp. 67–70.

Muñoz, P. and Cohen, B. (2017) 'Towards a social-ecological understanding of sustainable venturing', *Journal of Business Venturing Insights*, 7, pp. 1–8.

OECD (2018) *Global Material Resources Outlook to 2060: Economic Drivers and Environmental Consequences.* https://www.oecd-ilibrary.org/environment/global-material-resources-outlook-to-2060_9789264307452-en.

O'Neill, D. W., Fanning, A. L., Lamb, W. F. and Steinberger, J. K. (2018) 'A good life for all within planetary boundaries', *Nature Sustainability*, 1(2), pp. 88–95. https://doi.org/10.1038/s41893-018-0021-4.

Pache, A.-C. and Santos, F. (2013) 'Embedded in hybrid contexts: How individuals in organizations respond to competing institutional logics', in Lounsbury, M. and Boxenbaum, E. (eds.) *Institutional Logics in Action, Part B (Research in the Sociology of Organizations, Vol. 39 Part B)*. Bingley: Emerald Group Publishing Limited, pp. 3–35. https://doi.org/10.1108/S0733-558X(2013)0039AB014.

Page, A. and Katz, R. A. (2010) 'Is social enterprise the new corporate social responsibility', *Seattle University Law Review*, 34, 1351.

Parrish, B. D. (2010) 'Sustainability-driven entrepreneurship: Principles of organization design', *Journal of Business Venturing*, 25(5), pp. 510–523. https://doi.org/10.1016/j.jbusvent.2009.05.005.

Parrish, B. D. and Foxon, T. J. (2006) 'Sustainability entrepreneurship and equitable transitions to a low-carbon economy', *Greener Management International*, 2006(55), pp. 47–62.

Pastakia, A. (1998) 'Grassroots ecopreneurs: Change agents for a sustainable society', *Journal of Organizational Change Management*, 11(2), pp. 157–173.

Porter, M. E. and Kramer, M. R. (2019) 'Creating shared value', in G. Lenssen, and N. Smith (eds.) *Managing Sustainable Business*. Dordrecht: Springer, pp. 323–346. https://doi.org/10.1007/978-94-024-1144-7_16.

Ridley-Duff, R. and Bull, M. (2011) *Understanding Social Enterprise. Theory & Practice*. London: SAGE Publications Ltd.

Santos, F., Pache, A.-C. and Birkholz, C. (2015) 'Making hybrids work: Aligning business models and organizational design for social enterprises', *California Management Review*, 57(3), pp. 36–58.

Schaltegger, S., Hansen, E. G. and Lüdeke-Freund, F. (2016) Business models for sustainability: Origins, present research, and future avenues', *Organization & Environment*, 29(1), pp. 3–10. doi:10.1177/1086026615599806.

Schaltegger, S., Hörisch, J. and Freeman, R. E. (2019) 'Business cases for sustainability: A stakeholder theory perspective', *Organization & Environment*, 32(3), pp. 191–212.

Schaltegger, S. and Wagner, M. (2011) 'Sustainable entrepreneurship and sustainability innovation: Categories and interactions', *Business Strategy and the Environment*, 20(4), pp. 222–237.

Schaper, M. (2002) 'Introduction: the essence of ecopreneurship', *Greener Management International*, 2002(38), pp. 26–30.

Schneider, F., Kallis, G. and Martinez-Alier, J. (2010) 'Crisis or opportunity? Economic degrowth for social equity and ecological sustainability. Introduction to this special issue', *Journal of Cleaner Production*, 18(6), pp. 511–518.

Schneider, S. and Clauß, T. (2020) 'Business models for sustainability: Choices and consequences', *Organization & Environment*, 33(3), pp. 384–407.

Schröer, A. and Jäger, U. (2015) 'Beyond balancing? A research agenda on leadership in hybrid organizations', *International Studies of Management & Organization*, 45(3), pp. 259–281.

Scott, W. R. (2001) *Institutions and Organizations*. 2nd edn. Thousand Oaks, CA: Sage.

Sjåfjell, B., Johnston, A., Anker-Sørensen, L. and Millon, D. (2015) 'Shareholder primacy: The main barrier to sustainable companies', in B. Sjåfjell and B. J. Richardson (eds.), *Company Law and Sustainability: Legal Barriers and Opportunities*. Cambridge: Cambridge University Press, pp. 79–147. doi:10.1017/CBO9781107337978.005.

Smith, W. K. and Besharov, M. L. (2019) 'Bowing before dual gods: How structured flexibility sustains organizational hybridity', *Administrative Science Quarterly*, 64(1), pp. 1–44.

Smith, W. K., Gonin, M. and Besharov, M. L. (2013) 'Managing social-business tensions: A review and research agenda for social enterprise', *Business Ethics Quarterly*, 23(3), pp. 407–442.

Stenslie, E. (forthcoming). *An Institutional Analysis of Environmental Social Enterprises and Their Role in Building a Sustainable Economy*. Institute for international environment and development studies. Doctoral Thesis. Norwegian University of Life Sciences. Norway.

Stubbs, W. (2017) 'Sustainable entrepreneurship and B corps', *Business Strategy and the Environment*, 26(3), pp. 331–344.

Stubbs, W. and Cocklin, C. (2008) 'Conceptualizing a "sustainability business model"', *Organization & Environment*, 21(2), pp. 103–127.

Täuscher, K. and Abdelkafi, N. (2018) 'Scalability and robustness of business models for sustainability: A simulation experiment', *Journal of Cleaner Production*, 170, pp. 654–664.

Teece, D. J. (2010) 'Business models, business strategy and innovation', *Long Range Planning*, 43(2–3), pp. 172–194.

Thornton, P. H. and Ocasio, W. (2008) 'Institutional logics', *The Sage Handbook of Organizational Institutionalism*, 840(2008), pp. 99–128.

Tyler, J. (2010) 'Negating the legal problem of having two masters: A framework for L3C fiduciary duties and accountability', *Vermont Law Review*, 35, 117.

Van Zanten, J. A. and Van Tulder, R. (2018) 'Multinational enterprises and the sustainable development goals: An institutional approach to corporate engagement', *Journal of International Business Policy*, 1(3), pp. 208–233.

Vatn, A. (2005) *Institutions and the Environment*. Cheltenham: Edward Elgar Publishing.

Vickers, I. and Lyon, F. (2014) 'Beyond green niches? Growth strategies of environmentally-motivated social enterprises', *International Small Business Journal*, 32(4), pp. 449–470.

Wilson, F. and Post, J. E. (2013) 'Business models for people, planet (& profits): Exploring the phenomena of social business, a market-based approach to social value creation', *Small Business Economics*, 40(3), pp. 715–737.

Zahra, S. A., Gedajlovic, E., Neubaum, D. O. and Shulman, J. M. (2009) 'A typology of social entrepreneurs: Motives, search processes and ethical challenges', *Journal of Business Venturing*, 24(5), pp. 519–532. http://doi.org/10.1016/j.jbusvent.2008.04.007.

# 14

# SUSTAINABLE FUTURES AND THE CHANGING ROLE OF BUSINESS IN SOCIETY

*Anne Toppinen, Robert Kozak, and Dalia D'Amato*

## 1 A Renewed Sense of Urgency

Since 2007, of the top ten global risks estimated by the World Economic Forum through consultation with expert stakeholders, economic issues have progressively conceded their place to geopolitical, societal, technological, and – largely – environmental issues. Even after the pandemic, failure to act for climate change and the interlinked problem of extreme weather events head the list of short- and medium-term global risks (World Economic Forum, 2022). Climate-related risks, together with biodiversity loss, natural resource crises, and human-caused environmental damage, also dominated the long-term risks, according to the same report. Such risks will eventually materialise as severe disruptions to our existing economic systems, but the changes are only beginning to occur. Moreover, global environmental challenges are recognised as being wickedly intertwined both with each other and with other issues, such as economic conflicts, migration, infrastructure failures, or infamously, infectious diseases (ibid).

Already prior to the pandemic, the world had witnessed major widespread protests calling for more urgent environmental actions from governments, for example, Greta Thunberg and the school strike movement in Europe, the Extinction Rebellion movement, the activist-led lawsuits against the government's climate inactivity in the Netherlands and Canada, or the pipeline protests throughout North America. With global awareness of the climate change crisis gathering momentum, local-level extreme weather events are being extensively discussed in the public and media worldwide, creating a higher level of public awareness of the climate change-induced risks of flooding, forest fires, and extreme droughts.

On the one hand, the pandemic has, in the past two years, shifted some of the focus from the environmental crisis to human health and to the need for economic recoveries – perpetuating an erroneous siloed vision of human prosperity

DOI: 10.4324/9781003003588-18

and well-being. On the other hand, the health crisis has revealed and exacerbated the soft underbellies of a global society and economy that is experiencing increasingly polarised and conflictual political environments, power concentration and inequalities, new forms of poverty, rapid and unbridled technological changes, and overall, a more insecure and volatile future. For the luckiest, the government-imposed lockdowns and forced inactivity have been a dress rehearsal for a slower-paced lifestyle, with opportunities to work remotely in serene environments, and additional personal time, granted by the pause in local and international travel. The least lucky have been confronted with the harsh realities of fragile and insecure employment, difficult living conditions, and mental health challenges, with little support from weak welfare and health support systems. The pandemic has then overwhelmed parts of the global economy that earlier appeared robust, highlighting the reality that we live in a world connected by international trade, largely based on economic growth and increasing levels of consumption. This system has shown to be vulnerable and unprepared for external shocks.

Despite the increasing media coverage of both environmental problems and the pandemic, however, we are witnessing increasing political polarisation on both issues. In addition, during early 2022, when this chapter was written, geopolitical risks between nations have unexpectedly skyrocketed. Amidst a lot of chaos and fast-paced developments, common lessons can be drawn from the environmental crisis, the pandemic crisis, and the most recent geopolitical crisis. First, the interconnectedness of ecosystem and biodiversity conservation, energy security, supply chain security, national and global security, and human well-being; second, the role of international and regional policy coordination and that of international financial systems in managing crises and steering change; third, the role of information, disinformation, and information war in affecting beliefs, behaviours, and social acceptability of policy decisions or instruments; and fourth, the latent power of courageous leadership, as well as that of global citizens that can pressure and support the action of governments and other actors.

As the world waits in confusion for the pandemic crisis and the renewed geopolitical risks to finally and hopefully come under some sort of control, and in fear of the resulting economic fall-out, an impending, generalised sense of being at a crucial crossroads is palpable, especially as the resulting economic fall-out looms large. Perspective, needs, and perhaps deep leverage points such as human values, have shifted. An Overton window of policies and practices has been opened that would not be acceptable or feasible under 'normal' circumstances. But how will this shift manifest, and will it last in the long run?

Global and regional changes, tensions, and volatility at political and economic levels impact corporate behaviour and investment decisions, for example, by divesting in activities which are perceived as unethical or risky and/or shifting future emphasis from global to more local and regional supply chains. Throughout global and local pressures, companies in the private sector continue to make vital socio-economic contributions to the world in the forms of goods and employment. Doing business during this era, however, also means envisioning and developing economic models that can cater to societal needs within the planet's biophysical boundaries. The chapters have leveraged diverse topical cases, a barrage of scientific literature, and multiple practical examples to delineate a perimeter for the potential contribution of the private sector to sustainability. Drawing from the lessons presented by international scholars and practitioners in the 12 chapters following the introduction of this book, we now share our final reflections on the changing roles of business from the perspective of wider society. We focus on the elements that emerge and recur in several chapters, including key theoretical approaches (Section 2) and core areas of tension around the role of business in sustainability transformations (Section 3). We conclude more optimistically by offering a glimmer of hope (Section 4).

## 2 Sustainability Transitions and Transformations

Two chapters in this book, focusing respectively on sustainability management in the retail sector (see Chapter 6) and on sustainability-driven innovations (see Chapter 11), depart from the well-known theoretical framework of sustainability transitions in socio-technical systems (Geels, 2002, Geels and Schott, 2007; Markard et al., 2016; Rochracher et al., 2019). Materialising this systemic change calls for profound, long-term changes associated with the emergence of novel products, services, business models, organisations, regulations, norms, and user practices, which may either complement or substitute those that already exist. This requires the research community to adopt new practices, new forms of producing knowledge, and more inclusive co-creative approaches towards businesses when building more sustainable, viable solutions.

A transition also means phasing out current non-sustainable practices while simultaneously nurturing and accelerating the adoption of more sustainable ones and actively experimenting with and piloting new solutions. Efficient management of sociotechnical transition calls for a systemic view that emphasises the enforcement of feedback loops (e.g., Meadows, 2008). A field of transition management has emerged, which focuses on the systemic transitional and co-evolutionary changes that are required in both everyday life practices and cultural meanings to 'reconfigure' consumption and production systems for sustainability (Loorbach et al., 2017). This may also call upon new actors or breaking free from the unsustainable habits of old actors, and adopting new roles in making the change towards sustainability happen. For example, in many countries, stimulus packages have been directed toward green recovery (e.g., Allan et al., 2020), especially in the housing and construction sectors, with insulation retrofits and renewable materials, or towards accelerating the renewable energy transition, by building wind turbines or solar power. At the same time, infrastructure investments with less emphasis on the decarbonisation of economies remain prevalent, suggesting inertia in terms of change.

The term sustainability transformations, featuring in the title of this book, is used in the context of socio-ecological or socio-technical-ecological systems to envision and assess 'pathways of sustainable environmental and societal change within the looming Anthropocene' (Patterson et al., 2017, p. 2). Resilience is a key theoretical element in this context and has been widely applied in the scientific literature as a lens to understand the capacity of socio-ecological systems to reorganise and adapt through multi-scale interactions.

In addition to being related to other forms of resilience, such as purely ecological resilience or engineering resilience, socio-ecological resilience also represents the essential condition for business organisational resilience. In other words, organisational resilience is dependent on the resilience of broader socio-ecological systems in which firms are embedded. Williams et al. (2019) call for a more holistic and dynamic interpretation of multilevel resilience across social, ecological, and organisational boundaries. Evidently, resilient systems are only as strong as their weakest parts. An understanding of the feedback effects across nested systems is needed to discuss business sustainability.

Other notable theoretical perspectives covered in this book include emergent business models for sustainability (Bocken et al., 2014; Schaltegger et al., 2016) presented in Chapters 3, 5, 7, 12, and 13 and the notion of strong and weak sustainability (Munda, 1997) discussed in Chapters 12 and 13.

## 3 Core Tensions Around the Role of Business as a Transformative Power

Four core tensions emerge from the chapters of this book: the lack of a shared global sustainability vision; the dominance of some solution-oriented sustainability narratives over others; the interdependent roles and responsibilities of multiple societal actors; and the issue of asynchronous time horizons. These four critical tensions are also overlapping and interconnected (Figure 14.1).

### 3.1 Where Are We Going? A Global Vision of Sustainability

As also emphasised elsewhere in this book (e.g., Chapter 2), striving toward a sustainable society first requires clear objectives and political commitment to sustainability goals and means, and second, supporting the implementation of measures that convert this message about the desired ends to markets. A global vision and the transformative power of global commitments initially formulated with the Brundtlandt Report in 1987 have been refined for decades until the recent adoption of the Sustainable Development Goals by the United Nations.

Despite existing controversies and criticisms, the Sustainable Development Goals have come to represent a reference framework for a more sustainable and just world for national and local administrations, companies, and other societal actors, including scholars and civil society (Scheyvens et al., 2016; Vildåsen et al., 2017). As also emphasised in Chapter 12, however, the current mismatch between the agendas and priorities of most business actors and global sustainable development remains a key tension. Businesses face challenges in dealing with

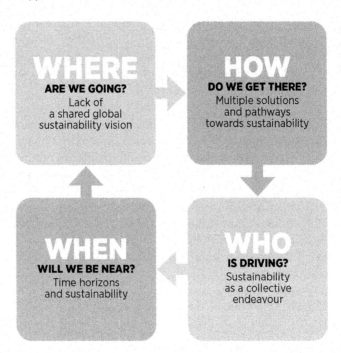

FIGURE 14.1   Four key areas of tension around the role of business in sustainability transformations.

complex, interconnected sustainability goals, and in translating their specific and diverse sets of sustainability activities into measurable impacts. As described in Chapter 2, the risk is 'rainbow washing' corporate responsibility, especially if the Sustainable Development Goals are not addressed as a full set of interdependent elements. At the same time, planetary boundaries, and consequently, biophysical limits to economic growth, are still rarely mentioned, let alone addressed with quantifiable targets, in both public and private decision-making (Whiteman et al., 2013; Bjørn et al., 2016; Haffar and Searcy, 2018). While climate change and resource efficiency dominate corporate reporting, biodiversity, which has also been at the centre of the political agenda for decades now, is still poorly acknowledged in terms of measurable outcomes (Addison et al., 2018). Notably, initiatives such as Capitals Coalition have recently emerged, which promote the integration of natural capital and ecosystem services in business (NCC, 2016).

Overall, better acknowledgment and quantification of the synergies and trade-offs across social and environmental goals seems to be the only way forward, as highlighted by, for example, applications of the Doughnut Economics framework (Fanning et al., 2021). Such a framework places human prosperity between planetary boundaries (e.g., biodiversity loss, climate change, disruption of biogeochemical flows, freshwater use) and social needs (e.g., food, health, housing, education, political voice, equality).

## 3.2 How Do We Get There? Multiple Solutions and Pathways Towards Sustainability

Many alternative pathways (all value-laden) are possible to reach ambitious climate and biodiversity targets, ranging from incremental to more radical ones (Leach et al., 2013). Narratives are the storylines used to frame sustainability problems and thus legitimise specific sets of solutions as the main interventions needed (D'Amato, 2021; D'Amato and Korhonen, 2021). Various societal actors, ranging from governmental institutions to businesses, think tanks, consultancies, and NGOs, adopt one or more narratives in their strategies and operations (D'Amato et al., 2017, 2019a, 2019b). Depending on the realm of society, certain sustainability narratives dominate others (Taherzadeh, 2021).

In this book, two worldwide mainstreamed narratives, the green economy and the (circular) bioeconomy, are examined in Chapters 4 and 5, respectively. Chapter 4 introduces the green economy as a United Nations-driven concept, largely founded on the centrality of biodiversity and natural capital in human social and economic well-being. The chapter showcases green economy business models and critically mobilising resources for monitoring progress towards the green economy. Chapter 5 describes the development of the circular bioeconomy in policymaking and academia and discusses, from a strategic management perspective, the potential challenges and opportunities for companies in the context of a new economy based on biomass resources and the circularity of production and consumption systems, as opposed to a linear fossil-based economy. The bioeconomy is also a recurrent element in Chapters 2, 3, 6, and 11.

Servitisation is presented as a third narrative, which is not as political as the other two, but is driven by market competitiveness forces (Chapter 7). Chapter 7 discusses the potential of servitisation, with particular reference to the forest industry and the circular bioeconomy, to help companies gain market competitiveness by including sustainability aspects in their supply of product–service systems and enabling the co-creation of value with customers and other actors. Coupled competitiveness and sustainability benefits may materialise by, for example, the company offering services that extend the lifecycle of products or materials (e.g., modularity, maintenance, refurbishment, and re-use), that improve waste management and recycling for customers, or that otherwise dematerialise the economy, decoupling it from resource consumption.

Clearly, companies are more likely to align with politically mainstreamed narratives or with narratives that offer visible economic or strategic benefits in the short term (e.g. compliance with legislation, efficiency of resource use), than with, for instance, narratives emerging from academia or bottom-up, citizen-led initiatives. However, increasingly solidifying and legitimising selected narratives may hamper the emergence and development of alternative ideas and paradigms (Taherzadeh, 2021). This relates to, for instance, the difficulty of mainstreaming sufficiency-based thinking in business model realms (Chapter 3).

Adopting specific narratives also bring about risks such as industry path dependency and lock-in, as pointed out in Chapter 5. For example, in the context of the forest bioeconomy (a thorough examination of the topic in a recent volume by Hetemäki et al., 2022), industry path dependence means that efforts are channelled towards incremental development rather than more radical changes (Luhas et al., 2021).

### 3.3 Who Is Driving? Sustainability as a Collective Endeavour

Key aspects enabling possibilities and potential towards sustainability are the scale and geographical scope of companies, including their sizes. A handful of transnational corporations dealing with food, forestry, construction, minerals, and fossil energy represent a major force that impacts intertwined ecological and social systems, while possessing sophisticated resources and a capability pool to implement positive change (Folke et al., 2019). However, another common view is that limited transformative potential lies within incumbent firms, whereas more is embedded in start-ups and SMEs, which having more agility, can adopt radically sustainable business models, and foster sustainability-oriented innovation (Chapters 3 and 11), although the scale of the impact may remain small. Aside from size, Chapter 13 proposes that core changes are needed in the DNA of business, with hybrid forms of business fostering sustainability by placing a stronger emphasis on social and environmental rather than commercial logics. As also explained by Bocken et al. (2020) '[o]rganizations of all types and sizes are pursuing such [sustainable] innovations. However, it should be noted that sustainability-oriented system-based innovations strongly benefit from hybrid forms of businesses (e.g., benefit corporations and social enterprises) that are emerging where the profit motive is less dominant, while social and environmental motives come to the foreground'.

Despite a company's size or motives, Waddock (2020, p. 1) suggests that 'while it is occasionally possible for leaders and companies to transform in the direction of sustainability or flourishing for all, it is unlikely that enough individual businesses can transform sufficiently while relying on an individual basis to achieve transformation. The context that constitutes the ecosystem in which businesses operate needs to change so that businesses themselves can change'. This means the discussion on the purpose of business in society (currently identified by the maximisation of profits or continual growth) must also account for changes in people's mind-sets and perceptions, power dynamics across stakeholders, businesses' performance criteria, and of course technical, legal, and normative frameworks.

In other words, in addition to understanding that the possibilities for business development may vary greatly between different companies and value networks, as also pointed out in Chapter 5, the orchestration of more radical changes requires bold actions from policymakers and legislators, value-chain actors (ranging from raw material suppliers to consumers), scientists, activists, and civil society (Luhas et al., 2021).

On the political (and partly the social) level, some 'taboos' are held in place (mostly by over-emphasising the power of incremental and relative sustainability improvements) in order to avoid the destabilisation of existing regimes and the related social and economic costs; in addition to postgrowth as an alternative paradigm to unsustainable economic growth (for more on this, see Chapter 12), examples of taboos include carbon taxation on internationally traded commodities, as well as policies and infrastructures favouring low-carbon alternatives to the *status quo*, such as plant-based diets, public transport, and non-fossil energy, while subsidies are still granted to unsustainable industries or activities. In their chapters, both Chapters 6 and 11 touch upon the role of governmental commitments, regulations, subsidies, and divestments to support the circular bioeconomy and, in general, sustainability-oriented innovations.

Going beyond the range of government actions, however, three chapters focus on opening up the role of private-led voluntary or 'soft' instruments. Chapter 8 examines how the growing emphasis on finance- and market-driven mechanisms in co-governing environmental challenges in the past three decades has not led to significant progress, despite being celebrated and supported by some intergovernmental processes, governments, and experts. Chapter 9 presents an overview of the mechanisms enabling cooperation between non-government organisations and businesses, based on the Forest Stewardship Council (FSC), a well-established certification scheme in the forest sector. Chapter 10 presents the potential of networked digital surveillance and open data, drawing from the case of pest management in forest ecosystems. The case offers reflections on how corporations, governmental institutions, and environmental organisations can co-govern grand challenges.

Chapters 6, 11, and 12 also highlight the role of consumers and how purchasing behaviour even at the household level is a key driver of changes. For example, according to a recent study by Moran et al. (2020), changes in consumer practices and consumption patterns could reduce carbon footprints further beyond business as usual by roughly one-fourth in Europe, with the primary actions targeting transport, food, and buildings. The question remains whether and how businesses in these fields can respond to the sensitivities and needs emerging from the demand side.

One final note is on the role of intermediary actors in aligning developments at niche and regime levels (Köhler et al., 2019). Effective involvement of intermediaries (such as championing public service organisations or industry associations) could offer the missing link between company and industry boundaries. The roles of intermediaries in sustainability transitions have been studied in urban development, especially in the building and energy sectors (Kivimaa et al., 2019). Intermediaries position themselves between other actors and may be able to facilitate or speed up transition processes or act as knowledge brokers by connecting actors when high transaction costs or communication challenges make direct interaction difficult. The roles of intermediaries in niche management, such as 'nurturing' or 'empowering' innovative niches, have been widely recognised. Previous studies have also attempted to identify potential complementarities and gaps across intermediaries to influence the diffusion of new technologies (e.g., Kivimaa et al., 2019). Fragmented structures and a low degree of coordination between intermediaries have been observed as weaknesses in terms of the efficiency of their role in accelerating transition processes (Vihemäki et al., 2020).

## 3.4 When Will We Be Near? Time Horizons and Sustainability

Related to the rate of change towards sustainability transformations, a prominent issue is that of perceived time horizons and perspectives across different actors. International agendas tend to be oriented towards the medium to the long term, aiming for 2030, 2050, or even beyond, whereas the political realities occur within four- to six-year timeframes (i.e., government election periods). The implementation of political processes tends to move slowly and lag behind visionary statements, at any level, from global to local. These different timeframes can lead to further tensions and difficulties in achieving realistically functioning programmes that would effectively also incorporate private-sector actors. For example, Chapter 11 concludes that sustainability-oriented innovations inevitably have their place in fostering sustainability, but – because of the long time-lags between the introduction of an innovation, its eventual large-scale adoption, and the expected sustainability benefits – an excessively innovation-centric approach to sustainability limits rather than facilitates the desired transitions, especially if return is expected in the short term.

At the business level, firm-specific benefits emerging from sustainability practices and measurement of the so-called business case of sustainability have been a topic of high research interest for decades. However, this field has been dominated by short-term, financial orientation, which may compromise longer-term resilience goals. According to Ortiz-de-Mandojana and Bansal (2016), firm-level sustainability practices significantly contribute to the long-term resilience of the organisation, even in the absence of short-term effects. This kind of thinking is slowly gaining ground, with a growing managerial awareness of the perils of climate change and the loss of valuable natural systems, which requires climate change adaptation, and natural capital valuation and preservation instead of short-term profit maximisation. The private sector is gradually awakening to the idea of developing a stronger capacity for opportunity and risk recognition by, for example, means of corporate foresight (see e.g., Rohrbeck et al., 2015). Indeed, this is one way to strengthen firm-level future awareness and organisational resilience[1] and is potentially beneficial for capturing salient business opportunities. Detecting discontinuous market and demand changes early and interpreting their consequences for the firm may effectively inform actors of future courses of action to ensure the firm's survival and value capture. In practice, however, these foresight tools are used with the mainstream mind-set and are still more financially and threat adaptation oriented than sustainability driven and proactive. Evidently, the temporality of sustainability practices and outcomes (or impacts) is an aspect that still needs abundant consideration, and the difficult struggle for reaching sufficient long-termism is ongoing.

## 4 Cynicism Is Not an Option

After presenting several areas of core tensions and sources of inertia in transformative change, we wish to end by offering a glimpse of hope. Long-term thinking has often emerged from times of crisis, and humanity is certainly living through exceptionally turbulent changes. As frightening and serious as these are, they may represent a window of opportunity to steer development within a safe operating space in ways that will allow humanity to prosper in the long term. Krznaric (2020) has recently suggested a potential S-curve inflection for humanity, inspired by the works of virologist Jonas Salk, responsible for the polio vaccine. According to Krznaric, after an early regime, dominated by short-termism, consumption, and their related aspects in the past two centuries, humanity can now proceed towards the twenty-first century seeking higher values in sustainability, mutual interdependence, and long-term planning. This calls for a so-called seventh generation or cathedral thinking, that is, envisioning decision-making in terms of multiple generations, rather than a few decades.

We also echo Goldin (2020, p. 9) in saying that 'Building a resilient and sustainable future requires action by all of us, from the individual level up to the global level. The networked problems of our time are amenable to networked solutions'. We re-iterate the importance of the context in which businesses operate, the need to exert strong pressure on business laggards to change, and sufficient support for frontrunners to thrive, the neglected role of the systemic approaches, and the need to strengthen future awareness and improve organisational resilience towards sustainability, along with moral consciousness. Capitalising on these opportunities remains the obligation of the current generation, especially of political decision-makers, at all levels and in all geographical areas; and of business management across sectoral boundaries. It is essentially the obligation of us all as consumers, citizens, and ultimately the guardians of nature, to preserve the Earth for unborn generations.

## Note

1 That said, we must also bear in mind what Kates et al. once wrote (2012, p. 7156) '...anticipatory transformational adaptation may be difficult to implement because of uncertainties about climate change risks and adaptation benefits, the high costs of transformational actions, and institutional and behavioral actions that tend to maintain existing resource systems and policies'.

## References

Addison, P. F. E., Bull, J. W. and Milner-Gulland, E. J. (2018) 'Using conservation science to advance corporate biodiversity accountability', *Conservation Biology*, 33(2), pp. 307–318. https://doi.org/10.1111/cobi.13190.

Allan, J., Donovan, C., Ekins, P., Gambhir, A., Hepburn, C., Robins, N., Reay, D., Shuckburgh, E. and Zenghelis, D. (2020). 'A net-zero emissions economic recovery from COVID-19', Working Paper 20–01, Smith School of Enterprise and the Environment, Oxford University. https://www.gla.ac.uk/media/Media_758105_smxx.pdf.

Bjørn, A., Bey, N., Georg, S., Røpke, I. and Hauschild, M. Z. (2016). 'Is Earth recognized as a finite system in corporate responsibility reporting?', *Journal of Cleaner Production*, 163, pp. 106–117. https://doi.org/10.1016/j.jclepro.2015.12.095.

Bocken, N., Ritala, P., Albareda, L. and Verburg, R. (2019) 'Introduction: Innovation for sustainability', *Palgrave Studies in Sustainable Business in Association with Future Earth*. Springer Nature. https://doi.org/10.1007/978-3-319-97385-2_1c.

Bocken, N. M. P., Short, S. W., Rana, P. and Evan, S. (2014) 'A literature and practice review to develop sustainable business model archetypes', *Journal of Cleaner Production*, 65, pp. 42–56. https://doi.org/10.1016/j.jclepro.2013.11.039.

D'Amato, D. (2021) 'Sustainability narratives as transformative solution pathways: Zooming in on the circular economy', *Circular Economy and Sustainability*, 1, pp. 231–242. https://doi.org/10.1007/s43615-021-00008-1.

D'Amato, D., Droste, N., Allen, B., Kettunen, M., Lähtinen, K., Korhonen, J., Leskinen, P., Matthies, B. D. and Toppinen, A. (2017) 'Green, circular, bio economy: A comparative analysis of sustainability avenues', *Journal of Cleaner Production*, 168, pp. 716–734. https://doi.org/10.1016/j.jclepro.2017.09.053.

D'Amato, D., Droste, N., Winkler, K. J. and Toppinen, A. (2019a) 'Thinking green, circular or bio: Eliciting researchers' perspectives on a sustainable economy with Q method', *Journal of Cleaner Production*, 230, pp. 460–476. https://doi.org/10.1016/j.jclepro.2019.05.099.

D'Amato, D., Korhonen, J. and Toppinen, A. (2019b) 'Circular, green, and bio economy: How do companies in land-use intensive sectors align with sustainability concepts?', *Ecological Economics*, 158, pp. 116–133. https://doi.org/10.1016/j.ecolecon.2018.12.026.

D'Amato, D. and Korhonen, J. (2021) 'Integrating the green economy, circular economy and bioeconomy in a strategic sustainability framework', *Ecological Economics*, 188, 107143. https://doi.org/10.1016/j.ecolecon.2021.107143.

Fanning, A. L., O'Neill, D. W., Hickel, J. and Roux, N. (2022) 'The social shortfall and ecological overshoot of nations', *Nature Sustainability*, 5, pp. 26–36. https://doi.org/10.1038/s41893-021-00799-z.

Folke, C., Biggs, R., Norström, A. V., Reyers, B. and Rockström, J. (2016) 'Social-ecological resilience and biosphere-based sustainability science', *Ecology and Society*, 21(3), 41. https://doi.org/10.5751/ES-08748-210341.

Folke, C., Österblom, H., Jouffray, J. B., Lambin, E. F., Adger, W. N., Scheffer, M., Crona, B. I., Nyström, M., Levin, S. A., Carpenter, S. R., Anderies, J. M., Chapin, S., Crépin, A. S., Dauriach, A., Galaz, V., Gordon, L. J., Kautsky, N., Walker, B. H., Watson, J. R., Wilen, J. and de Zeeuw, A. (2019) 'Transnational corporations and the challenge of biosphere stewardship', *Nature Ecology & Evolution*, 3, pp. 1396–1403. https://doi.org/10.1038/s41559-019-0978-z.

Geels, F. W. (2002) 'Technological transitions as evolutionary configuration processes: A multi-level perspective and a case-study', *Research Policy*, 31(8/9), 1257–1274. https://doi.org/10.1016/S0048-7333(02)00062-8.

Geels, F. W. and Schot, J. (2007) 'Typology of social transition pathways', *Research Policy*, 36(3), pp. 399–317. https://doi.org/10.1016/j.respol.2007.01.003.

Goldin, I. (2020). 'Rethinking global resilience', International Monetary Fund, Finance and Development, September 2020, pp. 5–9. https://www.elibrary.imf.org/view/journals/022/0057/003/article-A002-en.xml.

Haffar, M. and Searcy, C. (2018). 'Target-setting for ecological resilience: Are companies setting environmental sustainability targets in line with planetary thresholds?', *Business Strategy and the Environment*, 27(7), pp. 1079–1092. https://doi.org/10.1002/bse.2053.

Hetemäki, L., Kangas, J. and Peltola, H., eds. (2022). *Forest Bioeconomy and Climate Change*. Cham, Swizerland: Springer.

Kates, R., Travis, W. and Wilbanks, T. (2012). 'Transformational adaptation when incremental adaptations to climate change are insufficient', *Proceedings of the National Academy of Sciences*, 109(19), pp. 7156–7161. https://doi.org/10.1073/pnas.1115521109.

Kivimaa, P., Boon, W., Hyysalo, S. and Klerkx, L. (2019) 'Towards a typology of intermediaries in sustainability transitions: A systematic review and a research agenda', *Research Policy*, 48(4), pp. 1062–1075. https://doi.org/10.1016/j.respol.2018.10.006.

Köhler, J., Geels, F. W., Kern, F., Markard, J., Wieczorek, A., Alkemade, F., Avelino, F., Bergek, A., Boons, F., Fünfschilling, L., Hess, D., Holtz, G., Hyysalo, S., Jenkins, K., Kivimaa, P., Martiskainen, M., McMeekin, A., Mühlemeier, M. S., Nykvist, B., Onsongo, E., Pel, B., Raven, R., Rohracher, H., Sandén, B., Schot, J., Sovacool, B., Turnheim, B., Welch, D. and Wells, P. (2019) 'An agenda for sustainability transitions research: State of the art and future directions', *Environmental Innovation and Societal Transitions*, 31, pp. 1–32. https://doi.org/10.1016/j.eist.2019.01.004.

Krznaric, R. (2020) *The Good Ancestor*. London: Penguin Random House.

Leach, M., Raworth, K. and Rockström, J. (2013). 'Between social and planetary boundaries: Navigating pathways in the safe and just space for humanity', *World Social Science Report*. https://doi.org/10.1787/9789264203419-10-en.

Loorbach, D., Frantzeskaki, N. and Avelino, F. (2017) 'Sustainability transitions research: Transforming science and practice for societal change', *Annual Review of Environment and Resources*, 42, pp. 599–626. https://doi.org/10.1146/annurev-environ-102014-021340.

Luhas, J., Mikkilä, M., Miettinen, J., Kylkilahti, E., Malkamäki, A., Korhonen, J., Tuppura, A., Pätäri, S., Pekkanen, T.-L., Lähtinen, K., Autio, M., Linnanen, L., Ollikainen, M. and Toppinen, A. (2021) 'Pathways to a forest-based bioeconomy in 2060 within policy targets on climate change mitigation and biodiversity protection', *Forest Policy and Economics*, 131, 102551. https://doi.org/10.1016/j.forpol.2021.102551.

Markad, J., Suter, M. and Ingold, K. (2016) 'Socio-technical transitions and policy change – Advocacy Coalitions in Swiss energy policy', *Environmental Innovations and Societal Transitions*, 18, pp. 215–237.

Meadows, D. (2008) *Thinking in Systems: A Primer*. Vermont, USA: Chelsea Green Publishing Co.

Moran, D., Wood, R., Hertwitch, E., Mattson, K., Rodriguez, J., Schannes, K. and Barrett, J. (2020) 'Quantifying the potential for consumer-oriented policy to reduce European and foreign carbon emissions', *Climate Policy*, 20(1), pp. S28–S38. https://doi.org/10.1080/14693062.2018.1551186.

Munda, G. (1997) 'Environmental economics, ecological economics, and the concept of sustainable development', *Environmental Values*, 6, pp. 213–233. https://doi.org/10.3197/096327197776679158.

Ortiz-de-Mandojana, N. and Bansal, P. (2016) 'The long term benefits of organizational resilience through sustainable business practices', *Strategic Management Journal*, 37, pp. 1615–1631. https://doi.org/10.1002/smj.2410.

Patterson, J., Schulz, K., Vervoort, J., Hel, S., Widerberg, O., Adler, C., Hurlbert, M., Anderton, K., Sethi, M. and Barau, A. (2017). 'Exploring the governance and politics of transformations towards sustainability', *Environmental Innovation and Societal Transitions*, 24, pp. 1–16. https://doi.org/10.1016/j.eist.2016.09.001.

Raworth, K. (2017) *Doughnut Economics: Seven Ways to Think Like a 21st-Century Economist*. Vermont: Chelsea Green Publishing Co, USA.

Rohrbeck, R., Battistella, C. and Huizingh, E. (2015) 'Corporate foresight: An emerging field with a rich tradition', *Technological Forecasting and Social Change*, 101, pp. 1–9. https://doi.org/10.1016/j.techfore.2015.11.002.

Schaltegger, S., Hansen, E. G. and Lüdeke-Freund, F. (2016) 'Business models for sustainability: Origins, present research, and future avenues', *Organization and Environment*, 29(1), pp. 3–10. https://doi.org/10.1177/1086026615599806.

Scheyvens, R., Banks, G. and Hughes, E. (2016) 'The private sector and the SDGs: The need to move beyond "business as usual"', *Sustainable Development*, 24(6), pp. 371–382. https://doi.org/10.1002/sd.1623.

Taherzadeh, O. (2021) 'Promise of a green economic recovery post-Covid: Trojan horse or turning point?', *Global Sustainability*, 4, pe2. https://doi.org/10.1017/sus.2020.33.

Vihemäki, H., Toppinen, A. and Toivonen, R. (2020) 'Intermediaries to accelerate the diffusion of wooden multi-storey construction in Finland', *Environmental Innovation and Societal Transitions*, 36, pp. 433–448.

Vildåsen, S. S., Keitsch, M. and Fet, A. M. (2017) 'Clarifying the epistemology of corporate sustainability', *Ecological Economics*, 138, pp. 40–46. https://doi.org/10.1016/j.ecolecon.2017.03.029.

Waddock, S. (2020) 'Achieving sustainability requires systemic business transformation', *Global Sustainability*, 3(e12), pp. 1–12. https://doi.org/10.1017/sus.2020.9.

Weiss, G., Hansen, E., Ludvig, A., Nybakk, E. and Toppinen, A. (2021) 'Innovation governance in the forest sector: Reviewing concepts, trends and gaps', *Forest Policy and Economics*, 130, 102506. https://doi.org/10.1016/j.forpol.2021.102506.

Whiteman, G., Walker, B. and Perego, P. (2013) 'Planetary boundaries: Ecological foundations for corporate sustainability', *Journal of Management Studies*, 50(2), pp. 307–336. https://doi.org/10.1111/j.1467-6486.2012.01073.x.

Williams, A., Whiteman, G. and Kennedy, S. (2019) 'Cross-scale systemic resilience: Implications for organization studies', *Business and Society*, 60(1), pp. 95–104. https://doi.org/10.1177/0007650319825870.

World Economic Forum (2022) *The Global Risks Report 2022*. 17th ed.

# INDEX

Note: **Bold** page numbers refer to tables; *italic* page numbers refer to figures and page numbers followed by "n" denote endnotes.